Object-Oriented Design & Patterns

Second Edition

Cay Horstmann

San Jose State University

WILEY

John Wiley & Sons, Inc.

PUBLISHER: Bruce Spatz
SENIOR EDITORIAL ASSISTANT: Bridget Morrisey
PROJECT MANAGER: Cindy Johnson, Publishing Services
DIRECTOR OF MARKETING: Frank Lyman
SENIOR PRODUCTION MANAGER: Ken Santor
COVER DESIGNER: Harold Nolan
COVER PHOTO: © Corbis/Media Bakery

This book was set in Adobe Caslon by Publishing Services and printed and bound by Malloy, Inc. The cover was printed by Phoenix Color Corporation.

This book is printed on acid-free paper. ∞

ISBN 0-471-74487-5

Printed in the United States of America

10 9 8 7 6 5 4 3 2 1

Preface

Making Object-Oriented Design Accessible

This book is an introduction to object-oriented design and design patterns at an elementary level. It is intended for students with at least one semester of programming in an object-oriented language such as Java or C++.

I wrote this book to solve a common problem. When students first learn an object-oriented programming language, they cannot be expected to instantly master object-oriented design. Yet, students should learn the principles of object-oriented design early enough to put them to work throughout the computer science curriculum.

This book is suitable for a second or third course in computer science—no background in data structures is required, and students are not assumed to have experience with developing large software systems. Alternatively, the book can be used as a companion text in a course in software engineering. (If you need a custom version of this book for integration into another course, please contact your Wiley sales representative.)

This second edition is fully updated for Java 5.0, including

- the use of generic collections and the "for each" loop
- a detailed discussion of parameterized type constraints
- auto-boxing and varargs methods, particularly in the reflection API
- multithreading with the java.util.concurrent package

Integration of Design Patterns

The most notable aspect of this book is the manner in which the coverage of design patterns is interwoven with the remainder of the material. For example,

- Swing containers and components motivate the COMPOSITE pattern.
- Swing scroll bars motivate the DECORATOR pattern, and Swing borders are examined as a missed opportunity for that pattern.
- Java streams give a second example of the DECORATOR pattern. Seeing the pattern used in two superficially different ways greatly clarifies the pattern concept.

Without memorable examples, design patterns are just words. In order to visualize design patterns, this book uses examples from graphical user interface programming. Students will remember how a component is decorated by scroll bars, and how layout managers carry out different strategies. (A small and carefully selected subset of Swing is used for this purpose.)

A Foundation for Further Study

After covering the material in this book, students will have mastered the following topics in three subject areas:

1. Object-oriented design
   - A simple design methodology
   - CRC cards and UML diagrams
   - Design patterns

2. Advanced Java language
   - Interface types, polymorphism, and inheritance
   - Inner classes
   - Reflection
   - Generic types
   - Multithreading
   - Collections

3. User interface programming
   - Building Swing applications
   - Event handling
   - Java 2D graphics programming

These skills clearly form a useful foundation for advanced computer science courses. In fact, students who have completed this book will have encountered all features of the Java language (but not, of course, the entire standard Java library, which is too huge for any one person to master). One advantage of using Java is indeed that students can comprehend the entire language. Contrast that with C++, a language that is so complex that virtually no one can truthfully claim to understand all of its subtleties.

In summary: Use this book if you want your students to understand object-oriented design and design patterns early in the curriculum. As a bonus, your students will gain a complete overview of the Java language, and they will be able to program simple Swing user interfaces.

Programming and Design Tools

Another important aspect of this book is the coverage of tools. While many C++ programmers live their entire programming life in a large and complex integrated environment, the Java culture has embraced the use of different tools such as BlueJ, javadoc, and JUnit. Due to the reflective nature of the Java language, there are many interesting experimental tools. I highlight a number of them in the hope that students will gain an interest and aptitude in evaluating and selecting tools that fit their working style.

Students who learn object-oriented design also should become familiar with drawing UML diagrams. An easy-to-use and no-cost tool for this purpose, the Violet UML editor, is provided for their use. Chapter 8 of this book introduces the framework on which Violet is based. All UML diagrams in this book were drawn with Violet.

A Tour of the Book

Chapter 1 A Crash Course in Java

This chapter introduces the basic syntax of Java and can serve either as a refresher or as a transition for students with a background in C++. Topics covered include

- Defining classes and methods
- Objects and object references
- Exploring objects with BlueJ
- Documentation comments
- Numbers, strings, and arrays
- Packages
- Exception handling
- Common utility classes: `ArrayList` and `Scanner`
- Programming style guidelines

Chapter 2 The Object-Oriented Design Process

This chapter introduces the process of object-oriented design, CRC cards, and UML notation. It presents a case study of a simple voice mail system to illustrate the design process, starting with the project's specification and culminating in its Java implementation. Topics covered include

- Identifying classes and methods
- Relationships between classes
- CRC cards
- UML class, sequence, and state diagrams
- Case study

Chapter 3 Guidelines for Class Design

Unlike Chapter 2, which took a top-down view of the discovery of classes and their relationships, this chapter focuses on the design of a single class or a small group of related classes. Topics covered include

- Designing and implementing the interface of a class
- The importance of encapsulation
- Analyzing the quality of an interface
- Programming by contract: preconditions, postconditions, and invariants

Chapter 4 Interface Types and Polymorphism

This chapter introduces the notation of the Java interface type, without mentioning inheritance. This approach has an important advantage: The reader learns about polymorphism in its purest form, without being burdened by technical matters such as superclass construction or the invocation of superclass methods.

The chapter also introduces the Swing user interface toolkit and AWT drawing operations. It starts with the Icon interface type, which allows the placement of arbitrary drawings in a frame.

Anonymous classes are introduced as an easy mechanism for "ad-hoc" objects that implement a particular interface type. They are then put to use for Swing user interface actions.

Up to this point, all interface types have been supplied in the standard library. The chapter ends with the design of a custom interface type. Topics covered include

- Frames, images, and shapes
- The Icon interface type
- The Comparable and Comparator interface types
- Anonymous classes
- User interface actions
- Designing interface types

Chapter 5 Patterns and GUI Programming

This chapter introduces the concept of patterns and covers a number of patterns that arise in the Swing user interface toolkit and the Java collections library. Topics include

- Alexander's architectural patterns
- Software design patterns
- The ITERATOR pattern as an example of a design pattern
- The OBSERVER pattern, model/view/controller, and Swing listeners
- The STRATEGY pattern and layout managers
- The COMPOSITE pattern, user interface components and containers
- The DECORATOR pattern, scroll panes, and borders

Chapter 6 Inheritance and Abstract Classes

This chapter introduces the mechanics of inheritance using examples from the AWT graphics library. There is an extensive discussion of abstract classes, a topic that many beginners find challenging. An abstract shape class lays the foundation for the graph editor framework created in Chapter 8. Several inheritance hierarchies are examined, including the hierarchies of Swing components, geometric shapes, and exception classes. The chapter discusses advanced exception handling, including the definition of new exception classes (which, of course, requires inheritance). The chapter closes with a discussion of when *not* to use inheritance. Topics covered include

- Defining and implementing subclasses
- Invoking superclass constructors and methods
- Abstract classes and the TEMPLATE METHOD pattern
- The inheritance hierarchy of Swing components
- The inheritance hierarchy of graphical shapes in the `java.awt.geom` package
- The inheritance hierarchy of exception classes
- When not to use inheritance

Chapter 7 The Java Object Model

This chapter covers the Java type system in detail and introduces the important reflection capabilities of Java. It then moves on to a rigorous treatment of the fundamental methods of the `Object` class: `toString`, `equals`, `hashCode`, and `clone`. Generics are discussed at an intermediate level, going well beyond the basics but stopping short of discussing technical minutiae. As an application of reflection techniques, the JavaBeans component model and the implementation of JavaBeans properties are introduced. Topics covered include

- The Java type system, primitive types, wrappers, and array types
- Type inquiry and reflection
- Object equality and cloning
- Serialization
- Generic types
- Components and JavaBeans

Chapter 8 Frameworks

This capstone chapter culminates in the development of a graph editor framework and its specialization to a UML class diagram editor. Topics covered include

- The framework concept
- Applets as a simple framework
- The collections framework
- Application frameworks
- The graph editor framework

Chapter 9 Multithreading

This chapter introduces the multithreading primitives of the Java language, thus completing the students' introduction to Java language semantics. The synchronization primitives can be challenging for students to grasp because they tightly combine several related features. I first cover the `Lock` and `Condition` classes in the `java.util.concurrent` package, then use that background to explain the built-in locks and wait sets. Topics covered include

- Threads and the `Runnable` interface type
- Interrupting threads
- Thread synchronization
- The `java.util.concurrent` package
- An application: Algorithm animation

Chapter 10 More Design Patterns

The book concludes with a chapter that covers additional important design patterns. A summary at the end of the chapter briefly describes additional classical design patterns whose coverage is beyond the scope of this book. Topics covered include

- The ADAPTER pattern
- Actions and the COMMAND pattern
- The FACTORY METHOD pattern
- The PROXY pattern
- The SINGLETON pattern
- The VISITOR pattern
- Other design patterns

Figure 1 shows the dependencies between the chapters.

Pedagogical Structure

Each chapter begins with an introduction and listing of the chapter topics. Concepts and principles are presented in the context of programming examples, and many example programs are printed in their entirety in the text to encourage students to read and understand code listings. Complete source code for all of the examples in the text is available from the book's Web site at `http://www.wiley.com/college/horstmann` (see pages xvii–xix for a listing of the example programs that accompany this book).

Throughout the chapters, there are several kinds of special features to help your students. These features are specially marked so they don't interrupt the flow of the main material.

> Key concepts are highlighted with margin notes.

Margin notes highlight important topics and help students navigate the core material of each chapter by highlighting where new concepts are introduced.

Figure 1

Dependencies Between the Chapters

Special Topics introduce background material or advanced subjects that can be skipped. Several data structures that students in a second course may not have been introduced to are presented in these Special Topics, making them available as needed. Other Special Topics address features of languages other than Java that relate to the design principles in the chapter. (See page xvi for a list of these topics by chapter.)

 Design Patterns are specially marked with this icon. Each design pattern is presented in a standard format that includes the context in which the pattern is useful, the solution that the pattern provides, and a UML diagram of the pattern elements. Most design patterns are then followed by a table that shows students how the pattern's structure is applied to the example discussed in that section. (See page xvi for a list of patterns by chapter.)

 NOTE Notes highlight important or interesting material, such as tips or pointers for further reading.

 INTERNET Internet notes contain links to further information on the Internet, including locations for downloadable programming tools, documentation, and articles related to chapter topics.

 TIP Tips are used liberally throughout the text to explain good programming practices and to help students avoid common errors.

Web Resources

Additional resources can be found on the book's Web site at `http://www.wiley.com/college/horstmann`. These resources include:

- Solutions to selected exercises (accessible to students)
- Solutions to all exercises (for instructors only)
- Help with common compilers
- Presentation slides for lectures
- Source code for all examples in the book

The Violet UML Editor

Students may download Violet, an easy-to-use and no-cost UML editor, at `http://horstmann.com/violet`. Violet was used to draw the UML diagrams in the text, so students can use this same tool to create similar diagrams for the programs they design.

Acknowledgments

Many thanks to Bruce Spatz, Bill Zobrist, Bridget Morrisey, Catherine Shultz, Phyllis Cerys, Ken Santor, and Lisa Gee at John Wiley & Sons for their support for this book project.

I am very grateful to the many individuals who reviewed the manuscript, found embarrassing errors, made valuable suggestions, contributed to the supplements, and helped me make the book more student friendly:

Carl G. Alphonce, *University of Buffalo*

Bill Bane, *Tarleton State University*

Dwight Barnette, *Virginia Polytechnic Institute and State University*

Alfred Benoit, *Johnson & Wales University*

Richard Borie, *University of Alabama*

Bruce Char, *Drexel University*

Chia Chen, *Tuskegee University*

Ashraful Chowdhury, *Georgia Perimeter College*

David M. Dacus, *Mountain View College*

Roger deBry, *Utah Valley State College*

Preetam Desai, *University of Missouri, St. Louis*

Chris Dovolis, *University of Minnesota*

Robert Duvall, *Duke University*

Anne B. Horton, *AT&T Laboratories*

Robert Kelly, *State University of New York, Stony Brook*

Walter W. Kirchherr, *San Jose State University*

Blayne Mayfield, *Oklahoma State University*

Marlene Miller

Evelyn Obaid, *San Jose State University*

Edward G. Okie, *Radford University*

Jong-Min Park, *San Diego State University*

Richard Pattis, *Carnegie Mellon University*

Hao Pham, *San Jose State University*

Gary Pollice, *Worcester Polytechnic Institute*

Saeed Rajput, *Florida Atlantic University*

Gopal Rao, *California State University, Sacramento*

Mike Rowe, *University of Wisconsin, Platteville*

Ken Slonneger, *University of Iowa*

Richard L. Upchurch, *University of Massachusetts, Dartmouth*

Phil Ventura, *State University of West Georgia*

Victor Yu, *DeAnza College*

Steven J. Zeil, *Old Dominion University*

Rong Zhao, *State University of New York, Stony Brook*

I appreciate the enthusiasm and patience of my students at San Jose State University who participated in courses based on early versions of this book and provided valuable feedback for the development of this second edition.

Finally, a special thanks to Cindy Johnson of Publishing Services, who served as editor, production supervisor, liaison with the publisher, general troubleshooter, and in innumerable other roles. Her work was essential for quality, timeliness, and sanity, throughout the production of this book.

Contents

▶ Special Topics   ▶ Patterns

▶ Code in Text		▶ Companion Code

A Crash Course in Java

The purpose of this chapter is to teach you the elements of the Java programming language—or to give you an opportunity to review them— assuming that you know an object-oriented programming language. In particular, you should be familiar with the concepts of classes and objects. If you know C++ and understand classes, member functions, and constructors, then you will find that it is easy to make the switch to Java.

1.1   "Hello, World!" in Java

Classes are the building blocks of Java programs. Let's start our crash course by looking at a simple but typical class:

```java
public class Greeter
{
   public Greeter(String aName)
   {
      name = aName;
   }

   public String sayHello()
   {
      return "Hello, " + name + "!";
   }

   private String name;
}
```

This class has three features:

- A *constructor* Greeter(String aName) that is used to construct new objects of this class.

- A *method* sayHello() that you can apply to objects of this class. (Java uses the term "method" for a function defined in a class.)

- A *field* name. Every object of this class has an instance of this field.

> A class definition contains the implementation of constructors, methods, and fields.

Each feature is tagged as public or private. Implementation details (such as the name field) are private. Features that are intended for the class user (such as the constructor and sayHello method) are public. The class itself is declared as public as well. You will see the reason in the section on packages.

To construct an object, you use the new operator, which invokes the constructor.

```java
new Greeter("World")
```

The new operator returns the constructed object, or, more precisely, a reference to that object—we will discuss this distinction in detail in the section on object references.

> The new operator constructs new instances of a class.

The object that the new operator returns belongs to the Greeter class. In object-oriented parlance, we say that it is an *instance* of the Greeter class. The process of constructing an object of a class is often called "instantiating the class".

After you obtain an instance of a class, you can call (or *invoke*) methods on it. The call

```
(new Greeter("World")).sayHello()
```

creates a new object and causes the sayHello method to be executed. The result is the string "Hello, World!", the concatenation of the strings "Hello, ", name, and "!".

> Object-oriented programming follows the "client-server" model. The client code requests a service by invoking a method on an object.

The code that invokes a method is often called the *client code*. We think of the object as providing a service for the client.

You often need *variables* to store object references that are the result of the new operator or a method call:

```
Greeter worldGreeter = new Greeter("World");
String greeting = worldGreeter.sayHello();
```

Now that you have seen how to define a class, you're ready to build your first Java program, the traditional program that displays the words "Hello, World!" on the screen.

You will define a second class, GreeterTester, to produce the output.

Ch1/helloworld/GreeterTester.java

```
1 public class GreeterTester
2 {
3    public static void main(String[] args)
4    {
5       Greeter worldGreeter = new Greeter("World");
6       String greeting = worldGreeter.sayHello();
7       System.out.println(greeting);
8    }
9 }
```

> Execution of a Java program starts with the main method of a class.

This class has a main method, which is required to start a Java application. The main method is *static*, which means that it doesn't operate on an object. (We will discuss static methods—also called *class methods*—in greater detail later in this chapter.) When the application is launched, there aren't any objects yet. It is the job of the main method to construct the objects that are needed to start the program.

The args parameter of the main method holds the *command-line arguments*, which are not used in this example. We will discuss command-line arguments in the section on arrays.

You have already seen the first two statements inside the main method. They construct a Greeter object, store it in an object variable, invoke the sayHello method, and capture the result in a string variable. The last statement invokes the println method on the System.out object. The result is to print the message and a line terminator to the standard output stream.

To build and execute the program, put the Greeter class inside a file Greeter.java and the GreeterTester class inside a separate file GreeterTester.java. The directions for compiling and running the program depend on your development environment.

The Java Software Development Kit (SDK) from Sun Microsystems is a set of command-line programs for compiling, running, and documenting Java programs.

Versions for several platforms are available at `http://java.sun.com/j2se`. If you use the Java SDK, then follow these instructions:

1. Create a new directory of your choice to hold the program files.

2. Use a text editor of your choice to prepare the files `Greeter.java` and `GreeterTester.java`. Place them inside the directory you just created.

3. Open a shell window.

4. Use the `cd` command to change to the directory you just created.

5. Run the compiler with the command

   `javac GreeterTester.java`

   If the Java compiler is not on the search path, then you need to use the full path (such as `/usr/local/jdk1.5.0/bin/javac` or `c:\jdk1.5.0\bin\javac`) instead of just `javac`. Note that the `Greeter.java` file is automatically compiled as well since the `GreeterTester` class requires the `Greeter` class. If any compilation errors are reported, then make a note of the file and line numbers and fix them.

6. Have a look at the files in the current directory. Verify that the compiler has generated two *class files*, `Greeter.class` and `GreeterTester.class`.

7. Start the Java interpreter with the command

   `java GreeterTester`

Now you will see a message "Hello, World!" in the shell window (see Figure 1).

The structure of this program is typical for a Java application. The program consists of a collection of classes. One class has a `main` method. You run the program by launching the Java interpreter with the name of the class whose `main` method contains the instructions for starting the program activities.

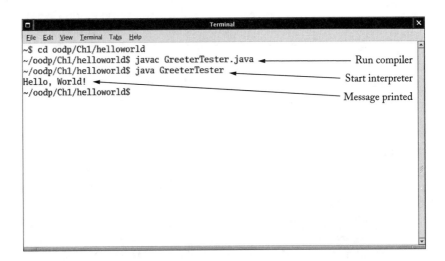

Figure 1

Running the "Hello, World!" Program in a Shell Window

> Some programming environments allow you to execute Java code without requiring a `main` method.

The BlueJ development environment, developed at Monash University, lets you test classes without having to write a new program for every test. BlueJ supplies an interactive environment for constructing objects and invoking methods on the objects. You can download BlueJ from `http://www.bluej.org`.

With BlueJ, you don't need a `GreeterTester` class to test the `Greeter` class. Instead, just follow these steps.

1. Select "Project → New..." from the menu; point the file dialog box to a directory of your choice and type in the name of the subdirectory that should hold your classes—this must be the name of a new directory. BlueJ will create it.

2. Click on the "New Class..." button and type in the class name `Greeter`. Right-click on the class rectangle and type in the code of the `Greeter` class.

3. Click on the "Compile" button to compile the class. Click on the "Close" button.

4. The class is symbolized as a rectangle. Right-click on the class rectangle and select "new Greeter(aName)" to construct a new object. Call the object `worldGreeter` and supply the constructor parameter `"World"` (including the quotation marks).

5. The object appears in the object workbench. Right-click on the object rectangle and select "String sayHello( )" to execute the `sayHello` method.

6. A dialog box appears to display the result (see Figure 2).

As you can see, BlueJ lets you think about objects and classes without fussing with `public static void main`.

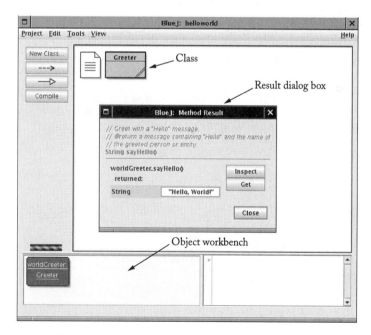

Figure 2

Testing a Class with BlueJ

1.2   Documentation Comments

Java has a standard form for comments that describe classes and their features. The Java development kit contains a tool, called javadoc, that automatically generates a convenient set of HTML pages that document your classes.

Documentation comments are delimited by /** and */. Both class and method comments start with freeform text. The javadoc utility copies the *first sentence* of each comment to a summary table. Therefore, it is best to write that first sentence with some care. It should start with an uppercase letter and end with a period. It does not have to be a grammatically complete sentence, but it should be meaningful when it is pulled out of the comment and displayed in a summary.

Method and constructor comments contain additional information. For each parameter, supply a line that starts with @param, followed by the parameter name and a short explanation. Supply a line that starts with @return to describe the return value. Omit the @param tag for methods that have no parameters, and omit the @return tag for methods whose return type is void.

Here is the Greeter class with documentation comments for the class and its public interface.

Ch1/helloworld/Greeter.java

```
 1  /**
 2      A class for producing simple greetings.
 3  */
 4  public class Greeter
 5  {
 6      /**
 7          Constructs a Greeter object that can greet a person or entity.
 8          @param aName  the name of the person or entity who should
 9          be addressed in the greetings.
10      */
11      public Greeter(String aName)
12      {
13          name = aName;
14      }
15
16      /**
17          Greet with a "Hello" message.
18          @return  a message containing "Hello" and the name of
19          the greeted person or entity.
20      */
21      public String sayHello()
22      {
23          return "Hello, " + name + "!";
24      }
25
26      private String name;
27  }
```

Your first reaction may well be "Whoa! I am supposed to write all this stuff?" These comments do seem pretty repetitive. But you should still take the time to write them, even if it feels silly at times. There are three reasons.

First, the javadoc utility will format your comments into a nicely formatted set of HTML documents. It makes good use of the seemingly repetitive phrases. The first sentence of each method comment is used for a *summary table* of all methods of your class (see Figure 3). The @param and @return comments are neatly formatted in the detail descriptions of each method (see Figure 4). If you omit any of the comments, then javadoc generates documents that look strangely empty.

> Supply comments for all methods and public fields of a class.

Next, it is possible to spend more time pondering whether a comment is too trivial to write than it takes just to write it. In practical programming, very simple methods are rare. It is harmless to have a trivial method overcommented, whereas a complicated method without any comment can cause real grief to future maintenance programmers. According to the standard Java documentation style, *every* class, *every* method, *every* parameter, and *every* return value should have a comment.

Finally, it is always a good idea to write the method comment *first*, before writing the method code. This is an excellent test to see that you firmly understand what you need to program. If you can't explain what a class or method does, you aren't ready to implement it.

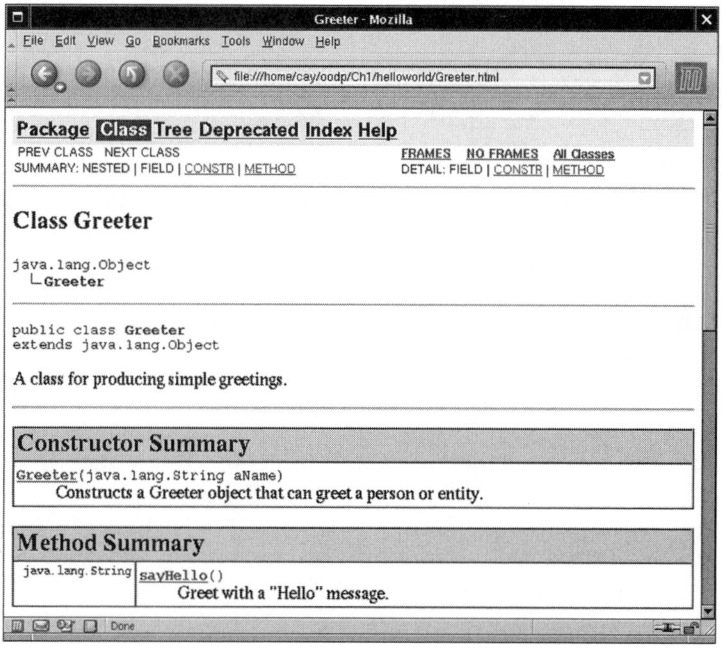

Figure 3

A javadoc Class Summary

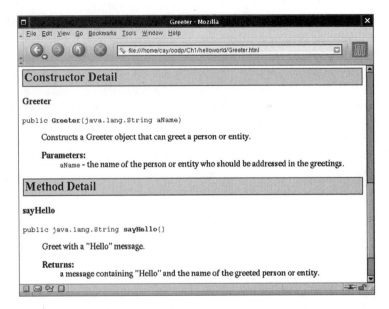

Figure 4

Parameter and Return Value Documentation in `javadoc`

After you have written the documentation comments, invoke the `javadoc` utility.

1. Open a shell window.
2. Use the `cd` command to change to the directory you just created.
3. Run the `javadoc` utility

   `javadoc *.java`

   If the Java development tools are not on the search path, then you need to use the full path (such as `/usr/local/jdk1.5.0/bin/javadoc` or `c:\jdk1.5.0\bin\java-doc`) instead of just `javadoc`.

> The `javadoc` utility extracts documentation comments and produces a set of cross-linked HTML files.

The `javadoc` utility then produces one HTML file for each class (such as `Greeter.html` and `GreeterTester.html`) as well as a file `index.html` and a number of other summary files. The `index.html` file contains links to all classes.

The `javadoc` tool is wonderful because it does one thing right: It allows you to put the documentation *together with your code*. That way, when you update your programs, you can see immediately which documentation needs to be updated. Hopefully, you will then update it right then and there. Afterwards, run `javadoc` again and get a set of nicely formatted HTML pages with the updated comments.

INTERNET The `DocCheck` program reports any missing `javadoc` comments. Download it from `http://java.sun.com/j2se/javadoc/doccheck/`.

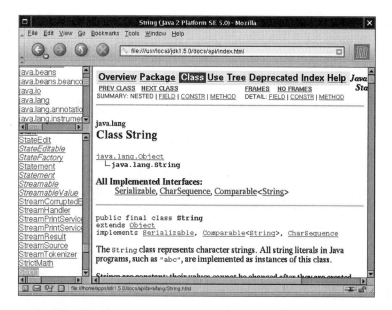

Figure 5

The Java API Documentation

The Java development kit contains the documentation for *all* classes in the Java library, also called the application programming interface or API. Figure 5 shows the documentation of the String class. This documentation is directly extracted from the library source code. The programmers who wrote the Java library documented every class and method and then simply ran javadoc to extract the HTML documentation.

TIP   Download the SDK documentation from http://java.sun.com/j2se. Install the documentation into the same location as the Java development kit. Point your browser to the docs/api/index.html file inside your Java development kit directory, and make a bookmark. Do it now! You will need to access this information frequently.

1.3   Primitive Types

> Java has eight primitive types for integers, floating-point numbers, bytes, characters, and boolean values.

In Java, numbers, characters, and Boolean values are not objects but values of a primitive type. Table 1 shows the eight primitive types of the Java language.

To indicate long constants, use a suffix L, such as 10000000000L. Similarly, float constants have a suffix F, such as 3.1415927F.

Characters are encoded in *Unicode,* a uniform encoding scheme for characters in many languages around the world. Character constants are enclosed in single quotes, such as 'a'. Several characters, such as a newline '\n', are represented as two-character escape

Type	Size	Range
int	4 bytes	−2,147,483,648 ... 2,147,483,647
long	8 bytes	−9,223,372,036,854,775,808L ... 9,223,372,036,854,775,807L
short	2 bytes	−32768 ... 32767
byte	1 byte	−128 ... 127
char	2 bytes	'\u0000' ... '\uFFFF'
boolean		false, true
double	8 bytes	approximately ±1.79769313486231570E+308
float	4 bytes	approximately ±3.40282347E+38F

Table 1

The Primitive Types of the Java Language

Escape Sequence	Meaning
\b	backspace (\u0008)
\f	form feed (\u000C)
\n	newline (\u000A)
\r	return (\u000D)
\t	tab (\u0009)
\\	backslash
\'	single quote
\"	double quote
\u$n_1n_2n_3n_4$	Unicode encoding

Table 2

Character Escape Sequences

sequences. Table 2 shows the most common permitted escape sequences. Arbitrary Unicode characters are denoted by a \u, followed by four hexadecimal digits enclosed in single quotes. For example, `'\u2122'` is the trademark symbol (™).

INTERNET   You can find the encodings of tens of thousands of letters in many alphabets at http://www.unicode.org.

Conversions that don't incur information loss (such as short to int or float to double) are always legal. Values of type char can be converted to int. All integer types can be converted to float or double, even though some of the conversions (such as long to double) lose precision. All other conversions require a *cast:*

```
double x = 10.0 / 3.0; // sets x to 3.3333333333333335
int n = (int) x; // sets n to 3
float f = (float) x; // sets f to 3.3333333
```

It is not possible to convert between the boolean type and number types.

The Math class implements useful mathematical methods. Table 3 contains some of the most useful ones. The methods of the Math class do not operate on objects. Instead, numbers are supplied as parameters. (Recall that numbers are not objects in Java.) For example, here is how to call the sqrt method:

```
double y = Math.sqrt(x);
```

Since the method doesn't operate on an object, the class name must be supplied to tell the compiler that the sqrt method is in the Math class. In Java, every method must belong to some class.

Method	Description
`Math.sqrt(x)`	Square root of x, $\sqrt{x}$
`Math.pow(x, y)`	x^y ($x > 0$, or $x = 0$ and $y > 0$, or $x < 0$ and y is an integer)
`Math.toRadians(x)`	Converts x degrees to radians (i.e., returns $x \cdot \pi/180$)
`Math.toDegrees(x)`	Converts x radians to degrees (i.e., returns $x \cdot 180/\pi$)
`Math.round(x)`	Closest integer to x (as a long)
`Math.abs(x)`	Absolute value $|x|$

Table 3

Mathematical Methods

1.4   Control Flow Statements

The `if` statement is used for conditional execution. The `else` branch is optional.

```
if (x >= 0) y = Math.sqrt(x); else y = 0;
```

The `while` and `do` statements are used for loops. The body of a `do` loop is executed at least once.

```
while (x < target)
{
   x = x * a;
   n++;
}

do
{
   x = x * a;
   n++;
}
while (x < target);
```

The `for` statement is used for loops that are controlled by a loop counter.

```
for (i = 1; i <= n; i++)
{
   x = x * a;
   sum = sum + x;
}
```

A variable can be defined in a `for` loop. Its scope extends to the end of the loop.

```
for (int i = 1; i <= n; i++)
{
   x = x * a;
   sum = sum + x;
}
// i no longer defined here
```

Java 5.0 introduces an enhanced form of the `for` loop. We will discuss that construct later in this chapter.

1.5   Object References

In Java, an object value is always a *reference* to an object, or, in other words, a value that describes the location of the object. For example, consider the statement

```
Greeter worldGreeter = new Greeter("World");
```

> An object reference describes the location of an object. In Java, you manipulate object references, not objects.

The value of the `new` expression is the location of the newly constructed object. The variable `worldGreeter` can hold the location of any `Greeter` object, and it is being filled with the location of the new object (see Figure 6.)

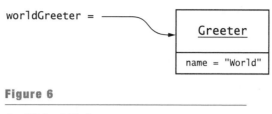

Figure 6

An Object Reference

There can be multiple variables that store references to the same object. For example, after the assignment

```
Greeter anotherGreeter = worldGreeter;
```

the two object variables refer to the same object (see Figure 7).

> When you copy object references, the copy accesses the same object as the original.

If the `Greeter` class has a `setName` method that allows modification of the object, and if that method is invoked on the object reference, then both variables access the modified object.

```
anotherGreeter.setName("Dave");
// now worldGreeter also refers to the changed object
```

To make a copy of the actual object, instead of just copying the object reference, use the `clone` method. Implementing the `clone` method correctly is a subtle process that is discussed in greater detail in Chapter 7. However, many library classes have a `clone` method. It is then a simple matter to make a copy of an object of such a class. For example, here is how you clone a `Date` object:

```
Date aDate = . . .;
Date anotherDate = (Date) aDate.clone();
```

The cast `(Date)` is necessary because `clone` is a generic method with return type `Object`. In Java, all classes extend the class `Object`.

The special reference `null` refers to no object. You can set an object variable to `null`:

```
worldGreeter = null;
```

You can test if an object reference is currently `null`:

```
if (worldGreeter == null) . . .
```

> The `null` reference refers to no object.

If you invoke a method on a `null` reference, a `NullPointerException` is thrown. Unless you supply a handler for the exception, the program terminates. (Exception handling is discussed later in this chapter.)

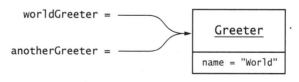

Figure 7

A Shared Object

It can happen that an object has no references pointing to it, namely when all object variables that previously referred to it are filled with other values or have been recycled. In that case, the memory that was used for storing the object will be automatically reclaimed by the garbage collector. In Java, you never need to manually recycle memory.

NOTE   If you are familiar with the C++ programming language, you will recognize that object references in Java behave just like *pointers* in C++. In C++, you can have multiple pointers to the same value, and a NULL pointer points to no value at all. Of course, in C++, pointers strike fear in the hearts of many programmers because it is so easy to create havoc with invalid pointers. It is sometimes said that Java is easier than C++ because it has no pointers. That statement is not true. Java *always* uses pointers (and calls them references), so you don't have to worry about the distinction between pointers and values. More importantly, the pointers in Java are *safe*. It is not possible to create invalid pointers, and the garbage collector automatically reclaims unused objects.

1.6   Parameter Passing

The object reference on which you invoke a method is called the *implicit parameter*. In addition, a method may have any number of *explicit parameters* that are supplied between parentheses. For example, in the call

```
myGreeter.setName("Mars");
```

the reference stored in myGreeter is the implicit parameter, and the string "Mars" is the explicit parameter. The explicit parameters are so named because they are explicitly defined in a method, whereas the implicit parameter is implied in the method definition.

Occasionally, you need to refer to the implicit parameter of a method by its special name, this. For example, consider the following implementation of the setName method:

```
public class Greeter
{
   . . .

   /**
       Sets this greeter's name to the given name.
       @param name  the new name for this greeter
   */
   public void setName(String name)
   {
       this.name = name;
   }

   . . .

}
```

> The this reference refers to the object on which a method was invoked.

The this reference refers to the object on which the method was invoked (such as myGreeter in the call myGreeter.setName("Mars")). The name field is set to the value of the explicit parameter that is also called name. In the example, the use of the this reference was necessary to resolve the ambiguity between the name field and the name parameter.

Occasionally, the `this` reference is used for greater clarity, as in the next example.

> A method can change the state of an object whose reference it receives.

In Java, a method can modify the state of an object because the corresponding parameter variable is set to a copy of the passed object reference. Consider this contrived method of the `Greeter` class:

```
public class Greeter
{
    . . .
    /**
        Sets another greeter's name to this greeter's name.
        @param other  a reference to the other Greeter
    */
    public void copyNameTo(Greeter other)
    {
        other.name = this.name;
    }
    . . .
}
```

Now consider this call:

```
Greeter worldGreeter = new Greeter("World");
Greeter daveGreeter = new Greeter("Dave");
worldGreeter.copyNameTo(daveGreeter);
```

Figure 8 shows how the `other` parameter variable is initialized with the `daveGreeter` reference. The `copyNameTo` method changes `other.name`, and after the method returns, `daveGreeter.name` has been changed.

However, in Java, a method can never update the *contents of a variable* that is passed as a parameter. For example, after the call

```
worldGreeter.copyNameTo(daveGreeter);
```

the contents of `daveGreeter` is the same object reference before and after the call. It is not possible to write a method that would change the contents of `daveGreeter` to another object reference. In this regard, Java differs from languages such as C++ and C# that have a "call by reference" mechanism.

To see that Java does not support call by reference, consider yet another set of contrived methods. These methods try to modify a parameter, but they have no effect at all.

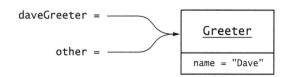

Figure 8

Accessing an Object through a Parameter Variable

```
public class Greeter
{
    . . .
    /**
        Tries to copy the length of this greeter's name into an integer variable.
        @param n  the variable into which the method tries to copy the length
    */
    public void copyLengthTo(int n)
    {
        // this assignment has no effect outside the method
        n = name.length();
    }

    /**
        Tries to set another Greeter object to a copy of this object.
        @param other  the Greeter object to initialize
    */
    public void copyGreeterTo(Greeter other)
    {
        // this assignment has no effect outside the method
        other = new Greeter(name);
    }
    . . .
}
```

Let's call these two methods:

```
int length = 0;
Greeter worldGreeter = new Greeter("World");
Greeter daveGreeter = new Greeter("Dave");
worldGreeter.copyLengthTo(length);
    // has no effect on the contents of length
worldGreeter.copyGreeterTo(daveGreeter);
    // has no effect on the contents of daveGreeter
```

> Java uses "call by value" when passing parameters.

Neither method call has any effect. Changing the value of the parameter variable does not affect the variable supplied in the method call. Thus, Java has no call by reference. Java uses the "call by value" mechanism for both primitive types and object references.

1.7 Packages

Java classes can be grouped into *packages*. Package names are dot-separated sequences of identifiers, such as

```
java.util
javax.swing
com.sun.misc
edu.sjsu.cs.cs151.alice
```

> Java uses packages to group related classes and to ensure unique class names.

To guarantee the uniqueness of package names, the inventors of Java recommend that you start a package name with a domain name in reverse (such as com.sun or edu.sjsu.cs), because domain names are guaranteed to be unique. Then use some other mechanism within your organization to ensure that the remainder of the package name is unique as well.

You place a class inside a package by adding a package statement as the first statement of the source file:

```
package edu.sjsu.cs.cs151.alice;
public class Greeter
{
    . . .
}
```

Any class without a package statement is in the "default package" with no package name.

The *full* name of a class consists of the package name followed by the class name, such as edu.sjsu.cs.cs151.alice.Greeter. Some full class name examples from the Java library are java.util.ArrayList and javax.swing.JOptionPane.

> The import directive allows programmers to omit package names when referring to classes.

It is tedious to use these full names in your code. Use the import statement to use the shorter class names instead. For example, after you place a statement

```
import java.util.Scanner;
```

into your source file, then you can refer to the class simply as Scanner. If you simultaneously use two classes with the same short name (such as java.util.Date and java.sql.Date), then you are stuck—you must use the full name for one of them.

You can also import all classes from a package:

```
import java.util.*;
```

However, you never need to import the classes in the java.lang package, such as String or Math.

> Organize your class files in directories that match the package names.

Large programs consist of many classes in multiple packages. The class files must be located in subdirectories that match the package names. For example, the class file Greeter.class for the class

```
edu.sjsu.cs.cs151.alice.Greeter
```

must be in a subdirectory

```
edu/sjsu/cs/cs151/alice
```

or

```
edu\sjsu\cs\cs151\alice
```

of the project's *base directory* (see Figure 9). The base directory is the directory that contains all package directories as well as any classes that are contained in the default package (that is, the package without a name).

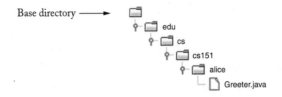

Base directory

edu
cs
cs151
alice
Greeter.java

Figure 9

Package Name Must Match the Directory Path

Always compile from the base directory, for example

```
javac edu/sjsu/cs/cs151/alice/Greeter.java
```

or

```
javac edu\sjsu\cs\cs151\alice\Greeter.java
```

Then the class file is automatically placed in the correct location.

To run a program, you must start the Java virtual machine in the base directory and specify the full class name of the class that contains the main method:

```
java edu.sjsu.cs.cs151.alice.Greeter
```

1.8 Basic Exception Handling

When a program carries out an illegal action, an *exception* is generated. Here is a common example. Suppose you initialize a variable with the null reference, intending to assign an actual object reference later, but then you accidentally use the variable when it is still null.

```
String name = null;
int n = name.length(); // Illegal
```

> When an exception occurs and there is no handler for it, the program terminates.

Applying a method call to null is illegal. The virtual machine now throws a NullPointerException. Unless your program handles this exception, it will terminate after displaying a *stack trace* (the sequence of pending method calls) such as this one:

```
Exception in thread "main" java.lang.NullPointerException
        at Greeter.sayHello(Greeter.java:25)
        at GreeterTester.main(GreeterTester.java:6)
```

Different programming errors lead to different exceptions. For example, trying to open a file with an illegal file name causes a FileNotFoundException.

> Throw an exception to indicate an error condition that the current method cannot handle.

You can also throw your own exceptions if you find that a programmer makes an error when using one of your classes. For example, if you require that the parameter of one of your methods should be positive, and the caller supplies a negative value, you can throw an `Illegal-ArgumentException`:

```
if (n <= 0) throw new IllegalArgumentException("n should be > 0");
```

> There are two categories of exceptions: checked and unchecked. If you call a method that might throw a checked exception, you must either declare it or catch it.

We will discuss the hierarchy of exception types in greater detail in Chapter 6. At this point you need to be aware of an important distinction between two kinds of exceptions, called *checked exceptions* and *unchecked exceptions*. The `NullPointerException` is an example of an unchecked exception. That is, the compiler does not check that your code handles the exception. If the exception occurs, it is detected at runtime and may terminate your program. The `IOException`, on the other hand, is a checked exception. If you call a method that might throw this exception, you must also specify how you want the program to deal with this failure.

In general, a checked exception is caused by an external condition beyond the programmer's control. Exceptions that occur during input and output are checked because the file system or network may spontaneously cause problems that the programmer cannot control. Therefore, the compiler insists that the programmer provide code to handle these situations.

On the other hand, unchecked exceptions are generally the programmer's fault. You should never get a `NullPointerException`. Therefore, the compiler doesn't tell you to provide a handler for a `NullPointerException`. Instead, you should spend your energy on making sure that the error doesn't occur in the first place. Either initialize your variables properly, or test that they aren't `null` before making a method call.

Whenever you write code that might cause a checked exception, you must take one of two actions:

1. Declare the exception in the method header.
2. Handle (or *catch*) the exception.

Consider this example. You want to read data from a file.

```
public void read(String filename)
{
    FileReader reader = new FileReader(filename);
    . . .
}
```

If there is no file with the given name, the `FileReader` constructor throws a `FileNotFoundException`. Because it is a checked exception, the compiler insists that you handle it. However, the implementor of the `read` method probably has no idea how to correct this situation. Therefore, the optimal remedy is to let the exception *propagate to its caller*. That means that the `read` method terminates, and that the exception is thrown to the method that called it.

Whenever a method propagates a *checked* exception, you must declare the exception in the method header, like this:

```
public void read(String filename) throws FileNotFoundException
{
    FileReader reader = new FileReader(filename);
    . . .
}
```

 TIP   There is no shame associated with acknowledging that your method might throw a checked exception—it is just "truth in advertising".

If a method can throw multiple exceptions, you list them all, separated by commas. Here is a typical example. As you will see in Chapter 7, reading objects from an object stream can cause both an IOException (if there is a problem with reading the input) and a ClassNotFoundException (if the input contains an object from an unknown class). A read method can declare that it throws both exceptions:

```
public void read(String filename)
        throws IOException, ClassNotFoundException
```

When you tag a method with a throws clause, the callers of this method are now put on notice that there is the possibility that a checked exception may occur. Of course, those calling methods also need to deal with these exceptions. Generally, the calling methods also add throws declarations. When you carry this process out for the entire program, the main method ends up being tagged as well:

```
public static void main(String[] args)
        throws IOException, ClassNotFoundException
{
    . . .
}
```

If an exception actually occurs, the main method is terminated, a stack trace is displayed, and the program exits.

However, if you write a professional program, you do not want the program to terminate whenever a user supplies an invalid file name. In that case, you want to *catch* the exception. Use the following syntax:

```
try
{
    . . .
    code that might throw an IOException
    . . .
}
catch (IOException exception)
{
    take corrective action
}
```

> When an exception is thrown, the program jumps to the closest matching catch clause.

An appropriate corrective action might be to display an error message and to inform the user that the attempt to read the file has failed.

In most programs, the lower-level methods simply propagate exceptions to their callers. Some higher-level method, such as main or a part of the user interface, catches exceptions and informs the user.

For debugging purposes, you sometimes want to see the stack trace. Call the print-StackTrace method like this:

```
try
{
    . . .
}
catch (IOException exception)
{
    exception.printStackTrace();
    take corrective action
}
```

Occasionally, a method must carry out an action even if a prior statement caused an exception. A typical example is closing a file. A program can only open a limited number of files at one time, and it should close all files that it opened. To ensure that a file is closed even if an exception occurred during file processing, use the finally clause:

```
FileReader reader = null;
reader = new FileReader(name);
try
{
    . . .
}
finally
{
    reader.close();
}
```

> Code in a finally clause is executed during normal processing and when an exception is thrown.

The finally clause is executed when the try block exits without an exception, and also when an exception is thrown inside the try block. In either case, the close method is called. Note that the FileReader constructor is *not* contained inside the try block. If the constructor throws an exception, then reader has not yet been assigned a value, and the close method should not be called.

1.9   Strings

Java strings are sequences of Unicode characters. The charAt method yields the individual characters of a string. String positions start at 0.

```
String greeting = "Hello";
char ch = greeting.charAt(1); // sets ch to 'e'
```

> A Java string is an immutable sequence of Unicode characters.

Java strings are *immutable*. Once created, a string cannot be changed. Thus, there is no setCharAt method. This may sound like a severe restriction, but in practice it isn't. For example, suppose you initialized greeting to "Hello". You can still change your mind:

```
greeting = "Goodbye";
```

The string object "Hello" hasn't changed, but greeting now refers to a different string object.

The length method yields the length of a string. For example, "Hello".length() is 5.

Figure 10

Extracting a Substring

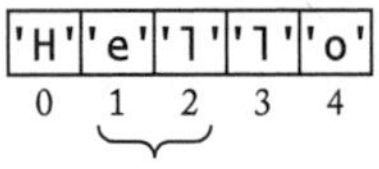

'H'	'e'	'l'	'l'	'o'
0	1	2	3	4

Note that the empty string "" of length 0 is different from null—a reference to no string at all.

The `substring` method computes substrings of a string. You need to specify the positions of the first character that you want to include in the substring and the first character that you no longer want to include. For example, `"Hello".substring(1, 3)` is the string `"el"` (see Figure 10). Note that the difference between the two positions equals the length of the substring.

Since strings are objects, you need to use the `equals` method to compare whether two strings have the same contents.

```
if (greeting.equals("Hello")) . . . // OK
```

If you use the `==` operator, you only test whether two string references have the identical *location*. For example, the following test fails:

```
if ("Hello".substring(1, 3) == "el") . . . // NO
```

The substring is not at the same location as the constant string `"el"`, even though it has the same contents.

You have already seen the string concatenation operator: `"Hello, " + name` is the concatenation of the string `"Hello, "` and the string object to which `name` refers.

If either argument of the `+` operator is a string, then the other is *converted to a string*. For example,

```
int n = 7;
String greeting = "Hello, " + n;
```

constructs the string `"Hello, 7"`.

If a string and an object are concatenated, then the object is converted to a string by invoking its `toString` method. For example, the `toString` method of the `Date` class in the `java.util` package returns a string containing the date and time that is encapsulated in the `Date` object. Here is what happens when you concatenate a string and a `Date` object:

```
// default Date constructor sets current date/time
Date now = new Date();
String greeting = "Hello, " + now;
// greeting is a string such as "Hello, Wed Jan 18 16:57:18 PST 2006"
```

Sometimes, you have a string that contains a number, for example the string `"7"`. To convert the string to its number value, use the `Integer.parseInt` and `Double.parseDouble` methods. For example,

```
String input = "7";
n = Integer.parseInt(input); // sets n to 7
```

If the string doesn't contain a number, or contains additional characters besides a number, the unchecked `NumberFormatException` is thrown.

1.10   Reading Input

> The Scanner class can be used to read input from the console or a file.

Starting with Java 5.0, the simplest way to read input in a Java program is to use the Scanner class. To read console input, construct a Scanner from System.in. Call the nextInt or nextDouble method to read an integer or a floating-point number. For example,

```
Scanner in = new Scanner(System.in);
System.out.print("How old are you? ");
int age = in.nextInt();
```

If the user types input that is not a number, an (unchecked) InputMismatchException is thrown. You can protect yourself against that exception by calling the hasNextInt or has-NextDouble method before calling nextInt or nextDouble.

The next method reads the next whitespace-delimited token, and nextLine reads the next input line.

You can read input from a file by constructing a Scanner from a FileReader. For example, the following loop reads all lines from the file input.txt:

```
Scanner in = new Scanner(new FileReader("input.txt"));
while (in.hasNextLine())
{
    String line = in.nextLine();
    . . .
}
```

1.11   Array Lists and Linked Lists

The ArrayList class of the java.util package lets you collect a sequence of objects of any type. The add method adds an object to the end of the array list.

```
ArrayList<String> countries = new ArrayList<String>();
countries.add("Belgium");
countries.add("Italy");
countries.add("Thailand");
```

Starting with Java 5.0, the ArrayList class is a *generic* class with a *type parameter*. The type parameter (String in our example) denotes the type of the list elements. You can form array lists of any type, except for primitive types. For example, you can use an ArrayList<Date> but not an ArrayList<int>.

The size method returns the number of elements in the array list. The get method returns the element at a given position; legal positions range from 0 to size() - 1. For example, the following loop prints all elements of the countries list:

```
for (int i = 0; i < countries.size(); i++)
{
    String country = countries.get(i);
    System.out.println(country);
}
```

Figure 11

Inserting into an Array List

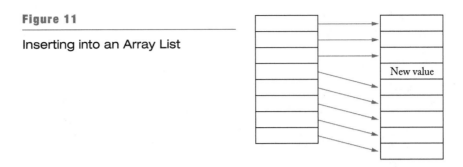

This loop is so common that Java 5.0 introduces a convenient shortcut: the *enhanced* for loop or "for each" loop:

```
for (String country : countries)
    System.out.println(country);
```

In each loop iteration, the variable before the : is set to the next element of the countries list.

The set method lets you overwrite an existing element with another:

```
countries.set(1, "France");
```

If you access a nonexistent position (< 0 or >= size()), then an IndexOutOfBounds-Exception is thrown.

Finally, you can insert and remove elements in the middle of the array list.

```
countries.add(1, "Germany");
countries.remove(0);
```

> An array list is a collection of objects that supports efficient access to all storage locations.

> A linked list is a collection of objects that supports efficient insertion and removal of elements. You use an iterator to traverse a linked list.

These operations move the remaining elements up or down. The name "array list" signifies that the public interface allows both array operations (get/set) and list operations (add/remove).

Inserting and removing elements in the middle of an array list is not efficient. All elements beyond the location of insertion or removal must be moved (see Figure 11). A *linked list* is a data structure that supports efficient insertion and removal at any location. When inserting or removing an element, all elements stay in place, and only the neighboring links are rearranged (see Figure 12). The standard Java library supplies a class LinkedList implementing this data structure.

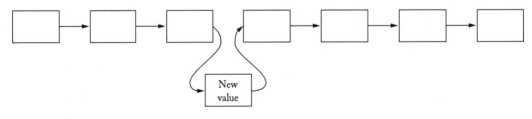

Figure 12

Inserting into a Linked List

As with array lists, you use the add method to add elements to the end of a linked list.

```
LinkedList<String> countries = new LinkedList<String>();
countries.add("Belgium");
countries.add("Italy");
countries.add("Thailand");
```

However, accessing elements in the middle of the linked list is not as simple. You don't want to access a position by an integer index. To find an element with a given index, it is necessary to follow a sequence of links, starting with the head of the list. That process is not very efficient. Instead, you need an *iterator*, an object that can access a position anywhere in the list:

```
ListIterator<String> iterator = countries.listIterator();
```

The next method advances the iterator to the next position of the list and returns the element that the iterator just passed (see Figure 13). The hasNext method tests whether the iterator is already past the last element in the list. Thus, the following loop prints all elements in the list:

```
while (iterator.hasNext())
{
    String country = iterator.next();
    System.out.println(country);
}
```

To add an element in the middle of the list, advance an iterator past the insert location and call add:

```
iterator = countries.listIterator();
iterator.next();
iterator.add("France");
```

To remove an element from the list, call next until you jump over the element that you want to remove, then call remove. For example, this code removes the second element of the countries list.

```
iterator = countries.listIterator();
iterator.next();
iterator.next();
iterator.remove();
```

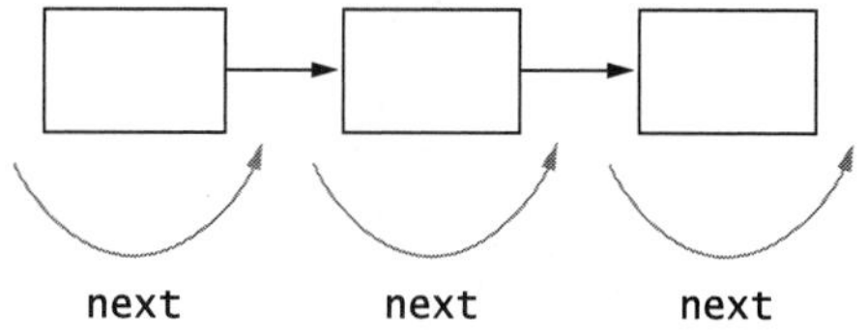

Figure 13

Iterator Movement

next   next   next

1.12   Arrays

Array lists and linked lists have one drawback—they can only hold objects, not values of primitive types. *Arrays*, on the other hand, can hold sequences of arbitrary values. You construct an array as

```
new T[n]
```

where T is any type and n any integer-valued expression. The array has type T[].

```
int[] numbers = new int[10];
```

> An array stores a fixed number of values of any given type.

Now numbers is a reference to an array of 10 integers—see Figure 14. When an array is constructed, its elements are set to zero, false, or null.

The length of an array is stored in the length field.

```
int length = numbers.length;
```

Note that an empty array of length 0

```
new int[0]
```

is different from null—a reference to no array at all.

You access an array element by enclosing the index in brackets, such as

```
numbers[i] = i * i;
```

If you access a nonexistent position (< 0 or >= length), then an ArrayIndexOutOf-BoundsException is thrown.

As with array lists, you can use the "for each" loop to traverse the elements of an array. For example, the loop

```
for (int n : numbers)
    System.out.println(n);
```

is a shorthand for

```
for (int i = 0; i < numbers.length; i++)
    System.out.println(numbers[i]);
```

There is a convenient shorthand for constructing and initializing an array. Enclose the array elements in braces, like this:

```
int[] numbers = { 0, 1, 4, 9, 16, 25, 36, 49, 64, 81 };
```

Occasionally, it is convenient to construct an *anonymous array*, without storing the array reference in a variable. For example, the Polygon class has a constructor

```
Polygon(int[] xvalues, int[] yvalues, int n);
```

You can construct a triangle by calling

```
Polygon triangle = new Polygon(
    new int[] { 0, 10, 5 }, // anonymous array of integers
    new int[] { 10, 0, 5 }, // another anonymous array
    3);
```

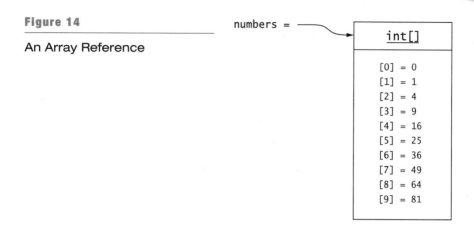

Figure 14

An Array Reference

After an array has been constructed, you cannot change its length. If you want a larger array, you have to construct a new array and move the elements from the old array to the new array.

You can obtain a two-dimensional array like this:

```
int[][] table = new int[10][20];
```

You access the elements as `table[row][column]`.

When you launch a program by typing its name into a command shell, then you can supply additional information to the program by typing it after the program name. The entire input line is called the command line, and the strings following the program name are the command-line arguments. The `args` parameter of the `main` method is an array of strings, the strings specified in the command line. The first string after the class name is `args[0]`. For example, if you invoke a program as

```
java GreeterTester Mars
```

then `args.length` is 1 and `args[0]` is `"Mars"` and not `"java"` or `"GreeterTester"`.

Java 5.0 introduces methods with a variable number of parameters. When you call such a method, you supply as many parameter values as you like. The parameter values are automatically placed in an array. Here is an example:

```
public double sum(double... values)
{
   double sum = 0;
   for (double v : values) sum += v;
   return sum;
}
```

The ... symbol indicates that the method takes a variable number of parameters of type `double`. The parameter variable `values` is actually an array of type `double[]`. If you call the method, for example as

```
double result = sum(0.25, -1, 10);
```

then the `values` parameter is initialized with `new double[] { 0.25, -1, 10 }`.

Static Fields and Methods

Occasionally, you would like to share a variable among all objects of a class. Here is a typical example. The `Random` class in the `java.util` package implements a random number generator. It has methods such as `nextInt`, `nextDouble`, and `nextBoolean` that return random integers, floating-point numbers, and Boolean values. For example, here is how you print 10 random integers:

```
Random generator = new Random();
for (int i = 1; i <= 10; i++)
    System.out.println(generator.nextInt());
```

Let's use a random number generator in the `Greeter` class:

```
public String saySomething()
{
    if (generator.nextBoolean())
        return "Hello, " + name + "!";
    else
        return "Goodbye, " + name + "!";
}
```

It would be wasteful to supply each `Greeter` object with its own random number generator. To share one generator among all `Greeter` objects, declare the field as `static`:

```
public class Greeter
{
    . . .
    private static Random generator = new Random();
}
```

> A static field belongs to the class, not to individual objects.

The term "static" is an unfortunate and meaningless holdover from C++. A static field is more accurately called a *class variable:* there is only a single variable for the entire class.

Class variables are relatively rare. A more common use for the `static` keyword is to define constants. For example, the `Math` class contains the following definitions:

```
public class Math
{
    . . .
    public static final double E = 2.7182818284590452354;
    public static final double PI = 3.14159265358979323846;
}
```

The keyword `final` denotes a constant value. After a `final` variable has been initialized, you cannot change its value.

These constants are public. You refer to them as `Math.PI` and `Math.E`.

A static method (or class method) is a method that does not operate on an object. You have already encountered static methods such as `Math.sqrt` and `JOptionPane.showInputDialog`. Another use for static methods is *factory methods*, methods that return an object, similar to a constructor. Here is a factory method for the `Greeter` class that returns a greeter object with a random name:

```
public class Greeter
{
    public static Greeter getRandomInstance()
    {
        if (generator.nextBoolean())
            return new Greeter("Venus");
        else
            return new Greeter("Mars");
    }
    . . .
}
```

> A static method is not invoked on an object.

You invoke this method as `Greeter.getRandomInstance()`. Note that static methods can access static fields but not instance fields—they don't operate on an object.

Static fields and methods have their place, but they are quite rare in object-oriented programs. If your programs contain many static fields and methods, then this may mean that you have missed an opportunity to discover sufficient classes to implement your program in an object-oriented manner. Here is a bad example that shows how you can write very poor non-object-oriented programs with static fields and methods:

```
public class BadGreeter
{
    public static void main(String[] args)
    {
        name = "World";
        printHello();
    }

    public static void printHello() // Bad style
    {
        System.out.println("Hello, " + name + "!");
    }

    private static String name; // Bad style
}
```

1.14   Programming Style

Class names should always start with an uppercase letter and use mixed case, such as `String`, `StringTokenizer`, and so on. Package names should always be lowercase, such as `edu.sjsu.cs.cs151.alice`. Field and method names should always start with a lowercase letter and use mixed case, such as `name` and `sayHello`. Underscores are not commonly used in class or method names. Constants should be in all uppercase with an occasional underscore, such as `PI` or `MAX_VALUE`.

> Follow the standard naming conventions for classes, methods, fields, and constants.

These are not requirements of the Java language but a convention that is followed by essentially all Java programmers. Your programs would look very strange to other Java programmers if you used classes that started with a lowercase letter or methods that started with an uppercase letter. It is not considered good style by most Java programmers to use prefixes for fields (such as _name or m_name).

It is very common to use `get` and `set` prefixes for methods that get or set a property of an object, such as

```
public String getName()
public void setName(String aName)
```

However, a Boolean property has prefixes `is` and `set`, such as

```
public boolean isPolite()
public void setPolite(boolean b)
```

Use a consistent style for braces. We suggest that you line up { and } in the same row or column.

There are two common brace styles: The "Allmann" style in which braces line up, and the compact but less clear "Kernighan and Ritchie" style. Here is the `Greeter` class, formatted in the Kernighan and Ritchie style.

```
public class Greeter {
    public Greeter(String aName) {
        name = aName;
    }

    public String sayHello() {
        return "Hello, " + name + "!";
    }

    private String name;
}
```

We use the Allmann style in this book.

Some programmers list fields before methods in a class:

```
public class Greeter
{
    private String name;
        // Listing private features first is not a good idea

    public Greeter(String aName)
    {
        . . .
    }
    . . .
}
```

However, from an object-oriented programming point of view, it makes more sense to list the public interface first. That is the approach we use in this book.

Make sure that you declare all instance fields `private`.

Except for `public static final` fields, all fields should be declared private. If you omit the access specifier, the field has *package visibility*—all methods of classes in the same package can access it—an unsafe practice that you should avoid. Anyone can add classes to a package at any time. Therefore, there is an open-ended and uncontrollable set of methods that can potentially access fields with package visibility.

It is technically legal—as a sop to C++ programmers—to declare array variables as

```
int numbers[]
```

You should avoid that style and use

```
int[] numbers
```

That style clearly shows the type `int[]` of the variable.

All classes, methods, parameters, and return values should have documentation comments.

You should put spaces *around* binary operators and after keywords, but not after method names.

Good	Bad
`x > y`	`x>y`
`if (x > y)`	`if(x > y)`
`Math.sqrt(x)`	`Math.sqrt (x)`

You should not use *magic numbers*. Use named constants (`final` variables) instead. For example, don't use

```
h = 31 * h + val[off]; // Bad—what's 31?
```

What is 31? The number of days in January? The position of the highest bit in an integer? No, it's the hash multiplier.

Instead, declare a local constant in the method

```
final int HASH_MULTIPLIER = 31
```

or a static constant in the class (if it is used by more than one method)

```
private static final int HASH_MULTIPLIER = 31
```

Then use the named constant:

```
h = HASH_MULTIPLIER * h + val[off]; // Much better
```

 INTERNET The CheckStyle program (`http://checkstyle.sourceforge.net`) can automatically check the quality of your code. It reports misaligned braces, missing documentation comments, and many other style errors.

EXERCISES

Exercise 1.1. Add a `sayGoodbye` method to the `Greeter` class and add a call to test the method in the `GreeterTester` class (or test it in BlueJ).

Exercise 1.2. What happens when you run the Java interpreter on the `Greeter` class instead of the `GreeterTester` class? Try it out and explain.

Exercise 1.3. Add comments to the `GreeterTester` class and the `main` method. Document `args` as "unused". Use `javadoc` to generate a file `GreeterTester.html`. Inspect the file in your browser.

Exercise 1.4. Bookmark `docs/api/index.html` in your browser. Find the documentation of the `String` class. How many methods does the `String` class have?

Exercise 1.5. Write a program that prints "Hello, San José". Use a `\u` escape sequence to denote the letter é.

Exercise 1.6. What is the Unicode character for the Greek letter "pi" (π)? For the Chinese character "bu" (不)?

Exercise 1.7. Run the `javadoc` utility on the `Greeter` class. What output do you get? How does the output change when you remove some of the documentation comments?

Exercise 1.8. Download and install the `DocCheck` utility. What output do you get when you remove some of the documentation comments of the `Greeter` class?

Exercise 1.9. Write a program that computes and prints the square root of 1000, rounded to the nearest integer.

Exercise 1.10. Write a program that computes and prints the sum of integers from 1 to 100 and the sum of integers from 100 to 1000. Create an appropriate class `Summer` that has no `main` method for this purpose. If you don't use BlueJ, create a second class with a `main` method to construct two objects of the `Summer` class.

Exercise 1.11. Add a `setName` method to the `Greeter` class. Write a program with two `Greeter` variables that refer to the same `Greeter` object. Invoke `setName` on one of the references and `sayHello` on the other. Print the return value. Explain.

Exercise 1.12. Write a program that sets a `Greeter` variable to `null` and then calls `sayHello` on that variable. Explain the resulting output. What does the number behind the file name mean?

Exercise 1.13. Write a test program that tests the `setName`, `copyNameTo`, `copyLengthTo`, and `copyGreeterTo` methods of the examples in Section 1.6, printing out the parameter variables before and after the method call.

Exercise 1.14. Write a method `void swapNames(Greeter other)` of the `Greeter` class that swaps the names of this greeter and another.

Exercise 1.15. Write a program in which `Greeter` is in the package `edu.sjsu.cs.`*yourcourse*`.`*yourname* and `GreeterTester` is in the default package. Into which directories do you put the source files and the class files?

Exercise 1.16. What is wrong with the following code snippet?

```
ArrayList<String> strings;
strings.add("France");
```

Exercise 1.17. Write a `GreeterTester` program that constructs `Greeter` objects for all command-line arguments and prints out the results of calling `sayHello`. For example, if your program is invoked as

```
java GreeterTester Mars Venus
```

then the program should print

```
Hello, Mars!
Hello, Venus!
```

Exercise 1.18. What are the values of the following?

(a) `2 + 2 + "2"`

(b) `"" + countries`, where `countries` is an `ArrayList` filled with several strings

(c) `"Hello" + new Greeter("World")`

Write a small sample program to find out, then explain your answers.

Exercise 1.19. Write a program that prints the sum of its command-line arguments (assuming they are numbers). For example,

```
java Adder 3 2.5 -4.1
```

should print `The sum is 1.4`

Exercise 1.20. Write a program that reads input data from a file and prints the minimum, maximum, and average value of the input data. The file name should be specified on the command line. Use a class `DataAnalyzer` and a separate class `DataAnalyzerTester`.

Exercise 1.21. Write a `GreeterTester` program that asks the user "What is your name?" and then prints out `"Hello, username"`.

Exercise 1.22. Write a class that can generate random strings with characters in a given set. For example,

```
RandomStringGenerator generator = new RandomStringGenerator();
generator.addRange('a', 'z');
generator.addRange('A', 'Z');
String s = generator.nextString(10);
    // A random string consisting of ten lowercase
    // or uppercase English characters
```

Your class should keep an `ArrayList<Range>` of Range objects.

Exercise 1.23. Write a program that plays TicTacToe with a human user. Use a class `TicTacToeBoard` that stores a 3×3 array of `char` values (filled with `'x'`, `'o'`, or space characters). Your program should use a random number generator to choose who begins. When it's the computer's turn, randomly generate a legal move. When it's the human's turn, read the move and check that it is legal.

Exercise 1.24. Improve the performance of the `getRandomInstance` factory method by returning one of two fixed `Greeter` objects (stored in static fields) rather than constructing a new object with every call.

Exercise 1.25. Use any ZIP utility or the `jar` program from the Java SDK to uncompress the `src.zip` file that is part of the Java SDK. Then look at the source code of the `String` class in `java/lang/String.java`. How many style rules do the programmers violate? Look at the `hashCode` method. How can you rewrite it in a less muddleheaded way?

Exercise 1.26. Look inside the source code of the class `java.awt.Window`. List the instance fields of the class. Which of them are private, and which of them have package visibility? Are there any other classes in the `java.awt` package that access those fields? If not, why do you think that they are not private?

The Object-Oriented Design Process

In this chapter, we will introduce the main topic of this book: object-oriented design. The chapter introduces a miniature version of a typical object-oriented design methodology that can guide you from the functional specification of a program to its implementation. You will see how to find and document classes and the relationships between them, using CRC cards and UML diagrams.

2.1   From Problem to Code

This book discusses the design and implementation of computer programs from the object-oriented point of view. We focus on small and medium-sized problems. Although much of what we say remains valid for large projects, there are added complexities with large projects that we will not address here.

Programming tasks originate from the desire to solve a particular problem. The task may be simple, such as writing a program that generates and formats a report, or complicated, such as writing a word processor. The end product is a working program. To this end, it is a common practice to break up the software development process into three phases:

- Analysis
- Design
- Implementation

> The software development process consists of analysis, design, and implementation phases.

This section briefly discusses the goals and methods of these phases. Of course, it is simplistic to assume that development is a simple linear progression through these phases. Successful software products evolve over time. Implementation experiences may suggest an improved design. New requirements are added, forcing another iteration through analysis and design. Experience suggests that object-oriented design can lead to software that facilitates the inevitable evolution better than software developed with traditional methods because the objects and classes that represent the concepts of a problem domain tend to be fairly stable.

2.1.1 — The Analysis Phase

> The goal of the analysis phase is a complete description of what the software product should do.

In the analysis phase, a vague understanding of the problem is transformed into a precise description of the tasks that the software system needs to carry out. The result of the analysis phase is a detailed textual description, commonly called a *functional specification*, that has the following characteristics:

- It completely defines the tasks to be performed.
- It is free from internal contradictions.
- It is readable both by experts in the problem domain and by software developers.
- It is reviewable by diverse interested parties.
- It can be tested against reality.

Consider, for example, the task of writing a word-processing program. The analysis phase must define terms, such as fonts, footnotes, multiple columns, and document sections, and the interaction of those features, such as how footnotes in multiple-column text ought to look on the screen and the printed page. The user interface must be documented, explaining, for example, how the user is to enter and move a footnote or specify the font for footnote numbers. One possible format for an analysis document is a user manual, very precisely worded to remove as much ambiguity as possible.

Another common format for describing the behavior of a system is a set of *use cases*. A use case is a description of a sequence of actions that yields a benefit for a user of a system. At least in principle, it should be possible to enumerate all benefits that a system can confer upon its users and supply use cases that show how they can be obtained.

The analysis phase concerns itself with the description of *what* needs to be done, not how it should be done. The selection of specific algorithms, such as those that insert page breaks or sort the index, will be handled in the implementation phase.

Although we do not do so in this book, it is possible to use object-oriented techniques in the analysis phase as well as the design phase. An advantage of that approach is that the object model of the analysis phase can be carried forward to the design phase. A potential pitfall is that customers of a software product are generally not familiar with the terminology of object orientation. Clients may not find it easy to tell whether the analysis will lead to a product that satisfies their needs.

2.1.2 — The Design Phase

In the design phase, the program designer must structure the programming tasks into a set of interrelated classes. Each class must be specified precisely, listing both its responsibilities and its relationship to other classes in the system. You will study this process in this book in some detail.

The designer must strive for a result in which the classes are crisply defined and class relationships are of manageable complexity. The exact choice of data structures, for example, hash tables or binary search trees for a collection, is not of concern in the design phase but is deferred until implementation. Even the choice of programming language is not a design issue. It is possible to map an object-oriented design to a programming language without object-oriented features, although that process can be somewhat unpleasant.

> The goal of object-oriented design is the identification of classes, their responsibilities, and the relationships among them.

Here are the major goals of the design phase:

- Identify the classes
- Identify the responsibilities of these classes
- Identify the relationships among these classes

These are goals, not steps. It is usually not possible to find all classes first, then give a complete description of their responsibilities, then elaborate on their relationships. The discovery process is iterative—the identification of one aspect of a class may force changes in or lead to the discovery of others.

The end result of the design process consists of a number of artifacts:

- A textual description of the classes and their most important responsibilities
- Diagrams of the relationships among the classes
- Diagrams of important usage scenarios
- State diagrams of objects whose behavior is highly state-dependent

Depending on the tool support, this information may be stored on paper, in text and graphics files, or in a CASE (computer-assisted software engineering) tool database.

The information gathered in this phase becomes the foundation for the implementation of the system in an actual programming language. Typically, the design phase is more time-consuming than the the actual programming, or—to put a positive spin on it—a good design greatly reduces the time required for implementation and testing.

2.1.3 — The Implementation Phase

> The goal of the implementation phase is the programming, testing, and deployment of the software product.

In the implementation phase, the classes and methods are coded, tested, and deployed. A part of this book concerns itself with the problems of implementing an object-oriented design in Java.

Traditional programming methods rely on completion and unit testing of procedural units, followed by an integration phase. This integration tends to be frustrating and disappointing. Few programs are born according to plan out of a successful "big bang" integration. Object-oriented development encourages the gradual growth of a program by successively attaching more working classes and class clusters and repeated testing.

It is quite common to defer the implementation of some operations and build a "rapid prototype" that displays some functionality of the final product. Such a prototype can be extremely helpful in influencing the design or even the problem analysis, especially in cases where a problem was so incompletely understood that seeing a prototype do some work gives more insights into the solutions that are really desired.

You should not rush the analysis and design phase just to get to a working prototype quickly, nor should you hesitate to reopen the previous phases if a prototype yields new insight.

Object-oriented design is particularly suited for prototyping. The objects supporting the prototype are likely to be the same that need to be present in the final product, and growing the prototype into a complete program often is feasible. Some developers welcome this; others caution against it because prototypes are often rushed and without sufficient time to work them over carefully. In fact, some people recommend implementing a prototype in a language such as Visual Basic and then writing the final product in another language such as Java. For small to medium-sized products, a prototype can expand into a complete product. If you follow this evolutionary approach, be sure that the transition from prototype to final product is well managed and that enough time is allocated to fix mistakes and implement newly discovered improvements.

For the remainder of this chapter, we will mainly be concerned with the design phase of a programming project, focusing on object-oriented design techniques.

2.2   The Object and Class Concepts

We assume that you have programmed with classes for some time, and that you are familiar with the mechanics of defining classes and constructing objects. Thus, you have a fairly good idea what objects and classes are in the context of Java. Let's take a higher-level view and think about the concepts of objects and classes outside any particular programming language.

> An object is characterized by its state, behavior, and identity.

Objects are entities in a computer program that have three characteristic properties:

- State
- Behavior
- Identity

An object can store information that is the result of its prior operations. That information may determine how the object behaves in the future. The collection of all information held by an object is the object's *state*. An object's state may change over time, but only when an operation has been carried out on the object that causes the state change.

Consider the example of a mailbox in a voice mail system. A mailbox object may be in an empty state (immediately after its creation) or full (after receiving a large number of messages). This state affects the behavior of the mailbox object: A full mailbox may reject new mail messages, whereas an empty mailbox may give a special response ("no messages waiting") when asked to list all new messages.

The *behavior* of an object is defined by the operations (or methods, as they are called in Java) that an object supports. Objects permit certain operations and do not support others. For example, a mailbox can add a mail message to its collection or retrieve a stored message, but it cannot carry out other operations such as "translate the stored messages into Lithuanian".

Object-oriented programs contain statements in which objects are asked to carry out certain operations. Because not all operations are suitable for all objects, there must be a mechanism for rejecting improper requests. Object-oriented programming systems differ in this regard. Some systems attempt to weed out unsupported operations at compile time; others generate run-time errors.

The momentary state and the collection of admissible operations, however, do not fully characterize an object. It is possible for two or more objects to support the same operations and to have the same state, yet to be different from each other. Each object has its own *identity*. For example, two different mailboxes may, by chance, have the same contents, yet the program can tell them apart.

Some researchers *define* objects as entities that have state, behavior, and identity. This definition is somewhat unsatisfactory—what, after all, is an "entity"? The definition is also quite broad. As one computer scientist has pointed out, it then follows that his cat is an object: It has a rich internal state (hungry, purring, sleeping); it carries out certain operations (scratch sofa, catch mouse) while not supporting others (solve system of linear equations); and it has an identity that differentiates it from its twin brother.

Of course, when designing software, we consider only objects that have an existence in a computer program and that are, by necessity, models of real or abstract entities. The physical cat exists in the real world and not in a computer program. But a software product (perhaps the software controlling a vacuum-cleaning robot) may well include `Cat` objects that simulate certain relevant aspects of real cats.

> A class specifies objects with the same behavior.

Most object-oriented programming languages support the grouping of similar objects into classes. A *class* describes a collection of related objects. Objects of the same class support the same collection of operations and have a common set of possible states. A class definition must therefore include the following:

- The operations that are allowed on the objects of the class
- The possible states for objects of the class

Consider, for example, a class `Mailbox` that describes those aspects common to all mailboxes. All mailboxes support the same operations (add a mail message, retrieve a stored message, delete a message, and so forth). All mailboxes must store the same kind of information (collection of messages, index of current message). Each object is constrained by the properties of its class. It supports only those operations that the class lists as admissible, and its legal states must stay within the range that the class permits.

> An instance of a class is an object that belongs to the given class.

Objects that conform to a class description are called *instances* of that class. For example, my mailbox in the voice mail system at my place of work is an instance of the `Mailbox` class. The message that my boss sent me yesterday is an instance of class `Message`.

SPECIAL TOPIC 2.1

ECMAScript—An Object-Oriented Language Without Classes

Some programming languages have objects but no classes. Consider for example the ECMA-Script language that is the foundation of the JavaScript and JScript languages used in Web programming.

INTERNET You can download the ECMAScript language specification at `http://www.ecma-international.org/publications/standards/Ecma-262.htm`. A tutorial that shows how to use JavaScript inside Web pages is at `http://developer.netscape.com/docs/manuals/communicator/jsguide4/index.htm`. The Rhino toolkit at `http://www.mozilla.org/rhino/` is an ECMAScript interpreter that is implemented in Java. You can download it to experiment with the language, or to add scripting capabilities to a Java program.

There is no relationship between Java and JavaScript—Netscape renamed their "LiveScript" language to JavaScript for marketing reasons. When the language was standardized by ECMA, the European Computer Manufacturers Association, it acquired the catchy name ECMAScript. ECMAScript lets you create objects without specifying a class, simply by setting values of fields and methods. Here we define an object that has a name field and a sayHello method.

```
worldGreeter =
    {
        name: "World",
        sayHello: function () { return "Hello, " + this.name + "!" },
    };
```

This object supports the sayHello method:

```
message = worldGreeter.sayHello();
```

To create multiple related objects, you can write a function that constructs them:

```
function Greeter(aName)
{
    return {
        name: aName,
        sayHello: function () { return "Hello, " + this.name + "!" }
    }
}

marsGreeter = Greeter("Mars");
message = marsGreeter.sayHello();
```

However, ECMAScript has no classes. Even though worldGreeter and marsGreeter have the same behavior and state set, the language does not recognize them as being related.

Note that variables in ECMAScript are *untyped*. The worldGreeter variable can refer to different objects at different times. You can store a string object in the variable at any time.

```
worldGreeter = "Welcome to Venus!";
```

Of course, if you now try to invoke the sayHello method, then a run-time error occurs, since the object to which the variable currently refers does not support that method.

2.3   Identifying Classes

To discover classes, look for nouns in the problem description.

A simple rule of thumb for identifying classes is to look for *nouns* in the functional specification. Later in this chapter, we will analyze, design, and implement a voice mail system. To follow the examples throughout the chapter, you may want to peek ahead at Section 2.12, or just use your general knowledge about voice mail systems.

The following nouns are typical of those that can be found in the functional description of a voice mail system:

- Mailbox
- Message
- User
- Passcode
- Extension
- Menu

Many, but not necessarily all of them, are good choices for classes.

 TIP   Make sure not to fall into the trap of making your designs too specific. Suppose you are designing software to process orders for kitchen appliances such as toasters and blenders. If you let the object-oriented design process run amok, you end up with classes Kitchen-Appliance, Toaster, and Blender. But wait—the kitchen appliance hierarchy is *irrelevant* to our problem, namely to process orders for products. A Product class is probably a better choice.

Don't fall into the opposite trap of making your designs unreasonably general. Consider the mail system example. A mailbox is a kind of component, and there are connections between various components. Connections can carry data (such as messages). Should you therefore design classes Component, Connection, and Data? No—those classes are too general. You would not be able to come up with clear responsibilities for them, and you would be no closer to a solution of your design problem.

After you have harvested the classes that are obvious from the program specification, you need to turn your attention to other classes that are required to carry out necessary work. For example, consider the storage of messages in a mailbox. The mailbox owner wants to listen to the messages in the order in which they were added. In other words, messages are inserted and retrieved in a *FIFO (first in, first out)* fashion. Computer scientists defined the *queue* data type to describe this behavior, and they have discovered several implementations of this data type, some of which are more efficient than others. (See the note at the end of this section for more information about queues.) During design time, it makes sense to describe a class MessageQueue and its FIFO behavior. However, the exact implementation of the queue is of no interest in the design phase.

> Class names should be nouns in the singular form.

Class names should be nouns in the singular form: Message, Mailbox. Sometimes the noun needs to be prefixed by an adjective or participle: RectangularShape, BufferedReader. Don't use Object in the class name (MailboxObject)—it adds no value. Unless you are solving a very generic problem, stay away from generic names such as Agent, Task, Item, Event, User. If you name your classes after verbs (such as Deliver or Printing), you are probably on the wrong track.

After you go beyond the technique of finding nouns in the functional specification, it is useful to look at other categories of classes that are often helpful. Here are some of these categories:

- Tangible things
- Agents
- Events and transactions
- Users and roles
- Systems
- System interfaces and devices
- Foundational classes

Tangible things are the easiest classes to discover because they are visible in the problem domain. We have seen many examples: `Mailbox`, `Message`, `Document`, `Footnote`.

Sometimes it is helpful to change an operation into an agent class. For example, the "compute page breaks" operation on a document could be turned into a `Paginator` class, which operates on documents. Then the paginator can work on a part of a document while another part is edited on the screen. In this case, the agent class is invented to express parallel execution.

The `Scanner` class is another example. As described in Chapter 1, a `Scanner` is used to scan for numbers and strings in an input stream. Thus, the operation of parsing input is encapsulated in the `Scanner` agent.

Agent classes often end in "er" or "or".

Event and transaction classes are useful to model records of activities that describe what happened in the past or what needs to be done later. An example is a `MouseEvent` class, which remembers when and where the mouse was moved or clicked.

User and role classes are stand-ins for actual users of the program. An `Administrator` class is a representation of the human administrator of the system. A `Reviewer` class in an interactive authoring system models a user whose role is to add critical annotations and recommendations for change. User classes are common in systems that are used by more than one person or where one person needs to perform distinct tasks.

System classes model a subsystem or the overall system being built. Their roles are typically to perform initialization and shutdown and to start the flow of input into the system. For example, we might have a class `MailSystem` to represent the voice mail system in its entirety.

System interface classes model interfaces to the host operating system, the windowing system, a database, and so on. A typical example is the `File` class.

Foundation classes are classes such as `String`, `Date`, or `Rectangle`. They encapsulate basic data types with well-understood properties. At the design stage, you should simply assume that these classes are readily available, just as the fundamental types (integers and floating-point numbers) are.

SPECIAL TOPIC   2.2

Queues

A *queue* is a very common data type in computer science. You add items to one end of the queue (the *tail*) and remove them from the other end of the queue (the *head*). To visualize a queue, simply think of people lining up (see Figure 1). People join the tail of the queue and wait until they have reached the head of the queue. Queues store items in a first in, first out or FIFO fashion. Items are removed in the same order in which they have been added.

There are many applications for queues. For example, the Java graphical user interface system keeps an event queue of all events, such as mouse and keyboard events. The events are inserted into the queue whenever the operating system notifies the application of the event. Another thread of control removes them from the queue and passes them to the appropriate event listeners. Another example is a print queue. A printer may be accessed by several applications, perhaps running on different computers. If all of the applications tried to access the printer at the same time, the printout would be garbled. Instead, each application places all bytes that need to be sent to the printer into a file and inserts that file into the print queue. When the printer is done printing one file, it retrieves the next one from the queue. Therefore, print jobs are printed using the FIFO rule, which is a fair arrangement for users of the shared printer.

The standard Java library defines a number of queue classes for multithreaded programming, but for simple queues, the library designers suggest that you just use the add and remove methods of the LinkedList class. We will consider a "circular array" implementation of a queue in the next chapter.

Figure 1

A Queue

2.4   Identifying Responsibilities

> To discover responsibilities, look for verbs in the problem description.

Just as classes correspond to nouns in the problem description, *responsibilities* correspond to *verbs*. If you read through the functional description of the voice mail system in Section 2.12, you will find that messages are *recorded*, *played*, and *deleted;* users *log in;* passcodes are *checked*. When you discover a responsibility, you must find one class (and only one class) that owns that responsibility.

> A responsibility must belong to exactly one class.

For some classes, finding responsibilities is quite easy because we are familiar with the territory. For example, any textbook on data structures will tell us the responsibilities of the MessageQueue class:

- Add a message to the tail of the queue.
- Remove a message from the head of the queue.
- Test whether the queue is empty.

With other classes, finding the right responsibilities is more difficult. Consider the following responsibility in a voice mail system.

- Add the message to a mailbox.

Is this is a responsibility of the Message class? That is not a good idea. To see the reason, think how a message could perform the responsibility. In order to add itself to a mailbox, the message would need to know the internal structure of the mailbox. The details would depend on whether the mailbox uses an array list, a queue, or another data structure to hold its messages. But we always assume that those implementation details are private to the Mailbox class, and that the Message class has no insight into them.

In our situation, the responsibility of adding a message to a mailbox lies with the mailbox, not with the message. The mailbox has sufficient understanding of its structure to perform the operation.

When discovering responsibilities, programmers commonly make wrong guesses and assign the responsibility to an inappropriate class. For that reason, it is helpful to have more than one person involved in the design phase. If one person assigns a responsibility to a particular class, another can ask the hard question, "How can an object of this class possibly carry out this responsibility?" The question is hard because we are not yet supposed to get to the nitty-gritty of implementation details. But it is appropriate to consider a "reasonable" implementation, or better, two different possibilities, to demonstrate that the responsibility can be carried out.

 TIP   When assigning responsibilities, respect the natural *layering of abstraction levels*. At the lowest levels of any system, we have files, keyboard and mouse interfaces, and other system services. At the highest levels there are classes that tie together the software system, such as MailSystem. The responsibilities of a class should stay at *one abstraction level*. A class Mailbox that represents a mid-level abstraction should not deal with processing keystrokes, a low-level responsibility, nor should it be concerned with the initialization of the system, a high-level responsibility.

2.5 Relationships Between Classes

Three relationships are common among classes:

- Dependency ("uses")
- Aggregation ("has")
- Inheritance ("is")

We will discuss these three relationships in detail in this section.

2.5.1 — Dependency

> A class depends on another class if it manipulates objects of the other class.

A class *depends on* another class if it manipulates objects of the other class in any way. For example, the class `Mailbox` in a voice mail system *uses* the `Message` class because `Mailbox` objects manipulate `Message` objects.

It is almost easier to understand when a class *doesn't* depend on another. If a class can carry out all of its tasks without being aware that the other class even exists, then it doesn't use that class. For example, the `Message` class does not need to use the `Mailbox` class at all. Messages need not be aware that they are stored inside mailboxes. However, the `Mailbox` class uses the `Message` class. This shows that dependency is an asymmetric relationship.

One important design goal is to minimize the number of dependency relationships; that is, to minimize the *coupling* between classes. If one class is unaware of the existence of another, it is also unconcerned about any changes in that other class. A low degree of coupling tends to make it much easier to implement changes in the future.

For example, consider this message class:

```
public class Message
{
    public void print() { System.out.println(text); }
    . . .
}
```

The `print` method prints the message to `System.out`. Therefore, the `Message` class is coupled with both the `System` and the `PrintStream` classes. (The `System.out` object is an instance of the `PrintStream` class.)

If the class is deployed in an embedded device such as a real voice message system or a toaster oven, then there is no `System.out`. It would be better to have a method

```
public String getText()
```

that returns the message text as a string. Then it is up to some other part of the system to send the string to `System.out`, to a dialog box, or to a speaker.

TIP   Minimize the number of dependencies between classes. When classes depend on each other, changes in one of them can force changes in the others.

2.5.2 — Aggregation

> A class aggregates another if its objects contain objects of the other class.

Aggregation takes place if objects of one class contain objects of another class over a period of time. For example, `MessageQueue` has `Message` objects, and we say that the `MessageQueue` class aggregates the `Message` class.

Aggregation is a special case of dependency. Of course, if a class contains objects of another class, then it is acutely aware of the existence of that class.

Aggregation is often informally described as the "has-a" relationship. A message queue *has a* message. Actually, a message queue has several messages. With aggregation relationships, it is useful to keep track of these *multiplicities*. There may be a 1:1 or 1:*n* relationship. For example, each mailbox has exactly one greeting (1:1), but each message queue may contain many messages (1:*n*).

Aggregation is usually implemented through instance fields. For example, if a mailbox has a greeting, then the Java implementation might look like this:

```
public class Mailbox
{
    . . .
    private Greeting myGreeting;
}
```

This particular implementation can serve as a 1:1 or 1:0...1 relationship (if you allow `myGreeting == null` to indicate that there is no greeting for a particular mailbox). For a 1:*n* relationship, you need an array or a collection object. For example,

```
public class MessageQueue
{
    . . .
    private ArrayList<Message> elements;
}
```

However, not all instance fields of a class correspond to aggregation. If an object contains a field of a very simple type such as a number, string, or date, it is considered merely an *attribute*, not aggregation. For example, suppose a message has a time stamp of type `Date`.

```
public class Message
{
    . . .
    private Date timestamp;
}
```

We consider `Date` a foundational type, just like a number or a string. Thus, we don't say that the `Message` class aggregates the `Date` class, but we consider the time stamp an attribute.

The distinction between aggregation and attributes depends on the context of your design. You'll need to make a judgment whether a particular class is "very simple", giving rise to attributes, or whether you should describe an aggregation relationship.

2.5.3 — Inheritance

> A class inherits from another if it incorporates the behavior of the other class.

A class *inherits* from another if all objects of its class are special cases of objects of the other class, capable of exhibiting the same behavior but possibly with additional responsibilities and a richer state.

Here is a typical example. Many voice mail systems let you forward a message that you received to another user. When the forwarded message is played, it first tells who forwarded it before playing the contents of the original message. We can model this feature by having the `ForwardedMessage` inherit from the `Message` class.

We call the more general class the *superclass* and the more specialized class the *subclass*. A subclass object must be usable in all situations in which a superclass object is expected. For example, a forwarded message object can be stored and played, just like any other message.

But a greeting in a voice mail system, even though it is in many respects similar to a message, is not usable in the same contexts as messages are. Users cannot store greetings in mailboxes. We conclude that `Greeting` may not inherit from `Message`.

Inheritance is often called the "is-a" relationship. This intuitive notion makes it easy to distinguish inheritance from aggregation. For example, a forwarded message *is a* message (inheritance) while a mailbox *has a* greeting (aggregation).

As you will see in Chapters 4 and 6, exploiting inheritance relationships can lead to very powerful and extensible designs. However, we must point out that inheritance is much less common than the dependency and aggregation relationships. Many designs can best be modeled by employing inheritance in a few selected places.

2.6   Use Cases

Use cases are an *analysis* technique to describe in a formal way how a computer system should work. Each use case focuses on a specific scenario, and describes the steps that are necessary to bring it to successful completion. Each step in a use case represents an interaction with people or entities outside the computer system (the *actors*) and the system itself. For example, the use case "Leave a message" describes the steps that a caller must take to dial an extension and leave a message. The use case "Retrieve messages" describes the steps needed to listen to the messages in the mailbox. In the first case, the actor is the caller leaving a message. In the second case, the actor is the mailbox owner.

> A use case lists a sequence of actions that yields a result that is of value to an actor.

An essential aspect of a use case is that it must describe a scenario that completes to a point that is of some *value* to one of the actors. In the case of "Leave a message", the value to the caller is the fact that the message is deposited in the appropriate mailbox. In contrast, merely dialing a telephone number and listening to a menu would not be considered a valid use case because it does not by itself have value to anyone.

Of course, most scenarios that potentially deliver a valuable outcome can also fail for one reason or another. Perhaps the message queue is full, or a mailbox owner enters the wrong password. A use case should include *variations* that describe these situations.

Minimally, a use case should have a name that describes it concisely, a main sequence of actions, and, if appropriate, variants to the main sequence. Some analysts prefer a more formal writeup that numbers the use cases, calls out the actors, refers to related use cases, and so on. However, in this book we'll keep use cases as simple as possible.

Here is a sample use case for a voice mail system.

Leave a Message

1. The caller dials the main number of the voice mail system.
2. The voice mail system speaks a prompt.

    `Enter mailbox number followed by #.`
3. The user types in the extension number of the message recipient.
4. The voice mail system speaks.

    `You have reached mailbox xxxx. Please leave a message now.`
5. The caller speaks the message.
6. The caller hangs up.
7. The voice mail system places the recorded message in the recipient's mailbox.

Variation #1

1.1. In Step 3, the user enters an invalid extension number.
1.2. The voice mail system speaks.

    `You have typed an invalid mailbox number.`
1.3. Continue with Step 2.

Variation #2

2.1. After Step 4, the caller hangs up instead of speaking a message.
2.2. The voice mail system discards the empty message.

 INTERNET   The Web site `http://www.usecases.org/` contains a template for a more elaborate use case format. The "Use Case Zone" at `http://www.pols.co.uk/use-case-zone/` has many useful links to articles that report on experiences with use cases, including some interesting cautionary tales.

2.7   CRC Cards

> A CRC card is an index card that describes a class, its high-level responsibilities, and its collaborators.

The CRC card method is an effective *design* technique for discovering classes, responsibilities, and relationships. A *CRC card* is simply an index card that describes one class and lists its responsibilities and *collaborators* (dependent classes). Index cards are a good choice for a number of reasons. They are small, thereby discouraging you from piling too much responsibility into a single class. They are low-tech, so that they can be used by groups of designers gathered around a table. They are more rugged than sheets of paper and can be handed around and rearranged during brainstorming sessions.

INTERNET   The original article describing CRC cards is: Kent Beck and Ward Cunningham, "A Laboratory for Teaching Object-Oriented Thinking", OOPSLA '89 Conference Proceedings October 1–6, 1989, New Orleans, Louisiana. You can find an electronic version at `http://c2.com/doc/oopsla89/paper.html`.

You make one card for each discovered class. Write the class name at the top of the card. Below, on the left-hand side, you describe the responsibilities. On the right-hand side, you list other classes that need to collaborate with this class so that it can fulfill its responsibilities.

The CRC card shown in Figure 2 indicates that we have discovered three responsibilities of the mailbox: to manage the passcode, to manage the greeting, and to manage new and saved messages. The latter responsibility requires collaboration with the `MessageQueue` class. That is, the mailbox needs to interact with `MessageQueue` objects in some unspecified way.

The responsibilities should be at a *high level*. Don't write individual methods. If a class has more responsibilities than you can fit on the index card, you may need to make two

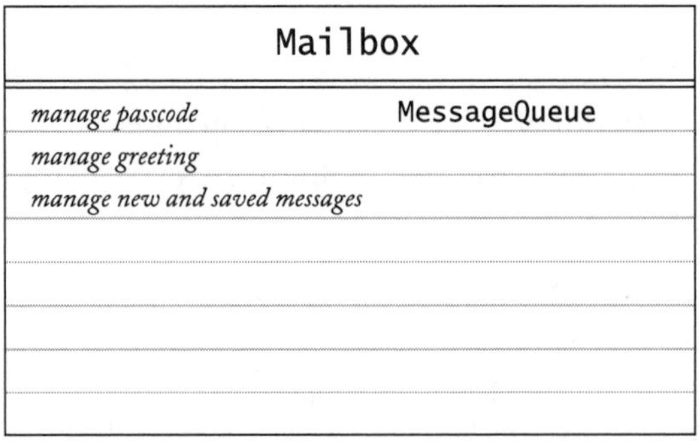

Mailbox	
manage passcode	MessageQueue
manage greeting	
manage new and saved messages	

Figure 2

A CRC Card

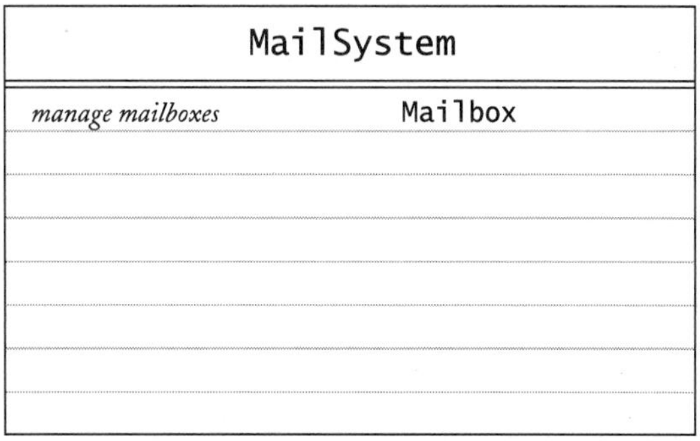

MailSystem	
manage mailboxes	Mailbox

Figure 3

Making the Mail System Responsible for
Managing Mailboxes

new cards, distribute the responsibilities among them, and tear up the old card. Between one and three responsibilities per card is ideal.

TIP Programmers who start out with the CRC card technique sometimes equate responsibilities with methods. Keep in mind that responsibilities are at a high level. A single responsibility may give rise to a number of methods. If you find that your card contains lots of related responsibilities, try to express some of them at a higher level. For example, you may want to replace "manage passcode" and "manage greeting" with "manage user options".

The collaborators don't have to be on the same lines as the responsibilities. Simply list collaborators as you discover them, without regard for the ordering.

CRC cards are quite intuitive for "walking through" use cases. Consider, for example, the use case "Leave a message". The caller dials the main number and is connected to the voice mail system. That happens through the public telephone system and is outside our concern. Next, the caller dials the extension. Now "someone" inside the voice mail program needs to locate the mailbox that has the given extension number. Neither the Mailbox nor the Message class can handle this responsibility. Perhaps a mailbox knows its own extension number, but it doesn't know about the extension numbers of the other mailboxes in the system. And a message doesn't know anything about mailboxes and extension numbers. A MailSystem knows about all of its mailboxes, so it would be a reasonable choice for a responsible agent. Let's create a new index card, shown in Figure 3.

TIP Beware of the omnipotent system class. You often need a class that is responsible for coordinating the working of the system that you are building, but there is a tremendous danger of overburdening that class with too many responsibilities. Have a look at the evolution of the MailSystem class throughout this chapter and see if we manage to keep it under control.

TIP   Beware of classes with magical powers that have no connection with the real world or computer systems. A `MailSystem` is actually quite real—when you buy a commercial voice mail system, you get a box into which you plug phone cables. But you can't just define your own "systems". If in doubt, check with experts that understand the problem domain.

Next, imagine *how* the mail system is going to locate the mailbox. Maybe each mailbox knows its number, and the mail system asks each one of the mailboxes "are you number *x*"? Or maybe the mailboxes don't know their numbers, and the mail system keeps a table that lists all extension numbers and their mailboxes? Either one is a reasonable mechanism, and you don't have to settle for one or the other at this stage. All that matters is that you are convinced that the mail system can do the job.

Let's finish the use case. The mail system has located the appropriate mailbox. It now needs to deliver the message to that mailbox. Look again at the `Mailbox` CRC card. It has a responsibility "manage new and saved messages". Thus, it seems to be up to the job of storing the message. Now you should add the `Mailbox` class as a collaborator of the `MailSystem` class. The mail system needs the collaboration of the mailbox to complete the delivery.

TIP   Avoid "mission creep". If a class acquires too many responsibilities, then consider splitting it in two. Ideally, a class should not have more than three high-level responsibilities.

TIP   Watch out for unrelated responsibilities. A class should represent a coherent concept, with related responsibilities. If the `Mailbox` class gets charged with storing messages *and* parsing input, make a new class and split the responsibilities.

TIP   Resist the temptation to add responsibilities just because they can be done. For example, someone may have suggested a `Mailbox` responsibility "sort messages". But the task at hand requires no sorting, and you shouldn't collect unused responsibilities.

TIP   A class with no responsibilities surely is not useful. Try eliminating classes that don't seem to contribute to solving the problem at hand. Typical candidates are vague mechanisms such as `Connector` and `Data`.

The walkthroughs with CRC cards are particularly suited for group discussion. Let's assume the analysts are done with their work and have left behind a stack of use cases. Get two or three designers together. Here is a good way to "break the ice" and get started. Let all participants use the "noun and verb" technique to come up with a pool of candidates for classes and operations. Then consider the first use case that looks interesting and perform a walkthrough. Have one person play the protagonist, who proposes a responsible agent and a method for carrying out the task. Invariably the description will be somewhat vague, and the other participants will find it easy to ask for clarification or to suggest different preferences. Rotate the protagonist role so that each participant gets to play "devil's advocate".

Arrange cards on the table so that classes are physically close to their collaborators. The visual arrangement of the cards can give clues to simple or overly complex relationships. You should not be afraid to tear up cards or to erase, modify, or reorganize operations. Experienced designers will cheerfully admit that they rarely hit upon an optimal division of responsibilities on the first try and that a fair amount of trial and error is necessary even in seemingly simple designs.

You do not necessarily need a group of people for effective class discovery. If you work on your own, though, it helps if you have a "Jekyll and Hyde" personality and can play your own devil's advocate.

CRC cards are a good tool for proposing designs, but they are not particularly suited for documenting them. The better the design discussions, the messier the cards look afterwards. The visual arrangement and movement of the cards are ephemeral. For this reason, the cards should be discarded after a design has been found. They are meant as a discovery tool, not as archival information. We will discuss more permanent documentation tools in the next sections.

In summary, CRC cards are a popular mechanism for discovering classes and operations. Making a new card for each class as the need arises and marking new operations on the cards is easy. Scenarios can be "played out" by moving the cards around while tracing the control flow.

2.8 UML Class Diagrams

Graphical notations are very popular for conveying design information, for a good reason. It is easier to extract relationship information by looking at a diagram than by reading documentation.

> A UML diagram illustrates an aspect of an object-oriented design, using a standardized notation.

To express design information, some convention is required. You may have seen flowcharts that use diamond-shaped symbols for decisions. Of course, there is no logical reason why decisions couldn't be denoted by triangles or circles. The diamond is just the standard choice. For quite some time, there was no similar standard for object-oriented design diagrams. A number of diagramming conventions had been proposed over time that differed greatly in their visual appearance. Finally, three well-known researchers, Booch, Rumbaugh, and Jacobson, got together to unify their disparate notations and developed *UML, the unified modeling language*. We will use UML for all diagrams in this book.

 INTERNET There are a number of tools available for drawing UML diagrams. The best-known commercial programs are

- Rational Rose (`http://www.ibm.com/software/rational/`)
- Together (`http://www.borland.com/together/`)

The commercial programs can be expensive. Freely available programs are

- ArgoUML (`http://argouml.tigris.org/`) and its commercial cousin Poseidon UML Community Edition (`http://www.gentleware.com/`)
- Dia (`http://www.gnome.org/projects/dia`; a Windows version is available from `http://hans.breuer.org/dia/`)

For simple UML diagrams, you can use the Violet tool that you can download from the companion Web site for this book or from `http://horstmann.com/violet`. In Chapter 8, you will learn more about the design of the Violet program.

> A class diagram shows classes and the relationships among them.

There are a number of different types of UML diagrams. In this book, we will use class diagrams, sequence diagrams, and state diagrams.

The basic UML notation for class diagrams is fairly simple. Classes are drawn as boxes, which contain the class name and, when appropriate, the names of attributes and methods in additional compartments (see Figure 4). The UML defines an attribute as a named property of a class that describes a range of values that instances of the property may hold. Often, an attribute simply corresponds to an instance field. Occasionally, an attribute is conceptually at a higher level than the actual implementation. You usually do not list all attributes and methods, only the most important ones.

 TIP   If you have lots of attributes, check whether you can group some of them into classes. For example, if a `Student` class has attributes `name`, `street`, `city`, `state`, and `zip`, then you missed the opportunity of discovering a class `Address`.

You can also specify the type of an attribute. Unlike in Java, where the type precedes a variable, the UML format is *attribute : Type*, for example,

```
text : String
```

Similarly, you can specify the parameter and return types of a method, for example

```
getMessage(index : int) : Message
```

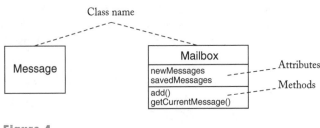

Figure 4

UML Notation for Classes

Figure 5

UML Connectors

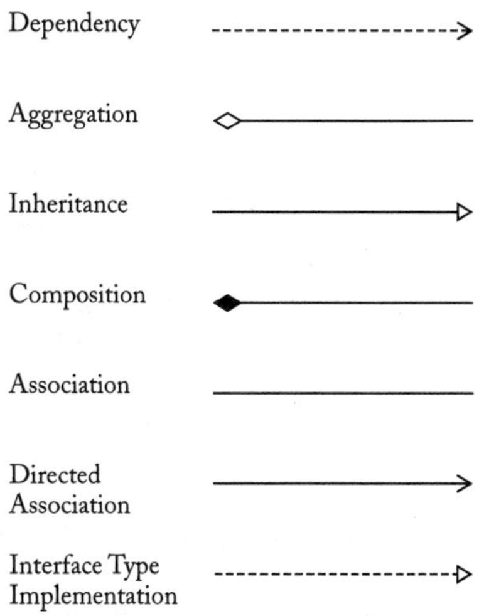

Dependency	- - - - - - - - - - - - ->
Aggregation	◇—————————
Inheritance	————————▷
Composition	◆—————————
Association	—————————
Directed Association	————————→
Interface Type Implementation	- - - - - - - - - - ▷

Often, the types of attributes, parameters, and return values are omitted to conserve space. Thus, if you see *methodName*(), you cannot automatically assume that the method has no parameters.

Classes are joined by various kinds of connections (see Figure 5). You are already familiar with the first three relationships. We will discuss the others in this section.

You have to be careful about the shapes of the arrow tips. The inheritance arrow is closed, whereas the dependency arrow is open. Also note that the arrow tips for inheritance and dependency are at the end of the dependent class, but the diamond for aggregation is at the end of the aggregating class.

For the "has" relationship, you can also write the multiplicity on the end points of the connection. The most common choices for the multiplicity are:

- any number (zero or more): *
- one or more: 1..*
- zero or one: 0..1
- exactly one: 1

For example, Figure 6 denotes that a message queue can hold any number of messages, and a message is in exactly one message queue.

Figure 6

Multiplicities of an Aggregation Relationship

TIP   Make sure that you use either aggregation or an attribute for a particular feature, but not both. For example, suppose the class Message has a field timestamp of type Date. If you consider the time stamp an attribute, then you should not draw a box and an aggregation connector for the Date class.

TIP   Challenge counts of one. Does a mailbox really only have one greeting? Many real systems have multiple greetings: one for inside callers and one for outside callers, and yet another one for weekends. Once you have a class, you can construct as many objects as you need.

Some designers differentiate between aggregation and composition. *Composition* is a stronger form of aggregation where the contained objects do not have an existence independent of their container. For example, in the voice mail system, the message queues are permanently contained in the mailboxes—a message queue never exists outside a mailbox. The UML notation for composition is a line with a solid diamond at the end (see Figure 7). In contrast, messages move throughout the mail system and don't always reside in a message queue. Thus, messages are aggregated in message queues, but a message queue is not composed of messages. We will not make that distinction in this book, but you may encounter it elsewhere.

TIP   Use aggregation (or composition) only if a class actively *manages* objects of another class. For example, does a gas station have cars? Of course it does. Should you therefore draw an aggregation between the class GasStation and the class Car? Not necessarily. If the gas station objects do not need to keep track of the cars, then aggregation is not appropriate.

Some designers do not like the aggregation relationship because they feel it is too implementation-specific. UML defines a more general *association* between classes. An association is drawn as a solid line without a diamond. You can write *roles* at the ends of the lines (see Figure 8).

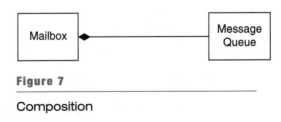

Figure 7

Composition

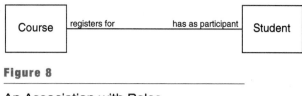

Figure 8

An Association with Roles

Here we model the fact that students register for courses and courses have students as participants. Early in a design, this general relationship makes a lot of sense. As you move closer to implementation, you will want to resolve whether a `Course` object manages a collection of students, a `Student` object manages a collection of courses, or both courses and students manage collections of each other.

The relationship between courses and students is bidirectional—`Course` objects will need to know about the students in the course, and `Student` objects need to know about the courses for which they are registered. Quite often, an association is directed, that is, it can only be navigated in one way. For example, a message queue needs to be able to locate the messages inside, but a message need not know in which message queue it is. A directed association is drawn with an open arrow tip (see Figure 9). It is easy to confuse that connector with inheritance—you have to pay close attention to the shapes of the arrow tips when drawing UML diagrams.

In Chapter 4, we will introduce the notion of an *interface type*. An interface type describes a set of methods, but it contains no implementation at all. A class can *implement* the interface by supplying implementations of its methods. In the UML notation, you denote an interface by adding the *stereotype descriptor* «`interface`» above the interface name. (The « and » characters are called *guillemets* or French quotation marks. They have Unicode values \u00AB = 171 and \u00BB = 187.) If a class implements an interface, you draw a dotted arrow with a closed arrow tip. Figure 10 shows an example.

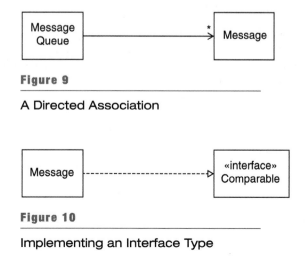

Figure 9

A Directed Association

Figure 10

Implementing an Interface Type

Because the javadoc documentation and the class browsers in integrated development environments only display the inheritance relationship, they give the false impression that inheritance is the most important of the relationships between classes. Actually, that is not the case—inheritance is simply easy to determine from the program code. The most important relationship to control is the dependency or "uses" relationship. Too many dependencies make it difficult to evolve a design over time.

 TIP You should *not* aim for a comprehensive diagram that shows all classes and relationships in the system. A diagram with too much information becomes just a blur. The reason for drawing diagrams is to communicate design decisions. To achieve this purpose, each UML diagram should focus on a particular aspect of the design, and it should be accompanied by text that explains its relevance. When drawing a diagram, you should only include those elements that are needed to make a particular point, and omit all distractions.

2.9 Sequence Diagrams

> A sequence diagram shows the time ordering of a sequence of method calls.

Class diagrams are static—they display the relationships among the classes that exist throughout the lifetime of the system. In contrast, a sequence diagram shows the dynamics of a particular scenario. You use sequence diagrams to describe communication patterns among objects. Figure 11 shows the key elements of a sequence diagram—a method call from one object to another.

Sequence diagrams describe interactions between objects. In UML, you use <u>underline</u> to distinguish object rectangles from class rectangles. The text inside an object rectangle has one of the following three formats:

- objectName : ClassName (full description)
- objectName (class not specified)
- : ClassName (object not specified)

The dashed vertical line that emanates from the object is called the *lifeline*. In some object-oriented programming languages, objects can be explicitly destroyed, which causes their lifeline to end at the point of destruction. However, we will always draw the lifeline so that it goes on indefinitely.

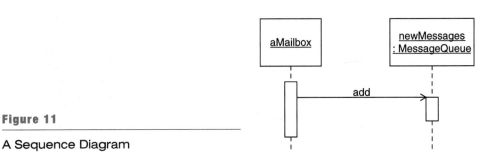

Figure 11

A Sequence Diagram

Figure 12

Self-Call

The rectangles along the lifeline are called *activation bars*. They show when the object has control, executing a method. When you call a method, start an activation bar at the end of the call arrow. The activation bar ends when the method returns. (Note that the activation bar of a called method should always be smaller than that of the calling method.)

In the most common form, a sequence diagram illustrates the behavior of a single method. Then the leftmost object has one long activation bar, from which one or more call arrows emanate. For example, the diagram in Figure 11 illustrates the add method of the MessageQueue class. A message is added to the message queue that holds the new messages. The diagram corresponds to the Java statement

```
newMessages.add(. . .)
```

You cannot tell from the diagram what parameter was passed to the method.

A method can call another method on the same object. Then draw the activation bar of the called method over the one of the calling method, as in Figure 12.

If a method constructs a new object, you can use the stereotype «create» to indicate the timing of the creation. Arrange the object rectangle of the created object as in Figure 13.

When drawing a sequence diagram, you omit a large amount of detail. Generally, you do not indicate branches or loops. (The UML defines a notation for that purpose, but it is a bit cumbersome and rarely used.) The principal purpose of a sequence diagram is to show the objects that are involved in carrying out a particular scenario and the order of the method calls that are executed.

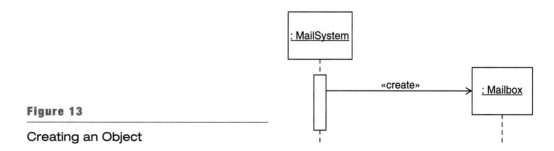

Figure 13

Creating an Object

Sequence diagrams are valuable for documenting complex interactions between objects. These interactions are common in object-oriented programs where any one object tends to have limited responsibilities and requires the collaboration of several other objects. You will see examples in the case study at the end of this chapter.

 TIP If you played through a use case when using CRC cards, then it is probably a good idea to use a sequence diagram to document that scenario. On the other hand, there is no requirement to use sequence diagrams to document every method call.

2.10   State Diagrams

Some objects have a discrete set of states that affect their behavior. For example, a voice mail system is in a "connected" state when a caller first connects to it. After the caller enters an extension number, the system enters the "recording" state where it records whatever the caller speaks. When the caller enters a passcode, the system is in the "mailbox menu" state. The state diagram in Figure 14 shows these states and the transitions between them.

> A state diagram shows the states of an object and the transitions between states.

The state has a noticeable impact on the behavior. If the caller speaks while the system is in the "mailbox menu" state, the spoken words are simply ignored. Voice input is recorded only when the system is in the "recording" state.

States are particularly common with objects that interact with the program user. For example, suppose a user wants to retrieve recent voice mail messages. The user must

- Enter the mailbox number.
- Enter the passcode.
- Enter a menu command to start playing messages.

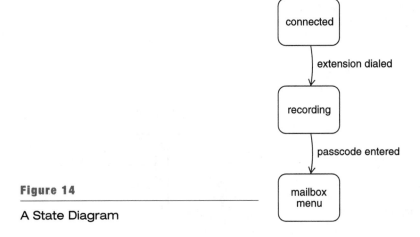

Figure 14

A State Diagram

The telephone touchpad has no concept of these steps—it keeps no state. Whenever the user presses a key, that key might be a part of the mailbox number, passcode, or menu command. Some part of the voice mail system must keep track of the current state so that it can process the key correctly. We will discuss this issue further in the case study at the end of this chapter.

2.11   Using javadoc for Design Documentation

> You can use javadoc to generate design information by applying comments to classes and methods that are not yet implemented.

You already saw in Chapter 1 how to use the javadoc tool to document classes and methods: Add documentation comments to your source file and run the javadoc tool to generate a set of hyperlinked documents. You can also use javadoc to document your designs. Simply write a skeleton class with no fields and leave all method implementations blank. Of course, supply the class and method comments.

Here is an example:

```
/**
    A mailbox contains messages that the mailbox owner can manage.
*/
public class Mailbox
{
    /**
        Adds a message to the end of the new messages.
        @param aMessage a message
    */
    public void add(Message aMessage)
    {
    }

    /**
        Returns the current message.
        @return the current message
    */
    public Message getCurrentMessage()
    {
    }
}
```

Do not compile this file—the compiler will complain about unknown types and methods with no return statements. Instead, simply run the javadoc program to extract the HTML documentation. This approach has two benefits. You can post the HTML documentation on the Web and easily share it with your team members. And you can carry the Java files into the implementation phase, with the comments for the key methods already in place.

Professional object-oriented design tools can also produce HTML reports of classes and methods as well as skeleton source code. If you use one of those tools for your design work, then you do not need to use javadoc.

2.12   Case Study: A Voice Mail System

To walk through the basic steps of the object-oriented design process, we will consider the task of writing a program that simulates a telephone voice mail system, similar to the message system that many companies use.

In a voice mail system, a person dials an extension number and, provided the other party does not pick up the telephone, leaves a message. The other party can later retrieve the messages, keep them, or delete them. Real-world systems have a multitude of fancy features: Messages can be forwarded to one or more mailboxes; distribution lists can be defined, retained, and edited; and authorized persons can send broadcast messages to all users.

We will design and implement a program that simulates a voice mail system, without creating a completely realistic working phone system. We will simply represent voice mail by text that is entered through the keyboard. We need to simulate the three distinct input events that occur in a real telephone system: speaking, pushing a button on the telephone touchpad, and hanging up the telephone. We use the following convention for input: An input line consisting of a single character 1 . . . 9 or # denotes a pressed button on the telephone touchpad. For example, to dial extension 13, you enter

```
1
3
#
```

An input line consisting of the single letter H denotes hanging up the telephone. Any other text denotes voice input.

The first formal step in the process that leads us toward the final product (the voice mail system) is the analysis phase. Its role is to crisply define the behavior of the system. In this example, we will define the behavior through a set of use cases. Note that the use cases by themselves are *not* a full specification of a system. The functional specification also needs to define system limitations, performance, and so on.

2.12.1   Use Cases for the Voice Mail System

Reach an Extension

1. The user dials the main number of the voice mail system.
2. The voice mail system speaks a prompt.
   ```
   Enter mailbox number followed by #.
   ```
3. The user types in the extension number of the message recipient.
4. The voice mail system speaks.
   ```
   You have reached mailbox xxxx. Please leave a message now.
   ```

Leave a Message

1. The caller carries out **Reach an Extension**.
2. The caller speaks the message.
3. The caller hangs up.
4. The voice mail system places the recorded message in the recipient's mailbox.

Log in

1. The mailbox owner carries out **Reach an Extension**.
2. The mailbox owner types the passcode, followed by the # key. (The default passcode is the same as the mailbox number. The mailbox owner can change it—see **Change the Passcode**.)
3. The voice mail system plays the mailbox menu:

```
Enter 1 to retrieve your messages.
Enter 2 to change your passcode.
Enter 3 to change your greeting.
```

Retrieve Messages

1. The mailbox owner carries out **Log in**.
2. The mailbox owner selects the "retrieve your messages" menu option.
3. The voice mail system plays the message menu:

```
Enter 1 to listen to the current message.
Enter 2 to save the current message.
Enter 3 to delete the current message.
Enter 4 to return to the mailbox menu.
```

4. The mailbox owner selects the "listen to the current message" menu option.
5. The voice mail system plays the current new message, or, if there are no new messages, the current old message. Note that the message is played, not removed from the queue.
6. The voice mail system plays the message menu.
7. The user selects "delete the current message". The message is permanently removed.
8. Continue with Step 3.

Variation #1. Saving a message

1.1. Start at Step 6.
1.2. The user selects "save the current message". The message is removed from its queue and appended to the queue of old messages.
1.3. Continue with Step 3.

Change the Greeting

1. The mailbox owner carries out **Log in**.
2. The mailbox owner selects the "change your greeting" menu option.
3. The mailbox owner speaks the greeting.
4. The mailbox owner presses the # key.
5. The mail system sets the new greeting.

Variation #1. Hang up before confirmation

1.1. Start at Step 3.
1.2. The mailbox owner hangs up the telephone.
1.3. The mail system keeps the old greeting.

Change the Passcode

1. The mailbox owner carries out **Log in**.
2. The mailbox owner selects the "change your passcode" menu option.
3. The mailbox owner dials the new passcode.
4. The mailbox owner presses the # key.
5. The mail system sets the new passcode.

Variation #1. Hang up before confirmation

1.1. Start at Step 3.
1.2. The mailbox owner hangs up the telephone.
1.3. The mail system keeps the old passcode.

2.12.2 — CRC Cards for the Voice Mail System

Let us walk through the process of discovering classes for the voice mail system. Some obvious classes, whose nouns appear in the functional specification, are

- `Mailbox`
- `Message`
- `MailSystem`

Let's start with `Mailbox` since it is both important and easy to understand. The principal job of the mailbox is to keep messages. The mailbox should keep track of which messages are new and which are saved. New messages may be deposited into the mailbox, and users should be able to retrieve, save, and delete their messages.

The messages need to be kept somewhere. Since we retrieve messages in a first-in, first-out fashion, a queue is an appropriate data structure. Since we need to differentiate between new and saved messages, we'll use two queues, one for the new messages and one for the saved messages. So far, the CRC cards looks like this:

Mailbox	
keep new and saved messages	MessageQueue

MessageQueue	
add and remove messages in	
FIFO order	

Where are the mailboxes kept? There needs to be a class that contains them all. We'll call it MailSystem. The responsibility of the mail system is to manage the mailboxes.

MailSystem	
manage mailboxes	Mailbox

We can't go much further until we resolve how input and output is processed. Since we have been simulating telephone equipment, let's start with a class `Telephone`. A telephone has two responsibilities: to take user input (button presses, voice input, and hangup actions), and to play voice output on the speaker.

Telephone
take user input from touchpad,
microphone, hangup
speak output

When the telephone gets user input, it must communicate it to some object. Could it tell the mail system? Superficially, that sounds like a good idea. But it turns out that there is a problem. In a real voice mail system, it is possible for multiple telephones to be connected to the voice mail system. *Each* connection needs to keep track of the current state (recording, retrieving messages, and so on). It is possible that one connection is currently recording a message while another is retrieving messages. It seems a tall order for the mail system to keep multiple states, one for each connection. Instead, let's have a separate `Connection` class. A connection communicates with a telephone, carries out the user commands, and keeps track of the state of the session.

Connection	
get input from telephone	`Telephone`
carry out user commands	`MailSystem`
keep track of state	

 TIP   Consider reasonable generalizations when designing a system. What features might the next update contain? What features do competing products implement already? Check that these features can be accommodated without radical changes in your design.

For example, to arrive at the design of the voice mail system in this chapter, I considered two reasonable generalizations:

- Can the system be extended to support two telephones?
- Can the system use a graphical user interface instead of a command-line interface?

Now that we have some idea of the components of the system, it is time for a simple scenario walkthrough. Let's start with the **Leave a Message** use case.

1. The user dials an extension. The `Telephone` sends the dialed extension number to the `Connection`. (Add `Connection` as a collaborator of `Telephone`. Place the two cards next to each other.)

2. The `Connection` asks the `MailSystem` to find the `Mailbox` object with the given extension number. (This is at least vaguely included in the "manage mailboxes" responsibility. Arrange the `MailSystem` and `Mailbox` cards close to the `Connection` card.)

3. The `Connection` asks the `Mailbox` for its greeting. (Add "manage greeting" to the `Mailbox` responsibilities, and add `Mailbox` as a collaborator of `Connection`.)

4. The `Connection` asks the `Telephone` to play the greeting on the speaker.

5. The user speaks the message. The `Telephone` asks the `Connection` to record it. (Add "record voice input" to the responsibilities of `Connection`.)

6. The user hangs up. The `Telephone` notifies the `Connection`.

7. The `Connection` constructs a `Message` object that contains the recorded message. (Add `Message` as a collaborator of `Connection`. Make a `Message` card with a responsibility "manage message contents".)

8. The `Connection` adds the `Message` object to the `Mailbox`.

As a result of this walkthrough, the `Telephone`, `Connection`, and `Mailbox` cards have been updated, and a `Message` card has been added.

Telephone	
take user input from touchpad,	Connection
microphone, hangup	
speak output	

Connection	
get input from telephone	Telephone
carry out user commands	MailSystem
keep track of state	Mailbox
record voice input	Message

Mailbox	
keep new and saved messages	MessageQueue
manage greeting	

Message
manage message contents

Now let's consider the use case **Retrieve Messages**. The first steps of the scenario are the same as that of the preceding scenario. Let's start at the point where the user types in the passcode.

1. The user types in the passcode. The Telephone notifies the Connection.

2. The Connection asks the Mailbox to check the passcode. (Add "manage passcode" to the responsibilities of the Mailbox class.)

3. Assuming the passcode was correct, the `Connection` sets the `Mailbox` as the current mailbox and asks the `Telephone` to speak the mailbox menu.

4. The user types in the "retrieve messages" menu option. The `Telephone` passes it on to the `Connection`.

5. The `Connection` asks the `Telephone` to speak the message menu.

6. The user types in the "listen to current message" option. The `Telephone` passes it on to the `Connection`.

7. The `Connection` gets the first `Message` from the current `Mailbox` and sends its contents to the `Telephone`. (Add "retrieve messages" to the responsibilities of `Mailbox`.)

8. The `Connection` asks the `Telephone` to speak the message menu.

9. The user types in the "save current message" menu option. The `Telephone` passes it on to the `Connection`.

10. The `Connection` tells the `Mailbox` to save the current message. (Modify the responsibilities of `Mailbox` to "retrieve, save, delete messages".)

11. The `Connection` asks the `Telephone` to speak the message menu.

That finishes the scenario. As a result, the `Mailbox` CRC card has been updated.

Mailbox	
keep new and saved messages	`MessageQueue`
manage greeting	
manage passcode	
retrieve, save, delete messages	

The remaining use cases do not add any new information, so we omit the scenarios here.

There are a few points to keep in mind when using CRC cards. It is not easy to reason about objects and scenarios at a high level. It can be extremely difficult to distinguish between operations that are easy to implement and those that sound easy but actually pose significant implementation challenges. The only solution to this problem is lots of practice. Try your best with the CRC cards, and when you run into trouble with the implementation, try again. There is no shame in redesigning the classes until a system actually works. In fact, I redesigned the mail system classes at least twice before arriving at the current design.

Also, don't be deceived by the seemingly logical progression of thoughts in this section. Generally, when using CRC cards, there are quite a few false starts and detours. Describing them in a book would be pretty boring, so the process descriptions that you get in books tend to give you a false impression. One purpose of CRC cards is to fail early, to fail often, and to fail inexpensively. It is a lot cheaper to tear up a bunch of cards than to reorganize a large amount of source code.

2.12.3 — UML Class Diagrams for the Voice Mail System

The "collaboration" parts of the CRC cards show the following dependency relationships:

- `Mailbox` depends on `MessageQueue`
- `MailSystem` depends on `Mailbox`
- `Connection` depends on `Telephone`, `MailSystem`, `Message`, and `Mailbox`
- `Telephone` depends on `Connection`

Figure 15 shows these dependencies.

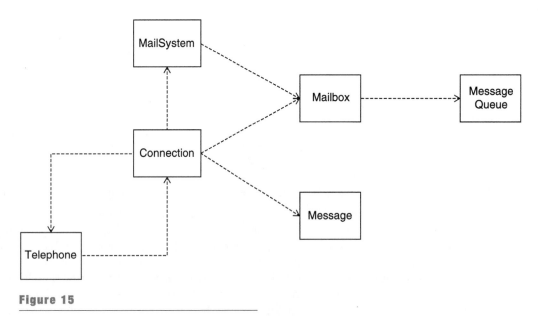

Figure 15

The Voice Mail System Dependencies from the CRC Cards

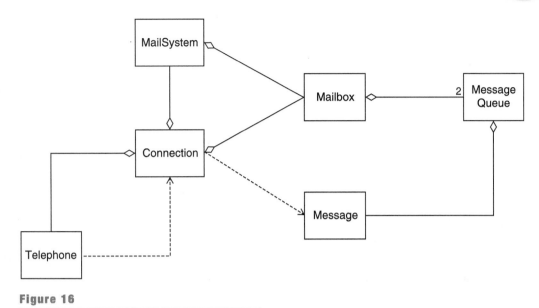

The UML Class Diagram for the Voice Mail System

Next, consider the aggregation relationships. From the previous discussion, we know the following:

- A mail system has mailboxes.

- A mailbox has two message queues.

- A message queue has some number of messages.

- A Connection has a current mailbox. It also has references to the MailSystem and Telephone objects that it connects.

There is no inheritance relationship between the classes. Figure 16 shows the completed UML diagram. Note that an aggregation relationship "wins" over a dependency relationship. If a class aggregates another, it clearly uses it, and you don't need to record the latter.

2.12.4 — UML Sequence and State Diagrams

The purpose of a sequence diagram is to understand a complex control flow that involves multiple objects, and to assure oneself at design time that there will be no surprises during the implementation.

In our case, the interactions between the Telephone, Connection, MailSystem, and Mailbox classes are not easy to understand. Let us draw a sequence diagram for the use case **Leave a Message** (see Figure 17).

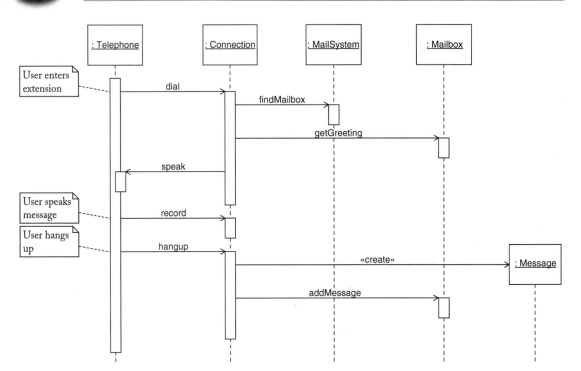

Figure 17

Sequence Diagram for Leaving a Message

The Telephone class reads user input one line at a time and passes it on to the Connection class. Let's postulate three methods for the Connection class:

- dial passes on a button press.
- record passes on speech.
- hangup tells the connection that the telephone has hung up.

First, the caller keys in the extension number, resulting in several calls to dial. We show only one of them—there is no advantage in modeling the repetition.

Once the Connection has the complete mailbox number, it needs to play the greeting. How does it know what greeting to play? It needs to get the mailbox and ask it for the greeting. How does it get the mailbox? It asks the mail system, calling a method that we call findMailbox.

The findMailbox method returns a Mailbox object. You don't see parameters and return values in the sequence diagram. You have to keep track of the objects yourself and realize that the Mailbox object to the right of the figure is meant to be the object returned by the findMailbox call.

Now that the connection has access to the mailbox, it needs the greeting. Thus, it invokes the getGreeting method on the mailbox and gets the greeting, which it then plays on the telephone speaker. Note that the greeting does not show up at all in the sequence diagram since it is entirely passive—no methods are invoked on it.

Next, the telephone reads the message text from the user and passes it on to the connection. Then the telephone reads the hangup signal and calls the hangup method. That is the signal for the connection to construct a message object and to add it to the mailbox.

Which mailbox? The same one that was previously obtained by calling findMailbox. How does the connection remember that mailbox? After all, it had called findMailbox in another method call. This is an indication that the Connection class holds on to the current mailbox.

Figure 18 shows the sequence diagram for the use case **Retrieve Messages**. It is a good exercise for you to analyze the sequence calls one by one. Ask yourself exactly where the objects of the diagram come from and how the calling methods have access to them.

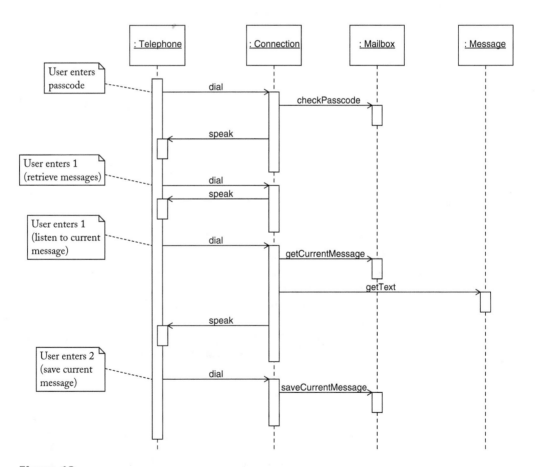

Figure 18

Sequence Diagram for Retrieving a Message

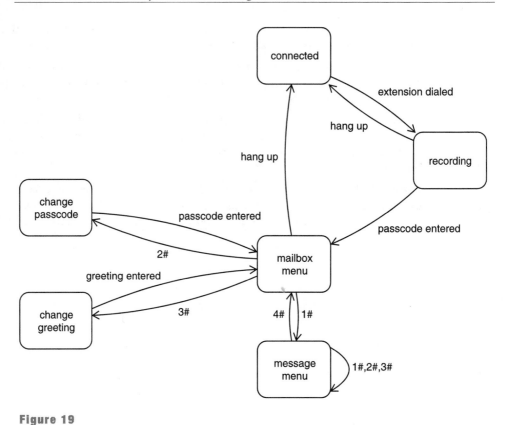

Figure 19

State Diagram for the Connection States

One complexity of the voice mail system is that it is not in control of the input. The user may provide touchpad or spoken input in any order, or simply hang up the phone. The telephone notifies the connection when such an event occurs. For example, notice that the connection is called at least three times in the "**Leave a Message**" scenario. (As already mentioned, the dial method is called for each separate key. The connection needs to aggregate keys until the user hits the # key. We didn't show that detail in the sequence diagrams.) The connection needs to keep track of the various states so that it can pick up at the right place when it receives the next user input. Figure 19 shows the state diagram.

2.12.5 — Java Implementation

Now we are ready to implement the system in Java. The files below give the implementation, which at this point is quite straightforward. You should compile and run the program to see the mail system in action. When you run the program, type Q to terminate it.

After running the program, have a look at each of the classes. Read the documentation comments and compare them with the CRC cards and the UML class diagrams. Look again at the UML sequence diagrams and trace the method calls in the actual code. Find the state transitions of the `Connection` class.

This simulation has a somewhat unsightly keyboard interface. In Chapter 5, you will see how to attach a graphical user interface (with buttons for the telephone keys and a text area to enter simulated voice). That change will require modification of just two classes: `Telephone` and `MailSystemTester`. Because the other classes have been decoupled from input and output, they require no changes whatsoever. Furthermore, in that program, you will be able to use two simulated telephones that can interact with the voice mail system at the same time, just like in a real voice mail system. This is possible because each connection between a telephone and the voice mail system is managed by a separate `Connection` object.

Ch2/mail/Message.java

```java
1  /**
2      A message left by the caller.
3  */
4  public class Message
5  {
6      /**
7          Construct a message object.
8          @param messageText the message text
9      */
10     public Message(String messageText)
11     {
12         text = messageText;
13     }
14
15     /**
16         Get the message text.
17         @return message text
18     */
19     public String getText()
20     {
21         return text;
22     }
23
24     private String text;
25 }
```

Ch2/mail/MessageQueue.java

```java
1  import java.util.ArrayList;
2
3  /**
4      A first-in, first-out collection of messages. This
5      implementation is not very efficient. We will consider
6      a more efficient implementation in Chapter 3.
7  */
8  public class MessageQueue
9  {
```

```
10      /**
11          Constructs an empty message queue.
12      */
13      public MessageQueue()
14      {
15          queue = new ArrayList<Message>();
16      }
17
18      /**
19          Remove message at head.
20          @return  message that has been removed from the queue
21      */
22      public Message remove()
23      {
24          return queue.remove(0);
25      }
26
27      /**
28          Append message at tail.
29          @param newMessage  the message to be appended
30      */
31      public void add(Message newMessage)
32      {
33          queue.add(newMessage);
34      }
35
36      /**
37          Get the total number of messages in the queue.
38          @return  the total number of messages in the queue
39      */
40      public int size()
41      {
42          return queue.size();
43      }
44
45      /**
46          Get message at head.
47          @return  message that is at the head of the queue, or null
48          if the queue is empty
49      */
50      public Message peek()
51      {
52          if (queue.size() == 0) return null;
53          else return queue.get(0);
54      }
55
56      private ArrayList<Message> queue;
57  }
```

 ## Ch2/mail/Mailbox.java

```
1  /**
2      A mailbox contains messages that can be listed, kept or discarded.
3  */
4  public class Mailbox
5  {
```

```
 6     /**
 7         Creates Mailbox object.
 8         @param aPasscode passcode number
 9         @param aGreeting greeting string
10     */
11     public Mailbox(String aPasscode, String aGreeting)
12     {
13         passcode = aPasscode;
14         greeting = aGreeting;
15         newMessages = new MessageQueue();
16         keptMessages = new MessageQueue();
17     }
18
19     /**
20         Check if the passcode is correct.
21         @param aPasscode a passcode to check
22         @return true if the supplied passcode matches the mailbox passcode
23     */
24     public boolean checkPasscode(String aPasscode)
25     {
26         return aPasscode.equals(passcode);
27     }
28
29     /**
30         Add a message to the mailbox.
31         @param aMessage the message to be added
32     */
33     public void addMessage(Message aMessage)
34     {
35         newMessages.add(aMessage);
36     }
37
38     /**
39         Get the current message.
40         @return the current message
41     */
42     public Message getCurrentMessage()
43     {
44         if (newMessages.size() > 0)
45             return newMessages.peek();
46         else if (keptMessages.size() > 0)
47             return keptMessages.peek();
48         else
49             return null;
50     }
51
52     /**
53         Remove the current message from the mailbox.
54         @return the message that has just been removed
55     */
56     public Message removeCurrentMessage()
57     {
58         if (newMessages.size() > 0)
59             return newMessages.remove();
60         else if (keptMessages.size() > 0)
61             return keptMessages.remove();
```

```
 62            else
 63                return null;
 64        }
 65
 66        /**
 67            Save the current message.
 68        */
 69        public void saveCurrentMessage()
 70        {
 71            Message m = removeCurrentMessage();
 72            if (m != null)
 73                keptMessages.add(m);
 74        }
 75
 76        /**
 77            Change mailbox's greeting.
 78            @param newGreeting the new greeting string
 79        */
 80        public void setGreeting(String newGreeting)
 81        {
 82            greeting = newGreeting;
 83        }
 84
 85        /**
 86            Change mailbox's passcode.
 87            @param newPasscode the new passcode
 88        */
 89        public void setPasscode(String newPasscode)
 90        {
 91            passcode = newPasscode;
 92        }
 93
 94        /**
 95            Get the mailbox's greeting.
 96            @return the greeting
 97        */
 98        public String getGreeting()
 99        {
100            return greeting;
101        }
102
103        private MessageQueue newMessages;
104        private MessageQueue keptMessages;
105        private String greeting;
106        private String passcode;
107 }
```

Ch2/mail/Connection.java

```
 1 /**
 2      Connects a phone to the mail system. The purpose of this
 3      class is to keep track of the state of a connection, because
 4      the phone itself is just a source of individual key presses.
 5 */
 6 public class Connection
 7 {
```

```
8     /**
9         Construct a Connection object.
10        @param s a MailSystem object
11        @param p a Telephone object
12    */
13    public Connection(MailSystem s, Telephone p)
14    {
15        system = s;
16        phone = p;
17        resetConnection();
18    }
19
20    /**
21        Respond to the user's pressing a key on the phone touchpad.
22        @param key the phone key pressed by the user
23    */
24    public void dial(String key)
25    {
26        if (state == CONNECTED)
27            connect(key);
28        else if (state == RECORDING)
29            login(key);
30        else if (state == CHANGE_PASSCODE)
31            changePasscode(key);
32        else if (state == CHANGE_GREETING)
33            changeGreeting(key);
34        else if (state == MAILBOX_MENU)
35            mailboxMenu(key);
36        else if (state == MESSAGE_MENU)
37            messageMenu(key);
38    }
39
40    /**
41        Record voice.
42        @param voice voice spoken by the user
43    */
44    public void record(String voice)
45    {
46        if (state == RECORDING || state == CHANGE_GREETING)
47            currentRecording += voice;
48    }
49
50    /**
51        The user hangs up the phone.
52    */
53    public void hangup()
54    {
55        if (state == RECORDING)
56            currentMailbox.addMessage(new Message(currentRecording));
57        resetConnection();
58    }
59
60    /**
61        Reset the connection to the initial state and prompt
62        for mailbox number.
63    */
```

```
64      private void resetConnection()
65      {
66         currentRecording = "";
67         accumulatedKeys = "";
68         state = CONNECTED;
69         phone.speak(INITIAL_PROMPT);
70      }
71
72      /**
73         Try to connect the user with the specified mailbox.
74         @param key the phone key pressed by the user
75      */
76      private void connect(String key)
77      {
78         if (key.equals("#"))
79         {
80            currentMailbox = system.findMailbox(accumulatedKeys);
81            if (currentMailbox != null)
82            {
83               state = RECORDING;
84               phone.speak(currentMailbox.getGreeting());
85            }
86            else
87               phone.speak("Incorrect mailbox number. Try again!");
88            accumulatedKeys = "";
89         }
90         else
91            accumulatedKeys += key;
92      }
93
94      /**
95         Try to log in the user.
96         @param key the phone key pressed by the user
97      */
98      private void login(String key)
99      {
100        if (key.equals("#"))
101        {
102           if (currentMailbox.checkPasscode(accumulatedKeys))
103           {
104              state = MAILBOX_MENU;
105              phone.speak(MAILBOX_MENU_TEXT);
106           }
107           else
108              phone.speak("Incorrect passcode. Try again!");
109           accumulatedKeys = "";
110        }
111        else
112           accumulatedKeys += key;
113     }
114
115     /**
116        Change passcode.
117        @param key the phone key pressed by the user
118     */
119     private void changePasscode(String key)
```

```
120    {
121       if (key.equals("#"))
122       {
123          currentMailbox.setPasscode(accumulatedKeys);
124          state = MAILBOX_MENU;
125          phone.speak(MAILBOX_MENU_TEXT);
126          accumulatedKeys = "";
127       }
128       else
129          accumulatedKeys += key;
130    }
131
132    /**
133       Change greeting.
134       @param key the phone key pressed by the user
135    */
136    private void changeGreeting(String key)
137    {
138       if (key.equals("#"))
139       {
140          currentMailbox.setGreeting(currentRecording);
141          currentRecording = "";
142          state = MAILBOX_MENU;
143          phone.speak(MAILBOX_MENU_TEXT);
144       }
145    }
146
147    /**
148       Respond to the user's selection from mailbox menu.
149       @param key the phone key pressed by the user
150    */
151    private void mailboxMenu(String key)
152    {
153       if (key.equals("1"))
154       {
155          state = MESSAGE_MENU;
156          phone.speak(MESSAGE_MENU_TEXT);
157       }
158       else if (key.equals("2"))
159       {
160          state = CHANGE_PASSCODE;
161          phone.speak("Enter new passcode followed by the # key");
162       }
163       else if (key.equals("3"))
164       {
165          state = CHANGE_GREETING;
166          phone.speak("Record your greeting, then press the # key");
167       }
168    }
169
170    /**
171       Respond to the user's selection from message menu.
172       @param key the phone key pressed by the user
173    */
174    private void messageMenu(String key)
175    {
```

```
176          if (key.equals("1"))
177          {
178             String output = "";
179             Message m = currentMailbox.getCurrentMessage();
180             if (m == null) output += "No messages." + "\n";
181             else output += m.getText() + "\n";
182             output += MESSAGE_MENU_TEXT;
183             phone.speak(output);
184          }
185          else if (key.equals("2"))
186          {
187             currentMailbox.saveCurrentMessage();
188             phone.speak(MESSAGE_MENU_TEXT);
189          }
190          else if (key.equals("3"))
191          {
192             currentMailbox.removeCurrentMessage();
193             phone.speak(MESSAGE_MENU_TEXT);
194          }
195          else if (key.equals("4"))
196          {
197             state = MAILBOX_MENU;
198             phone.speak(MAILBOX_MENU_TEXT);
199          }
200       }
201
202       private MailSystem system;
203       private Mailbox currentMailbox;
204       private String currentRecording;
205       private String accumulatedKeys;
206       private Telephone phone;
207       private int state;
208
209       private static final int DISCONNECTED = 0;
210       private static final int CONNECTED = 1;
211       private static final int RECORDING = 2;
212       private static final int MAILBOX_MENU = 3;
213       private static final int MESSAGE_MENU = 4;
214       private static final int CHANGE_PASSCODE = 5;
215       private static final int CHANGE_GREETING = 6;
216
217       private static final String INITIAL_PROMPT
218             = "Enter mailbox number followed by #";
219       private static final String MAILBOX_MENU_TEXT
220             = "Enter 1 to listen to your messages\n"
221             + "Enter 2 to change your passcode\n"
222             + "Enter 3 to change your greeting";
223       private static final String MESSAGE_MENU_TEXT
224             = "Enter 1 to listen to the current message\n"
225             + "Enter 2 to save the current message\n"
226             + "Enter 3 to delete the current message\n"
227             + "Enter 4 to return to the main menu";
228 }
```

Ch2/mail/MailSystem.java

```java
1  import java.util.ArrayList;
2
3  /**
4      A system of voice mailboxes.
5  */
6  public class MailSystem
7  {
8      /**
9          Constructs a mail system with a given number of mailboxes.
10         @param mailboxCount the number of mailboxes
11     */
12     public MailSystem(int mailboxCount)
13     {
14         mailboxes = new ArrayList();
15
16         // Initialize mailboxes.
17
18         for (int i = 0; i < mailboxCount; i++)
19         {
20             String passcode = "" + (i + 1);
21             String greeting = "You have reached mailbox " + (i + 1)
22                     + ". \nPlease leave a message now.";
23             mailboxes.add(new Mailbox(passcode, greeting));
24         }
25     }
26
27     /**
28         Locate a mailbox.
29         @param ext the extension number
30         @return the mailbox or null if not found
31     */
32     public Mailbox findMailbox(String ext)
33     {
34         int i = Integer.parseInt(ext);
35         if (1 <= i && i <= mailboxes.size())
36             return mailboxes.get(i - 1);
37         else return null;
38     }
39
40     private ArrayList<Mailbox> mailboxes;
41 }
```

Ch2/mail/Telephone.java

```java
1  import java.util.Scanner;
2
3  /**
4      A telephone that takes simulated keystrokes and voice input
5      from the user and simulates spoken text.
6  */
7  public class Telephone
8  {
```

```
 9     /**
10         Construct phone object.
11         @param aScanner that reads text from a character-input stream
12     */
13     public Telephone(Scanner aScanner)
14     {
15         scanner = aScanner;
16     }
17
18     /**
19         Speak a message to System.out.
20         @param output the text that will be "spoken"
21     */
22     public void speak(String output)
23     {
24         System.out.println(output);
25     }
26
27     /**
28         Loops reading user input and passes the input to the
29         Connection object's methods dial, record, or hangup.
30         @param c the connection that connects this phone to the
31         voice mail system
32     */
33     public void run(Connection c)
34     {
35         boolean more = true;
36         while (more)
37         {
38             String input = scanner.nextLine();
39             if (input == null) return;
40             if (input.equalsIgnoreCase("H"))
41                 c.hangup();
42             else if (input.equalsIgnoreCase("Q"))
43                 more = false;
44             else if (input.length() == 1
45                     && "1234567890#".indexOf(input) >= 0)
46                 c.dial(input);
47             else
48                 c.record(input);
49         }
50     }
51
52     private Scanner scanner;
53 }
```

Ch2/mail/MailSystemTester.java

```
1 import java.util.Scanner;
2
3 /**
4     This program tests the mail system. A single phone
5     communicates with the program through System.in/System.out.
6 */
7 public class MailSystemTester
8 {
```

```
 9     public static void main(String[] args)
10     {
11        MailSystem system = new MailSystem(MAILBOX_COUNT);
12        Scanner console = new Scanner(System.in);
13        Telephone p = new Telephone(console);
14        Connection c = new Connection(system, p);
15        p.run(c);
16     }
17
18     private static final int MAILBOX_COUNT = 20;
19  }
```

EXERCISES

Exercise 2.1. Consider the development of an online course registration system that allows students to add and drop classes at a university. Describe the activities that will take place during the analysis, design, and implementation phases. Give specific examples of activities that relate to the registration system.

Exercise 2.2. What is the difference between an object and a class? What is the difference between a class and a type?

Exercise 2.3. Consider cars in a car-racing video game. Explain the notions of state, behavior, and identity as they relate to car objects.

Exercise 2.4. Download the Mozilla Rhino implementation of ECMAScript. Implement the Greeter class and write a program that tests two instances of Greeter.

Exercise 2.5. Implement a class Car in ECMAScript. A car has a fuel efficiency (in miles per gallon or the metric equivalent) and a certain fuel level. Supply methods to add fuel, find out the fuel remaining in the tank, and drive a given distance.

Exercise 2.6. List at least eight classes that can be used in an online course registration system that allows students to add and drop classes at a university.

Exercise 2.7. Consider the development of a computer system for car rentals. Name one class that might be useful in this context from each of the following categories:

(a) Tangible things

(b) Agents

(c) Events and transactions

(d) Users and roles

(e) Systems

(f) System interfaces and devices

(g) Foundational classes

Exercise 2.8. What relationship is appropriate between the following classes: aggregation, inheritance, or neither?

(a) `University–Student`

(b) `Student–TeachingAssistant`

(c) `Student–Freshman`

(d) `Student–Professor`

(e) `Car–Door`

(f) `Truck–Vehicle`

(g) `Traffic–TrafficSign`

(h) `TrafficSign–Color`

Exercise 2.9. Consider an online course registration system that allows students to add and drop classes at a university. Give the multiplicities of the associations between these class pairs.

(a) `Student–Course`

(b) `Course–Section`

(c) `Section–Instructor`

(d) `Section–Room`

Exercise 2.10. Consider an airline reservation system with classes `Passenger`, `Itinerary`, `Flight`, and `Seat`. Consider a scenario in which a passenger adds a flight to an itinerary and selects a seat. What responsibilities and collaborators will you record on the CRC cards as a result?

Exercise 2.11. How does the design of the preceding exercise change if you have a group of passengers that fly together?

Exercise 2.12. Consider an online store that enables customers to order items from a catalog and pay for them with a credit card. Draw a UML diagram that shows the relationships between these classes:

```
Customer
Order
RushOrder
Product
Address
CreditCard
```

Exercise 2.13. Consider this test program:

```java
public class Tester
{
   public static void main(String[] args)
   {
      String s = "Hello World";
      Scanner in = new Scanner(s);
      while (in.hasNext())
         System.out.println(tokenizer.next());
   }
}
```

Draw a sequence diagram that shows the method calls of the main method.

Exercise 2.14. Consider a program that plays TicTacToe with a human user. A class TicTacToeBoard stores the game board. A random number generator is used to choose who begins and to generate random legal moves when it's the computer's turn. When it's the human's turn, the move is read from a Scanner, and the program checks that it is legal. After every move, the program checks whether the game is over. Draw a sequence diagram that shows a scenario in which the game starts, the computer gets the first turn, and the human gets the second turn. Stop the diagram after the second turn.

Exercise 2.15. Look up the API documentation of the URLConnection class and draw a state diagram of the states of an object of this class.

Exercise 2.16. Consider the scenario "A user changes the mailbox passcode" in the voice mail system. Carry out a walkthrough with the mail system's CRC cards. What steps do you list in your walkthrough? What collaborations and responsibilities do you record as a result of the walkthrough?

Exercise 2.17. In our voice mail simulation, the Connection objects hold a reference to the "current mailbox". Explain how you can change the design so that the Connection class does not depend on the Mailbox class. *Hint:* Add responsibilities to the MailSystem class.

Exercise 2.18. Design and implement a program that simulates a vending machine. Products can be purchased by inserting the correct number of coins into the machine. A user selects a product from a list of available products, adds coins, and either gets the product or gets the coins returned if insufficient money was supplied or if the product is sold out. Products can be restocked and money removed by an operator. Follow the design process that was described in this chapter.

Exercise 2.19. Design and implement a program that manages an appointment calendar. An appointment includes the description, date, starting time, and ending time; for example,

```
Dentist 2006/10/1 17:30 18:30
CS1 class 2006/10/2 08:30 10:00
```

Supply a user interface to add appointments, remove canceled appointments, and print out a list of appointments for a particular day. Follow the design process that was described in this chapter.

Exercise 2.20. *Airline seating.* Design and implement a program that assigns seats on an airplane. Assume the airplane has 20 seats in first class (5 rows of 4 seats each, separated by an aisle) and 180 seats in economy class (30 rows of 6 seats each, separated by an aisle). Your program should take three commands: add passengers, show seating, and quit. When passengers are added, ask for the class (first or economy), the number of passengers traveling together (1 or 2 in first class; 1 to 3 in economy), and the seating preference (aisle or window in first class; aisle, center, or window in economy). Then try to find a match and assign the seats. If no match exists, print a message. Follow the design process that was described in this chapter.

Guidelines for Class Design

In the preceding chapter, we discussed how to find classes for solving a practical programming problem. We looked at all classes in a program and the relationships among them. In this chapter, we take a very different, "bottom up" point of view, and explore how to write a single class well.

There are a number of useful rules and concepts that can dramatically improve the quality of the classes and interfaces that you design. It is well worth spending time on "good craftsmanship" of class design. The result is classes that are useful and reusable, and increased pride and satisfaction for you, the designer.

3.1   An Overview of the Date Classes in the Java Library

Many programs need to process dates such as "Saturday, February 4, 2006". The Java library has a Date class in the java.util package that can help. For example, the following statements print out the current date and time:

```
Date now = new Date();
   // constructs current date/time
System.out.println(now.toString());
   // prints date such as Sat Feb 04 16:34:10 PST 2006
```

As you can see, a Date object keeps track of both the date and the time. Look at the principal methods in the Date class:

Method	Description
boolean after(Date when)	Tests if this date is after the specified date
boolean before(Date when)	Tests if this date is before the specified date
int compareTo(Date anotherDate)	Compares two Date objects for ordering
long getTime()	Returns the number of milliseconds since 1970-01-01 00:00:00 GMT represented by this Date object
void setTime(long time)	Sets this Date object to represent a point in time that is time milliseconds after 1970-01-01 00:00:00 GMT

NOTE This table omits a number of *deprecated* methods—methods that the class designers had originally provided but then decided not to support any longer. You should not use deprecated methods because they may be withdrawn from a future version of the library without further notice. And, of course, there is a reason they were deprecated—someone realized that they were poorly thought out and should not have been included in the first place.

The Date class implements a very straightforward abstraction—a point in time, measured in milliseconds. (Time might have been a better name for this class.)

If you have two Date objects, it makes sense to ask which one comes before the other—see Figure 1. In mathematical terms, points in time have a *total ordering*. The before and after methods compute the ordering relationship.

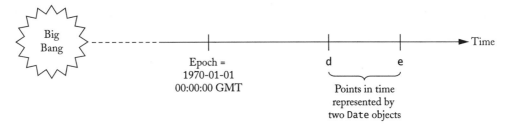

Figure 1

Two Points in Time

SPECIAL TOPIC   **3.1**

Total Orderings

A *total ordering* is a relation between the elements in a set that fulfills certain properties. In particular, a total ordering defines how elements can be sorted. Since sorting is an important operation, we are often interested in total orderings for objects of a class.

Let us review the definition of a total ordering. In mathematical notation, it is customary to use $\leq$ or a similar symbol (such as $\preccurlyeq$) to denote an ordering relation. With the $\leq$ symbol, the characteristic properties of a total ordering are:

1. Transitivity: If $x \leq y$ and $y \leq z$, then $x \leq z$
2. Reflexivity: $x \leq x$
3. Antisymmetry: If $x \leq y$ and $y \leq x$, then $x = y$
4. Totality: For any x and y, $x \leq y$ or $y \leq x$

(A relation that fulfills only the first three properties is called a *partial ordering*.)

The totality condition means that all elements can be compared with each other. An example of a total ordering is the standard $\leq$ relationship on the real numbers. Here is another example: For two Date objects x and y, you can define x $\leq$ y as

```
x.before(y) || x.equals(y)
```

This ordering lets you sort objects of the Date class.

It is not always so easy to find total orderings. Consider for example objects of the Rectangle class. Does the set of rectangles in the plane have a total ordering? That is, is there some way of comparing rectangles such that any two rectangles are comparable to each other? The first ordering relationship that comes to mind is containment (or $\subseteq$ in mathematical notation). A rectangle is considered "smaller" than another if it is contained in the other.

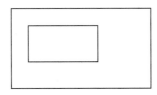

▼

▼

▼

▼

▼

This relationship is indeed a partial ordering, but it is not total. It is easy to find two rectangles that are not comparable to each other:

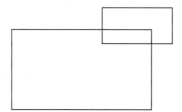

It is possible to define a total ordering on the set of rectangles, but it requires more effort. We will take up this issue again in Chapter 4 when we discuss the `Comparable` interface type.

The `Date` class provides a second service beyond supplying a total ordering. The `getTime` and `setTime` methods convert between `Date` objects and another common measurement of time—the number of milliseconds from the "epoch", 1970-01-01 00:00:00 GMT.

```
Date d = new Date();
long n = d.getTime();
    // sets n to the number of milliseconds since the epoch
```

In other words, the call

```
d.after(e)
```

is equivalent with the condition

```
d.getTime() > e.getTime()
```

But if you have a `Date` object and would like to know in what month or year it occurs, then you are out of luck. The `Date` class has no methods for computing that information. (We do not consider the deprecated methods or the `toString` method—that method is only intended for debugging.)

Instead, the responsibility of determining months, years, weekdays, and so on, is handled by a class `GregorianCalendar` that knows about the intricacies of our calendar such as the fact that January has 31 days and February has 28 or sometimes 29. The Gregorian calendar is named after Pope Gregory XIII. In 1582, he ordered the implementation of the calendar that is in common use throughout the world today. Its predecessor was the Julian calendar, instituted by Julius Caesar in the first century BCE. The Julian calendar introduced the rule that every fourth year is a leap year. The Gregorian calendar refines that rule by specifying that years divisible by 100 are not leap years, unless they are divisible by 400. Thus, the year 1900 was not a leap year but the year 2000 was.

NOTE   The Microsoft Excel program treats 1900 as a leap year. The explanation at http://support.microsoft.com/default.aspx?scid=kb;en-us;214326 claims that this choice was intentional to provide greater compatibility with another spreadsheet program that had the same error. Apparently, one group of programmers was not diligent enough to research leap years, and another group of programmers couldn't figure out how to rectify that problem. Details do matter.

Defining the `GregorianCalendar` class separate from the `Date` class is good class design. There are many possible descriptions of a point in time. For example, February 3, 2001 is

- Année 209 de la République Mois de Pluviôse Décade 2 Jour du Quintidi in the French Revolutionary Calendar
- 12.19.7.17.1 in the Mayan Long Count

While you aren't likely to have customers using the French Revolutionary or Mayan calendar, there are other calendars in active use around the world, such as the Chinese, Jewish, and Islamic calendars.

 INTERNET   You can find a detailed discussion of the French Revolutionary, Mayan, Chinese, Jewish, and Islamic calendars at `http://www.tondering.dk/claus/calendar.html`.

Thus, the responsibility of the `GregorianCalendar` class is to assign descriptions to points in time, and conversely, to compute the point in time that corresponds to such a description. It would be possible in principle to design a class `FrenchRevolutionaryCalendar` or `IslamicCalendar` that converts between `Date` values and descriptions in those calendar systems.

For that reason, the Java library designers provide a superclass `Calendar` that is supposed to help implementors of other calendars. Figure 2 shows the relationship between these classes in UML notation.

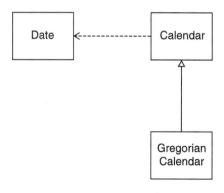

Figure 2

The Date Handling Classes in the Java Library

The following table shows some of the most important methods of the `Calendar` class:

Method	Description
`int get(int field)`	Gets a field value; `field` is a `Calendar` class constant such as YEAR, MONTH, DATE, HOUR, MINUTE, SECOND
`void set(int field, int value)`	Sets a field value
`void add(int field, int increment)`	Adds to a field value
`Date getTime()`	Converts to a `Date` value
`void setTime(Date d)`	Converts from a `Date` value

3.2   Designing a Day Class

This section explores a variety of possible designs for a `Day` class, a class that represents a calendar day in the Julian/Gregorian calendar, such as February 4, 2006. You are encouraged to always use the standard Java class library in your own programs, but the behavior of calendar days is just subtle enough to make other class examples interesting.

For simplicity, we do not deal with time, and we fix a place on the globe, ignoring the fact that elsewhere it may be a day earlier or later. We assume that the switchover from the Julian to the Gregorian calendar is on October 15, 1582, even though different countries adopted the Gregorian calendar at different times.

A `Day` object encapsulates a particular day. Unlike the designers of the `Date` class, who felt that the most useful operation for the `Date` class is the total ordering (`before`, `after`), we will implement a stronger set of methods. In particular, we want to be able to answer questions such as

- How many days are there between now and the end of the year?
- What day is 100 days from now?

Day
relate calendar days to day counts

The `daysFrom` method computes the number of days between two days. For example, if bday is your birthday, and today is today's day, then

```
int n = today.daysFrom(bday);
```

computes how many days you have lived. The value of `d1.daysFrom(d2)` is negative if d1 comes before d2, it is 0 if they are the same, and positive if d1 comes after d2. Thus, Day objects also have a total ordering.

Conversely, if n is a number of days (either positive or negative), then the `addDays` method computes the day that is n days away from the current day. For example, here is how you compute 999 days from today:

```
Day later = today.addDays(999);
```

However, unlike the Date class, the Day class does not reveal an "epoch", a fixed day 0 such as January 1, 1970. If it uses an epoch for its internal computations, it is a hidden implementation detail.

In other words, we define the "difference" between two days as an integer, and we define an "addition" operation that takes a day and an integer and yields another day. These operations are inverses of each other, in the sense that

```
d.addDays(n).daysFrom(d) is the same as n
```

and

```
d1.addDays(d2.daysFrom(d1)) is the same as d2
```

This becomes clearer if you write `addDays` as + and `daysFrom` as -.

```
(d + n) - d is the same as n
```

and

```
d1 + (d2 - d1) is the same as d2
```

Clearly, there is a mathematical structure here. We don't want to overemphasize this fact, but neither do we want to hide it. Often times, the existence of a mathematical structure can be used to define the behavior of a class in a precise and unambiguous manner.

 NOTE If you are familiar with pointers into arrays in C or C++, you will recognize that pointers have the same mathematical structure as our Day objects. The difference between two pointers is an integer (or, to be precise, a `ptrdiff_t` value). The sum of a pointer and an integer is another pointer.

Finally, we want a constructor that constructs a Day object from a given year, month, and day, and we want methods to obtain the year, month, and day of the month. For example,

```
Day today = new Day(2006, 2, 4); // February 4, 2006
Day later = today.addDays(999);
System.out.println(later.getYear()
      + "-" + later.getMonth()
      + "-" + later.getDate()); // prints 2008-10-30
System.out.println(later.daysFrom(today)); // prints 999
```

Note that the constructor expects the year, followed by the month, and finally the day, as defined in the ISO 8601 standard. That international standard recommends always presenting days in a standard order: four-digit year, month, and day. This convention avoids confusion with dates such as 02/04/06, which are interpreted differently in different countries.

INTERNET   The official ISO 8601 standard document is available for purchase from `http://www.iso.ch`. See `http://www.cl.cam.ac.uk/~mgk25/iso-time.html` for a nice explanation of the main points of the standard.

Thus, our Day class has the following public interface:

```
public class Day
{
    /**
        Constructs a day with a given year, month, and day
        of the Julian/Gregorian calendar. The Julian calendar
        is used for all days before October 15, 1582.
        @param aYear a year != 0
        @param aMonth a month between 1 and 12
        @param aDate a date between 1 and 31
    */
    public Day(int aYear, int aMonth, int aDate) { . . . }

    /**
        Returns the year of this day.
        @return the year
    */
    public int getYear() { . . . }

    /**
        Returns the month of this day.
        @return the month
    */
    public int getMonth() { . . . }

    /**
        Returns the day of the month of this day.
        @return the day of the month
    */
    public int getDate() { . . . }

    /**
        Returns a day that is a certain number of days away from
        this day.
        @param n the number of days, can be negative
        @return a day that is n days away from this one
    */
    public Day addDays(int n) { . . . }
```

```
/**
    Returns the number of days between this day and another
    day.
    @param other the other day
    @return the number of days that this day is away from
    the other (> 0 if this day comes later)
*/
public int daysFrom(Day other) { . . . }
}
```

Special Topic   3.2

Operator Overloading

The Day class has a method to compute the "difference" between two Day objects, that is, the number of days between two Day objects. In some programming languages, you can actually use the familiar subtraction operator (-) to denote this conceptual difference. That is, you can use the statement

```
int n = today - bday;
```

instead of

```
int n = today.daysFrom(bday);
```

This mechanism is called *operator overloading*. In C++, you achieve operator overloading by defining methods with special names. For example, you define a method called `operator-` to overload the subtraction operator. Whenever you use the subtraction operator, the compiler checks whether you want to subtract numbers or values of another type. When you subtract two Day objects, the compiler locates the `operator-` method of the Day class and invokes it. That method should of course have the same functionality as the daysFrom method.

Operator overloading can make programs easier to read, particularly when dealing with mathematical objects such as big numbers, vectors, and matrices. For example, the expression

```
x + y * z
```

is much clearer than the equivalent

```
x.add(y.multiply(z))
```

The Java programming language does not support operator overloading. The language desigers felt that operator overloading was a complex feature that would make Java harder to learn. Furthermore, operator overloading seems to have limited applicability outside scientific computing.

Not everyone agrees with this decision. Mathematicians have extensive experience with designing notation that makes complex expressions easier to read. It would be desirable to make use of some of that expertise and make computer programs easier to read as well.

3.3   Three Implementations of the Day Class

Let us consider a straightforward implementation of the Day class, where the state of a Day object is represented as

```
private int year;
private int month;
private int date;
```

Then the constructor and the three get methods are trivial to implement.

```
public Day(int aYear, int aMonth, int aDate)
{
    year = aYear;
    month = aMonth;
    date = aDate;
}

public int getYear()
{
    return year;
}
. . .
```

Of course, the addDays and daysFrom methods are tedious. Consider the following facts:

1. April, June, September, and November have 30 days.
2. February has 28 days, except in leap years, when it has 29 days.
3. All other months have 31 days.
4. Leap years are years that are divisible by 4, except after 1582, when years that are divisible by 100 but not 400 are not leap years.
5. There is no year 0; year 1 is preceded by year −1.
6. In the switchover to the Gregorian calendar, 10 days were dropped so that October 15, 1582, followed immediately after October 4.

You will find a solution in Section 3.3.1. Have a look at it and note how it depends on helper methods nextDay and previousDay.

These helper methods have been declared as private and not public. It may not be immediately obvious why this is a good arrangement. After all, since you went through the trouble of implementing the methods, shouldn't you make them available for others to use?

There are three reasons why you should be cautious about making helper methods public:

- They can clutter up the public interface, making it harder for class users to understand your class.
- Sometimes, helper methods require a special protocol or calling order. You may not trust your class users to understand the subtleties, or you may not want to document them as carefully as you document the public interface.

- Sometimes, helper methods depend on a particular implementation. Their need goes away when you switch to another implementation. But if you make them public, then there is the possibility that one of the users of your class has actually called the method. Now you need to keep it working under the new implementation, or you risk the wrath of the user who will not want you to take it away. "Once public, always public".

TIP   Choose private visibility for those methods that are of no concern to the class user and for those methods that could not easily be supported if the class implementation changed.

Our first implementation of the Day class is quite inefficient because all computations increment or decrement one day at a time. Now let us turn to a completely different implementation. Rather than storing the year, month, and date, the second implementation will store the *Julian day number*. The Julian day number is the number of days from January 1, 4713 BCE. For example, the Gregorian calendar day May 23, 1968, corresponds to the Julian day number 2,440,000. Standard functions can compute the Julian day number from a calendar date and a calendar date from the Julian day number—see the source code in Section 3.3.2 for the formulas.

NOTE   The Julian day number is unrelated to the Julian calendar enacted by Julius Caesar. The sixteenth-century historian Joseph Scaliger used the recurrence intervals for certain astronomical events and the 15-year Roman tax cycle to find a synchronization point, January 1, 4713 BCE. He used that point as a zero for mapping every event in written history reliably to a positive day number. Scaliger named this day number after his father Julius. Julian day numbers are used today by astronomers throughout the world.

With the Julian day number, the addDays and daysFrom methods become trivial and very efficient.

```
public class Day
{
   public Day addDays(int n)
   {
      return new Day(julian + n); // Calls private constructor
   }

   public int daysFrom(Day other)
   {
      return julian - other.julian;
   }

   . . .

   private int julian;
}
```

Of course, now the public Day(int aYear, int aMonth, int aDate) constructor and the getYear, getMonth, and getDate methods are not very efficient. In particular, consider the call

```
System.out.println(later.getYear()
    + "-" + later.getMonth()
    + "-" + later.getDate());
```

The computation for converting a Julian day number back to the calendar day now runs three times, once for each accessor.

This problem can be overcome with a third implementation that combines the benefits of the two. Keep both the year-month-date representation *and* the julian representation, converting between them as needed. The conversion should be *lazy*—the julian value should be computed only when it is required. That way, we pay no conversion cost if a Day object never executes any date arithmetic. Conversely, if an object is constructed with the private Day(int julian) constructor, the year-month-date representation should only be generated when one of the get methods is called. After all, maybe the object is used for intermediate calculations only.

To implement the lazy conversion between the two representations, use two boolean variables ymdValid and julianValid. See the source code for the third implementation in Section 3.3.3 for details.

Which of these three implementations is best? There is no one answer—it depends on the application. If little date arithmetic is required, then the first implementation is entirely acceptable. The last implementation is the most efficient, but it is undeniably complex and requires more storage.

3.3.1 — Implementation #1

Ch3/day1/Day.java

```
 1  public class Day
 2  {
 3     /**
 4        Constructs a day with a given year, month, and day
 5        of the Julian/Gregorian calendar. The Julian calendar
 6        is used for all days before October 15, 1582.
 7        @param aYear a year != 0
 8        @param aMonth a month between 1 and 12
 9        @param aDate a date between 1 and 31
10     */
11     public Day(int aYear, int aMonth, int aDate)
12     {
13        year = aYear;
14        month = aMonth;
15        date = aDate;
16     }
17
18     /**
```

```
19            Returns the year of this day.
20            @return the year
21     */
22     public int getYear()
23     {
24         return year;
25     }
26
27     /**
28            Returns the month of this day.
29            @return the month
30     */
31     public int getMonth()
32     {
33         return month;
34     }
35
36     /**
37            Returns the day of the month of this day.
38            @return the day of the month
39     */
40     public int getDate()
41     {
42         return date;
43     }
44
45     /**
46            Returns a day that is a certain number of days away from
47            this day.
48            @param n the number of days, can be negative
49            @return a day that is n days away from this one
50     */
51     public Day addDays(int n)
52     {
53         Day result = this;
54         while (n > 0)
55         {
56             result = result.nextDay();
57             n--;
58         }
59         while (n < 0)
60         {
61             result = result.previousDay();
62             n++;
63         }
64         return result;
65     }
66
67     /**
68            Returns the number of days between this day and another
69            day.
70            @param other the other day
71            @return the number of days that this day is away from
72            the other (> 0 if this day comes later)
73     */
74     public int daysFrom(Day other)
```

```
75    {
76       int n = 0;
77       Day d = this;
78       while (d.compareTo(other) > 0)
79       {
80          d = d.previousDay();
81          n++;
82       }
83       while (d.compareTo(other) < 0)
84       {
85          d = d.nextDay();
86          n--;
87       }
88       return n;
89    }
90
91    /**
92       Compares this day with another day.
93       @param other  the other day
94       @return  a positive number if this day comes after the
95       other day, a negative number if this day comes before
96       the other day, and zero if the days are the same
97    */
98    private int compareTo(Day other)
99    {
100      if (year > other.year) return 1;
101      if (year < other.year) return -1;
102      if (month > other.month) return 1;
103      if (month < other.month) return -1;
104      return date - other.date;
105   }
106
107   /**
108      Computes the next day.
109      @return  the day following this day
110   */
111   private Day nextDay()
112   {
113      int y = year;
114      int m = month;
115      int d = date;
116      if (y == GREGORIAN_START_YEAR
117            && m == GREGORIAN_START_MONTH
118            && d == JULIAN_END_DAY)
119         d = GREGORIAN_START_DAY;
120      else if (d < daysPerMonth(y, m))
121         d++;
122      else
123      {
124         d = 1;
125         m++;
126         if (m > DECEMBER)
127         {
128            m = JANUARY;
129            y++;
130            if (y == 0) y++;
```

```
131            }
132        }
133        return new Day(y, m, d);
134    }
135
136    /**
137        Computes the previous day.
138        @return the day preceding this day
139    */
140    private Day previousDay()
141    {
142        int y = year;
143        int m = month;
144        int d = date;
145
146        if (y == GREGORIAN_START_YEAR
147                && m == GREGORIAN_START_MONTH
148                && d == GREGORIAN_START_DAY)
149            d = JULIAN_END_DAY;
150        else if (d > 1)
151            d--;
152        else
153        {
154            m--;
155            if (m < JANUARY)
156            {
157                m = DECEMBER;
158                y--;
159                if (y == 0) y--;
160            }
161            d = daysPerMonth(y, m);
162        }
163        return new Day(y, m, d);
164    }
165
166    /**
167        Gets the days in a given month.
168        @param y the year
169        @param m the month
170        @return the last day in the given month
171    */
172    private static int daysPerMonth(int y, int m)
173    {
174        int days = DAYS_PER_MONTH[m - 1];
175        if (m == FEBRUARY && isLeapYear(y))
176            days++;
177        return days;
178    }
179
180    /**
181        Tests if a year is a leap year.
182        @param y the year
183        @return true if y is a leap year
184    */
185    private static boolean isLeapYear(int y)
186    {
```

```
187        if (y % 4 != 0) return false;
188        if (y < GREGORIAN_START_YEAR) return true;
189        return (y % 100 != 0) || (y % 400 == 0);
190    }
191
192    private int year;
193    private int month;
194    private int date;
195
196    private static final int[] DAYS_PER_MONTH
197        = { 31, 28, 31, 30, 31, 30, 31, 31, 30, 31, 30, 31 };
198
199    private static final int GREGORIAN_START_YEAR = 1582;
200    private static final int GREGORIAN_START_MONTH = 10;
201    private static final int GREGORIAN_START_DAY = 15;
202    private static final int JULIAN_END_DAY = 4;
203    private static final int JANUARY = 1;
204    private static final int FEBRUARY = 2;
205    private static final int DECEMBER = 12;
206 }
```

3.3.2 — Implementation #2

Ch3/day2/Day.java

```
 1 public class Day
 2 {
 3     /**
 4         Constructs a day with a given year, month, and day
 5         of the Julian/Gregorian calendar. The Julian calendar
 6         is used for all days before October 15, 1582.
 7         @param aYear  a year != 0
 8         @param aMonth  a month between 1 and 12
 9         @param aDate  a date between 1 and 31
10     */
11     public Day(int aYear, int aMonth, int aDate)
12     {
13         julian = toJulian(aYear, aMonth, aDate);
14     }
15
16     /**
17         Returns the year of this day.
18         @return  the year
19     */
20     public int getYear()
21     {
22         return fromJulian(julian)[0];
23     }
24
25     /**
26         Returns the month of this day.
27         @return  the month
28     */
```

```
29    public int getMonth()
30    {
31        return fromJulian(julian)[1];
32    }
33
34    /**
35        Returns the day of the month of this day.
36        @return the day of the month
37    */
38    public int getDate()
39    {
40        return fromJulian(julian)[2];
41    }
42
43    /**
44        Returns a day that is a certain number of days away from
45        this day.
46        @param n the number of days, can be negative
47        @return a day that is n days away from this one
48    */
49    public Day addDays(int n)
50    {
51        return new Day(julian + n);
52    }
53
54    /**
55        Returns the number of days between this day and another day.
56        @param other the other day
57        @return the number of days that this day is away from
58        the other (> 0 if this day comes later)
59    */
60    public int daysFrom(Day other)
61    {
62        return julian - other.julian;
63    }
64
65    private Day(int aJulian)
66    {
67        julian = aJulian;
68    }
69
70    /**
71        Computes the Julian day number of the given day.
72        @param year a year
73        @param month a month
74        @param date a day of the month
75        @return The Julian day number that begins at noon of
76        the given day
77        Positive year signifies CE, negative year BCE.
78        Remember that the year after 1 BCE is 1 CE.
79
80        A convenient reference point is that May 23, 1968, noon
81        is Julian day number 2,440,000.
82
83        Julian day number 0 is a Monday.
84
```

```
 85        This algorithm is from Press et al., Numerical Recipes
 86        in C, 2nd ed., Cambridge University Press, 1992.
 87     */
 88     private static int toJulian(int year, int month, int date)
 89     {
 90        int jy = year;
 91        if (year < 0) jy++;
 92        int jm = month;
 93        if (month > 2) jm++;
 94        else
 95        {
 96           jy--;
 97           jm += 13;
 98        }
 99        int jul = (int) (java.lang.Math.floor(365.25 * jy)
100              + java.lang.Math.floor(30.6001 * jm) + date + 1720995.0);
101
102        int IGREG = 15 + 31 * (10 + 12 * 1582);
103           // Gregorian calendar adopted October 15, 1582
104
105        if (date + 31 * (month + 12 * year) >= IGREG)
106           // Change over to Gregorian calendar
107        {
108           int ja = (int) (0.01 * jy);
109           jul += 2 - ja + (int) (0.25 * ja);
110        }
111        return jul;
112     }
113
114     /**
115        Converts a Julian day number to a calendar date.
116
117        This algorithm is from Press et al., Numerical Recipes
118        in C, 2nd ed., Cambridge University Press, 1992.
119
120        @param j the Julian day number
121        @return an array whose 0 entry is the year, 1 the month,
122        and 2 the date
123     */
124     private static int[] fromJulian(int j)
125     {
126        int ja = j;
127
128        int JGREG = 2299161;
129        // The Julian day number of the adoption of the Gregorian calendar
130
131        if (j >= JGREG)
132        // Crossover to Gregorian calendar produces this correction
133        {
134           int jalpha = (int) ((((float) (j - 1867216) - 0.25)
135                 / 36524.25);
136           ja += 1 + jalpha - (int) (0.25 * jalpha);
137        }
138        int jb = ja + 1524;
139        int jc = (int) (6680.0 + ((float) (jb - 2439870) - 122.1)
140              / 365.25);
```

```
141        int jd = (int) (365 * jc + (0.25 * jc));
142        int je = (int) ((jb - jd) / 30.6001);
143        int date = jb - jd - (int) (30.6001 * je);
144        int month = je - 1;
145        if (month > 12) month -= 12;
146        int year = jc - 4715;
147        if (month > 2) --year;
148        if (year <= 0) --year;
149        return new int[] { year, month, date };
150    }
151
152    private int julian;
153 }
```

3.3.3 — Implementation #3

Ch3/day3/Day.java

```
 1 public class Day
 2 {
 3    /**
 4        Constructs a day with a given year, month, and day
 5        of the Julian/Gregorian calendar. The Julian calendar
 6        is used for all days before October 15, 1582.
 7        @param aYear a year != 0
 8        @param aMonth a month between 1 and 12
 9        @param aDate a date between 1 and 31
10    */
11    public Day(int aYear, int aMonth, int aDate)
12    {
13        year = aYear;
14        month = aMonth;
15        date = aDate;
16        ymdValid = true;
17        julianValid = false;
18    }
19
20    /**
21        Returns the year of this day.
22        @return the year
23    */
24    public int getYear()
25    {
26        ensureYmd();
27        return year;
28    }
29
30    /**
31        Returns the month of this day.
32        @return the month
33    */
34    public int getMonth()
35    {
```

```
36          ensureYmd();
37          return month;
38      }
39
40      /**
41          Returns the date of this day.
42          @return the date
43      */
44      public int getDate()
45      {
46          ensureYmd();
47          return date;
48      }
49
50      /**
51          Returns a day that is a certain number of days away from
52          this day.
53          @param n the number of days, can be negative
54          @return a day that is n days away from this one
55      */
56      public Day addDays(int n)
57      {
58          ensureJulian();
59          return new Day(julian + n);
60      }
61
62      /**
63          Returns the number of days between this day and another
64          day.
65          @param other the other day
66          @return the number of days that this day is away from
67          the other (> 0 if this day comes later)
68      */
69      public int daysFrom(Day other)
70      {
71          ensureJulian();
72          other.ensureJulian();
73          return julian - other.julian;
74      }
75
76      private Day(int aJulian)
77      {
78          julian = aJulian;
79          ymdValid = false;
80          julianValid = true;
81      }
82
83      /**
84          Computes the Julian day number of this day if
85          necessary.
86      */
87      private void ensureJulian()
88      {
89          if (julianValid) return;
90          julian = toJulian(year, month, date);
91          julianValid = true;
```

```
92    }
93
94    /**
95       Converts this Julian day number to a calendar date if necessary.
96    */
97    private void ensureYmd()
98     {
99       if (ymdValid) return;
100      int[] ymd = fromJulian(julian);
101      year = ymd[0];
102      month = ymd[1];
103      date = ymd[2];
104      ymdValid = true;
105    }
106
```

. . .

A number of repetitive methods are omitted here

. . .

```
190    private int year;
191    private int month;
192    private int date;
193    private int julian;
194    private boolean ymdValid;
195    private boolean julianValid;
196  }
```

3.4 The Importance of Encapsulation

The three implementations in the previous section illustrate an important point: Even a seemingly simple class such as the Day class can be implemented in different ways, each with its own benefits and drawbacks. By using encapsulation, the users of the Day class can be blissfully unaware of the implementation details, and the implementor of the class can switch implementations without inconveniencing the class users.

Suppose we had started out with a Day class that used public instance variables

```
public class Day
{
   . . .
   public int year;
   public int month;
   public int date;
}
```

But then we decide to speed up date calculations by using a Julian day number instead. We remove the year, month, and date fields and supply an int julian field. What is the impact of this change on the class user? Of course, none of the class user's code that accessed the public fields will compile after the change has been made. Code such as

```
m = d.month;
```

must be replaced by

```
m = d.getMonth();
```

How about

```
d.year++;
```

That gets trickier, and also less efficient.

```
d = new Day(d.getDay(), d.getMonth(), d.getYear() + 1);
```

What should be a simple change of representation turns into a major effort. In practical programming situations, many worthwhile improvements are not undertaken simply because they would force other programmers to go through an effort just like this.

> Private data fields are essential for improving the implementation of a class without disruption to its users.

In this scenario, it is still possible to identify all places that require change, simply by recompiling and following the compiler's error messages. But suppose we want to switch from the first to the third implementation, adding the julian field and the flags to indicate which of the two representations is currently valid. Now the compiler will accept code containing d.year. The programmers using the Day class must inspect each line of the program to see whether it is affected by the change. They have to be trusted to set the flags correctly. If any one of them makes a mistake, data may be corrupted and time-consuming debugging sessions may result.

Thus, even though encapsulation forces programmers to spend more time on planning and design, it is an essential feature for larger programs. Successful software products evolve over time. New user requirements must be implemented, and obsolete features are sometimes retired. The existing code must be maintainable. Rewriting all code for every product release would be too slow and expensive. (Novice programmers initially find it hard to envision this—if the lifetime of your homework assignment is three weeks, then you are much more interested in coding quickly than in keeping the code maintainable.)

Data encapsulation provides a mechanism for restricting the range of the program that is affected by a change to a small subset, namely the methods of a class. Once that subset has been updated to track a change, the programmer can state with confidence that no other portion of the program needs attention in this regard.

3.4.1 — Accessors and Mutators

> A mutator method modifies the state of an object; an accessor method leaves the state unchanged.

We make a conceptual distinction between *mutator methods*, which change the state of an object, and *accessor methods*, which merely read its instance fields.

For example, the Day class of the preceding section has no mutators. It is an *immutable* class, just like the String class. In contrast, the java.util.Date class has a mutator, setTime. The GregorianCalendar class has several mutators as well—look at the set and add methods in the API documentation.

> Objects of an immutable class cannot be changed after they have been constructed.

Should we add methods `void setYear(int aYear)`, `void setMonth(int aMonth)`, and `void setDate(int aDate)`? These methods are actually not a good idea. Consider this sequence of events.

```
Day deadline = new Day(2006, 1, 31);
```

Now we want to move the deadline by a month:

```
deadline.setMonth(2);
```

Clearly, this won't work—there is no February 31. Or should the day have rolled over to March 3? The `set` method in the `GregorianCalendar` class actually does that! The results aren't pretty. Consider the following sequence, where the desired outcome is to move the deadline by a day:

```
deadline.setMonth(2);
deadline.setDate(1);
```

Oops—now the deadline has been set to March 1! Silly me, you'll say. I should have *first* set the date. But that won't always work either:

```
Day deadline = new Day(2006, 2, 1);
deadline.setDate(30);
deadline.setMonth(4);
```

If `setDate` rolls over to the next valid day, then the deadline is first set to March 2, then to April 2. Clearly, these `set` methods are a disaster waiting to happen.

There is no need to supply `set` methods for every instance field or as a counterpart of every `get` method. However, some tools that generate code from UML diagrams automatically supply `get` and `set` methods for all attributes. If you use such a tool, you should use this feature with caution.

   TIP   Don't automatically supply `set` methods for every instance field.

There is one great advantage to classes without mutator methods: Their object references can be freely shared. In contrast, you need to be careful about sharing of mutable objects. In particular, it is dangerous for an accessor method to give out a reference to a mutable instance field. Consider the following example:

```
class Employee
{
    . . .
    public String getName()
    {
        return name;
    }

    public double getSalary()
    {
        return salary;
```

```
    }

    public Date getHireDate()
    {
        return hireDate;
    }

    private String name;
    private double salary;
    private Date hireDate;
}
```

The get methods look quite harmless—Java programmers write many methods like this. But actually, there is a hidden danger. The getHireDate method breaks encapsulation. Since the Date class is a mutable class, anyone can apply a mutator method to the returned reference and thereby modify the Employee object.

```
Employee harry = . . .;
Date d = harry.getHireDate();
d.setTime(t); // Changes Harry's state! (See Figure 3)
```

Clearly, this is not what the designer of the Employee class intended. The getHireDate method was designed to give information about the Employee object, not to permit modification of it. The remedy is to *clone* the object before giving it out.

```
public Date getHireDate()
{
    return (Date) hireDate.clone();
}
```

The clone method of the Object class makes a copy of the object with the same fields as the original. The recipient of the cloned object is of course still able to modify it, but those modifications don't affect the Date object held by the employee.

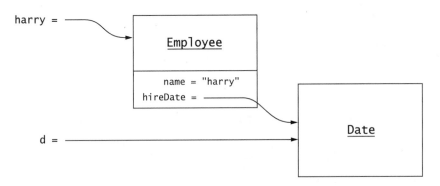

Figure 3

Changing Object State Through a Reference to a Subobject

Cloning is more subtle than it appears at first sight—you will see all the details in Chapter 7.

However, the getName method is safe. The String class is immutable. Nobody can modify the name object, so it is not a problem to return a reference to it.

TIP An accessor method should never return a reference to a mutable instance field. Instead, clone the field. However, it is safe to return primitive types and references to immutable objects.

There is a second potential problem with Date references in the Employee class. When you construct an Employee object, you supply a Date reference. Suppose the constructor looks like this:

```
public Employee(String aName, Date aHireDate)
{
   name = aName;
   hireDate = aHireDate;
}
```

Then an evil or clueless programmer could construct an Employee object and later mutate the construction parameter:

```
Date d = new Date();
Employee e = new Employee("Harry Hacker", d);
d.setTime(. . .);
```

Once again, the encapsulation is broken. The remedy is to clone the value in the constructor. As you can see, properly dealing with mutable classes is quite tedious.

TIP Immutability is a valuable feature. If you can make your class immutable, you should.

3.4.2 — Final Instance Fields

You can mark an instance field as final to indicate that it doesn't change once it has been constructed. For example,

```
public class Date
{
   . . .
   private final int day;
   private final int month;
   private final int year;
}
```

This is a good way of expressing that this class is immutable. However, the final keyword only refers to the contents of the variable, not to the state of the object to which it refers.

For example, you can declare a variable containing an `ArrayList` reference as `final`.

```
public class MessageQueue
{
   . . .
   private final ArrayList elements;
}
```

But that merely guarantees that no other `ArrayList` object is ever attached to the `elements` field. The `final` keyword does *not* prevent changes to the contents of the array list.

3.4.3 — Separation of Accessors and Mutators

We've been pretty negative on mutators in this section. Let's put mutators in perspective. Of course, many classes require mutators. In fact, a benefit of using objects is to represent states that mutate over time.

When you have a class that has both accessors and mutators, then it is a good idea to keep their roles separate. A method that returns information about an object should ideally not change the object state. A method that changes the object state should ideally have return type `void`.

For example, in a `BankAccount` class, you don't expect the `getBalance` method to affect the balance by deducting a "balance inquiry" charge. You expect that you can call accessors as often as you like and always get the same result, as long as no mutator changed the object state.

Let's look at a couple of examples that violate this rule. The `next` method of the `Scanner` class returns a value: the next token from the input. Therefore, it appears to be an accessor method. But it *also* changes the state of the `Scanner` object. The next time you call `next`, you get a different token. Thus, it is a mutator as well.

Could the two be separated? Of course—by using two methods:

- `String getCurrent()` // Gets the current token
- `void next()` // Advances to next token

This approach has one advantage: Suppose that you wanted to look at the current token twice. With the original interface, you have to store the return value of `next` because it's gone for good once you call the method. With the redesigned interface, the tokenizer remembers the current token and you can retrieve it as often as you like.

Why didn't the designers of the standard library think of this approach? Maybe they wanted to avoid a method call? Maybe they never explored the various alternatives and simply implemented the first solution that came to mind? Maybe they didn't know that it is a good idea to keep accessors and mutators separate? We don't know, but the standard library is not perfect, and you should not follow its designs blindly.

Let's look at the `MessageQueue` class of Chapter 2. There is a `remove` method that removes and returns the first message in the queue. Of course, removing the message changes the state of the queue. Isn't that a violation of the "mutators should return `void`" rule?

We need to refine that rule a bit. Indeed, it would not be good if the *only* way of getting the object at the front of the queue was to remove it. What if you just wanted to look at the head without removing it? Once you remove it, you can't put it back to the front. A queue only lets you insert to the back. Therefore, a queue interface should offer a method peek that returns the front object without removing it. Then you could declare the remove method to return void. That way, a user of the queue class can always call peek and then remove.

Then again, it seems cruel to force the class user to make an added method call. It is a convenience for the user if the remove method returns the removed object. A user who just wants to remove without looking at the object can just ignore the return value. Thus, a mutator can return a value for the user's convenience. But there also should be an accessor that gets the same value, so that the class user isn't forced to mutate the object. In the example of the Scanner class, there is nothing wrong with the next method—the real problem is that there isn't a getCurrent method.

TIP   Whenever possible, keep accessors and mutators separate. Ideally, mutators return void. It is OK to return a value for the user's convenience, provided that there is an accessor that returns the same value without mutating the object.

3.4.4 — Side Effects

A *side effect* of a method is any data modification that is observable when the method is called. If a method has no side effects, you can call it as often as you like, and you always get the same answer (provided, of course, that no other methods with a side effect have been called in the meantime). This is clearly a desirable property.

Some programming languages (called *functional* programming languages) can improve the efficiency of code that avoids side effects altogether. In an object-oriented programming language, however, it is accepted that mutator methods have a side effect, namely the mutation of the implicit parameter.

A method can modify other objects besides the implicit parameter, namely

- Explicit parameters
- Accessible static fields

Generally, users of your class expect that its methods do not modify the explicit parameters that they supply. For example, consider this example from the standard library. You can add all elements from one array list to another with the call

```
a.addAll(b);
```

After this call, all elements from the array list b have been added to a. Thus, the implicit parameter of the call has been modified. That is to be expected—the addAll method is a mutator. However, if the call changed the contents of b, for example by removing elements, then an undesirable side effect would occur. Fortunately, the addAll method does not modify the object b, which is the behavior that most programmers expect.

The standard library does not have many methods that mutate an explicit parameter. Here is one of the few examples. The `SimpleDateFormat` class has a method `parse` to parse a string describing a date into a `Date` object:

```
SimpleDateFormat formatter = new SimpleDateFormat("yyyy-MM-dd");
String dateString = "2001-02-03";
Date d = formatter.parse(dateString);
```

There is a second version of `parse` that analyzes a string containing a date description together with other characters. That method has an additional parameter of type `Field-Position` that describes a position in the field. The call

```
Date d = formatter.parse(dateString, position);
```

parses the date that starts at the given position, and then moves the position object to the index immediately following the date substring. There is a side effect: The explicit parameter is modified.

Is this side effect necessary? Not really. The `formatter` object could remember the field position. That design would eliminate the side effect. Of course, then a particular `SimpleDateFormat` object would only be able to parse one string at a time.

Another kind of side effect is changing the state of an accessible static field, such as `System.out`. This too is a side effect that you should avoid if possible. In particular, printing error messages to `System.out` is reprehensible:

```
public void addMessage()
{
   if (newMessages.isFull())
      System.out.println("Sorry--no space"); // DON'T DO THAT!
   . . .
}
```

Instead, throw an exception to report an error condition. Exceptions give a great deal of flexibility to the programmers that use your classes.

 TIP   Minimize side effects that go beyond mutating the implicit parameter.

3.4.5 — The Law of Demeter

In the voice mail system example of Chapter 2, we had one method that purposefully returned an object so that other methods could mutate it. The `findMailbox` method of the `MailSystem` class returned a `Mailbox` object, and the `Connection` object changed its contents by adding and removing messages. That too breaks the encapsulation of the `MailSystem` class. Perhaps a future version of the program no longer uses `Mailbox` classes to hold the messages, but instead holds the messages in one large queue or a database. Now the `MailSystem` class might have to manufacture `Mailbox` objects for backwards compatibility!

Some researchers believe that this object promiscuity is a sign of poor organization that is likely to lead to maintenance headaches. Karl Lieberherr has formulated the *Law of Demeter* that states that a method should only use

- Instance fields of its class

- Parameters

- Objects that it constructs with new

> A method that follows the Law of Demeter does not operate on global objects or objects that are a part of another object.

In particular, a method should not ask another object to give it a part of its internal state to work on.

The law was named after the Greek goddess Demeter, the goddess of agriculture and the sister of Zeus. The researchers first chose the name Demeter because they were working on another project called Zeus and they needed a related name. Also, they were promoting the concept of growing software—hence the agricultural theme.

Like so many laws, the Law of Demeter tells you what not to do, but it doesn't tell you what to do instead. For example, how can the Connection class avoid working on the Mailbox object that the MailSystem finds for it? We can give the mail system more responsibilities, such as "add this message to the mailbox with that number", "return the current message of the mailbox with that number", and so on. Then the MailSystem class needs to delegate those method calls to the mailbox that it manages.

All that delegation can get tedious to implement. The Demeter researchers claim that this tedium is not so much a problem with the law but a limitation of the programming language. You can find tools on the Demeter Web site that translate an expression of the programmer's intent at a higher level into the Java methods that carry out the intent.

You should not take the Law of Demeter as a natural or mathematical law. Simply consider it, together with other and possibly conflicting design guidelines, when you design your programs.

INTERNET   The site http://www.ccs.neu.edu/research/demeter/ covers the Law of Demeter and the tools that support it. You can find an electronic version of the overview article by Karl J. Lieberherr and Ian Holland, "Assuring Good Style for Object-Oriented Programs," *IEEE Software*, September 1989, pages 38–48, at ftp://ftp.ccs.neu.edu/pub/research/demeter/documents/papers/LH89-law-of-demeter.ps.

TIP   The Law of Demeter implies that a class should not return a reference to an object that is a part of its internal implementation. Rather than letting some other code interact with the subobject, the class should take on the responsibility for that work. If you follow the Law of Demeter, you can reorganize the internal structure of your classes extensively without having to modify the public interface.

3.5   Analyzing the Quality of an Interface

The design and implementation of classes must be approached from two points of view simultaneously. Programmers design and implement classes to be used in code by other programmers who are often referred to as class users. Class users are different from the end users of the final software application who, of course, wish to know nothing about the application code. The customer of the class designer is another programmer, the class user. As in any relationship between service providers and customers, the service provider must consider the needs of the customer.

The class designer has certain objectives, such as efficient algorithms and convenient coding. Programmers who use the classes in their code have different priorities. They want to be able to understand and use the operations without having to comprehend the internal data representations. They want a set of operations that is large enough to solve their programming tasks yet small enough to be comprehensible.

Beginning programmers in an object-oriented language often find it difficult to separate these two aspects because, in their first programming projects, they are both the class designer and the class user. Getting together with a colleague for a project is very helpful. Each programmer designs a set of classes, then you switch roles and complete the assignment with the other programmer's classes. Of course, no substantial changes to the classes should be made after the switch. This will give you a feel for the difficulty of anticipating the needs of another programmer *and* of working with classes that were produced with less-than-perfect anticipation of these needs. In a project where group work is not possible, you must play Dr. Jekyll and Mr. Hyde and envision both roles yourself.

In this section, we discuss several criteria used to analyze the quality of the interface of a class.

3.5.1 — Cohesion

A class is cohesive if all of its methods are related to a single abstraction.

A class is an abstraction of a single concept. All class operations must logically fit together to support a single, coherent purpose.

Consider this mailbox class:

```
public class Mailbox
{
    public void addMessage(Message aMessage) { . . . }
    public Message getCurrentMessage() { . . . }
    public Message removeCurrentMessage() { . . . }
    public void processCommand(String command) { . . . }
    . . .
}
```

The processCommand operation sticks out as being different from all other operations. The other operations deal with a single abstraction: a mailbox that holds messages. The processCommand operation adds another wrinkle to it, the ability to process commands. How? In what format? It would be better to have a different class deal with commands and leave the mailbox to do what it does best: store messages.

TIP   The public interface of a class should be cohesive: The class features should be related to a single abstraction. If a class has unrelated responsibilities, split it up into two classes.

3.5.2 — Completeness

A class interface should be complete. It should support all operations that are a part of the abstraction that the class represents.

Consider the `Date` class in the Java library. Suppose you have two `Date` objects and would like to know how many milliseconds have elapsed between them.

```
Date start = new Date();
// Do some work
Date stop = new Date();
// How many milliseconds between start and stop?
```

The `before` and `after` methods indicate that `start` came before `stop`. But they won't tell you how big the difference between them was. The designer of the `Date` class may argue that this responsibility falls outside the scope of the `Date` class. But that is not a credible argument. The `Date` class is willing to map any `Date` object to an absolute number of milliseconds. Why is measuring the distance between two points so unrelated to the mission of the `Date` class, when checking their ordering is something it is willing to undertake?

Of course, this is not a fatal flaw. You can use the `getTime` method and compute

```
long difference = stop.getTime() - start.getTime();
```

Generally, the classes that you find in the standard library are complete enough that you can achieve what you need to, even if it sometimes requires heroic effort. (Consider, for example, the task of computing the number of days between two `GregorianCalendar` objects.)

But when you are working on a project in which new classes are designed, it is common that you come across a class that is simply missing an essential method. Then you must negotiate with the class designer to have that method added.

3.5.3 — Convenience

An interface may be complete in the sense that it supplies sufficient tools to achieve any necessary task. However, programmers should not have to jump through hoops to solve conceptually simple tasks. A good interface shouldn't merely make all tasks possible, it should also make common tasks easy.

Consider the common task of reading input from `System.in`. Unfortunately, `System.in` has no methods for reading lines of text or numbers. Before Java 5.0, you had to wrap `System.in` into an `InputStreamReader` and then into a `BufferedReader`, which was very inconvenient indeed. This problem was finally fixed with the `Scanner` class.

Why did it take the library designers such a long time to remove the inconvenience? I suspect they had a wrong view of their customers. The layered stream and reader classes are very convenient for other *library programmers* who need to program other kinds of streams. But nobody paid attention to the convenience of the *application programmers*.

When a class designer has the wrong customer in mind, the result is all too often a set of classes that makes all tasks possible and common tasks difficult.

TIP   Your interfaces should provide convenient ways to accomplish common tasks.

3.5.4 — Clarity

The interface of a class should be clear to programmers, without generating confusion. Confused programmers write buggy code.

Lack of clarity can come from unnecessarily complex call protocols. Consider list iterators in the standard Java library. Here we construct a linked list and add some elements.

```
LinkedList<String> list = new LinkedList<String>();
list.add("A");
list.add("B");
list.add("C");
```

To iterate through the elements in the linked list, you use a list iterator:

```
ListIterator<String> iterator = list.listIterator();
while (iterator.hasNext())
    System.out.println(iterator.next());
```

As you can see, the iterator is similar to the string tokenizer.

An iterator position indicates a position *between* two list elements, just like the "I-beam" cursor in your word processor that sits between two characters. The add method of the ListIterator class adds an element before the cursor, just like your word processor does. For example, here is how to insert an element before the second element of a list:

```
ListIterator<String> iterator = list.listIterator(); // |ABC
iterator.next(); // A|BC
iterator.add("X"); // AX|BC
```

But the remove method is *not* intuitive. The word processor analogy would suggest that remove removes the element to the left of the cursor. For example, you'd expect that two calls to remove delete the first two elements of the list.

```
// This isn't how it works
iterator.remove(); // A|BC
iterator.remove(); // |BC
```

Instead, both calls are illegal. The API documentation describes the remove method this way:

"Removes from the list the last element that was returned by next or previous. This call can only be made once per call to next or previous. It can be made only if add has not been called after the last call to next or previous."

In other words, to remove these two elements, you have to first jump over them and then remove them immediately afterwards. If your word processor worked like that, you'd be pretty unhappy.

Whenever the explanation of a method is complex, you should pause and think whether the complexity is necessary; in this case, it plainly isn't. It would be straightforward to implement a `remove` operation that removes the element to the left of the iterator (like the BACKSPACE key).

3.5.5 — Consistency

The operations in a class should be consistent with each other with respect to names, parameters and return values, and behavior.

The Java library has its share of minor inconsistencies. To specify a day in the `Gregorian-Calendar` class, you call

```
new GregorianCalendar(year, month - 1, day)
```

because the constructor expects a month between 0 and 11. But the day is between 1 and 31. That's not consistent. (The reason is presumably compatibility with a C library that has the same convention.)

To check if two strings are equal, you call

```
s.equals(t);
```

or

```
s.equalsIgnoreCase(t);
```

That's simple enough, and there is a pair of methods `compareTo/compareToIgnoreCase` that follows the same scheme. But then there is an inconsistent pair

```
boolean regionMatches(int toffset, String other, int ooffset, int len)
boolean regionMatches(boolean ignoreCase, int toffset, String other,
    int ooffset, int len)
```

Why not `regionMatchesIgnoreCase`? Or, if it is such a good idea to have a parameter for ignoring case, why not use that scheme for `equals` and `compareTo`? This seems like a minor matter, but it can be extremely irritating to class users. If nothing else, it is a sign of shoddy craftsmanship. Your class users are like any other customers—they will enjoy using your classes if they perceive quality and attention to detail, and they will use them reluctantly otherwise.

 TIP   In this section, we recommend that you strive for cohesion, completeness, convenience, clarity, and consistency. You will often find that these requirements conflict with each other. As with any engineering task, you need to use your judgment to balance these conflicts.

3.6   Programming by Contract

As you have seen, encapsulation makes it possible to produce dramatically more reliable code than the traditional programming style in which every function was able to modify data fields. Once we ensure that all constructors of a class create only objects with valid state and that all mutator operations preserve the valid state, then we can never have invalid objects. No operation should waste a lot of time checking for invalid objects. Bertrand Meyer, the pioneering designer of the Eiffel language, uses the metaphor of a *contract* to describe these guarantees. This chapter explores the ideas surrounding the concepts of programming by contract.

3.6.1 — Preconditions

Consider the MessageQueue class of Chapter 2.

```
public class MessageQueue
{
    public void add(Message aMessage) { . . . }
    public Message remove() { . . . }
    public Message peek() { . . . }
    public int size() { . . . }
    . . .
}
```

What should happen if a programmer using this class attempts to remove a message from an empty queue?

There are two ways to answer this question. The designer of the queue class may declare this behavior as an error. Users of the queue are plainly forbidden to invoke remove on an empty queue. Or, the designer of the queue class may decide to tolerate potential abuses and build in a robust failure mechanism, such as returning a null reference.

In the terminology of "Programming by Contract" that is advocated by Bertrand Meyer and other computer scientists, methods are viewed as agents fulfilling a contract. The remove method promises to deliver the correct result when applied to a nonempty queue. For an empty queue, you must read the fine print. Maybe remove is free to take any action, however disastrous, when applied to an empty queue. Maybe it promises to handle the error gracefully.

Consider the contract you have with your bank. When you write a check that is not covered by the funds in your checking account, what happens? Your bank may, as a courtesy, pay the check if you have been a reliable customer in the past. But if the bank refuses to pay the check, then you have no reason to complain. Some banks offer—for an extra fee, of course—an overdraft protection plan where they cover checks for you. Should you pay that extra fee for an overdraft protection plan? Or would you rather save the money and take the risk? It's a tradeoff.

The same tradeoff holds for programs. Would you rather use classes that check for all possible abuses (even though you never intend to abuse them) if the cost is a significant reduction in performance?

> A precondition of a method is a condition that must be fulfilled before the method may be called.

The important point is that the class that provides a service and its caller should have a formal agreement on these issues. The terminology of pre- and postconditions serves to formalize the contract between a method and its caller. A *precondition* is a condition that must be true before the service provider promises to do its part of the bargain. If the precondition is not true and the service is still requested, the provider can choose any action that is convenient for it, no matter how disastrous the outcome may be for the service requester. A *postcondition* is a condition that the service provider guarantees upon completion. We will discuss postconditions in the next section.

Thus, we can define a precondition for the `remove` method:

```
/**
    Remove message at head.
    @return  the message that has been removed from the queue
    @precondition size() > 0
*/
public Message remove()
{
    return elements.remove(0);
}
```

NOTE   Here we use `@precondition` as if it were a valid `javadoc` tag. Actually, the standard `javadoc` program skips all tags that it doesn't know, so the `@precondition` information won't make it into the documentation. To include preconditions, run `javadoc` with the option `-tag precondition:cm:"Precondition:"`. (The letters `cm` instruct `javadoc` to look for this tag only in constructors and methods.)

This `remove` method makes *no promises* to do anything sensible when you call it on an empty queue. In fact, this particular implementation causes an `IndexOutOfBoundsException` in that situation that might terminate the program. However, a different implementation is free to act differently. Consider a change in implementation.

The `remove` method of the `MessageQueue` class of Chapter 2 is quite inefficient. If you remove a message, all other references are moved down in the array (see Figure 4).

You can avoid this problem with a "circular array" implementation of a queue. In this implementation, we use two index variables head and `tail` that contain the index of the

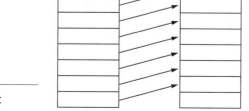

Figure 4

Inefficient Removal of an Element

Figure 5

Adding and Removing Queue Elements
in a Circular Array

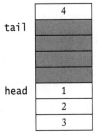

Figure 6

A Queue Element Set That Wraps
around the End of the Array

next element to be removed and the next element to be added. After an element is removed or added, the index is incremented (see Figure 5).

After a while, the `tail` element will reach the top of the array. Then it "wraps around" and starts again at 0—see Figure 6. For that reason, the array is called "circular".

Here is an implementation of a queue as a circular array. This implementation supplies a *bounded* queue—it can eventually fill up. It is not difficult to enhance the implementation to remove that limitation, by allocating a larger array when the original array fills up (see Exercise 3.25).

Ch3/queue/MessageQueue.java

```
1  /**
2     A first-in, first-out bounded collection of messages.
3  */
4  public class MessageQueue
5  {
6     /**
7        Constructs an empty message queue.
8        @param capacity the maximum capacity of the queue
9     */
10    public MessageQueue(int capacity)
11    {
12       elements = new Message[capacity];
13       count = 0;
14       head = 0;
15       tail = 0;
```

```
16       }
17
18       /**
19          Removes message at head.
20          @return the message that has been removed from the queue
21          @precondition size() > 0
22       */
23       public Message remove()
24       {
25          Message r = elements[head];
26          head = (head + 1) % elements.length;
27          count--;
28          return r;
29       }
30
31       /**
32          Appends a message at tail.
33          @param aMessage the message to be appended
34       */
35       public void add(Message aMessage)
36       {
37          elements[tail] = aMessage;
38          tail = (tail + 1) % elements.length;
39          count++;
40       }
41
42       /**
43          Gets the total number of messages in the queue.
44          @return the total number of messages in the queue
45       */
46       public int size()
47       {
48          return count;
49       }
50
51       /**
52          Gets message at head.
53          @return the message that is at the head of the queue
54          @precondition size() > 0
55       */
56       public Message peek()
57       {
58          return elements[head];
59       }
60
61       private Message[] elements;
62       private int head;
63       private int tail;
64       private int count;
65    }
```

Now, if you call remove on an empty queue, you may get some element that still happens to be in the elements array from a prior assignment; also, you might mess up the state of the head index and set count to −1. All these effects may cause strange and seemingly random behavior during debugging. Thus, here the cost of violating the precondition is high.

One important aspect of preconditions is that they need to be checkable by the caller. Consider again the circular array implementation of the `MessageQueue` class. A precondition of the `add` method is that the array is not full:

```
/**
    Appends a message at the tail.
    @param aMessage the message to be appended
    @precondition size() < elements.length;
*/
public void add(Message aMessage) { . . . }
```

But the caller cannot check this precondition because the `elements` field is private. There is no way for the caller to find out the capacity of the queue. To remedy that situation, add a method `isFull` that tests whether the queue is already full. Then the precondition can be reworded as

```
@precondition !isFull()
```

 TIP   The class user must be able to check the precondition of a method. Preconditions of public methods must only involve public methods of the class.

3.6.2 — Assertions

When you implement a method with a precondition, what action should you take if the method is called with one of its preconditions violated? The easiest choice is to do nothing at all. That is certainly a permissible strategy, but it can result in difficult debugging sessions.

Alternatively, you may want to alert the user of your class whenever you detect a precondition violation. The Java language has a special feature for alerts of this kind: the assertion mechanism.

The statement

```
assert condition;
```

checks that the condition is true. If so, then execution simply continues. However, if the condition fails, then an `AssertionError` is thrown. Normally, the program terminates as a result.

There is a second form of the `assert` statement, in which an explanation is supplied to the `AssertionError` object:

```
assert condition : explanation;
```

An assertion is a condition that a programmer expects to be true.

The explanation is usually a string. If it is an expression of another type, it is converted to a string.

Here is a typical example of an assertion.

```
/**
    Removes message at head.
    @return the message that has been removed from the queue
    @precondition size() > 0
*/
public Message remove()
{
    assert count > 0 : "violated precondition size() > 0";
    Message r = elements[head];
    head = (head + 1) % elements.length;
    count--;
    return r;
}
```

If a user invokes this method on an empty queue, then the program terminates with an assertion error. In most execution environments, an error message is displayed that contains the file and line number of the failed assertion statement, as well as the explanation string.

It appears as if assertions negate an advantage of preconditions—to free the implementation from the computational cost of checking for violations. However, assertions can be turned off completely after testing is completed.

The mechanism for enabling or disabling assertions depends on your execution environment. With the virtual machine launcher in the JDK, you use the `-enableassertions` (or `-ea`) switch to turn assertions on. For example:

```
java -enableassertions MailSystemTest
```

By default, assertions are disabled.

Some computer scientists think that assertions shouldn't be turned off after debugging is completed. After all, would you wear a life vest only while sailing close to the shore and throw it overboard when you reach the middle of the ocean? Unfortunately, it's not that simple. If assertion checking slows down the program too much, then you need to turn off some or all of the checks. Assertions let you make that choice, which is better than not having the choice at all.

Would it be "nicer" to drop preconditions and instead return "harmless" values? For example,

```
/**
    Removes message at head.
    @return the message that has been removed from the queue
*/
public Message remove()
{
    if (count == 0) return null;
    . . .
}
```

Actually, this is not a benefit for the caller. The `null` return value may also cause problems later when the cause of the error is less clear. The "tough love" approach of terminating the program with an assertion error makes it possible to locate the error precisely.

TIP In some programming languages (in particular C and C++), assertions are implemented in the *compiler.* To activate or deactivate assertions, you need to recompile the source files that contain the assertion statements. However, in Java, assertions are handled by the Java class loader. When a class is loaded and assertions are disabled, the class loader simply strips out the virtual machine instructions for assertion checking.

As a consequence, you can selectively enable and disable assertions in different classes and packages. See `http://java.sun.com/j2se/1.4/docs/guide/lang/assert.html` for more information.

3.6.3 — Exceptions in the Contract

A common strategy for dealing with problem cases is throwing an exception. Here is an example:

```
public Message remove()
{
    if (count <= 0)
        throw new NoSuchElementException(
                "violated precondition size() > 0");
    . . .
}
```

Unlike an assertion test, this check cannot be turned off and therefore always incurs a small performance penalty.

That does not mean that you should stay away from exceptions. In fact, exceptions are often *a part of the contract.* Consider this constructor.

```
/**
    Creates a new FileReader, given the name of the file to read from.
    @param fileName the name of the file to read from
    @throws FileNotFoundException if the named file does not exist, is
    a directory rather than a regular file, or for some other reason
    cannot be opened for reading
*/
public FileReader(String fileName)
```

As you can see, the constructor promises to throw a `FileNotFoundException` if there is no file with the given name.

There is an important distinction between a precondition and a contractually specified exception. This constructor has *no precondition.* In particular, "fileName must be the name of a valid file" is *not* a precondition. Recall that a method may do anything at all if the precondition is violated. But this particular constructor makes a very definite promise, namely to throw a `FileNotFoundException`, when there is no file with the given name. Programmers calling this constructor are entitled to rely on this behavior.

You may wonder why the implementors of this constructor didn't simply set a precondition. Couldn't a caller of this constructor have checked that the file exists? Not really, because another program could have removed the file immediately after that check and before the constructor call. Thus, existence of the file is not a *verifiable* precondition. In such a situation, throwing an exception is entirely appropriate.

3.6.4 — Postconditions

> A postcondition of a method is a condition that holds after the method has completed.

Of course, every operation promises to do "the right thing", provided that the precondition was fulfilled when it was called. For example, the remove operation of the MessageQueue class promises to return the element that has been in the queue for the longest time. Such a promise is called a *postcondition*.

In general, a postcondition is any condition that a method promises to fulfill after it is called. For example, the add method of the MessageQueue class has a useful postcondition that after adding an element, size() > 0. This condition is useful because it *implies the precondition* of the remove method. After you add an element, it is always safe to call remove.

```
q.add(m);
// Postcondition of add: q.size() > 0
// Precondition of remove: q.size() > 0
m = q.remove();
```

TIP It is useful to document postconditions that go beyond the description of the method purpose and @return tag, such as

```
@postcondition size() > 0
```

But don't repeat the @return comment in a @postcondition comment—that adds no value.

If a postcondition is not fulfilled, you should *not* throw an exception. After all, that is a failure in your own code. But you can use assertions to check for postconditions.

3.6.5 — Class Invariants

> A class invariant is a condition that is fulfilled by all objects of the class after the completion of any constructor or method.

A *class invariant* is a logical condition that holds for all objects of a class, except possibly those that are undergoing mutation. In other words, the condition must be true before and after every method call, but it can be temporarily violated inside a method call.

Here is a class invariant of the circular array implementation of the MessageQueue class.

$$0 \leq head \text{ and } head < elements.length$$

To prove an invariant you need to check that

1. It is true after every constructor has completed execution.
2. It is preserved by every mutator.

That means, if it is true at the start of the mutator, then it is again true when the mutator returns. We don't worry about accessor operations because they don't change the object state.

The first point above guarantees that no invalid objects can be created. Thus, the first time a mutator is applied, we know the invariant is true at the outset. The second point guarantees that it is again true when the first mutator operation completes. By the same logic, the second mutator operation must preserve the invariant condition, as must all subsequent operations. As a consequence we know that the invariant must be true upon entry and exit of all operations.

After the `MessageQueue` constructor has been executed, the invariant is true because `head` has been set to zero. But wait—how do we know that `elements.length` is positive? Let's give the constructor a precondition:

```
/**
    Constructs an empty queue.
    @param capacity the maximum size of the queue
    @precondition capacity > 0
*/
public MessageQueue(int capacity) { . . . }
```

Now we know that `elements.length` must be positive. Therefore, the invariant is true at the end of the constructor.

There is only one method that changes the value of `head`, namely `remove`. We need to show that it preserves the invariant. The method carries out the assignment

$head_{new}$ = ($head_{old}$ + 1) % elements.length.

Here $head_{old}$ denotes the value of the `head` instance field before the method was called, and $head_{new}$ denotes the value after the method returns. Now since we assume that $head_{old}$ fulfilled the invariant at the beginning of the method, we know that

$head_{old}$ + 1 > 0.

Hence

$head_{new}$ = ($head_{old}$ + 1) % elements.length $\geq$ 0

And, by the definition of the % operator, it is less than `elements.length`. That proves the invariant. But what good is it?

We can now reason that every array access of the form `elements[head]` is legal. You can similarly prove that

0 $\leq$ tail and tail < elements.length

is an invariant. That invariant guarantees that array accesses of the form `elements[tail]` are always legal. In other words, we have just *proven* that there will never be an array exception raised in the `MessageQueue` class.

NOTE The % operator computes the remainder that is left when dividing an integer by another. For example, 17 % 5 is 2 since $17 = 5 \cdot 3 + 2$. Unfortunately, many programming languages (including Java) have a quirk in the behavior of the % operator. Instead of computing a proper remainder, which would always be 0 or a positive number, the result of % can be negative when one or both of the arguments are negative. For example, -17 % 5 is -2 , even though the mathematical remainder is 3 since $-17 = 5 \cdot (-4) + 3$. For that reason, we had to be careful to verify that the argument `head + 1` of the % operator was not negative. In general, negative remainders are a common cause for programming errors. It is unfortunate that programming language designers ignored the experience of mathematicians who had hundreds of years to figure out the best definition for remainders.

Of course, the invariant that we have just proven is quite simple, but it is very typical. As long as the instance fields of a class are private, you have complete control over all operations that modify the instance fields. You can usually guarantee that certain values are within a legal range or that certain references are never null. Invariants are the appropriate tool for documenting such guarantees.

We distinguish between interface invariants and implementation invariants. *Interface invariants* are conditions that involve only the public interface of a class. *Implementation invariants* involve the details of a particular implementation. Interface invariants are of interest to the class user because they give a behavior guarantee for any object of the class. Implementation invariants can be used by the class implementor to ensure the correctness of the implementation algorithms.

The invariants that we discussed in the queue examples were implementation invariants. The values of `head` and `elements` are meaningless for the class user.

Interface invariants must be stated in terms of the public interface of a class. For example, an interface invariant of the Day class is that

```
1 <= getMonth() && getMonth() <= 12
```

 INTERNET   Invariants are useful for bringing out those properties of your classes that ensure freedom from bad casts, null pointers, or array bounds errors. Using theorem-proving technology, it is even possible to automate some of these checks. Check out Compaq Extended Static Checker for Java (ESC/Java) from `http://research.compaq.com/SRC/esc/` to see this technology in action.

3.7 Unit Testing

> A unit test of a class tests the class in isolation.

In this chapter, you have seen design rules that apply to a single class. We will conclude the chapter with a look at *unit testing:* testing a single class by itself, outside a complete program.

When implementing a class, it is a good idea to think about test cases that demonstrate that the class works correctly. For example, when writing the specification of a class, or when formulating postconditions or invariants, you can also think about test cases that demonstrate the correct working of the class.

Having a collection of test cases is particularly valuable when changing the implementation. Running the test cases again after the change gives you confidence that you have not broken the functionality of the class.

Experience has shown that programmers are much less reluctant to improve the implementation when they have a collection of test cases that they can use to validate their changes.

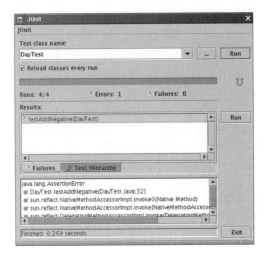

Figure 7

Unit Testing with JUnit

One popular tool for unit testing is JUnit. JUnit makes it very simple to collect and run test cases. Figure 7 shows the graphical user interface of JUnit.

To test a class with JUnit, you need to design a companion class that contains the test cases. Each test case needs to be placed in a method whose name starts with `test`. Follow this template:

```
import junit.framework.*;
public class DayTest extends TestCase
{
    public void testAdd() { . . . }
    public void testDaysBetween() { . . . }
    . . .
}
```

Each test case executes some code and then checks a condition. Here is a typical test case for testing the addDays method of the Day class:

```
public void testAdd()
{
    Day d1 = new Day(1970, 1, 1);
    int n = 1000;
    Day d2 = d1.addDays(n);
    assertTrue(d2.daysFrom(d1) == n);
}
```

If the test fails, then the testing framework catches the assertion error and records the failure.

When compiling the test class, you need to add the `junit.jar` file to the class path:

```
javac -classpath .:junit.jar DayTest.java
```

To run all tests in the graphical test runner, execute

```
java -classpath .:junit.jar junit.swingui.TestRunner DayTest
```

If all tests pass, the user interface shows a green bar, and you can relax. Otherwise, there is a red bar and a detailed set of error messages. That's great too. It is much easier for you to fix the class in isolation than it would be to track down the error when the class is part of a complex program.

 INTERNET You can download the JUnit tool from `http://junit.org`. The documentation describes a number of advanced options for fine-tuning the testing process.

EXERCISES

Exercise 3.1. Find two total orderings for `String` objects. Find a partial ordering that is not a total ordering.

Exercise 3.2. Find a total ordering for `Rectangle` objects. *Hint:* Use lexicographic ordering on (*x, y, width, height*).

Exercise 3.3. Search the Internet for a description of the French Revolutionary calendar. How do you convert your birthday to that calendar?

Exercise 3.4. Implement a class `FrenchRevolutionaryCalendar` that extends the `Calendar` class.

Exercise 3.5. Have a look at the `Calendar` and `GregorianCalendar` classes in the standard library. The `Calendar` class is supposed to be a general class that works for arbitrary calendars, not just the Gregorian calendar. Why does the public interface fall short of that ideal?

Exercise 3.6. Write a program that computes the number of days that have elapsed since you were born. Use the `GregorianCalendar` class, not the `Day` class of this chapter.

Exercise 3.7. Write a program that computes the number of days that have elapsed since you were born. Use the `Day` class of this chapter, not the `GregorianCalendar` class.

Exercise 3.8. Write a program that prints the calendar of a given month. For example,

```
June 2006
 S  M  T  W  T  F  S
             1  2  3
 4  5  6  7  8  9 10
11 12 13 14 15 16 17
18 19 20 21 22 23 24
25 26 27 28 29 30 31
```

Use the `getFirstDayOfWeek` method of the `Calendar` class to find the first day of the week—it's Monday in most of the world (so that Saturday and Sunday fall on the week's end). The `DateFormatSymbols` class yields the names of the months and the weekdays.

Exercise 3.9. Add `before` and `after` methods that define a total ordering on `Day` objects to the first implementation of the `Day` class.

Exercise 3.10. Implement a class `TimeOfDay` that stores a time between 00:00:00 and 23:59:59. Supply a constructor `TimeOfDay(int hours, int minutes, int seconds)` and accessor methods to get the current hours, minutes, and seconds. Supply methods

```
TimeOfDay addSeconds(int seconds)
int secondsFrom(TimeOfDay other)
```

The first method returns a `TimeOfDay` object that is the given number of seconds away from the current object. The second method computes the number of seconds between two `TimeOfDay` objects. Use three integers for the hours, minutes, and seconds as the internal representation.

Exercise 3.11. Reimplement the `TimeOfDay` class of Exercise 3.10 by using a different internal representation: the number of seconds since midnight.

Exercise 3.12. Implement a class `Matrix` that represents a matrix of the form

$$
\begin{bmatrix}
a_{00} & a_{01} & \cdots & a_{0,\,c-1} \\
a_{10} & a_{11} & \cdots & a_{1,\,c-1} \\
\vdots & \vdots & \ddots & \vdots \\
a_{r-1,\,0} & a_{r-1,\,1} & \cdots & a_{r-1,\,c-1}
\end{bmatrix}
$$

Here r and c are the number of rows and columns of the matrix. Your class should support the following operations:

- Constructs a matrix with a given number of rows and columns.

- Gets and sets the element at a particular row and column position.

- Adds and multiplies two compatible matrices. (You may need to look up the definition for matrix addition and multiplication in a linear algebra book or on the Web.)

As the internal representation, store the elements in a two-dimensional array

```
private double[][] elements;
```

In the constructor, initialize the array as

```
elements = new double[r][c];
```

Then you can access the element at row i and column j as `elements[i][j]`.

Exercise 3.13. In many applications, matrices are *sparse*. They have mostly values of zero off the diagonal, values of one on the diagonal, and a few other values:

$$
\begin{bmatrix}
1 & 0 & a & 0 \\
0 & 1 & 0 & 0 \\
0 & 0 & b & 1 \\
c & 0 & 0 & 1
\end{bmatrix}
$$

Such a matrix can be stored more efficiently by simply keeping track of the special values and their row and column positions. Reimplement the Matrix class of Exercise 3.12 using a representation that is optimized for sparse matrices.

Exercise 3.14. Reimplement the Matrix class of Exercises 3.12 and 3.13 so that you switch between a full and a sparse representation, depending on the number of elements in the matrix that are not zero off the diagonal or one on the diagonal.

Exercise 3.15. List all accessors and mutators of the Date class (but skip the deprecated methods).

Exercise 3.16. This chapter discusses the drawbacks of mutator methods for setting the year, month, and date of a Day object. However, the Calendar class of the standard library has a set method for just that purpose. Does that method solve the issues that were raised in our discussion?

Exercise 3.17. List three immutable classes from the standard Java library.

Exercise 3.18. The implementation of the SimpleDateFormat class in JDK 5.0 (and possibly other versions of the JDK) contains a subtle flaw that makes it possible to break the behavior of the class by applying a mutator to an object that one of the accessor methods returns. Find the flaw. *Hint:* Look at the mutable instance fields.

Exercise 3.19. Implement a variant of the standard StringTokenizer class with two methods

```
String nextToken() // Gets the current token and advances to the next token
String getToken() // Gets the current token and doesn't advance
```

Exercise 3.20. Reimplement the voice mail system of Chapter 2 so that the Law of Demeter holds. In particular, the MailSystem class should not give out Mailbox objects. Instead, you need to add additional methods to the MailSystem class.

Exercise 3.21. Critique the java.io.File class. Where is it inconsistent? Where does it lack clarity? Where is it not cohesive?

Exercise 3.22. The job of the NumberFormat class is to format numbers so that they can be presented to a human reader in a format such as an invoice or table. For example, to format a floating-point value with two digits of precision and trailing zeroes, you use the following code:

```
NumberFormat formatter = NumberFormat.getNumberInstance();
formatter.setMinimumFractionDigits(2);
formatter.setMaximumFractionDigits(2);
String formattedNumber = formatter.format(x);
```

Critique this class. Is it convenient? Is it clear? Is it complete? (*Hint:* How would you format a table of values so that the columns line up?)

Exercise 3.23. In many text-processing applications, it is useful to "peek" at the next character in a file without actually reading it. For example, if the next character is a digit, then one may want to call a method readNumber, without first consuming the initial digit. The standard library offers a PushbackReader for this purpose. Is that class a convenient solution to the "one character lookahead" problem?

Exercise 3.24. According to the API documentation, what are the preconditions of the following methods?

```
int java.util.BitSet.nextSetBit(int fromIndex)
String java.util.Properties.get(String key)
int java.util.Arrays.binarySearch(int[] a, int key)
```

How accurate is the API documentation when stating the prerequisites of the methods in this exercise? Can you find conditions under which the methods fail to work properly? *Hint:* Try null parameters.

Exercise 3.25. Improve the circular array implementation of the bounded queue by growing the elements array when the queue is full.

Exercise 3.26. Add assertions to check all preconditions of the methods of the bounded queue implementation.

Exercise 3.27. Show that (tail - head - count) % elements.length == 0 is an invariant of the bounded queue implementation.

Exercise 3.28. Design a test class to test the MessageQueue class with JUnit.

Interface Types and Polymorphism

A class defines a set of operations (the interface) *and* statements that specify how to carry out the operations and how to represent object state (the implementation). However, it is often useful to *separate* the interface concept from that of a class. This can help in the development of reusable code.

Multiple classes can *implement* the same interface type. That is, these classes all have the methods that the interface type requires, which makes it possible to write programs that can operate on a mixture of objects from any of these classes. This behavior is called *polymorphism*. By focusing on interface types first, you will study polymorphism in its purest and simplest form. Chapter 6 will cover inheritance, which gives rise to polymorphism in a more complex setting.

In this chapter, you will study several useful interface types in the Java library. At the end of the chapter, you will learn how to design a new interface type.

4.1 The Icon Interface Type

You can display a dialog box that contains a simple message with the following call:

```
JOptionPane.showMessageDialog(null, "Hello, World!");
```

Figure 1 shows the result. (The first parameter of the method is the parent window of the dialog box; a null parameter indicates that the dialog box should be placed at the center of the screen.)

Note the icon at the left side of the message dialog box. You can show a different icon by using a more complex version of the showMessageDialog method. In that method, you need to supply the window title, message type, and icon, in addition to the parent and the message. Here is an example:

```
JOptionPane.showMessageDialog(
        null, // parent window
        "Hello World!", // message
        "Message", // window title
        JOptionPane.INFORMATION_MESSAGE, // message type
        new ImageIcon("globe.gif"));
```

Figure 2 shows the result. Note that the image from the GIF file is displayed instead of the standard information icon.

However, suppose you want to draw shapes without first producing an image file, such as the outline of the planet Mars in Figure 3.

Figure 1

Displaying a Message

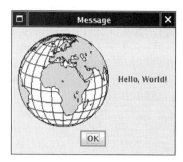

Figure 2

Displaying an Image Icon

Fortunately, you can use the same showMessageDialog call as in the preceding example. The showMessageDialog method is declared as

```
public static void showMessageDialog(
        Component parent,
        Object message,
        String title,
        int messageType,
        Icon anIcon)
```

> If a method has a parameter of an interface type, then you can supply an object of any class that implements the interface type.

Note that the last parameter is of type Icon. That means that you do not have to supply an ImageIcon object. You can supply an object of any class that implements the Icon *interface type*. The ImageIcon class is one such class, but we can write our own classes that also implement the Icon interface type.

> An interface type specifies a set of methods, but it does not implement them.

Here is the definition of the Icon interface type:

```
public interface Icon
{
    int getIconWidth();
    int getIconHeight();
    void paintIcon(Component c, Graphics g, int x, int y);
}
```

Figure 3

Drawing a Shape

> When a class implements an interface type, it defines implementations for the methods that the interface type specifies.

An interface type has *no implementation*. It merely specifies a set of methods. Note that the methods in the interface type are not declared as public—all methods of an interface type are automatically public. A class *implements* the interface type by providing an implements clause and supplying implementations for the methods that are declared in the interface type.

```
public class MyIcon implements Icon
{
   public int getIconWidth()
   {
      implementation
   }

   public int getIconHeight()
   {
      implementation
   }

   public void paintIcon(Component c, Graphics g, int x, int y)
   {
      implementation
   }
   . . .
}
```

An interface type cannot specify instance variables. Instance variables are implementation details that need to be supplied by implementing classes. The interface type only specifies *what* needs to be done, not how to do it.

NOTE The interface keyword of the Java language is used to define an interface type: a type with a set of methods but no implementation. However, the term "interface" is often used more loosely to describe the set of methods of a class. When reading about interfaces, you need to infer from the context whether the term refers to a data type or a set of methods.

Any class that implements the Icon interface type has two responsibilities:

- Give the size of the icon.
- Paint the icon.

You may wonder why the paintIcon method receives a parameter of type Component. That parameter is the user interface component containing the icon. You can query properties of the component such as the background color or font, which allows the painting code to produce a drawing that matches the component. The x and y parameters tell the location of the icon inside the component. Generally, it is safe to ignore these parameters.

Section 4.9 discusses the Graphics class in detail. However, it should be clear that by varying the painting instructions, you can paint different kinds of images. Because the paint instructions are executed as the program runs, you have a great deal of flexibility and can achieve effects that would not be possible by just displaying image files.

Let's design a class MarsIcon that implements the Icon interface type. The MarsIcon class must

- Declare that it implements the Icon interface type.

- Supply implementations for the methods of the Icon interface type.

Here is the complete code for the MarsIcon class. Its paintIcon method simply draws a red circle.

Ch4/icon2/MarsIcon.java

```
 1 import java.awt.*;
 2 import java.awt.geom.*;
 3 import javax.swing.*;
 4
 5 /**
 6    An icon that has the shape of the planet Mars.
 7 */
 8 public class MarsIcon implements Icon
 9 {
10    /**
11       Constructs a Mars icon of a given size.
12       @param aSize the size of the icon
13    */
14    public MarsIcon(int aSize)
15    {
16       size = aSize;
17    }
18
19    public int getIconWidth()
20    {
21       return size;
22    }
23
24    public int getIconHeight()
25    {
26       return size;
27    }
28
29    public void paintIcon(Component c, Graphics g, int x, int y)
30    {
31       Graphics2D g2 = (Graphics2D) g;
32       Ellipse2D.Double planet = new Ellipse2D.Double(x, y,
33          size, size);
34       g2.setColor(Color.RED);
35       g2.fill(planet);
36    }
37
38    private int size;
39 }
```

Figure 4 shows the Icon interface type and the classes that implement it.

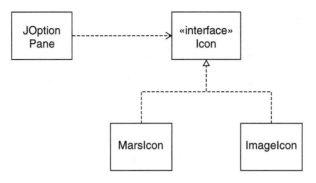

Figure 4

The Icon Interface Type and Implementing Classes

 TIP   When you implement a method that has been defined in an interface type, you need not supply a `javadoc` comment if the comment in the interface type is sufficient. The `javadoc` utility automatically inserts links to the documentation of the interface type. If the interface type belongs to the standard library, you should run the `javadoc` utility with the `-link` option and supply a URL for the standard library documentation. For example:

```
javadoc -link http://java.sun.com/j2se/1.5.0/docs/api *.java
```

This section ends with a couple of technical remarks about interface types.

An interface type cannot specify any implementation details. In particular, an interface type never specifies instance variables. It is, however, legal to supply variables in an interface type definition. These variables are automatically declared as `public static final` variables. For example, the interface type `ImageObserver` defines a number of constants:

```
public interface ImageObserver
{
    . . .
    int ABORT = 128; // a public static final constant
}
```

A class can implement as many interface types as it likes. For example, the `MarsIcon` class can choose to implement two interface types:

```
public class MarsIcon implements Icon, Shape { . . . }
```

Of course, then the class must supply definitions for the methods of all of its interface types.

An interface type can extend another by adding additional requirements. For example, you can define an interface type `MoveableIcon` that extends the `Icon` interface and also requires that the icon shape can be moved around:

```
public interface MoveableIcon extends Icon
{
    void translate(int x, int y);
}
```

A class that chooses to implement this interface type must supply the translate method and all methods of the Icon interface type.

4.2   Polymorphism

Recall that the showMessageDialog method is declared as

```
public static void showMessageDialog(. . ., Icon anIcon)
```

Now put yourself into the shoes of the programmer who implemented this method. That programmer must show a dialog box that contains

- The icon
- The message
- The "OK" button

The programmer needs to compute the size of the dialog box. The width of the dialog box is computed by adding the icon width, the message width, and some blank space to separate the components. How can the programmer compute the icon width? Fortunately, the Icon interface type provides a method for that purpose:

```
int iconWidth = anIcon.getIconWidth();
```

> If a class implements an interface type, its objects can be assigned to variables of the interface type.

Note that the implementor of the showMessageDialog class has *no idea* what kind of icon is passed as a parameter. Maybe it is an ImageIcon. Maybe it is a MarsIcon. (Since the MarsIcon was invented by the author of this textbook, the library implementor did not even know about this class!) Of course, it doesn't matter what object was used to initialize the parameter variable, as long as it belongs to a class that implements the Icon interface type.

> The type of an object is never an interface type. However, the type of a variable can be an interface type. Such a variable contains a reference to an object whose class implements the interface type.

Let's have a closer look at the anIcon parameter variable. It contains a reference to an object. What do we know about the class of that object? We know that the class is *not* Icon. The Icon type is an interface type, not a class type. There are *no* objects whose class is Icon.

In fact, we do not know the exact class, but we know one fact about it: It must implement the Icon interface type (see Figure 5). Thus, we are certain that the class has a getIconWidth method.

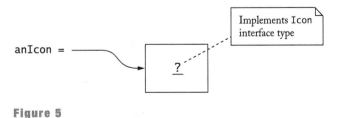

Figure 5

A Variable of Interface Type

When the call `anIcon.getIconWidth()` is executed, the Java interpreter first looks up the actual type of the object, then it locates the `getIconWidth` method of that type, and finally invokes that method. For example, suppose you pass a `MarsIcon` to the `showMessageDialog` method:

```
JOptionPane.showMessageDialog(. . ., new MarsIcon(50));
```

Then the `getIconWidth` method of the `MarsIcon` class is invoked. But if you supply an `ImageIcon`, then the `getIconWidth` method of the `ImageIcon` class is called. These two methods have nothing in common beyond their name and return type. The `MarsIcon` version simply returns the `size` instance field, whereas the `ImageIcon` version returns the width of the bitmap image.

> Polymorphism refers to the ability to select different methods according to the actual type of an object.

The ability to select the appropriate method for a particular object is called *polymorphism*. (The term "polymorphic" literally means "having multiple shapes".)

An important use of polymorphism is to promote *loose coupling*. Have another look at Figure 4. As you can see, the `JOptionPane` class uses the `Icon` interface, but it is decoupled from the `ImageIcon` class. Thus, the `JOptionPane` class need not know anything about image processing. It is only concerned with those aspects of images that are captured in the `Icon` interface type.

Another important use of polymorphism is *extensibility*. By using the `Icon` interface type, the designers of the `JOptionPane` class don't lock you into the use of bitmap icons. You can supply icons of your own design.

4.3 The `Comparable` Interface Type

> The `Collections.sort` method can sort objects of any class that implements the `Comparable` interface type.

For another useful example of code reuse, we turn to the `Collections` class in the Java library. This class has a static `sort` method that can sort an array list:

```
Collections.sort(list);
```

The objects in the array list can belong to any class that implements the `Comparable` interface type. That type has a single method:

```
public interface Comparable<T>
{
    int compareTo(T other);
}
```

This interface is a generic type, similar to the `ArrayList` class. We will discuss generic types in greater detail in Chapter 7, but you can use the `Comparable` type without knowing how to implement generic types. Simply remember to supply a type parameter, such as `Comparable<String>`. The type parameter specifies the parameter type of the `compareTo` method. For example, the `Comparable<Country>` interface defines a `compareTo(Country other)` method.

The call

```
object1.compareTo(object2)
```

is expected to return a negative number if `object1` should come before `object2`, zero if the objects are equal, and a positive number otherwise.

Why does the `sort` method require that the objects that it sorts implement the `Comparable` interface type? The reason is simple. Every sorting algorithm compares objects in various positions in the collection and rearranges them if they are out of order. The code for the `sort` method contains statements such as the following:

```
if (object1.compareTo(object2) > 0)
    rearrange object1 and object2;
```

For example, the `String` class implements the `Comparable<String>` interface type. Therefore, you can use the `Collections.sort` method to sort a list of strings:

```
ArrayList<String> countries = new ArrayList<String>();
countries.add("Uruguay");
countries.add("Thailand");
countries.add("Belgium");
Collections.sort(countries); // Now the array list is sorted
```

> If you design a class whose objects need to be compared to each other, your class should implement the `Comparable` interface type.

If you have an array list of objects of your own class, then you need to make sure your class implements the `Comparable` interface type. Otherwise, the `sort` method will throw an exception.

For example, here is a class `Country` that implements the `Comparable<Country>` interface type. The `compareTo` method compares two countries by area. The test program demonstrates sorting by area.

Ch4/sort1/Country.java

```
 1  /**
 2      A country with a name and area.
 3  */
 4  public class Country implements Comparable<Country>
 5  {
 6      /**
 7          Constructs a country.
 8          @param aName the name of the country
 9          @param anArea the area of the country
10      */
11      public Country(String aName, double anArea)
12      {
13          name = aName;
14          area = anArea;
15      }
16
17      /**
18          Gets the name of the country.
19          @return the name
20      */
21      public String getName()
22      {
```

```
23        return name;
24     }
25
26     /**
27        Gets the area of the country.
28        @return the area
29     */
30     public double getArea()
31     {
32        return area;
33     }
34
35     /**
36        Compares two countries by area.
37        @param otherObject the other country
38        @return a negative number if this country has a smaller
39        area than otherCountry, 0 if the areas are the same,
40        a positive number otherwise
41     */
42     public int compareTo(Country other)
43     {
44        if (area < other.area) return -1;
45        if (area > other.area) return 1;
46        return 0;
47     }
48
49     private String name;
50     private double area;
51  }
```

Ch4/sort1/CountrySortTester.java

```
1  import java.util.*;
2
3  public class CountrySortTester
4  {
5     public static void main(String[] args)
6     {
7        ArrayList<Country> countries = new ArrayList<Country>();
8        countries.add(new Country("Uruguay", 176220));
9        countries.add(new Country("Thailand", 514000));
10       countries.add(new Country("Belgium", 30510));
11
12       Collections.sort(countries);
13       // Now the array list is sorted by area
14       for (Country c : countries)
15          System.out.println(c.getName() + " " + c.getArea());
16    }
17 }
```

4.4   The Comparator Interface Type

Now suppose you want to sort an array of countries by the country name instead of the area. It's not practical to redefine the compareTo method every time you want to change the sort order. Instead, there is a second sort method that is more flexible. You can use *any* sort order by supplying an object that implements the Comparator interface type. The Comparator<T> interface type requires one method

```
int compare(T first, T second)
```

that returns a negative number, zero, or a positive number depending on whether first is less than, equal to, or greater than second in the particular sort order.

Similar to the Comparable interface type, the Comparator interface type is also generic. The type parameter specifies the type of the compare method parameters. For example, to compare Country objects, you would use an object of a class that implements the Comparator<Country> interface type.

> You can sort a collection in any sort order by supplying an object of a class that implements the Comparator interface type.

Note the method is called compare, not compareTo—it compares two explicit parameters rather than comparing the implicit parameter to the explicit parameter.

If comp is an object of a class that implements the Comparator interface type, then

```
Collections.sort(list, comp)
```

sorts the objects in list according to the sort order that comp defines. Now list can contain any objects—they don't have to belong to classes that implement any particular interface type. For example, to sort the countries by name, define a class CountryComparatorByName whose compare method compares two Country objects.

```java
public class CountryComparatorByName implements Comparator<Country>
{
    public int compare(Country country1, Country country2)
    {
        return country1.getName().compareTo(country2.getName());
    }
}
```

Now make an object of this class and pass it to the sort method:

```java
Comparator<Country> comp = new CountryComparatorByName();
Collections.sort(countries, comp);
```

An object such as comp is often called a *function object* because its sole purpose is to execute the comparison function.

The CountryComparatorByName class has no state—all objects of this class behave in exactly the same way. However, it is easy to see that some state might be useful. Here is a comparator class that can sort in either ascending or descending order.

```java
public class CountryComparator implements Comparator<Country>
{
    public CountryComparator(boolean ascending)
    {
```

```
        if (ascending) direction = 1; else direction = -1;
      }

      public int compare(Country country1, Country country2)
      {
         return direction * country1.getName().compareTo(country2.getName());
      }

      private int direction;
   }
```

Then an object

```
   Comparator<Country> reverseComp = new CountryComparator(false);
```

can be used to sort an array of Country objects from Z to A.

4.5 Anonymous Classes

Consider again the call to the sort method of the preceding section:

```
   Comparator<Country> comp = new CountryComparatorByName();
   Collections.sort(countries, comp);
```

There is actually no need to explicitly name the comp object. You can pass an *anonymous object* to the sort method since you only need it once.

```
   Collections.sort(countries, new CountryComparatorByName());
```

> An anonymous object is an object that is not stored in a variable.

After the call to sort, the comparator object is no longer needed. Thus, there is no reason to store it in the comp variable.

Is it good style to use anonymous objects? It depends. Sometimes, the variable name gives useful information to the reader. But in our situation, the variable comp did not make the code clearer. If you look at your own programs, you will find that you often use anonymous values of type int or String. For example, which of these two styles do you prefer?

```
   countryNames.add("Uruguay");
```

or

```
   String countryName1 = "Uruguay";
   countryNames.add(countryName1);
```

Most programmers prefer the shorter style, particularly if they have to type the code themselves.

> An anonymous class is a class without a name. When defining an anonymous class, you must also construct an object of that class.

An anonymous object is handy if you only need an object once. The same situation can arise with classes. Chances are good that you only need the CountryComparatorByName class once as well—it is a "throwaway" class that fulfills a very specialized purpose.

If you only need a class once, you can make the class anonymous by defining it inside a method and using it to make a single object.

```
Comparator<Country> comp = new
    Comparator<Country>() // Make object of anonymous class
    {
        public int compare(Country country1, Country country2)
        {
            return country1.getName().compareTo(country2.getName());
        }
    };
```

The new expression:

- Defines a class with no name that implements the `Comparator<Country>` interface type.
- Has only one method, `compare`.
- Constructs one object of the class.

NOTE   An anonymous class is a special case of an *inner class*. An inner class is a class that is defined inside another class.

TIP   Most programmers find it easier to learn about anonymous classes by rewriting the code and explicitly introducing a class name. For example:

```
class MyComparator implements Comparator<Country> // Give a name to the class
{
    public int compare(Country country1, Country country2)
    {
        return country1.getName().compareTo(country2.getName());
    }
}
Comparator<Country> comp = new MyComparator();
```

After you have gained experience with anonymous classes, they will become quite natural, and you will find that you no longer need to rewrite the code.

Anonymous classes are very useful because they relieve you from the drudgery of having to name and document classes that are merely of a technical nature. Unfortunately, the syntax is rather cryptic. You have to look closely at the call `new` to find out that it constructs an object of an anonymous class.

The opening brace after the constructor parameter

```
new Comparator<Country>() { . . . }
```

shows that a new class is being defined.

Of course, in this situation, you know that `new Comparator<Country>()` couldn't have been a regular constructor call—`Comparator<Country>` is an interface type and you can't construct instances of an interface type.

Note the semicolon after the closing brace of the anonymous class definition. It is part of the statement

```
Comparator<Country> comp = an object;
```

TIP   To make anonymous classes easier to read, you should start the anonymous class definition on a new line, like this:

```
Comparator<Country> comp = new // Break line here
   Comparator<Country>() // Indent one tab stop
   {
      . . .
   };
```

The line break after the new keyword tips you off that something special is going to happen. Furthermore, the interface type name lines up nicely with the braces surrounding the definitions of the features of the anonymous class.

NOTE   Anonymous classes look tricky when first encountered. However, they are a programming idiom that has become extremely popular with professional Java programmers. You will encounter anonymous classes frequently when looking at professional Java code, and it is important that you spend time mastering the idiom. Fortunately, with a little practice, it quickly becomes second nature to most programmers.

In our first example, we made a single short-lived object of the anonymous class, making it truly into a "throwaway" class. But it is easy to create multiple objects of the anonymous class, simply by putting the construction inside a method. For example, the Country class can have a static method that returns a comparator object that compares countries by name:

```
public class Country
{
   . . .
   public static Comparator<Country> comparatorByName()
   {
      return new
         Comparator<Country>() // Make object of anonymous class
         {
            public int compare(Country country1, Country country2)
            {
               return country1.getName().compareTo(country2.getName());
            }
         };
   }
   . . .
}
```

You can now sort an array list of countries like this:

```
Collections.sort(countries, Country.comparatorByName());
```

Actually, for a class that doesn't have one natural ordering, this is a very nice setup, much better than implementing the Comparable interface type. Rather than defining a compareTo method that sorts rather arbitrarily by area or name, the Country class can define two methods that return Comparator objects.

```
comparatorByName
comparatorByArea
```

This design gives both comparisons equal preference. Using anonymous classes in these methods makes it easier to define them.

4.6   Frames and User Interface Components

We will now turn to an important example of Java interface types from the domain of graphical user interface programming. A graphical user interface contains buttons, menus, and other components that a user can activate. In Java, you specify the actions that occur upon activation by defining classes that implement the ActionListener interface type.

However, before we are ready to attach action listeners to buttons, we need to cover some basic material about graphical user interfaces. In this section, you will learn how to display a window and how to add user interface components to it.

> A frame window is a top-level window, usually decorated with borders and a title bar.

Let's start with a very simple application that contains two buttons and a text field (see Figure 6).

The window containing the components is called a *frame window*.

A frame window is displayed as follows:

```
JFrame frame = new JFrame();
frame.pack();
frame.setVisible(true);
```

The pack command sets the size of the frame to the smallest size needed to display its components. Alternatively, you can set the size of the frame to a given width and height (in pixels):

```
frame.setSize(FRAME_WIDTH, FRAME_HEIGHT);
```

If you don't pack the frame or set the size, then the window is displayed at a rather useless size of 0 by 0 pixels.

For a simple demo program, add the following line:

```
frame.setDefaultCloseOperation(JFrame.EXIT_ON_CLOSE);
```

Then the program exits when the user closes the frame window. If you don't include this setting and if you don't provide for some other way of exiting the program, then the program will stay alive after the user closes the frame window.

Figure 6

A Frame with Several User Interface Components

Now it is time to construct the buttons.

```
JButton helloButton = new JButton("Say Hello");
JButton goodbyeButton = new JButton("Say Goodbye");
```

> A layout manager sets the positions and dimensions of components. The FlowLayout lines up components side by side.

You must decide on a *layout manager* for the frame to have multiple user interface components lined up. We will discuss layout management in Chapter 5. For now, we'll just use the FlowLayout. This layout manager simply lays out the components by placing them next to each other.

```
frame.setLayout(new FlowLayout());
```

Finally, you can add the components to the frame.

```
frame.add(helloButton);
frame.add(goodbyeButton);
```

To finish the user interface, place a *text field* next to the buttons. The text field is constructed as follows:

```
final int FIELD_WIDTH = 20;
JTextField textField = new JTextField(FIELD_WIDTH);
```

Use the setText method to place text inside the field:

```
textField.setText("Click a button!");
```

Of course, the text field must also be added to the frame. Here is the complete program.

Ch4/frame/FrameTester.java

```
1  import java.awt.*;
2  import javax.swing.*;
3
4  public class FrameTester
5  {
6     public static void main(String[] args)
7     {
8        JFrame frame = new JFrame();
9
10       JButton helloButton = new JButton("Say Hello");
11       JButton goodbyeButton = new JButton("Say Goodbye");
12
13       final int FIELD_WIDTH = 20;
14       JTextField textField = new JTextField(FIELD_WIDTH);
15       textField.setText("Click a button!");
16
17       frame.setLayout(new FlowLayout());
18
19       frame.add(helloButton);
20       frame.add(goodbyeButton);
21       frame.add(textField);
22
23       frame.setDefaultCloseOperation(JFrame.EXIT_ON_CLOSE);
24       frame.pack();
25       frame.setVisible(true);
26    }
27 }
```

When you run this program, you will notice that the user interface is displayed correctly. However, clicking on the buttons has no effect. In the next section, you will learn how to attach actions to the buttons.

NOTE   If you look closely at the program that displays a frame, you may wonder why the program doesn't quit immediately after showing the frame and exiting the `main` method. Indeed, the *main thread* of the program quits, but the `setVisible` method spawns another thread. This thread keeps running until the user closes the frame window. You will learn more about threads in Chapter 9.

4.7   User Interface Actions

> To define the action of a button, add an object of a class that implements the `ActionListener` interface type. When the button is clicked, the code of the `actionPerformed` method is executed.

Now that the user interface displays correctly, it's time to specify the actions of the "Say Hello" and "Say Goodbye" buttons. When a user clicks on the "Say Hello" button, you want to display the message "Hello, World!" in the text field. And, of course, when the user clicks the "Say Goodbye" button, you want to display "Goodbye, World!" instead.

In the Java user interface toolkit, the code that executes when a button is clicked is defined in a *listener class*. You make an object of that listener class and attach it to the button as an *action listener*. A button can have any number of action listener objects. When the button is clicked, each of them is notified.

Of course, just as with the `sort` method, there is a catch—there needs to be a standard method call for the notification. In the case of a button, the listener objects must belong to classes that implement the `ActionListener` interface type.

```
public interface ActionListener
{
   void actionPerformed(ActionEvent event);
}
```

The `ActionEvent` parameter contains information about the event, such as the event source. However, we do not need that information in most listener methods.

To define the action of the `helloButton`, add an action listener and use an anonymous class to implement the `ActionListener` interface type.

```
helloButton.addActionListener(new
   ActionListener()
   {
      public void actionPerformed(ActionEvent event)
      {
         // Button action goes here
         textField.setText("Hello, World!");
      }
   });
```

    TIP   Action listeners are a bit tedious to read. The best way to deal with them is to glaze over the routine code and focus on the code inside the `actionPerformed` method, like this:

```
helloButton.addActionListener(new
    ActionListener()
    {
        public void actionPerformed(ActionEvent event)
        {
            textField.setText("Hello, World!");
        }
    });
```

This looks pretty intuitive: When the button is clicked, set the text field to a new greeting.

Let's review how buttons do their jobs.

1. When setting up the user interface, you construct a listener object and add it to the button.

```
helloButton.addActionListener(new ActionListener() {. . .};);
```

The button simply stores the listener object. Note that the `actionPerformed` method is not yet called.

2. Whenever the button detects that it has been clicked, it calls the `actionPerformed` method of its listeners:

```
ActionEvent event = . . .;
for (listener : listeners)
    listener.actionPerformed(event);
```

In our example, each button has only one listener.

3. The `actionPerformed` methods execute.

> Methods of inner classes can access variables that are visible in the enclosing scope.

If you look closely at the statement inside the `actionPerformed` method of our example, you will notice something very remarkable: The methods of an inner class can access *variables from the enclosing scope*. In our example, the `actionPerformed` method of the anonymous listener class accesses the `textField` variable of the enclosing `main` method. This is clearly a very useful feature.

> If you access a local variable from an inner class, you must declare it as `final`.

There is just one technicality that you need to keep in mind. If an inner class accesses a *local* variable from an enclosing scope, that variable must be declared as `final`. If you look at the complete source code for the example at the end of this section, you will note that the text field is declared as

```
final JTextField textField = new TextField(FIELD_WIDTH);
```

The keyword `final` denotes the fact that the `textField` variable refers to the same object during its lifetime.

Here is the complete program:

Ch4/action1/ActionTester.java

```java
1  import java.awt.*;
2  import java.awt.event.*;
3  import javax.swing.*;
4
5  public class ActionTester
6  {
7     public static void main(String[] args)
8     {
9        JFrame frame = new JFrame();
10
11       final int FIELD_WIDTH = 20;
12       final JTextField textField = new JTextField(FIELD_WIDTH);
13       textField.setText("Click a button!");
14
15       JButton helloButton = new JButton("Say Hello");
16
17       helloButton.addActionListener(new
18          ActionListener()
19          {
20             public void actionPerformed(ActionEvent event)
21             {
22                textField.setText("Hello, World!");
23             }
24          });
25
26       JButton goodbyeButton = new JButton("Say Goodbye");
27
28       goodbyeButton.addActionListener(new
29          ActionListener()
30          {
31             public void actionPerformed(ActionEvent event)
32             {
33                textField.setText("Goodbye, World!");
34             }
35          });
36
37       frame.setLayout(new FlowLayout());
38
39       frame.add(helloButton);
40       frame.add(goodbyeButton);
41       frame.add(textField);
42
43       frame.setDefaultCloseOperation(JFrame.EXIT_ON_CLOSE);
44       frame.pack();
45       frame.setVisible(true);
46    }
47 }
```

NOTE It is very convenient that an inner class method can access variables that are visible in the scope of the class definition. If you think about it, it is actually quite remarkable that an inner class can have this capability. After all, the main method has exited by the time the `actionPerformed` method is called, and its local variables no longer exist. In order to overcome this problem, the inner class actually makes a copy of all variables that its methods use. Thus, the action listener object has its own `textField` reference that is initialized with the value from the `textField` in the `main` method. You don't really have to worry about this—it is all automatic. However, this mechanism explains why you can only refer to `final` local variables of the enclosing scope. That way, the meaning of `textField` cannot change during the execution of `main`, and there is no ambiguity about the object reference that the inner class should copy.

You should know about a very useful trick that comes in handy when you have several action listeners with similar actions. Consider the two button actions in our example. They only differ in the message string. It is very appropriate in this case to construct two objects of the same listener class with an instance field that stores the message text.

However, anonymous classes don't have constructors. To construct multiple objects of the same anonymous class, you must instantiate the anonymous class in a helper method, and then call that method twice. In the following code example, the `createGreeting-ButtonListener` helper method is called twice to construct two instances of the same listener class. The helper method is `static` because it is called from the `static main` method.

```
public class ActionTester
{
   public static void main(String[] args)
   {
      . . .
      textField = new JTextField(FIELD_WIDTH);
      helloButton.addActionListener(
         createGreetingButtonListener("Hello, World!"));
      goodbyeButton.addActionListener(
         createGreetingButtonListener("Goodbye, World!"));
      . . .
   }

   public static ActionListener createGreetingButtonListener(
         final String message)
   {
      return new
         ActionListener()
         {
            public void actionPerformed(ActionEvent event)
            {
               textField.setText(message);
            }
         };
   }

   private static JTextField textField;
}
```

Note that `message` is a parameter variable of the `createGreetingButtonListener` method. It too needs to be tagged as `final` so that you can reference it in the method of an anonymous class. However, the `textfield` variable need not be declared as `final` because inner class methods always have access to fields of enclosing classes. The field is static because the inner class is defined inside a static method.

This program constructs two objects of the same anonymous class. Each object stores the message value that was supplied when the createGreetingButtonListener method was called.

4.8   Timers

The Timer class in the javax.swing package generates a sequence of action events, spaced apart at equal time intervals, and notifies a designated action listener. To set up the timer, you supply the delay between the events (in milliseconds) and a listener:

```
ActionListener listener = . . .;
final int DELAY = 1000; // 1000 milliseconds delay between action events
Timer t = new Timer(DELAY, listener);
```

Then start the timer.

```
t.start();
```

The start method returns immediately. A new thread of execution is started that issues action events in the specified frequency.

Timers are useful for animation. In the next section, you will see how to use a timer to move a car across a window.

The program at the end of this section displays a simple digital clock (see Figure 7).

The program displays a text field inside a frame. A timer is set up to notify a listener once per second:

```
ActionListener listener = new
   ActionListener()
   {
      public void actionPerformed(ActionEvent event)
      {
         Date now = new Date();
         textField.setText(now.toString());
      }
   };
Timer t = new Timer(DELAY, listener);
```

Every second, the actionPerformed method of the listener class will be called. The text field is then updated to the current time.

Figure 7

The TimerTester Program

NOTE   There are two classes named `Timer` in the Java library: one in the `javax.swing` package, and another one in the `java.util` package. If you write a program that imports all classes from both packages, and then refer to `Timer`, the compiler reports an ambiguity. To resolve that ambiguity, you can use the fully qualified name:

```
javax.swing.Timer t = new javax.swing.Timer(DELAY, listener);
```

Alternatively, you can add a directive to import a single class:

```
import javax.swing.Timer;
```

Ch4/timer/TimerTester.java

```java
 1 import java.awt.*;
 2 import java.awt.event.*;
 3 import java.util.*;
 4 import javax.swing.*;
 5 import javax.swing.Timer;
 6
 7 /**
 8    This program shows a clock that is updated once per second.
 9 */
10
11 public class TimerTester
12 {
13    public static void main(String[] args)
14    {
15       JFrame frame = new JFrame();
16
17       final int FIELD_WIDTH = 20;
18       final JTextField textField = new JTextField(FIELD_WIDTH);
19
20       frame.setLayout(new FlowLayout());
21       frame.add(textField);
22
23       ActionListener listener = new
24          ActionListener()
25          {
26             public void actionPerformed(ActionEvent event)
27             {
28                Date now = new Date();
29                textField.setText(now.toString());
30             }
31          };
32
33       final int DELAY = 1000;
34          // Milliseconds between timer ticks
35       Timer t = new Timer(DELAY, listener);
36       t.start();
37
38       frame.setDefaultCloseOperation(JFrame.EXIT_ON_CLOSE);
39       frame.pack();
40       frame.setVisible(true);
41    }
42 }
```

4.9   Drawing Shapes

> The Graphics parameter of a paint method carries out drawing operations. To use the powerful 2D drawing operations, you need to cast it to the Graphics2D type.

In Section 4.1, you saw how an icon can paint a circle. This section gives a brief overview of the classes that the Java library provides for drawing geometric shapes. Let's have a closer look at the paintIcon method of the Icon interface type. That method has the signature

```
public void paintIcon(
        Component c, Graphics g, int x, int y)
```

The Graphics object is a *graphics context*. You invoke methods on that object whenever you want to draw a shape or change the current color or font. In general, a "context" object is usually an object that has some specialized knowledge of how to carry out complex tasks. You don't have to worry how the context object works; you just create it and pass it along as required.

Recent versions of Java have been enhanced to use a more powerful Graphics2D class. However, for historical reasons, most methods still use the older Graphics parameter type, even though a Graphics2D object is always passed into the methods. To take advantage of the more powerful type, you need to apply a cast:

```
public void paintIcon(Component c, Graphics g, int x, int y)
{
    Graphics2D g2 = (Graphics2D) g;
    . . .
}
```

> You can draw objects of any class that implements the Shape interface type, such as rectangles, ellipses, and line segments.

Then you are ready to draw an object of any class that implements the Shape interface type.

```
Shape s = . . .;
g2.draw(s);
```

The Java library supplies a number of classes that implement the Shape interface type. In this book, we will only draw shapes that are composed of line segments, rectangles, and ellipses. More complex shapes can be drawn by using arbitrary quadratic and cubic curve segments; those shape classes will not be covered here.

To draw a rectangle, construct and draw a Rectangle2D.Double object:

```
Shape rectangle = new Rectangle2D.Double(x, y, width, height);
g2.draw(rectangle);
```

You need to specify the top left corner, the width, and the height of the rectangle. (The strange class name Rectangle2D.Double is explained in Chapter 6.)

Constructing an ellipse is very similar. You must supply the *bounding* rectangle of the ellipse (see Figure 8). In particular, note that x and y do not form the center of the ellipse—in fact, they don't even lie on the ellipse.

```
Shape ellipse = new Ellipse2D.Double(x, y, width, height);
g2.draw(ellipse);
```

Figure 8

An Ellipse and Its
Bounding Rectangle

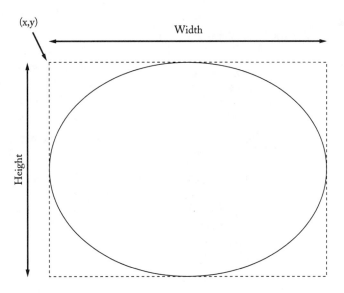

To draw a line segment, construct an object of type `Line2D.Double` as follows:

```
Point2D.Double start = new Point2D.Double(x1, y1);
Point2D.Double end = new Point2D.Double(x2, y2);
Shape segment = new Line2D.Double(start, end);
g2.draw(segment);
```

Figure 9 shows the relationships among these classes.

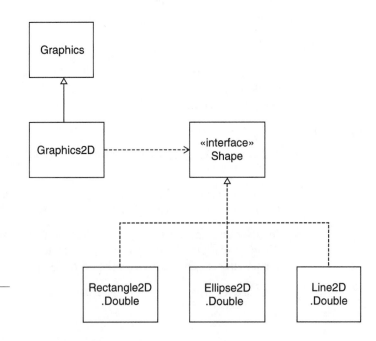

Figure 9

Commonly Used
Classes for Drawing Shapes

Figure 10

A Car Icon

You can also *fill* a shape instead of drawing the outline. For example, the call

```
g2.fill(ellipse);
```

fills the inside of the ellipse with the current color. To change the color, make a call such as

```
g2.setColor(Color.RED);
```

To draw text, call the `drawString` method:

```
g2.drawString(text, x, y);
```

This call draws the given text so that its *basepoint* falls on the given coordinates (see Figure 11 and the Special Topic note at the end of this section for more information on text placement).

The following program puts these shapes to work to draw a sketch of a car (see Figure 10).

Ch4/icon3/CarIcon.java

```
 1  import java.awt.*;
 2  import java.awt.geom.*;
 3  import javax.swing.*;
 4
 5  /**
 6      An icon that has the shape of a car.
 7  */
 8  public class CarIcon implements Icon
 9  {
10      /**
11          Constructs a car of a given width.
12          @param width  the width of the car
13      */
14      public CarIcon(int aWidth)
15      {
16          width = aWidth;
17      }
18
19      public int getIconWidth()
20      {
```

```
21        return width;
22     }
23
24     public int getIconHeight()
25     {
26        return width / 2;
27     }
28
29     public void paintIcon(Component c, Graphics g, int x, int y)
30     {
31        Graphics2D g2 = (Graphics2D) g;
32        Rectangle2D.Double body
33            = new Rectangle2D.Double(x, y + width / 6,
34            width - 1, width / 6);
35        Ellipse2D.Double frontTire
36            = new Ellipse2D.Double(x + width / 6, y + width / 3,
37            width / 6, width / 6);
38        Ellipse2D.Double rearTire
39            = new Ellipse2D.Double(x + width * 2 / 3, y + width / 3,
40            width / 6, width / 6);
41
42        // The bottom of the front windshield
43        Point2D.Double r1
44            = new Point2D.Double(x + width / 6, y + width / 6);
45        // The front of the roof
46        Point2D.Double r2
47            = new Point2D.Double(x + width / 3, y);
48        // The rear of the roof
49        Point2D.Double r3
50            = new Point2D.Double(x + width * 2 / 3, y);
51        // The bottom of the rear windshield
52        Point2D.Double r4
53            = new Point2D.Double(x + width * 5 / 6, y + width / 6);
54
55        Line2D.Double frontWindshield
56            = new Line2D.Double(r1, r2);
57        Line2D.Double roofTop
58            = new Line2D.Double(r2, r3);
59        Line2D.Double rearWindshield
60            = new Line2D.Double(r3, r4);
61
62        g2.fill(frontTire);
63        g2.fill(rearTire);
64        g2.setColor(Color.RED);
65        g2.fill(body);
66        g2.draw(frontWindshield);
67        g2.draw(roofTop);
68        g2.draw(rearWindshield);
69     }
70
71     private int width;
72  }
```

Special Topic   4.1

Accurate Positioning of Text

When drawing text on the screen, you usually need to position it accurately. For example, if you want to draw two lines of text, one below the other, then you need to know the distance between the two basepoints. Of course, the size of a string depends on the shapes of the letters, which in turn depends on the font face and point size. You will need to know a few typographical measurements (see Figure 11):

- The *ascent* of a font is the height of the largest letter above the baseline.
- The *descent* of a font is the depth below the baseline of the letter with the lowest descender.

These values describe the *vertical extent* of strings. The *horizontal extent* depends on the individual letters in a string. In a `monospaced font`, all letters have the same width. Monospaced fonts are still used for computer programs, but for plain text they are as outdated as the typewriter. In a *proportionally spaced font*, different letters have different widths. For example, the letter *l* is much narrower than the letter *m*.

To measure the size of a string, you need to construct a `FontRenderContext` object, which you obtain from the `Graphics2D` object by calling `getFontRenderContext`. A font render context is an object that knows how to transform letter shapes (which are described as curves) into pixels. The `Graphics2D` object is another example of a context object—many people call it a "graphics context".

To get the size of a string, you call the `getStringBounds` method of the `Font` class. For example,

```
String text = "Message";
Font font = g2.getFont();
FontRenderContext context = g2.getFontRenderContext();
Rectangle2D bounds = font.getStringBounds(text, context);
```

The returned rectangle is positioned so that the origin (0, 0) falls on the basepoint (see Figure 11). Therefore, you can get the ascent, descent, and extent as

```
double ascent = -bounds.getY();
double descent = bounds.getHeight() - ascent;
double extent = bounds.getWidth();
```

Figure 11

Drawing Text

4.10   Designing an Interface Type

In this section, we will put a timer to work in an animation program (see Figure 12).

Ten times per second, the car shape will move and the window will be repainted so that the new position is displayed.

In order to paint the car shape, define a class that implements the `Icon` interface type:

```
public class ShapeIcon implements Icon
{
   public void paintIcon(Component c, Graphics g, int x, int y)
   {
      paint the shape
   }
   . . .
}
```

Exercise 4.20 asks you to enhance this class to paint multiple shapes.

We place the icon inside a `JLabel`:

```
ShapeIcon icon = new ShapeIcon(. . .);
JLabel label = new JLabel(icon);
```

Then we place the label inside a frame in the usual way.

The timer action moves the shape and repaints the label.

```
ActionListener listener = new
   ActionListener()
   {
      public void actionPerformed(ActionEvent event)
      {
         move the shape
         label.repaint();
      }
   };
```

The `repaint` method causes the label to be repainted as soon as possible. When the label paints itself, it erases its contents and paints its icon. The `paintIcon` method then redraws the shape in the new position.

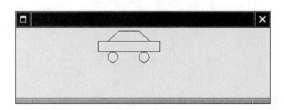

Figure 12

An Animated Car

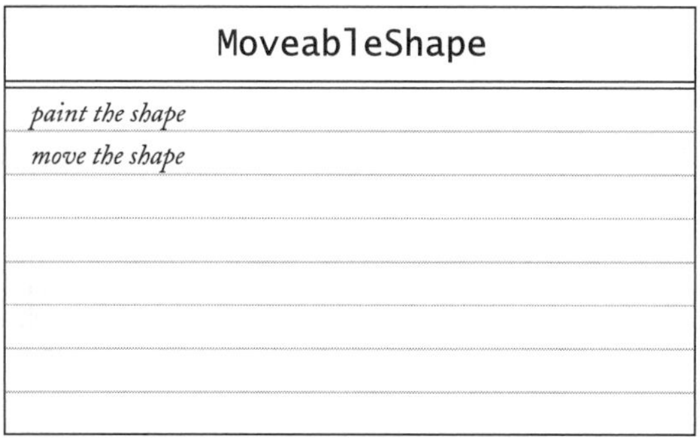

MoveableShape
paint the shape
move the shape

Figure 13

CRC Card for the MoveableShape Interface Type

If you review this plan, you will note that it doesn't matter what the shape looks like, as long as it can be painted and moved. The same plan will work for animating any shape.

Therefore, it is a good idea to *design a new interface type* that recognizes the basic shape operations (see Figure 13).

The interface has two methods, to paint the shape and move it by a given amount. In order to be consistent with the method names of the Java library, we call these methods draw and translate.

```
public interface MoveableShape
{
    void draw(Graphics2D g2);
    void translate(int dx, int dy);
}
```

We then supply a CarShape class that implements the MoveableShape interface type. You will find the code at the end of this section. The implementation is straightforward. The draw method draws the geometric shapes that make up the car. The translate method moves the top left corner position:

```
public void translate(int dx, int dy)
{
    x += dx;
    y += dy;
}
```

> Design your own interface types to decouple general mechanisms from specific implementation details.

By introducing the MoveableShape interface type, we have decoupled the animation from the specifics of the car shape. As you can see in Figure 14, the animation only depends on the MoveableShape interface type. It is an easy matter to change the program so that it animates another shape. Designing your programs so that they can be easily extended and modified is an important part of object-oriented design. In this example, we achieved this flexibility by defining a custom interface type.

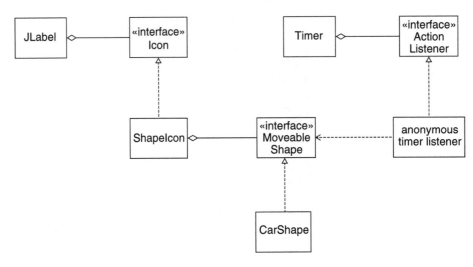

Figure 14

Classes in the Animation Program

TIP Whenever you design a mechanism that asks someone else to supply an object of a class, you should consider whether it would be more appropriate to specify an interface type instead. By using interface types, you give added flexibility to the programmers that use the services that you provide.

Ch4/animation/MoveableShape.java

```
 1  import java.awt.*;
 2
 3  /**
 4      A shape that can be moved around.
 5  */
 6  public interface MoveableShape
 7  {
 8      /**
 9          Draws the shape.
10          @param g2 the graphics context
11      */
12      void draw(Graphics2D g2);
13
14      /**
15          Moves the shape by a given amount.
16          @param dx the amount to translate in x-direction
17          @param dy the amount to translate in y-direction
18      */
19      void translate(int dx, int dy);
20  }
```

Ch4/animation/ShapeIcon.java

```
1  import java.awt.*;
2  import java.util.*;
3  import javax.swing.*;
4
5  /**
6     An icon that contains a moveable shape.
7  */
8  public class ShapeIcon implements Icon
9  {
10    public ShapeIcon(MoveableShape shape,
11          int width, int height)
12    {
13       this.shape = shape;
14       this.width = width;
15       this.height = height;
16    }
17
18    public int getIconWidth()
19    {
20       return width;
21    }
22
23    public int getIconHeight()
24    {
25       return height;
26    }
27
28    public void paintIcon(Component c, Graphics g, int x, int y)
29    {
30       Graphics2D g2 = (Graphics2D) g;
31       shape.draw(g2);
32    }
33
34    private int width;
35    private int height;
36    private MoveableShape shape;
37 }
```

Ch4/animation/AnimationTester.java

```
1  import java.awt.*;
2  import java.awt.event.*;
3  import javax.swing.*;
4
5  /**
6     This program implements an animation that moves
7     a car shape.
8  */
9  public class AnimationTester
10 {
11    public static void main(String[] args)
12    {
13       JFrame frame = new JFrame();
14
```

```
15          final MoveableShape shape
16              = new CarShape(0, 0, CAR_WIDTH);
17
18          ShapeIcon icon = new ShapeIcon(shape,
19              ICON_WIDTH, ICON_HEIGHT);
20
21          final JLabel label = new JLabel(icon);
22          frame.setLayout(new FlowLayout());
23          frame.add(label);
24
25          frame.setDefaultCloseOperation(JFrame.EXIT_ON_CLOSE);
26          frame.pack();
27          frame.setVisible(true);
28
29          final int DELAY = 100;
30          // milliseconds between timer ticks
31          Timer t = new Timer(DELAY, new
32             ActionListener()
33             {
34                 public void actionPerformed(ActionEvent event)
35                 {
36                     shape.translate(1, 0);
37                     label.repaint();
38                 }
39             });
40          t.start();
41      }
42
43      private static final int ICON_WIDTH = 400;
44      private static final int ICON_HEIGHT = 100;
45      private static final int CAR_WIDTH = 100;
46  }
```

Ch4/animation/CarShape.java

```
1   import java.awt.*;
2   import java.awt.geom.*;
3   import java.util.*;
4
5   /**
6       A car that can be moved around.
7   */
8   public class CarShape implements MoveableShape
9   {
10      /**
11          Constructs a car item.
12          @param x the left of the bounding rectangle
13          @param y the top of the bounding rectangle
14          @param width the width of the bounding rectangle
15      */
16      public CarShape(int x, int y, int width)
17      {
```

```
18          this.x = x;
19          this.y = y;
20          this.width = width;
21       }
22
23       public void translate(int dx, int dy)
24       {
25          x += dx;
26          y += dy;
27       }
28
29       public void draw(Graphics2D g2)
30       {
31          Rectangle2D.Double body
32               = new Rectangle2D.Double(x, y + width / 6,
33               width - 1, width / 6);
34          Ellipse2D.Double frontTire
35               = new Ellipse2D.Double(x + width / 6, y + width / 3,
36               width / 6, width / 6);
37          Ellipse2D.Double rearTire
38               = new Ellipse2D.Double(x + width * 2 / 3, y + width / 3,
39               width / 6, width / 6);
40
41          // The bottom of the front windshield
42          Point2D.Double r1
43               = new Point2D.Double(x + width / 6, y + width / 6);
44          // The front of the roof
45          Point2D.Double r2
46               = new Point2D.Double(x + width / 3, y);
47          // The rear of the roof
48          Point2D.Double r3
49               = new Point2D.Double(x + width * 2 / 3, y);
50          // The bottom of the rear windshield
51          Point2D.Double r4
52               = new Point2D.Double(x + width * 5 / 6, y + width / 6);
53          Line2D.Double frontWindshield
54               = new Line2D.Double(r1, r2);
55          Line2D.Double roofTop
56               = new Line2D.Double(r2, r3);
57          Line2D.Double rearWindshield
58               = new Line2D.Double(r3, r4);
59
60          g2.draw(body);
61          g2.draw(frontTire);
62          g2.draw(rearTire);
63          g2.draw(frontWindshield);
64          g2.draw(roofTop);
65          g2.draw(rearWindshield);
66       }
67
68       private int x;
69       private int y;
70       private int width;
71    }
```

EXERCISES

Exercise 4.1. When sorting a collection of objects that implements the `Comparable` type, the sorting method compares and rearranges the objects. Explain the role of polymorphism in this situation.

Exercise 4.2. In Java, a method call on an object such as `x.f()` is resolved when the program executes, not when it is compiled, in order to support polymorphism. Name two situations where the Java compiler can determine the exact method to be called before the program executes.

Exercise 4.3. Write a class that implements the `Icon` interface type and draws an image of a coffee mug by drawing and filling shapes.

Exercise 4.4. Write a class `BankAccount` that implements the `Comparable` interface type. Order bank accounts by increasing balance. Supply a test program that sorts an array list of bank accounts.

Exercise 4.5. Write a method

```
public static Object minimum(ArrayList a)
```

that computes the smallest element in the array list. Assume that the elements of the array list implement the `Comparable` interface type, and that the array is not empty. Document these preconditions. (Here, we use the "raw" `ArrayList` and `Comparable` types without type parameters. As a result, the compiler will issue warnings that you may ignore. You will see in Chapter 7 how to properly deal with generic type parameters.)

Exercise 4.6. Write a method

```
public static String maximum(ArrayList<String> a, Comparator<String> c)
```

that computes the largest string in the array list, using the ordering relationship that is defined by the given comparator. Supply a test program that uses this method to find the longest string in the list.

Exercise 4.7. Define an interface type `Measurer` as follows:

```
public interface Measurer
{
   double measure(Object x);
}
```

Then supply a method

```
public static Object maximum(Object[] a, Measurer m)
```

that computes the object in the array with the largest measure. Test your method by populating an array list with rectangles and finding the one with the largest area.

Exercise 4.8. Define an interface type `Filter` as follows:

```
public interface Filter
{
   boolean accept(String x);
}
```

Then supply a method

```
public static String[] filter(String[] a, Filter f)
```

that returns an array containing all elements of a that are accepted by the filter. Test your class by filtering an array of strings and accepting all strings that contain at most three characters.

Exercise 4.9. Define an interface type `Drawable` as follows:

```
public interface Drawable
{
    void draw(Graphics2D g2);
}
```

Then provide a class `Car` that implements the `Drawable` interface type and a class `DrawableIcon` that can paint any drawable shape. Reimplement the program in Section 4.9 that shows the car icon in an option pane. What is the benefit of this redesign?

Exercise 4.10. Write a class `RectangleComparator` that defines a total ordering on objects of type `Rectangle2D.Double`. Then write a test program that sorts an array of rectangles. The challenge is to define a *total* ordering. *Hint:* Use lexicographic ordering on (x, y, *width*, *height*). First compare the x-values. If they are the same, then compare the y-values. If they are also the same, compare the widths and finally, if necessary, the heights.

Exercise 4.11. Rewrite the program that displays the Mars icon by creating an anonymous class that implements the `Icon` interface type.

Exercise 4.12. Add two methods

```
public static Comparator<Country> createComparatorByName(
        final boolean increasing)
public static Comparator<Country> createComparatorByArea(
        final boolean increasing)
```

to the `Country` class. The methods should return instances of anonymous classes that implement the `Comparator` interface type. The `boolean` parameters indicate whether the comparison should be in increasing or decreasing order. The parameters are declared `final` so that you can access them in your `compare` methods.

Exercise 4.13. Write a program that shows a frame with a button labeled "Date" and a text field. Whenever the user clicks the button, the current date and time should be displayed in the text field. You can obtain the current date and time as follows:

```
String dateAndTime = new Date().toString();
```

Exercise 4.14. Write a program that shows a frame with three buttons labeled "Red", "Green", and "Blue", and a label containing an icon showing a circle that is initially red. As the user clicks the buttons, the fill color of the circle should change. When you change the color, you need to invoke the `repaint` method on the label. The call to `repaint` ensures that the `paintIcon` method is called so that the icon can be repainted with the new color.

Exercise 4.15. Write a program that shows a frame with two buttons labeled "Zoom in", and "Zoom out", and a label containing a car icon. As the user clicks the buttons, the car should get larger or smaller. As in Exercise 4.14, you need to invoke the `repaint` method on the label to trigger a redisplay of the image.

Exercise 4.16. You have seen how you can define action listeners with similar behavior by using a helper method. In this exercise, you will explore another way to achieve the same effect. Define a listener class with an explicit name, and then construct two objects:

```
helloButton.addActionListener(
    new GreetingButtonListener("Hello, World"));
goodbyeButton.addActionListener(
    new GreetingButtonListener("Goodbye, World"));
```

Your task is to define the `GreetingButtonListener` class and complete the program that shows the message text selected by the buttons. Do not use inner classes.

Exercise 4.17. Construct a `javax.swing.Timer` object and supply an action listener such that the message "Hello, World" is printed to `System.out` once per second.

Exercise 4.18. Write a class `ClockIcon` that implements the `Icon` interface type. Draw an analog clock whose hour, minute, and second hands show the current time. To get the current hours and minutes, construct an object of type `GregorianCalendar` with the default constructor.

Exercise 4.19. Continue Exercise 4.18 by adding a `javax.swing.Timer` object to your program. The timer's action listener should invoke the `repaint` method once per second.

Exercise 4.20. Enhance the `ShapeIcon` class so that it displays multiple moveable shapes. Then modify the animation program to show a number of moving cars. *Hint:* Store all shapes in an array list.

Exercise 4.21. Modify the animation program to show a moving airplane.

Exercise 4.22. Modify the animation program to make the moving shape reappear on the left-hand side after it disappears from the frame.

Patterns and GUI Programming

In this chapter, we introduce the concept of *patterns*. A pattern is a description of a problem and its solution that you can apply to many programming situations. In recent years, a number of useful patterns have been formulated and standardized. They now have become a part of the everyday vocabulary of many software developers. Some of the most common patterns are introduced in this chapter. When possible, the patterns are explained with examples from the Swing user interface toolkit, so that you can learn about patterns and GUI programming at the same time.

5.1   The Iterator as a Pattern

Recall how you use a list iterator to iterate through the elements of a linked list in Java.

```
LinkedList<String> list = . . .;
ListIterator<String> iterator = list.listIterator();
while (iterator.hasNext())
{
    String current = iterator.next();
    . . .
}
```

The hasNext method tests whether the iterator is at the end of the list. The next method returns the current element and advances the iterator to the next position.

Why does the Java library use an iterator to traverse a linked list?

If you look at a classical data structures book, you will find traversal code that looks quite different. In the traditional approach, the programmer manipulates the links directly:

```
Link currentLink = countries.head;
while (currentLink != null)
{
    do something with currentLink.data;
    currentLink = currentLink.next;
}
```

> Iterators do not expose the internal structure of a collection class.

This approach has two disadvantages. From a high-level point of view, it is not satisfactory because it exposes the links to the user of the list. But the links are just an artifact of the implementation that should be hidden from the user. As you may know, there are several variations for list implementations, such as circular lists or lists with a dummy header node. List users certainly should not have to worry about those implementation details.

Furthermore, as anyone who has ever implemented a linked list knows, it is very easy to mess up links and corrupt the link structure of a linked list. Thus, survival instinct dictates that list users should be shielded from the raw links.

Let's return to the high-level point of view. In Chapter 2, we used a queue class and had no problem defining the methods that make up a queue (see Figure 1):

```
void add(E x)
E peek()
E remove()
int size()
```

Insert in back   Remove from front

Figure 1

The Queue Interface

Figure 2

The Array Interface

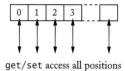

Here, E denotes the type of the queue elements. Similarly, it is an easy matter to define the methods that make up an array structure with random access (see Figure 2):

```
E get(int i)
void set(int i, E x)
void add(E x)
int size()
```

But the interface for a linked list is not so simple. We want to be able to add and remove elements in the middle of the linked list, but it would be very inefficient to specify a position in a linked list with an integer index.

One implementation that you sometimes see is a list with a cursor (see Figure 3). A list cursor marks a position similar to the cursor in a word processor. The list with cursor has the following interface:

```
E getCurrent()    // Get element at cursor
void set(E x)     // Set element at cursor to x
E remove()    // Remove element at cursor
void insert(E x)    // Insert x before cursor
void reset()    // Reset cursor to head
void next()    // Advance cursor
boolean hasNext()    // Check if cursor can be advanced
```

The state of such a list consists of

- The sequence of the stored elements

- A cursor that points to one of the elements

The reset method resets the cursor to the beginning. The next method advances it to the next element. The get, set, insert, and remove methods are relative to the cursor position. For example, here is how you traverse such a list.

```
for (list.reset(); list.hasNext(); list.next())
{
    do something with list.getCurrent();
}
```

At first glance, a list with a cursor seems like a good idea. The links are not exposed to the list user. No separate iterator class is required.

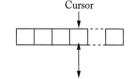

Figure 3

A List with a Cursor

> Iterators are preferred over cursors since you can attach more than one iterator to a collection.

However, that design has severe limitations. Since there is only one cursor, you can't implement algorithms that compare different list elements. You can't even print the contents of the list for debugging purposes. Printing the list would have the side effect of moving the cursor to the end!

> The iterator concept occurs in many different programming situations.

Thus, the iterator is a superior concept. A list can have any number of iterators attached to it. That means that you should supply iterators, and not a cursor, whenever you implement a collection class.

Furthermore, the iterator concept is useful outside the domain of collection classes. For example, the Scanner is an iterator through the tokens in a character sequence. An InputStream is an iterator through the bytes of a stream. This makes the iterator into a *pattern*. We will explain the concept of patterns in the next section.

5.2 The Pattern Concept

The architect Christopher Alexander formulated over 250 patterns for architectural design. (See Christopher Alexander et al., *A Pattern Language: Towns, Buildings, Construction*, Oxford University Press, 1977.) Those patterns lay down rules for building houses and cities. Alexander uses a very distinctive format for these rules. Every pattern has

- A short *name*
- A brief description of the *context*
- A lengthy description of the *problem*
- A prescription for a *solution*

Here is a typical example, showing the context and solution exactly as they appear in Alexander's book. The problem description is long; it is summarized here.

PATTERN

◆ **SHORT PASSAGES**

◆ ### Context

1. "… long, sterile corridors set the scene for everything bad about modern architecture."

◆ ### Problem

◆ This section contains a lengthy description of the problem of long corridors, with a depressing picture of a long, straight, narrow corridor with closed doors, similar to the one on the facing page.

◆ Alexander discusses issues of light and furniture. He cites research results about patient anxiety in hospital corridors. According to the research, corridors that are longer than 50 feet are perceived as uncomfortable.

Solution

Keep passages short. Make them as much like rooms as possible, with carpets or wood on the floor, furniture, bookshelves, beautiful windows. Make them generous in shape and always give them plenty of light; the best corridors and passages of all are those that have windows along an entire wall.

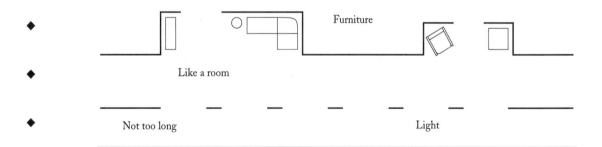

As you can see, this pattern distills a design rule into a simple format. If you have a design problem, it is easy to check whether the pattern is useful to you. If you decide that the pattern applies in your situation, then you can easily follow the recipe for a solution. Because that solution has been successful in the past, there is a good chance that you will benefit from it as well.

> A pattern presents proven advice in a standard format.

Alexander was interested in patterns that solve problems in architecture. Of course, our interest lies in software development. In this chapter, you will see patterns that give you guidance on object-oriented design.

> A design pattern gives advice about a problem in software design.

> The ITERATOR pattern teaches how to access the elements of an aggregate object.

Let's start by presenting the ITERATOR pattern. As you saw in the preceding section, iterators are useful for traversing the elements of a linked list, but they also occur in other programming situations. String tokenizers and input streams are both examples of the ITERATOR pattern.

PATTERN

ITERATOR

Context

1. An object (which we'll call the *aggregate*) contains other objects (which we'll call *elements*).
2. Clients (that is, methods that use the aggregate) need access to the elements.
3. The aggregate should not expose its internal structure.
4. There may be multiple clients that need simultaneous access.

Solution

1. Define an iterator class that fetches one element at a time.
2. Each iterator object needs to keep track of the position of the next element to fetch.
3. If there are several variations of the aggregate and iterator classes, it is best if they implement common interface types. Then the client only needs to know the interface types, not the concrete classes.

Note that the names of the interface types, classes, and methods (such as `Aggregate`, `ConcreteIterator`, `createIterator`, `isDone`) are *examples*. In an actual realization of the pattern, the names may be quite different.

For example, in the case of linked list iterators, we have:

Name in Design Pattern	Actual Name
Aggregate	List
ConcreteAggregate	LinkedList
Iterator	ListIterator
ConcreteIterator	An anonymous class that implements the ListIterator interface type
createIterator()	listIterator()
next()	next()
isDone()	Opposite of hasNext()
currentItem()	Return value of next()

The influential book, *Design Patterns* by Gamma, Helm, Johnson, and Vlissides, contains a description of many patterns for software design, including the ITERATOR pattern. Because the book has four authors, it is sometimes referred to as the "Gang of Four" book.

NOTE   The original Gang of Four—Jiang Qing (Mao Zedong's wife), Zhang Chunqiao, Yao Wenyuan, and Wang Hongwen—were radical Chinese communists who were strong advocates of the Cultural Revolution. There is no apparent connection between the two "gangs" beyond the fact that they each have four members.

INTERNET   Since the publication of the "Gang of Four" book, many authors have been bitten by the pattern bug. You can find many patterns for specialized problem domains on the Web. A good starting point for exploration is http://hillside.net/patterns/. There is even a column on "bug patterns", detailing common Java bugs, at http://www.ibm.com/developerworks/java/library/j-diag1.html.

NOTE   Design patterns give you constructive advice. *Antipatterns* are the opposite of design patterns—examples of design that are so bad that you should avoid them at all cost. Among the commonly cited antipatterns are:

- The Blob: A class that has gobbled up many disparate responsibilities.
- The Poltergeist: A spurious class whose objects are short-lived and carry no significant responsibilities.

5.3   The OBSERVER Pattern

Have you ever used a program that shows you two editable views of the same data, such as a "what you see is what you get" (WYSIWYG) and a structural view of a document? (See Figure 4.) When you edit one of the views, the other updates automatically and instantaneously.

You may well wonder how such a feature is programmed. When you type text into one of the windows, how does it show up in the other window? What happens if you have a third view of the same information?

The key to implementing this behavior is the *model/view/controller architecture*. One object, the *model*, holds the information in some data structure—an array of numbers, or a tree of document parts. The model has no visual appearance at all. It just holds the raw data. Several other objects, the *views*, draw the visible parts of the data, in a format that is specific to the view. For example, the table view displays numbers in a table. The graph view displays the same numbers in a bar chart. Finally, each view has a *controller*, an object that processes user interaction. The controller may process mouse and keyboard events from the windowing system, or it may contain user interface elements such as buttons and menus.

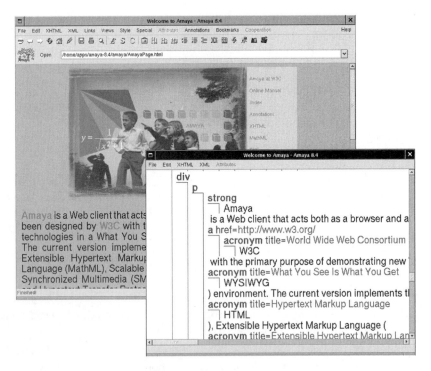

Figure 4

A WYSIWYG and a Structural View of the Same HTML Page

Some people are confused by the term "model". Don't think of an airplane model that approximates a real airplane. In the model/view/controller architecture (see Figure 5), the model is the real thing, and the views approximate it. Think instead of a model that poses for a painting. The model is real, and different artists can observe the same model and draw different views.

Here is what happens when a user types text into one of the windows:

- The controller tells the model to insert the text that the user typed.
- The model notifies all views of a change in the model.
- All views repaint themselves.
- During painting, each view asks the model for the current text.

This architecture minimizes the coupling between the model, views, and controllers. The model knows nothing about the views, except that they need to be notified of all changes. The views know nothing of the controllers. It is easy to add more views to a model. It is also easy to change the controller of a view, for example to facilitate voice input.

Let's have a closer look at the notification mechanism. The model knows about a number of *observers*, namely, the views. An observer is an object that is interested in state changes of the model. The model knows nothing in detail about the observers except that it should notify them whenever the model data changes.

> The OBSERVER pattern teaches how an object can tell other objects about events.

You have seen a similar situation in Chapter 4. An event source such as a button holds a number of *listeners*. When something interesting happens to the button, such as a button click, then the button notifies its listeners. The button knows nothing about its listeners except that they implement a particular interface type.

The fact that this arrangement occurs as a solution in two separate problems shows that it may be useful to distill the solution into a pattern. This notification pattern is called the OBSERVER pattern.

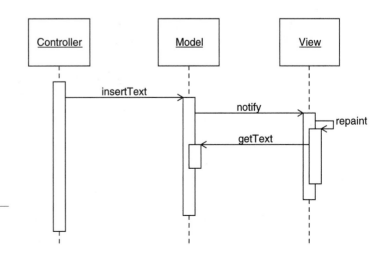

Figure 5

Sequence Diagram for
Inserting Text into a View

OBSERVER

Context

1. An object (which we'll call the *subject*) is the source of *events* (such as "my data has changed").
2. One or more objects (called the *observers*) want to know when an event occurs.

Solution

1. Define an observer interface type. Observer classes must implement this interface type.
2. The subject maintains a collection of observer objects.
3. The subject class supplies methods for attaching observers.
4. Whenever an event occurs, the subject notifies all observers.

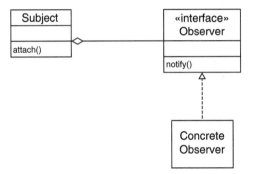

As you know, the names of the classes, interface types, and methods in the pattern description are examples. In the case of a button and its event listeners, we have:

Name in Design Pattern	Actual Name
Subject	JButton
Observer	ActionListener
ConcreteObserver	The class that implements the ActionListener interface type
attach()	addActionListener
notify()	actionPerformed

The OBSERVER pattern is pervasive in user interface programming with Java. All user interface elements—buttons, menus, check boxes, sliders, and so on—are subjects that are willing to tell observers about events.

5.4   Layout Managers and the STRATEGY Pattern

> You add user interface components to a container.

You build up user interfaces from individual user interface *components:* buttons, text fields, sliders, and so on. You place components into *containers*. For example, the content pane of a frame is a container.

When you add a component to a container, the container must put it somewhere on the screen. In some user interface toolkits, the programmer (or a layout tool) specifies pixel positions for each component. However, that is not a good idea. Component sizes can change from the original design, usually for one of two reasons:

1. The user chooses a different "look and feel". The Swing user interface toolkit allows users of Java programs to switch between various "look and feel" implementations, such as the native Windows or Macintosh look and feel or a cross-platform look and feel called "Metal". A Windows button has a different size than a Macintosh or Metal button.

2. The program gets translated into a different language. Button and label strings can become much longer (in German) or shorter (in Chinese).

> A layout manager arranges the components in a container.

Suppose a programmer painstakingly defines the pixel position for all components to have them line up nicely. Then the look and feel or the language changes and the components no longer line up nicely. The Java layout managers are a better idea. By choosing an appropriate layout manager, you describe how the components should be aligned. The layout manager looks at the sizes of the components and computes their positions.

5.4.1 — Using Predefined Layout Managers

There are several built-in layout managers in Java (see Figure 6).

- The FlowLayout lays out components left to right, then starts a new row when there isn't enough room in the current one.

- The BoxLayout lays out components horizontally or vertically without starting additional rows and columns.

- The BorderLayout has five areas, NORTH, SOUTH, EAST, WEST, and CENTER. You specify in which area each component should appear. Unlike the FlowLayout and BoxLayout, the BorderLayout grows each component to fill its area. Not all of the areas need to be occupied. It is common to leave one or more of the areas completely empty.

- The GridLayout arranges components in a rectangular grid. All components are resized to an identical size.

- The GridBagLayout also arranges components in a grid, but the rows and columns can have different sizes and components can span multiple rows and columns.

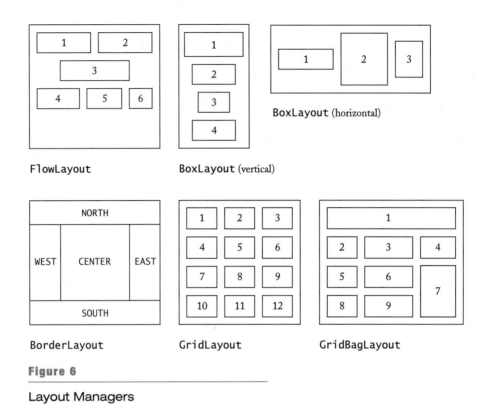

FlowLayout   BoxLayout (vertical)   BoxLayout (horizontal)

BorderLayout   GridLayout   GridBagLayout

Figure 6

Layout Managers

To set a layout manager, pick an appropriate layout manager class and add it to a container. For example,

```
JPanel keyPanel = new JPanel();
keyPanel.setLayout(new GridLayout(4, 3));
```

Figure 7 shows the relationships between these classes.

Let's put layout managers to work and write a GUI front end for the voice mail system of Chapter 2. We want to arrange the components so that they resemble a real telephone,

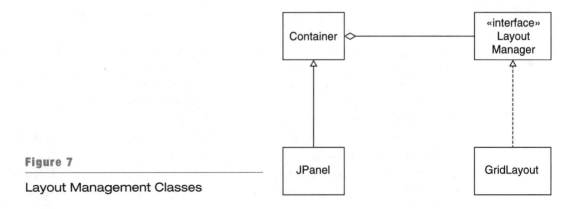

Figure 7

Layout Management Classes

with the speaker on top, the keypad in the middle, and the microphone on the bottom (see Figure 8). (The speaker and microphone are simulated with text areas.) Figure 9 shows the layout of the frame window.

You will find the complete code for the telephone layout at the end of this section. Because there are so many components to lay out, the code looks complicated. However, the basic concepts are straightforward.

When a user interface has a large number of components, it can be difficult to use a single layout manager to achieve the desired layout effect. However, by nesting *panels*, each with its own layout manager, you can achieve complex layouts easily. A panel is simply a container without visible decorations that can hold components.

First, note that the keypad is arranged in a grid. Clearly, the grid layout is the appropriate layout manager for this arrangement. We will therefore add the buttons to a panel that is controlled by a GridLayout.

```
JPanel keyPanel = new JPanel();
keyPanel.setLayout(new GridLayout(4, 3));
for (int i = 0; i < 12; i++)
{
   JButton keyButton = new JButton(. . .);
   keyPanel.add(keyButton);
   keyButton.addActionListener(. . .);
}
```

Figure 8

Telephone Handset

Figure 9

A GUI Front End for the Mail System

Figure 10

Laying out the Microphone
Components

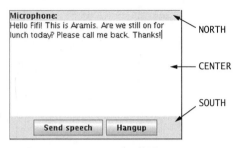

Just as we collect the keypad buttons in a panel, we will use a separate panel to hold the label and the text area for the simulated speaker. We use a border layout to place the label in the NORTH position and the text area in the CENTER position.

```
JPanel speakerPanel = new JPanel();
speakerPanel.setLayout(new BorderLayout());
speakerPanel.add(new JLabel("Speaker:"), BorderLayout.NORTH);
speakerField = new JTextArea(10, 25);
speakerPanel.add(speakerField, BorderLayout.CENTER);
```

We'll apply the same layout manager to the simulated microphone. However, now we need to add two buttons to the SOUTH area. Since each of the areas of a border layout can only hold a single component, we place the buttons inside a panel and add that button panel to the SOUTH area of the microphone panel (see Figure 10).

Finally, we need to stack up the panels for the speaker, keypad, and microphone. We take advantage of the fact that the default content pane of a frame has a border layout and add the three panels to the NORTH, CENTER, and SOUTH areas of the content pane (see Figure 11).

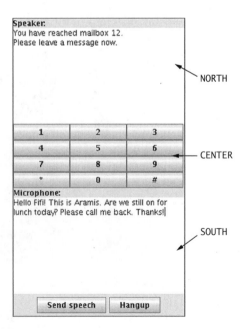

Figure 11

The Content Pane of the
Telephone Frame

In Chapter 2, we defined a `Telephone` class for reading simulated voice and key presses from `System.in` and sending simulated speech output to `System.out`. Remarkably, you can simply replace that class with the new `Telephone` class. None of the other classes of the voice mail system need to be changed.

Ch5/mailgui/Telephone.java

```java
1  import java.awt.*;
2  import java.awt.event.*;
3  import javax.swing.*;
4
5  /**
6      Presents a phone GUI for the voice mail system.
7  */
8  public class Telephone
9  {
10     /**
11         Constructs a telephone with a speaker, keypad,
12         and microphone.
13     */
14     public Telephone()
15     {
16        JPanel speakerPanel = new JPanel();
17        speakerPanel.setLayout(new BorderLayout());
18        speakerPanel.add(new JLabel("Speaker:"),
19            BorderLayout.NORTH);
20        speakerField = new JTextArea(10, 25);
21        speakerPanel.add(speakerField,
22            BorderLayout.CENTER);
23        String keyLabels = "123456789*0#";
24        JPanel keyPanel = new JPanel();
25        keyPanel.setLayout(new GridLayout(4, 3));
26        for (int i = 0; i < keyLabels.length(); i++)
27        {
28           final String label = keyLabels.substring(i, i + 1);
29           JButton keyButton = new JButton(label);
30           keyPanel.add(keyButton);
31           keyButton.addActionListener(new
32              ActionListener()
33              {
34                 public void actionPerformed(ActionEvent event)
35                 {
36                    connect.dial(label);
37                 }
38              });
39        }
40
41        final JTextArea microphoneField = new JTextArea(10,25);
42
43        JButton speechButton = new JButton("Send speech");
44        speechButton.addActionListener(new
45           ActionListener()
46           {
```

```
47              public void actionPerformed(ActionEvent event)
48              {
49                  connect.record(microphoneField.getText());
50                  microphoneField.setText("");
51              }
52          });
53
54          JButton hangupButton = new JButton("Hangup");
55          hangupButton.addActionListener(new
56              ActionListener()
57              {
58                  public void actionPerformed(ActionEvent event)
59                  {
60                      connect.hangup();
61                  }
62              });
63
64          JPanel buttonPanel = new JPanel();
65          buttonPanel.add(speechButton);
66          buttonPanel.add(hangupButton);
67
68          JPanel microphonePanel = new JPanel();
69          microphonePanel.setLayout(new BorderLayout());
70          microphonePanel.add(new JLabel("Microphone:"),
71                  BorderLayout.NORTH);
72          microphonePanel.add(microphoneField, BorderLayout.CENTER);
73          microphonePanel.add(buttonPanel, BorderLayout.SOUTH);
74
75          JFrame frame = new JFrame();
76          frame.setDefaultCloseOperation(JFrame.EXIT_ON_CLOSE);
77          frame.add(speakerPanel, BorderLayout.NORTH);
78          frame.add(keyPanel, BorderLayout.CENTER);
79          frame.add(microphonePanel, BorderLayout.SOUTH);
80
81          frame.pack();
82          frame.setVisible(true);
83      }
84
85      /**
86          Give instructions to the mail system user.
87      */
88      public void speak(String output)
89      {
90          speakerField.setText(output);
91      }
92
93      public void run(Connection c)
94      {
95          connect = c;
96      }
97
98      private JTextArea speakerField;
99      private Connection connect;
100 }
```

5.4.2 — **Implementing a Custom Layout Manager**

It is not difficult to write your own layout manager. Figure 12 shows a custom layout manager that aligns the odd-numbered components towards the right and the even-numbered components towards the left. This layout is useful for simple forms.

A layout manager must support the `LayoutManager` interface type:

```
public interface LayoutManager
{
    Dimension minimumLayoutSize(Container parent);
    Dimension preferredLayoutSize(Container parent);
    void layoutContainer(Container parent);
    void addLayoutComponent(String name, Component comp);
    void removeLayoutComponent(Component comp);
}
```

The `minimumLayoutSize` and `preferredLayoutSize` methods determine the minimum and preferred size of the container when the components are laid out. The `layout-Container` method lays out the components in the container, by setting the position and size for each component. The last two methods exist for historical reasons and can be implemented as do-nothing methods.

When you write a layout manager, start out with the `preferredLayoutSize` method. Compute the preferred width and height of your layout by combining the widths and heights of the individual components. For example, the form layout manager computes the width as follows: It finds the widest component on the left and the widest component on the right. Then it adds their widths and adds a small gap value. The computation of the height is slightly different. The height is obtained by adding up the heights of all rows. The height of each row is the maximum of the heights of the components in the row. Have a look at the `preferredLayoutSize` computation in `FormLayout.java` at the end of this section. It is not difficult to follow the process.

When the container is ready to lay out its contents, it calls the `layoutContainer` method of its layout manager. Then the layout manager positions the components according to its rules. The exact positioning is more tedious than just computing the preferred width, but the concepts are the same. If you look at the `layoutContainer` method of the `Form-Layout`, you can see that the method computes the positions of each component and then calls the `setBounds` method to put the component into the correct location. You don't have to worry about the details of the computation. The point of showing you this example is simply to demonstrate how flexible layout management can be. This flexibility is a direct consequence of separating layout management into a separate class.

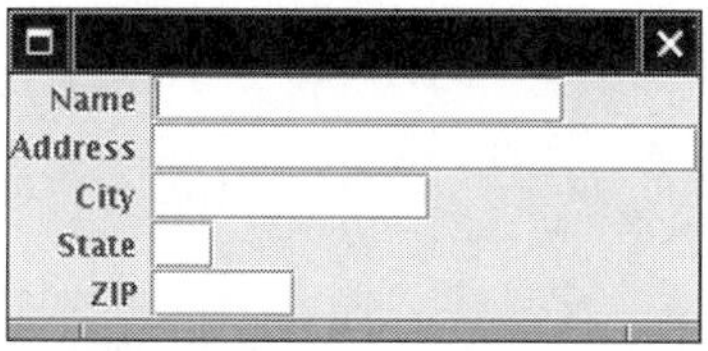

Figure 12

The FormLayout Custom
Layout Manager

The FormLayoutTester program shows how to put the custom layout to work. Simply set the layout manager of the content pane to a FormLayout object. Then add the components to the container.

Ch5/layout/FormLayout.java

```
 1  import java.awt.*;
 2
 3  /**
 4      A layout manager that lays out components along a central axis.
 5  */
 6  public class FormLayout implements LayoutManager
 7  {
 8     public Dimension preferredLayoutSize(Container parent)
 9     {
10        Component[] components = parent.getComponents();
11        left = 0;
12        right = 0;
13        height = 0;
14        for (int i = 0; i < components.length; i += 2)
15        {
16           Component cleft = components[i];
17           Component cright = components[i + 1];
18
19           Dimension dleft = cleft.getPreferredSize();
20           Dimension dright = cright.getPreferredSize();
21           left = Math.max(left, dleft.width);
22           right = Math.max(right, dright.width);
23           height = height + Math.max(dleft.height,
24                 dright.height);
25        }
26        return new Dimension(left + GAP + right, height);
27     }
28
29     public Dimension minimumLayoutSize(Container parent)
30     {
31        return preferredLayoutSize(parent);
32     }
33
34     public void layoutContainer(Container parent)
35     {
36        preferredLayoutSize(parent); // Sets left, right
37
38        Component[] components = parent.getComponents();
39
40        Insets insets = parent.getInsets();
41        int xcenter = insets.left + left;
42        int y = insets.top;
43
44        for (int i = 0; i < components.length; i += 2)
45        {
46           Component cleft = components[i];
47           Component cright = components[i + 1];
```

```
48
49            Dimension dleft = cleft.getPreferredSize();
50            Dimension dright = cright.getPreferredSize();
51
52            int height = Math.max(dleft.height, dright.height);
53
54            cleft.setBounds(xcenter - dleft.width, y + (height
55                  - dleft.height) / 2, dleft.width, dleft.height);
56
57            cright.setBounds(xcenter + GAP, y + (height
58                  - dright.height) / 2, dright.width, dright.height);
59         y += height;
60      }
61   }
62
63   public void addLayoutComponent(String name, Component comp)
64   {}
65
66   public void removeLayoutComponent(Component comp)
67   {}
68
69   private int left;
70   private int right;
71   private int height;
72   private static final int GAP = 6;
73 }
```

Ch5/layout/FormLayoutTester.java

```
1  import java.awt.*;
2  import javax.swing.*;
3
4  public class FormLayoutTester
5  {
6     public static void main(String[] args)
7     {
8        JFrame frame = new JFrame();
9        frame.setLayout(new FormLayout());
10       frame.add(new JLabel("Name"));
11       frame.add(new JTextField(15));
12       frame.add(new JLabel("Address"));
13       frame.add(new JTextField(20));
14       frame.add(new JLabel("City"));
15       frame.add(new JTextField(10));
16       frame.add(new JLabel("State"));
17       frame.add(new JTextField(2));
18       frame.add(new JLabel("ZIP"));
19       frame.add(new JTextField(5));
20       frame.setDefaultCloseOperation(JFrame.EXIT_ON_CLOSE);
21       frame.pack();
22       frame.setVisible(true);
23    }
24 }
```

5.4.3 — The STRATEGY Pattern

> The STRATEGY pattern teaches how to supply variants of an algorithm.

You have seen how the layout manager concept gives user interface programmers a great deal of flexibility. You can use one of the standard layout manager classes or provide a custom layout manager. To produce a particular layout, you simply make an object of the layout manager class and give it to the container. When the container needs to execute the layout algorithm, it calls the appropriate methods of the layout manager object. This is an example of the STRATEGY pattern. The STRATEGY pattern applies whenever you want to allow a client to supply an algorithm. The pattern tells us to place the essential steps of the algorithm in a strategy interface type. By supplying objects of different classes that implement the strategy interface type, the algorithm can be varied.

PATTERN

◆ **STRATEGY**

Context

1. A class (which we'll call the *context* class) can benefit from different variants of an algorithm.
2. Clients of the context class sometimes want to supply custom versions of the algorithm.

Solution

1. Define an interface type that is an abstraction for the algorithm. We'll call this interface type the *strategy*.
2. Concrete strategy classes implement the strategy interface type. Each strategy class implements a version of the algorithm.
3. The client supplies a concrete strategy object to the context class.
4. Whenever the algorithm needs to be executed, the context class calls the appropriate methods of the strategy object.

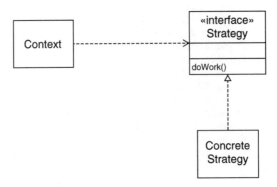

Here is the relationship between the names in the STRATEGY design pattern and the layout management manifestation.

Name in Design Pattern	Actual Name
Context	Container
Strategy	LayoutManager
ConcreteStrategy	A layout manager such as BorderLayout
doWork()	A method of the LayoutManager interface type such as layoutContainer

In Chapter 4, you encountered a different manifestation of the STRATEGY pattern. Recall how you can pass a Comparator object to the Collections.sort method to specify how elements should be compared.

```
Comparator comp = new CountryComparatorByName();
Collections.sort(countries, comp);
```

The comparator object encapsulates the comparison algorithm. By varying the comparator, you can sort by different criteria. Here is the mapping from the pattern names to the actual names:

Name in Design Pattern	Actual Name
Context	Collections
Strategy	Comparator
ConcreteStrategy	A class that implements the Comparator interface type
doWork()	compare()

5.5   Components, Containers, and the COMPOSITE Pattern

In the preceding section, you saw how one can use layout managers to organize components in a container. As you have seen in the telephone example, you often need to group components into a panel in order to achieve a satisfactory layout.

> The COMPOSITE pattern teaches how to combine several objects into an object that has the same behavior as its parts.

There is just one technical issue. User interface components are contained in containers. If a JPanel can contain other components, it must be a Container. But if we want to add it to the content pane, it must also be a Component. Can a container itself be a component?

The COMPOSITE pattern gives a solution to this problem. This pattern addresses situations where primitive objects can be grouped into composite objects, and the composites themselves are considered primitive objects.

There are many examples of this pattern. Later in this chapter you will see a program that deals with selling items. It is sometimes useful to sell a *bundle* of items as if it were a single item. The solution is to make a Bundle class that contains a collection of items and that also implements the Item interface type.

Similarly, the Container class contains components, and it also extends the Component class.

One characteristic of the COMPOSITE design pattern is how a method of the composite object does its work. It must apply the method to all of its primitive objects and then combine the results.

For example, to compute the price of a bundle, the bundle class computes the prices of each of its items and returns the sum of these values.

Similarly, consider the task of computing the preferred size of a container. The container must obtain the preferred sizes of all components in the container and combine the results. In the preceding section, you saw how a container carries out that work by delegating it to a layout manager.

PATTERN

COMPOSITE

Context

1. Primitive objects can be combined into composite objects.
2. Clients treat a composite object as a primitive object.

Solution

1. Define an interface type that is an abstraction for the primitive objects.
2. A composite object contains a collection of primitive objects.
3. Both primitive classes and composite classes implement that interface type.
4. When implementing a method from the interface type, the composite class applies the method to its primitive objects and combines the results.

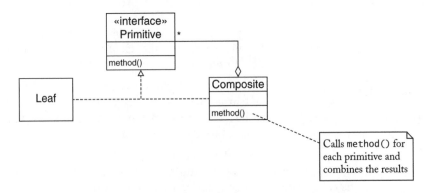

As with the previous patterns, we show how the names in the design pattern map to the the Swing user interface toolkit.

Name in Design Pattern	Actual Name
Primitive	Component
Composite	Container or a subclass such as JPanel
Leaf	A component that has no children such as JButton or JTextArea
method()	A method of the Component interface such as getPreferredSize

5.6   Scroll Bars and the DECORATOR Pattern

When a component contains more information than can be shown on the screen, it becomes necessary to add scroll bars (see Figure 13). Scroll bars make the most sense for text areas and lists, but other components, such as tables and trees, can also benefit from them.

For example, here is how you add scroll bars to a text area:

```
JTextArea area = new JTextArea(10, 25);
JScrollPane scroller = new JScrollPane(area);
```

Figure 14 shows the relationships between these classes. Because the scroll bars add functionality to the underlying text area, they are called a *decoration*.

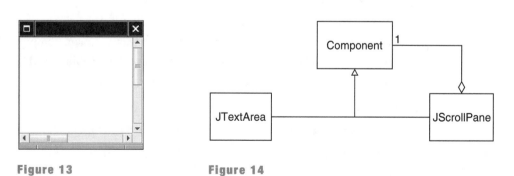

Figure 13

Scroll Bars

Figure 14

Adding a Scroll Bar to a Text Area

> The DECORATOR pattern teaches how to form a class that adds functionality to another class while keeping its interface.

You can decorate any component with a scroll pane, not just text areas. The important point is that a JScrollPane decorates a component *and is again a component.* Therefore, all of the functionality of the Component class still applies to scroll bars. For example, you can add the scroll pane into a container.

```
contentPane.add(scroller, BorderLayout.CENTER);
```

The JScrollPane class is an example of the DECORATOR pattern. The DECORATOR pattern applies whenever a class enhances the functionality of another class while preserving its interface. A key aspect of the DECORATOR pattern is that the decorated component is entirely passive. The text area does nothing to acquire scroll bars.

An alternate design would be to make the JTextArea class responsible for supplying scroll bars. An older version of that class (called TextArea without a J) does just that. If you want scroll bars, you have to pass a flag to the constructor.

There are two advantages to using decorators. First, it would be a bother if lots of different components (such as text areas, panels, tables, and so on) would each have to independently supply an option for scroll bars. It is much better if these component classes can wash their hands of that responsibility and leave it to a separate class.

Moreover, there is a potentially unbounded set of decorations, and the component classes can't anticipate all of them. Maybe you want a zoom bar, a slider that automatically shrinks or magnifies a component? There is no support for zoom bars in the Swing user interface toolkit, but nothing prevents an enterprising programmer from supplying a zoom bar decorator.

As with the COMPOSITE pattern, we note that the decorator implements a method from the component interface by invoking the same method on the component and then augmenting the result. For example, the paint method of a scroll pane paints the decorated component and also the scroll bars.

PATTERN

♦ ████ **DECORATOR** ████ ██████████████████

Context

1. You want to enhance the behavior of a class. We'll call it the component class.
2. A decorated component can be used in the same way as a plain component.
3. The component class does not want to take on the responsibility of the decoration.
4. There may be an open-ended set of possible decorations.

Solution

1. Define an interface type that is an abstraction for the component.
2. Concrete component classes implement this interface type.
3. Decorator classes also implement this interface type.
4. A decorator object manages the component object that it decorates.

5. When implementing a method from the component interface type, the decorator class applies the method to the decorated component and combines the result with the effect of the decoration.

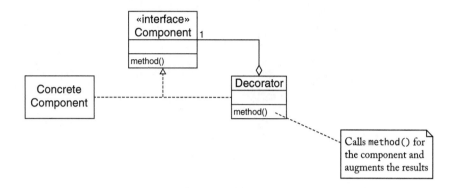

Superficially, the DECORATOR pattern looks very similar to the COMPOSITE pattern. However, there is an essential difference. A decorator enhances the behavior of a *single* component, whereas a composite collects *multiple* components. There is also a difference in intent. A decorator aims to enhance, whereas a composite merely collects.

Here is the mapping of pattern names to actual names in the case of the JScrollPane decorator.

Name in Design Pattern	Actual Name
Component	Component
ConcreteComponent	JTextArea
Decorator	JScrollPane
method()	A method of the Component interface. For example, the paint method paints a part of the decorated component and the scroll bars.

5.6.1 — Stream Decorators

Another example for the DECORATOR pattern is the set of stream filters in the I/O library. The Reader class supports basic input operations: reading a single character or an array of characters. The FileReader subclass implements these methods, reading characters from a file. However, a FileReader has no method for reading a line of input.

The BufferedReader class adds the ability of reading line-oriented input to any reader. Its readLine method keeps calling read on the underlying reader until the end of a line is encountered. Here is how you use it:

```
BufferedReader in  = new BufferedReader(new FileReader("input.txt"));
String firstLine = in.readLine();
```

The `BufferedReader` class adds another useful service. It asks the reader that it decorates to read data in larger blocks. The `BufferedReader`'s read method then gives out the characters that are stored in the buffer. This buffering increases efficiency.

The `BufferedReader` class is a decorator. It takes an arbitrary reader and yields a reader with additional capabilities.

Name in Design Pattern	Actual Name
Component	Reader
ConcreteComponent	FileReader
Decorator	BufferedReader
method()	The read method. Calling read on a buffered reader invokes read on the component reader if the buffer is empty.

The Java library contains a number of decorators for readers. The `PushbackReader` is designed for applications that require you to "peek ahead" at input. For example, suppose you process input and need to skip past a sequence of space characters. You read characters until you find a character that is not a space. But now you wish that you hadn't read that character because another part of the program wants to process it. With a `PushbackReader`, you can call the unread method to push the character back.

```
PushbackReader reader = new PushbackReader(
      new FileReader("input.txt"));
. . .
char c = reader.read();
if (. . .) reader.unread(c);
```

A `PushbackReader` simply keeps a small buffer of pushed back characters. Its `read` method looks inside that buffer before reading from the decorated reader.

Other common decorators for readers are decryptors and decompressors (see Exercise 5.12).

Of course, writers can be decorated as well. A basic `Writer` simply sends characters to some destination. The `PrintWriter` decorator takes on the responsibility of formatting numbers and strings.

5.7   How to Recognize Patterns

Students of object-oriented design often have trouble recognizing patterns. The descriptions of many patterns look superficially alike. As we discussed, the descriptions of the COMPOSITE and DECORATOR patterns appear to be almost identical. As you encounter additional patterns, you will find it increasingly difficult to tell them apart if you merely try to memorize the pattern descriptions.

One solution is to focus on the *intent* of the pattern. The intent of the COMPOSITE pattern is to group components into a whole, whereas the intent of the DECORATOR pattern is to decorate a component. The intent of the STRATEGY pattern is completely different, namely to wrap an algorithm into a class.

Another solution is to remember a place where the pattern is put to use. Many programmers remember the STRATEGY pattern as the pattern for layout managers and DECORATOR as the pattern for scroll bars. Of course, a pattern is more general than any of its manifestations, but there is nothing wrong with using the examples as a memorization aid.

Students often fall into another trap. The patterns have such intuitive names (such as OBSERVER or STRATEGY) that it is tempting to suspect their usage in many situations where they don't actually apply. Just because something seems strategic does not mean that the STRATEGY pattern is at work. Patterns are not vague concepts. They are very specific. The STRATEGY pattern only applies when a number of conditions are fulfilled:

- A context class must want to use different variants of an algorithm.
- There must be an interface type that is an abstraction for the algorithm.
- Concrete strategy classes must implement the strategy interface type.
- A client must supply an object of a concrete strategy class to the context class.
- The context class must use the strategy object to invoke the algorithm.

In other words, you should turn every statement in the "Context" and "Solution" parts of the pattern description into a litmus test.

Let's put this litmus test to work in another situation.

Figure 15 shows a decoration that you can apply to a component—a *border*. Typically, you place a border around a panel that holds related buttons. But you can apply a border to any Swing component. There are a number of classes that implement the `Border` interface type, such as the `EtchedBorder` and `BevelBorder` classes. Pass an object of any of these classes to the `setBorder` method:

```
Border b = new EtchedBorder();
panel.setBorder(b);
```

Figure 15

Borders Around Panels

While a border is undeniably decorative, it is *not* a manifestation of the DECORATOR pattern. To see why, let's go through the context elements of the DECORATOR pattern.

- You want to enhance the behavior of a class. We'll call it the component class.

This condition holds true. We want to enhance the behavior of a Swing component.

- A decorated component can be used in the same way as a plain component.

This condition still holds true. A component with a border is a component.

- The component class does not want to take on the responsibility of the decoration.

This condition doesn't apply here. The component class has a setBorder method. It is responsible for applying the border.

Thus, Swing borders are not a manifestation of the DECORATOR pattern.

5.8   Putting Patterns to Work

In this section, we will put several patterns to work in a simple application. We will implement an *invoice* that is composed of *line items*. A line item has a description and a price. Here is the LineItem interface type:

Ch5/invoice/LineItem.java

```
1  /**
2      A line item in an invoice.
3  */
4  public interface LineItem
5  {
6      /**
7          Gets the price of this line item.
8          @return the price
9      */
10     double getPrice();
11
12     /**
13         Gets the description of this line item.
14         @return the description
15     */
16     String toString();
17 }
```

We will encounter different kinds of line items. The simplest one is a product. Here is the Product class:

Ch5/invoice/Product.java

```
1  /**
2      A product with a price and description.
3  */
4  public class Product implements LineItem
5  {
```

```
 6    /**
 7        Constructs a product.
 8        @param description the description
 9        @param price the price
10    */
11    public Product(String description, double price)
12    {
13        this.description = description;
14        this.price = price;
15    }
16    public double getPrice() { return price; }
17    public String toString() { return description; }
18    private String description;
19    private double price;
20 }
```

 NOTE   Because roundoff errors are inevitable with floating-point numbers, it is actually not a good idea to use a `double` variable to store a monetary value. For financial accuracy, it would be better to store the price in pennies, as an `int` or `long` value, or to use the `BigDecimal` class.

Now let's consider a more complex situation. Sometimes, stores will sell *bundles* of related items (such as a stereo system consisting of a tuner, amplifier, CD player, and speakers). It should be possible to add a bundle to an invoice. That is, a bundle contains line items and is again a line item. This is precisely the situation of the COMPOSITE pattern (see Figure 16).

The COMPOSITE pattern teaches us that the `Bundle` class should implement the `LineItem` interface type. When implementing a `LineItem` method, the `Bundle` class should apply the method to the individual items and combine the result. For example, observe how the `getPrice` method of the `Bundle` class adds the prices of the items in the bundle.

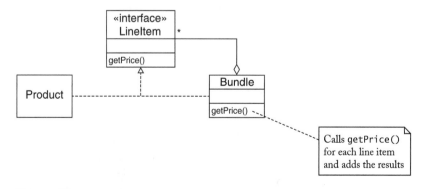

Figure 16

A Bundle of Line Items

Here is the code for the Bundle class.

Ch5/invoice/Bundle.java

```java
1  import java.util.*;
2
3  /**
4     A bundle of line items that is again a line item.
5  */
6  public class Bundle implements LineItem
7  {
8     /**
9        Constructs a bundle with no items.
10    */
11    public Bundle() { items = new ArrayList<LineItem>(); }
12
13    /**
14       Adds an item to the bundle.
15       @param item the item to add
16    */
17    public void add(LineItem item) { items.add(item); }
18
19    public double getPrice()
20    {
21       double price = 0;
22
23       for (LineItem item : items)
24          price += item.getPrice();
25       return price;
26    }
27
28    public String toString()
29    {
30       String description = "Bundle: ";
31       for (int i = 0; i < items.size(); i++)
32       {
33          if (i > 0) description += ", ";
34          description += items.get(i).toString();
35       }
36       return description;
37    }
38
39    private ArrayList<LineItem> items;
40 }
```

A store may give a discount for a bundle, or, for that matter, for other line items. We can use the DECORATOR pattern to implement discounts. That pattern teaches us to design a decorator class that holds a LineItem object and whose methods enhance the LineItem methods. For example, the getPrice method of the DiscountedItem class calls the getPrice method of the discounted item and then applies the discount (see Figure 17).

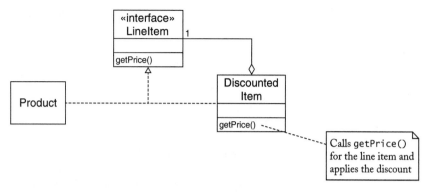

Figure 17

The `DiscountedItem` Decorator

Here is the code for the `DiscountedItem` class.

Ch5/invoice/DiscountedItem.java

```java
 1  /**
 2      A decorator for an item that applies a discount.
 3  */
 4  public class DiscountedItem implements LineItem
 5  {
 6     /**
 7         Constructs a discounted item.
 8         @param item the item to be discounted
 9         @param discount the discount percentage
10     */
11     public DiscountedItem(LineItem item, double discount)
12     {
13        this.item = item;
14        this.discount = discount;
15     }
16
17     public double getPrice()
18     {
19        return item.getPrice() * (1 - discount / 100);
20     }
21
22     public String toString()
23     {
24        return item.toString() + " (Discount " + discount
25           + "%)";
26     }
27
28     private LineItem item;
29     private double discount;
30  }
```

Now let's look at the Invoice class. An invoice holds a collection of line items.

```
public class Invoice
{
    public void addItem(LineItem item) { items.add(item); }
    . . .
    private ArrayList<LineItem> items;
}
```

Our sample program will have a graphical user interface in which we show the invoice text in a text area. When items are added to the invoice, the invoice text should be updated. Of course, we could make the "Add" button responsible for updating the text area, but we prefer a solution that decouples adding items from the invoice display. If we just knew when new items are added to the invoice, then we could simply refresh the text area at that time. The OBSERVER pattern teaches us how to proceed.

1. Define an observer interface type. Observer classes must implement this interface type.
2. The subject maintains a collection of observer objects.
3. The subject class supplies methods for attaching observers.
4. Whenever an event occurs, the subject notifies all observers.

These steps are easy to follow. Rather than designing an interface type from scratch, use the ChangeListener type from the Swing library:

```
public interface ChangeListener
{
    void stateChanged(ChangeEvent event);
}
```

The subject is the Invoice class. You are told to supply a collection of observers and a method to attach observers.

```
public class Invoice
{
    public void addChangeListener(ChangeListener listener)
    {
        listeners.add(listener);
    }
    . . .
    private ArrayList<ChangeListener> listeners;
}
```

Furthermore, when the invoice changes, you must notify all observers. This is easily achieved by appending the following code to the addItem method:

```
ChangeEvent event = new ChangeEvent(this);
for (ChangeListener listener : listeners)
    listener.stateChanged(event);
```

This completes the modifications to the Invoice class that are needed to support the OBSERVER pattern.

We were motivated to use that pattern because we wanted the text area to update itself automatically whenever the invoice changes. That goal is now easily achieved (see Figure 18).

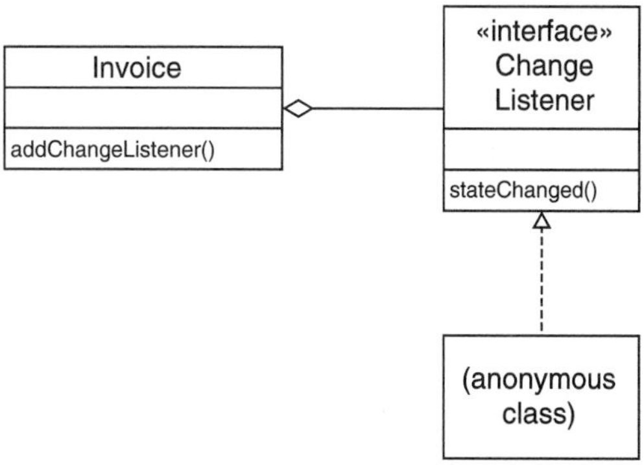

Figure 18

Observing the Invoice

```java
final Invoice invoice = new Invoice();
final JTextArea textArea = new JTextArea(20, 40);
ChangeListener listener = new
   ChangeListener()
   {
      public void stateChanged(ChangeEvent event)
      {
         String formattedInvoice = . . .;
         textArea.setText(formattedInvoice);
      }
   };
invoice.addChangeListener(listener);
```

Clients of the Invoice class may need to know the line items inside an invoice. However, we do not want to reveal the structure of the Invoice class. For example, it would be unwise to return the items array list. That simple-minded approach causes problems if we later change the internal implementation, storing the items in another data structure or in a relational database table. Instead, we will follow the ITERATOR pattern.

For simplicity, we make use of the Iterator interface of the Java library. This interface has three methods:

```java
public interface Iterator<E>
{
   boolean hasNext();
   E next();
   void remove();
}
```

The remove method is described as an "optional operation". When defining an iterator class, this method cannot be skipped because it belongs to the interface type. But you can implement it trivially by throwing an UnsupportedOperationException. We will discuss the optional operations of the Java library in more detail in Chapter 8.

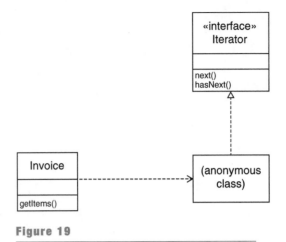

Figure 19

Iterating Through the Items of an Invoice

The following method returns an iterator. The returned object belongs to an anonymous class that implements the Iterator interface (see Figure 19). If you follow the definitions of the next and hasNext methods, you can see how the iterator object traverses the array list.

```
public Iterator<LineItem> getItems()
{
   return new
      Iterator<LineItem>()
      {
         public boolean hasNext()
         {
            return current < items.size();
         }

         public LineItem next()
         {
            LineItem r = items.get(current);
            current++;
            return r;
         }

         public void remove()
         {
            throw new UnsupportedOperationException();
         }

         private int current = 0;
      };
}
```

NOTE   The `ArrayList` class has an `iterator` method that yields an iterator for traversing the array list. The `getItems` method could have simply returned `items.iterator()`. We chose to implement the iterator explicitly so that you can see the inner workings of an iterator object.

Figure 20

The `InvoiceTester` Program

Finally, let's take a closer look at the task of formatting an invoice. Our sample program formats an invoice very simply (see Figure 20). As you can see, we have a string "INVOICE" on top, followed by the descriptions and prices of the line items, and a total at the bottom.

However, that simple format may not be good enough for all applications. Perhaps we want to show the invoice on a Web page. Then the format should contain HTML tags, and the line items should be rows of a table. Thus, it is apparent that there is a need for multiple algorithms for formatting an invoice.

The STRATEGY pattern addresses this issue. This pattern teaches us to design an interface to abstract the essential steps of the algorithm. Here is such an interface:

 Ch5/invoice/InvoiceFormatter.java

```
1  /**
2      This interface describes the tasks that an invoice
3      formatter needs to carry out.
4  */
5  public interface InvoiceFormatter
6  {
7      /**
8          Formats the header of the invoice.
9          @return the invoice header
10     */
```

```
11    String formatHeader();
12
13    /**
14       Formats a line item of the invoice.
15       @return  the formatted line item
16    */
17    String formatLineItem(LineItem item);
18
19    /**
20       Formats the footer of the invoice.
21       @return  the invoice footer
22    */
23    String formatFooter();
24 }
```

We make a strategy object available to the format method of the Invoice class:

```
public String format(InvoiceFormatter formatter)
{
   String r = formatter.formatHeader();
   Iterator<LineItem> iter = getItems();
   while (iter.hasNext())
   {
      LineItem item = iter.next();
      r += formatter.formatLineItem(item);
   }
   return r + formatter.formatFooter();
}
```

The SimpleFormatter class implements the strategy interface type. Figure 21 shows the relationships between the classes used for formatting.

This particular version provides a very simple formatting algorithm. Exercise 5.16 asks you to supply an invoice formatter that produces HTML output.

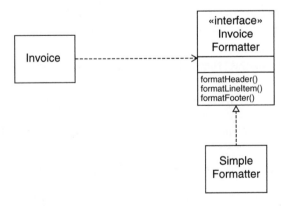

Figure 21

Formatting an Invoice

Ch5/invoice/SimpleFormatter.java

```
1  /**
2      A simple invoice formatter.
3  */
4  public class SimpleFormatter implements InvoiceFormatter
5  {
6     public String formatHeader()
7     {
8        total = 0;
9        return "      I N V O I C E\n\n\n";
10    }
11
12    public String formatLineItem(LineItem item)
13    {
14       total += item.getPrice();
15       return (String.format(
16           "%s: $%.2f\n", item.toString(), item.getPrice()));
17    }
18
19    public String formatFooter()
20    {
21       return (String.format("\n\nTOTAL DUE: $%.2f\n", total));
22    }
23
24    private double total;
25 }
```

This concludes the design of the invoice program. We have made use of five separate patterns during the design. Here are the complete `Invoice` class and the test program.

Ch5/invoice/Invoice.java

```
1  import java.util.*;
2  import javax.swing.event.*;
3
4  /**
5      An invoice for a sale, consisting of line items.
6  */
7  public class Invoice
8  {
9     /**
10        Constructs a blank invoice.
11    */
12    public Invoice()
13    {
14       items = new ArrayList<LineItem>();
15       listeners = new ArrayList<ChangeListener>();
16    }
17
18    /**
19        Adds an item to the invoice.
20        @param item the item to add
21    */
22    public void addItem(LineItem item)
23    {
```

```
24          items.add(item);
25          // Notify all observers of the change to the invoice
26          ChangeEvent event = new ChangeEvent(this);
27          for (ChangeListener listener : listeners)
28             listener.stateChanged(event);
29       }
30
31       /**
32          Adds a change listener to the invoice.
33          @param listener the change listener to add
34       */
35       public void addChangeListener(ChangeListener listener)
36       {
37          listeners.add(listener);
38       }
39
40       /**
41          Gets an iterator that iterates through the items.
42          @return an iterator for the items
43       */
44       public Iterator<LineItem> getItems()
45       {
46          return new
47             Iterator<LineItem>()
48             {
49                public boolean hasNext()
50                {
51                   return current < items.size();
52                }
53
54                public LineItem next()
55                {
56                   return items.get(current++);
57                }
58
59                public void remove()
60                {
61                   throw new UnsupportedOperationException();
62                }
63
64                private int current = 0;
65             };
66       }
67
68       public String format(InvoiceFormatter formatter)
69       {
70          String r = formatter.formatHeader();
71          Iterator<LineItem>iter = getItems();
72          while (iter.hasNext())
73             r += formatter.formatLineItem(iter.next());
74          return r + formatter.formatFooter();
75       }
76
77       private ArrayList<LineItem> items;
78       private ArrayList<ChangeListener> listeners;
79 }
```

Ch5/invoice/InvoiceTester.java

```
 1  import java.awt.*;
 2  import java.awt.event.*;
 3  import javax.swing.*;
 4  import javax.swing.event.*;
 5
 6  /**
 7     A program that tests the invoice classes.
 8  */
 9  public class InvoiceTester
10  {
11     public static void main(String[] args)
12     {
13        final Invoice invoice = new Invoice();
14        final InvoiceFormatter formatter = new SimpleFormatter();
15
16        // This text area will contain the formatted invoice
17        final JTextArea textArea = new JTextArea(20, 40);
18
19        // When the invoice changes, update the text area
20        ChangeListener listener = new
21           ChangeListener()
22           {
23              public void stateChanged(ChangeEvent event)
24              {
25                 textArea.setText(invoice.format(formatter));
26              }
27           };
28        invoice.addChangeListener(listener);
29
30        // Add line items to a combo box
31        final JComboBox combo = new JComboBox();
32        Product hammer = new Product("Hammer", 19.95);
33        Product nails = new Product("Assorted nails", 9.95);
34        combo.addItem(hammer);
35        Bundle bundle = new Bundle();
36        bundle.add(hammer);
37        bundle.add(nails);
38        combo.addItem(new DiscountedItem(bundle, 10));
39
40        // Make a button for adding the currently selected
41        // item to the invoice
42        JButton addButton = new JButton("Add");
43        addButton.addActionListener(new
44           ActionListener()
45           {
46              public void actionPerformed(ActionEvent event)
47              {
48                 LineItem item = (LineItem) combo.getSelectedItem();
49                 invoice.addItem(item);
50              }
51           });
52
53        // Put the combo box and the add button into a panel
54        JPanel panel = new JPanel();
```

```
55          panel.add(combo);
56          panel.add(addButton);
57
58          // Add the text area and panel to the content pane
59          JFrame frame = new JFrame();
60          frame.add(new JScrollPane(textArea),
61                BorderLayout.CENTER);
62          frame.add(panel, BorderLayout.SOUTH);
63          frame.setDefaultCloseOperation(JFrame.EXIT_ON_CLOSE);
64          frame.pack();
65          frame.setVisible(true);
66      }
67  }
```

You have now seen a number of common patterns. You have seen how they are used in GUI programming, and you have seen simple code examples that put them to work. We will introduce additional patterns throughout this book.

EXERCISES

Exercise 5.1. Write a program that contains two frames, one with a column of text fields containing numbers, and another that draws a bar graph showing the values of the numbers. When the user edits one of the numbers, the graph should be redrawn. Use the OBSERVER pattern. Store the data in a model. Attach the graph view as a listener. When a number is updated, the number view should update the model, and the model should tell the graph view that a change has occured. As a result, the graph view should repaint itself.

Exercise 5.2. Improve Exercise 5.1 by making the graph view editable. Attach a mouse listener to the panel that paints the graph. When the user clicks on a point, move the nearest data point to the mouse click. Then update the model and ensure that both the number view and the graph view are notified of the change so that they can refresh their contents. *Hint:* Look up the API documentation for the MouseListener interface type. In your listener, you need to take action in the mousePressed method. Implement the remaining methods of the interface type to do nothing.

Exercise 5.3. A *slider* is a user interface component that allows a user to specify a continuum of values. To be notified of slider movement, you need to attach a class that implements the ChangeListener interface type. Read the API documentation for JSlider and ChangeListener. Make a table of pattern names and actual names that shows how this is a manifestation of the OBSERVER pattern.

Exercise 5.4. Implement a program that contains a slider and a car icon. The size of the car should increase or decrease as the slider is moved.

Exercise 5.5. Read about the GridBagLayout and reimplement the Telephone class by adding all components directly to the content pane controlled by a single grid bag layout.

Exercise 5.6. Add two telephone handsets to the GUI version of the voice mail program. When you test your program, add a message through one of the handsets and retrieve it through the other.

Exercise 5.7. Improve the program of Exercise 5.6 so that the program does not terminate as soon as one of the handset frames is closed. *Hint:* Don't use a default close operation but install a `WindowListener` into the frames. The `windowClosing` method of the listener should call `System.exit(0)` when the last frame is being closed.

Exercise 5.8. Add scroll bars to the text areas of the telephone frame.

Exercise 5.9. Use the COMPOSITE pattern to define a class `CompositeIcon` that implements the `Icon` interface type and contains a list of icons. Supply a method

```
void addIcon(Icon icon, int x, int y)
```

Exercise 5.10. You can give a title to a border by using the `TitledBorder` class. For example,

```
panel.setBorder(new TitledBorder(new EtchedBorder(),
    "Select one option"));
```

Which pattern is at work here? Explain.

Exercise 5.11. A `Scanner` can be used to read numbers and lines from a `Reader`. Is this an example of the DECORATOR pattern?

Exercise 5.12. Supply decorator classes `EncryptingWriter` and `DecryptingReader` that encrypt and decrypt the characters of the underlying reader or writer. Make sure that these classes are again readers and writers so that you can apply additional decorations. For the encryption, simply use the *Caesar cipher*, which shifts the alphabet by three characters (i.e., A becomes D, B becomes E, and so on).

Exercise 5.13. Improve the classes of Exercise 5.12 so that it is possible to vary the encryption algorithm. Which design pattern are you employing?

Exercise 5.14. Suppose you want to combine the benefits of the `PushbackReader` and `BufferedReader` decorators and call both the `readLine` and `unread` methods. What problem might you encounter? What redesign could fix the problem? What design lesson can you draw from your observation?

Exercise 5.15. Make tables for the five patterns of the invoice program that show how the names used in the pattern descriptions map to the actual names in the implementations.

Exercise 5.16. Provide a class that implements the `InvoiceFormatter` interface type, using HTML to format the output prettily.

Exercise 5.17. Write a new pattern from your own programming experience. Think of a problem that you ended up solving more than once, and describe the problem and solution in the pattern format.

Inheritance and Abstract Classes

In this chapter we discuss the important class relationship of *inheritance*. A class inherits from another class if it describes a specialized subset of objects. For example, a class Manager may inherit from a class Employee. All methods that apply to employees also apply to managers. But managers are more specialized because they have methods that are not applicable to employees in general. For example, managers may get bonuses that regular employees do not enjoy.

We start with a very simple example to show the mechanics of inheritance. Then we progress to a series of interesting graphical programs that demonstrate advanced techniques. Finally, we examine how inheritance is used in the Java class libraries.

6.1   The Concept of Inheritance

6.1.1   Using Inheritance for Modeling Specialization

> Specialized subclasses inherit from superclasses that represent more general concepts.

You use inheritance to model a relationship between classes in which one class represents a more general concept and another a more specialized concept. For example, consider a class `Manager` that inherits from the class `Employee`. This is a valid use of inheritance because managers are a special type of employee. Every manager is an employee, but not every employee is a manager. The more general class is called the *superclass* and the more specialized class the *subclass*.

> A subclass can define additional methods and fields.

Generally, the subclass extends the capabilities of the superclass. The specialized subclass objects may have additional methods and fields.

Consider this simple `Employee` class:

```java
public class Employee
{
    public Employee(String aName) { name = aName; }
    public void setSalary(double aSalary) { salary = aSalary; }
    public String getName() { return name; }
    public double getSalary() { return salary; }
    private String name;
    private double salary;
}
```

> Subclasses can override methods by giving a new definition for a method that exists in the superclass.

Here is a `Manager` class that adds a new method and a new field. The subclass also *overrides* an existing method of the superclass, giving a new definition. The `Manager` version of `getSalary` will compute the sum of the base salary and the bonus.

```java
public class Manager extends Employee
{
    public Manager(String aName) { . . . }
    public void setBonus(double aBonus) { bonus = aBonus; } // new method
    public double getSalary() { . . . } // overrides Employee method
    private double bonus; // new field
}
```

Note that Java uses the extends keyword to denote inheritance. You will see the code for the `Manager` constructor and the `getSalary` method later in this chapter.

Figure 1 shows the class diagram.

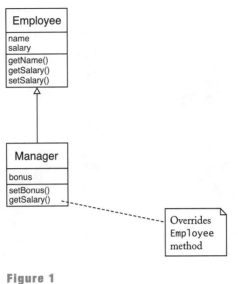

Figure 1

The Manager Class Inherits from the Employee Class

> Subclasses inherit the methods of the superclass.

When inheriting from a superclass, you need to declare only the *difference* between the subclass and superclass. The subclass automatically inherits all features from the superclass, unless the subclass overrides them.

In the example, the Manager subclass has the following methods and fields:

- Methods setSalary and getName (inherited from Employee)
- A method getSalary (overridden in Manager)
- A method setBonus (defined in Manager)
- Fields name and salary (inherited from Employee)
- A field bonus (defined in Manager)

NOTE   If a method is tagged as final, it cannot be overridden in a subclass, which is useful for particularly sensitive methods (such as security checks). It is also possible to declare a class as final. A final class cannot be extended. For example, the String class is a final class.

6.1.2 — The Super/Sub Terminology

Beginners are often confused by the super/sub terminology. Isn't a manager superior to employees in some way? After all, each Manager object contains all the fields of an Employee object. Why then is Manager the subclass and Employee the superclass?

Figure 2

The Set of Managers is a Subset of the Set of Employees

> Subclass objects form a subset of the set of superclass objects.

The terminology becomes clear when you think of a class as a set of objects. The set of managers is a *subset* of the set of employees, as shown in Figure 2.

6.1.3 — Inheritance Hierarchies

In the real world, concepts are often categorized into *hierarchies*. Hierarchies are frequently represented as trees, with the most general concepts at the root of the hierarchy and more specialized ones towards the branches.

> Sets of classes can form complex inheritance hierarchies.

In object-oriented design, it is equally common to group classes into complex inheritance hierarchies. Figure 3 shows a part of a hierarchy of classes that represent various kinds of employees. We place the class `Object` at the base of the hierarchy because all other classes in Java extend the `Object` class. You will learn more about that class in Chapter 7.

When designing a hierarchy of classes, you ask yourself which features are common to all classes that you are designing. Those common properties are collected in superclasses at the base of the hierarchy. For example, all employees have a name and a salary. More specialized properties are only found in subclasses. In our model, only managers receive a bonus.

Later in this chapter, we will analyze several important hierarchies of classes that occur in the Java library.

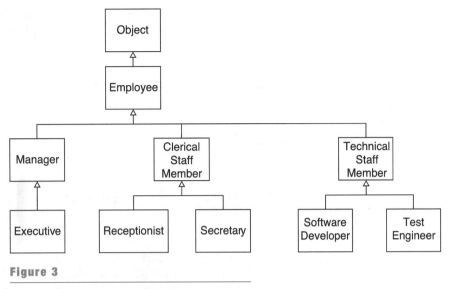

Figure 3

A Hierarchy of Employee Classes

6.1.4 — The Substitution Principle

According to the Liskov substitution principle, you can use a subclass object whenever a superclass object is expected.

Since a subclass inherits the behavior of its superclass, you can substitute subclass objects whenever a superclass object is expected. This rule is called the *Liskov substitution principle*, named after Barbara Liskov, a professor at MIT and pioneering researcher in the field of object-oriented programming.

For example, consider the following instructions:

```
Employee e;
. . .
System.out.println("name=" + e.getName());
System.out.println("salary=" + e.getSalary());
```

The Liskov substitution principle states that the instructions work equally well if you supply a `Manager` object where an `Employee` object is expected.

```
e = new Manager("Bernie Smith");
```

Let's look at each of the calls in turn. The call

```
e.getName()
```

poses no particular problem. The `Manager` class inherits the `getName` method from the `Employee` class.

However, the call

```
e.getSalary()
```

is more interesting. There are two versions of the `getSalary` method, one defined in the `Employee` class, and another in the `Manager` class. As you already saw in Chapter 4, the Java virtual machine automatically executes the correct version of the method, depending on the type of object to which e refers. If e refers to a `Manager` object, then the `Manager` version of the `getSalary` method is invoked. Recall that this phenomenon is called polymorphism.

6.1.5 — Invoking Superclass Methods

Now let's implement the `getSalary` method of the `Manager` class. This method returns the sum of the base salary and the bonus.

```
public class Manager extends Employee
{
    public double getSalary()
    {
        return salary + bonus; // ERROR—private field
    }
    . . .
}
```

> A subclass cannot access private features of its superclass.

However, we have a problem. The `salary` field is a private field of the `Employee` class. The methods of the `Manager` class have no right to access that field. A subclass has to play by the same rules as any other class, and use the public `getSalary` method.

```
public double getSalary()
{
    return getSalary() + bonus; // ERROR—recursive call
}
```

> Use the `super` keyword to call a superclass method.

Unfortunately, now we have a different problem. If you call `getSalary` inside a method that is also called `getSalary`, then the method calls itself. However, we want to call the superclass method to retrieve the employee salary. You use the `super` keyword to express that intention.

```
public double getSalary()
{
    return super.getSalary() + bonus;
}
```

Note that `super` is *not* a variable; in particular, it is not like the `this` variable. Of course, if you called

```
this.getSalary();
```

then the `Manager` version of the `getSalary()` method would call itself—and produce an infinite regression of calls.

Also note that you can't simply convert the `this` reference to the superclass type. Consider this attempt:

```
Employee superThis = this;
return superThis.getSalary() + bonus;
```

However, the call `superThis.getSalary` *still* invokes the `Manager` method! This is the effect of polymorphism. The actual type of the object to which a variable refers, and not the declared type of the variable, determines which method is called. Since the object to which `superThis` refers is of type `Manager`, the `getSalary` method of the `Manager` class is invoked.

The super keyword suppresses the polymorphic call mechanism and forces the superclass method to be called instead.

 TIP As you just saw, subclasses have no right to access the private features of a superclass. Beginners sometimes try to "solve" this problem by redeclaring fields in the subclass:

```
public class Manager extends Employee
{
    . . .
    private double salary; // ERROR—replicated field
}
```

Now a Manager object has *two* fields named salary! One of them is manipulated by the Employee methods and the other by the Manager methods. Be sure to avoid this common design error.

6.1.6 — Invoking Superclass Constructors

> Use the super keyword to call a superclass constructor at the start of a subclass constructor.

To complete the implementation of the Manager class, we need to supply the Manager constructor. The constructor receives a string for the name of the manager. As already discussed, you cannot simply set the name field to the parameter value, because that field is a private field of the Employee class. Instead, you must call the Employee constructor. You also use the super keyword for this purpose:

```
public Manager(String aName)
{
    super(aName); // Calls superclass constructor to initialize private fields of superclass
    bonus = 0;
}
```

The call to the superclass constructor must be the *first* statement of the subclass constructor.

> If a subclass constructor does not call a superclass constructor, then the superclass constructor with no parameters is called automatically.

If the superclass has a constructor with no parameters, then a subclass constructor doesn't have to call any superclass constructor. By default, the superclass is constructed automatically with its no-parameter constructor. For example, later in this chapter, we will form subclasses of the JComponent and JFrame classes. Because those classes have constructors JComponent() and JFrame() with no parameters, the subclass constructors needn't call super.

If all superclass constructors require parameters, then the subclass must call super or the compiler reports an error.

6.1.7 — Preconditions and Postconditions of Inherited Methods

Recall from Chapter 3 that a precondition of a method is a condition that must be true before the method can be called. The caller of the method is responsible for making the call only when the precondition holds.

> A subclass method can only require a precondition that is at most as strong as the precondition of the method that it overrides.

When a subclass overrides a method, the precondition of that method cannot be stronger than the precondition of the superclass method that it overrides.

For example, let's give a reasonable precondition to the `setSalary` method of the `Employee` class: The salary should be a positive value.

```
public class Employee
{
    /**
        Sets the employee salary to a given value.
        @param aSalary the new salary
        @precondition aSalary > 0
    */
    public void setSalary(double aSalary) { . . . }
    . . .
}
```

Now consider a subclass `Manager`. Can the `Manager` class set a precondition of the `set-Salary` method that the salary is always at least $100,000? No. The precondition in the subclass method cannot be stronger than the precondition in the superclass method.

To see the reason, consider these statements.

```
Employee e = . . . ;
e.setSalary(50000);
```

This code would appear to be correct because the method parameter is > 0, fulfilling the precondition of the `Employee` method. However, if e referred to a `Manager` object, then the precondition that the salary be at least $100,000 would be violated. This conflicts with the concept that preconditions must be checkable by the programmer making the call.

To summarize: When a subclass overrides a method, its precondition may be *at most as strong* as the precondition of the superclass method. In particular, if a superclass method has no precondition, the subclass method may not have a precondition either.

> A subclass method must ensure a postcondition that is at least as strong as the postcondition of the method that it overrides.

Conversely, when a subclass overrides a method, its postcondition must be *at least as strong* as the postcondition of the superclass method. For example, suppose `Employee.setSalary` promises not to decrease the employee's salary. Then all methods that override `set-Salary` must make the same promise or a stronger promise.

 NOTE You just saw that preconditions of subclass methods cannot be more restrictive than the preconditions of the superclass methods that they override. The same reasoning holds for a number of other conditions. In particular:

- When you override a method, you cannot make it less accessible.

- When you override a method, you cannot throw more checked exceptions than are already declared in the superclass method.

6.2   Graphics Programming with Inheritance

6.2.1 — Designing Subclasses of the JComponent Class

In this section, we will put inheritance to work in practical programming situations.

In Chapter 4, you saw how to draw shapes by using classes that implement the Icon interface type.

```java
public class MyIcon implements Icon
{
    public void paintIcon(Component c, Graphics g, int x, int y)
    {
        drawing instructions go here
    }
    . . .
}
```

> To draw shapes, subclass the JComponent class and override the paintComponent method.

Another common technique is to form a subclass of JComponent. You redefine its paintComponent method, like this:

```java
public class MyComponent extends JComponent
{
    public void paintComponent(Graphics g)
    {
        drawing instructions go here
    }
    . . .
}
```

There is one advantage to this approach—the JComponent class has a rich behavior that you automatically inherit. For example, you can attach a mouse listener to the component and receive notification when the user clicks on the component with the mouse.

This is an important difference between implementing an interface type and extending a class. When you implement an interface type, you start with nothing—the interface type supplies only the names and signatures of the methods you must support. When you extend a class, you inherit all features that the superclass offers.

We will develop a program that allows a user to move a car by dragging it with the mouse. In the following sections, that program will be enhanced to show a scene composed of arbitrary shapes.

The CarComponent class stores a reference to a CarShape object. Its paintComponent method draws the shape:

```java
public class CarComponent extends JComponent
{
    . . .
    public void paintComponent(Graphics g)
    {
        Graphics2D g2 = (Graphics2D) g;
        car.draw(g2);
    }
    private CarShape car;
}
```

6.2.2 — Listener Interface Types and Adapter Classes

To complete the car drawing program, we need to add mouse event handlers. When the user presses the mouse button, we want to check whether the mouse position is inside the car. If so, we will initiate the dragging process. When the user drags the mouse, we move the car to follow the mouse position.

> To track mouse actions, you attach mouse listeners and mouse motion listeners to components.

To enable mouse tracking, you attach a listener to the component. Actually, there are two listener types, one for listening to mouse clicks and another for listening to mouse movement. These two event types are separated because listening for mouse movement is fairly expensive. Program users move the mouse a lot, causing frequent calls to mouse motion listeners. If a client is only interested in mouse clicks, then it is best not to install a mouse motion listener.

Here are the interface types:

```
public interface MouseListener
{
    void mouseClicked(MouseEvent event);
    void mousePressed(MouseEvent event);
    void mouseReleased(MouseEvent event);
    void mouseEntered(MouseEvent event);
    void mouseExited(MouseEvent event);
}

public interface MouseMotionListener
{
    void mouseMoved(MouseEvent event);
    void mouseDragged(MouseEvent event);
}
```

> Listener interface types with many methods have corresponding adapter classes with do-nothing methods. Extend the adapter rather than implementing the listener.

Both the `MouseListener` and `MouseMotionListener` interface types have several methods, yet an actual listener usually wants a nontrivial action in only one or two of them. To simplify the implementation of listeners, some friendly soul has produced two *classes*, `MouseAdapter` and `MouseMotionAdapter`, that implement all methods to do nothing.

Here is the implementation of the `MouseAdapter` class:

```
public class MouseAdapter implements MouseListener
{
    public void mouseClicked(MouseEvent event) {}
    public void mousePressed(MouseEvent event) {}
    public void mouseReleased(MouseEvent event) {}
    public void mouseEntered(MouseEvent event) {}
    public void mouseExited(MouseEvent event) {}
}
```

To define your own listener, just extend these adapter classes and override the methods you care about. For example, the mouse listener of the `CarComponent` only cares about the `mousePressed` method, not the other four methods of the `MouseListener` interface type.

TIP If *most* subclasses need one version of the method, and a few need a different one, move the most common method to the superclass. The few subclasses that need a different version can override the default, but most classes need to do nothing.

Use an anonymous class to define the mouse listener. The anonymous listener class extends MouseAdapter rather than implementing MouseListener. (Note that the extends keyword is not used in the definition of an anonymous subclass.)

```java
public class CarComponent extends JComponent
{
    public CarComponent()
    {
        . . .
        addMouseListener(new
            MouseAdapter()
            {
                public void mousePressed(MouseEvent event)
                {
                    // mouse action goes here
                    mousePoint = event.getPoint();
                    if (!car.contains(mousePoint)) mousePoint = null;
                }
            });
    }
    . . .
    private CarShape car;
    private Point mousePoint;
}
```

The CarComponent class inherits the addMouseListener method from its superclass.

The mousePressed method is overridden so that we gain control as soon as the mouse button is depressed. The mouseClicked method is not appropriate here—it's only called after the mouse button has been depressed and released.

The mousePressed method remembers the position at which the mouse was pressed. That position is needed later when dragging the car. Therefore, we store it in the mouse-Point instance field. However, if the mouse position was not inside the car, we set the mousePoint field to null. That is an indication that dragging the mouse should not move the car.

Next, we need a mouse motion listener. We want to track when the mouse is dragged (moved while a mouse button is depressed). Whenever the mouse position changes, the mouseDragged method is called. We compute the difference between the previous and the current mouse positions, update the car position, and ask the component to repaint itself so that the car is drawn in the new position.

```java
addMouseMotionListener(new
    MouseMotionAdapter()
    {
        public void mouseDragged(MouseEvent event)
        {
            // mouse drag action goes here
```

```
            if (mousePoint == null) return;
            Point lastMousePoint = mousePoint;
            mousePoint = event.getPoint();

            double dx = mousePoint.getX() - lastMousePoint.getX();
            double dy = mousePoint.getY() - lastMousePoint.getY();
            car.translate((int) dx, (int) dy);
            repaint();
         }
      });
```

Here is the complete program. (The code for the CarShape class is in Section 4.10.)
Figure 4 shows the class diagram.

Ch6/car/CarComponent.java

```
 1  import java.awt.*;
 2  import java.awt.event.*;
 3  import java.awt.geom.*;
 4  import javax.swing.*;
 5  import java.util.*;
 6
 7  /**
 8     A component that shows a scene composed of items.
 9  */
10  public class CarComponent extends JComponent
11  {
12     public CarComponent()
13     {
14        car = new CarShape(20, 20, 50);
15        addMouseListener(new
16           MouseAdapter()
17           {
18              public void mousePressed(MouseEvent event)
19              {
20                 mousePoint = event.getPoint();
21                 if (!car.contains(mousePoint))
22                    mousePoint = null;
23              }
24           });
25
26        addMouseMotionListener(new
27           MouseMotionAdapter()
28           {
29              public void mouseDragged(MouseEvent event)
30              {
31                 if (mousePoint == null) return;
32                 Point lastMousePoint = mousePoint;
33                 mousePoint = event.getPoint();
34
35                 double dx = mousePoint.getX() - lastMousePoint.getX();
36                 double dy = mousePoint.getY() - lastMousePoint.getY();
37                 car.translate((int) dx, (int) dy);
38                 repaint();
39              }
40           });
```

```
41        }
42
43        public void paintComponent(Graphics g)
44        {
45           Graphics2D g2 = (Graphics2D) g;
46           car.draw(g2);
47        }
48
49        private CarShape car;
50        private Point mousePoint;
51 }
```

Ch6/car/CarMover.java

```
1 import java.awt.*;
2 import java.awt.geom.*;
3 import java.awt.event.*;
4 import javax.swing.*;
5
6 /**
7     A program that allows users to move a car with the mouse.
8 */
9 public class CarMover
10 {
11    public static void main(String[] args)
12    {
13       JFrame frame = new JFrame();
14       frame.setDefaultCloseOperation(JFrame.EXIT_ON_CLOSE);
15
16       frame.add(new CarComponent());
17       frame.setSize(FRAME_WIDTH, FRAME_HEIGHT);
18       frame.setVisible(true);
19    }
20
21    private static final int FRAME_WIDTH = 400;
22    private static final int FRAME_HEIGHT = 400;
23 }
```

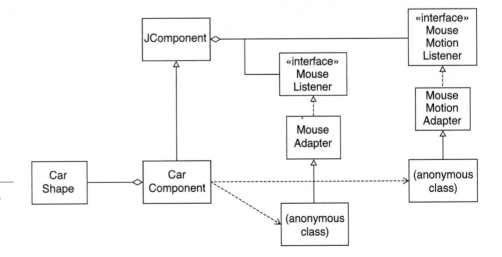

Figure 4

The Classes
of the
Car Mover
Program

6.3 Abstract Classes

As a practical example of object-oriented design techniques, we will develop a scene editor program. A scene consists of shapes such as cars, houses, and so on.

The scene editor draws the shapes and allows the user to add, move, and delete shapes (see Figure 5). As is common with programs of this kind, we allow the user to *select* a shape with the mouse. Clicking on a shape selects it, clicking again unselects it. The selection is used when dragging the mouse or clicking on the "Remove" button. Only the selected shapes are moved or deleted. Shapes need to draw themselves in a different way when they are selected. In this version of our scene editor, the houses and cars use a black fill to denote selection.

There are a number of operations that the shapes must carry out (see Figure 6):

- Keep track of the selection state.
- Draw a plain or selected shape.
- Move a shape.
- Find out whether a point (namely the mouse position) is inside a shape.

Therefore, a natural next step is to design an interface type

```java
public interface SceneShape
{
    void setSelected(boolean b);
    boolean isSelected();
    void draw(Graphics2D g2);
    void drawSelection(Graphics2D g2);
    void translate(int dx, int dy);
    boolean contains(Point2D aPoint);
}
```

SceneShape
manage selection state
draw the shape
move the shape
containment testing

Figure 5

The Scene Editor

Figure 6

A CRC Card of the SceneShape Interface Type

We'll then define classes `CarShape` and `HouseShape` that implement this interface type.

However, there is some commonality between these classes. Every shape needs to keep a selection flag. The naive approach would be to supply the selection flag separately in each class:

```
public class HouseShape implements SceneShape
{
    . . .
    public void setSelected(boolean b) { selected = b; }
    public boolean isSelected() { return selected; }
    private boolean selected;
}

public class CarShape implements SceneShape
{
    . . .
    public void setSelected(boolean b) { selected = b; }
    public boolean isSelected() { return selected; }
    private boolean selected;
}
```

> Move common fields and methods into a superclass.

Clearly, it is a better idea to design a class that expresses this commonality. We will call this class `SelectableShape`.

```
public class SelectableShape implements SceneShape
{
    public void setSelected(boolean b) { selected = b; }
    public boolean isSelected() { return selected; }
    private boolean selected;
}

public class CarShape extends SelectableShape { . . . }
public class HouseShape extends SelectableShape { . . . }
```

Figure 7 shows the relationships between these types.

However, there is a problem with the `SelectableShape` class. It does not define all of the methods of the `SceneShape` interface type. Four methods are left undefined in this class.

- `void draw(Graphics2D g2)`
- `void drawSelection(Graphics2D g2)`
- `void translate(double dx, double dy)`
- `boolean contains(Point2D aPoint)`

> An abstract method is undefined and must be defined in a subclass. A class with one or more abstract methods must be declared as abstract.

We say that these methods are undefined or *abstract* in the `Selectable-Shape` class. It is the job of further subclasses to define them. For that reason, the `SelectableShape` class must be tagged as `abstract`:

```
public abstract class SelectableShape implements
        SceneShape { . . . }
```

The `HouseShape` and `CarShape` classes are *concrete* subclasses that define the remaining methods.

Figure 7

Relationships Between
SelectableShape Types

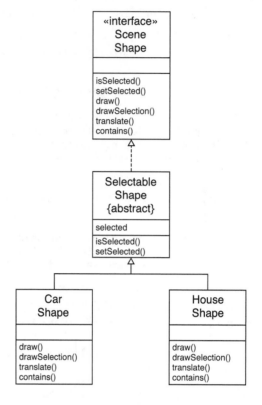

You cannot construct objects of an abstract class.

Abstract classes are convenient placeholders for factoring out common behavior. They behave exactly the same as any other classes, with a single exception: You cannot *instantiate* an abstract class. That is, it is an error to construct a SelectableShape object:

```
SelectableShape shape = new SelectableShape(); // ERROR
```

Such an object would be dangerous—an error would occur if one of its missing methods was called.

However, it is perfectly legal to have variables whose type is an abstract class. Naturally, they must contain a reference to an object of a concrete subclass (or null).

```
SelectableShape shape = new HouseShape(); // OK
```

TIP   Students are often scared about abstract classes, equating "abstract" with "hard to understand", and then believing that any class that is hard to understand should therefore be abstract. Don't fall into that trap. An abstract class is simply a class that cannot be instantiated, generally because it has unimplemented methods.

The SelectableShape class is abstract because it lacks the definition of several methods. However, you can tag any class as abstract, thereby making it impossible to construct objects of that class. That mechanism is useful for supplying a class that defines useful services for subclasses but that, for conceptual reasons, should not be instantiated. You will see an example later in this chapter.

An abstract class is somewhere between an interface type and a concrete class. It requires that subclasses implement methods with a given signature. However, an abstract class usually has some implementation—methods, fields, or both.

 TIP It is a common misconception that abstract classes have no instance fields, or that all methods of an abstract class should be abstract. That is not so; abstract classes can have instance fields and methods. You always want to move as much common functionality as possible into the superclass, whether or not it is abstract. For example, the SelectableShape class is an abstract class. But that doesn't mean it can't have fields or methods. An abstract shape does know how to do *something*, namely manage the selection flag. But it doesn't know *everything*; hence, it is abstract.

Abstract classes have an advantage over interface types: they can define common behavior. But they also have a severe disadvantage: A class can only extend one abstract class, but it can implement several different interface types.

For that reason, we have both a SceneShape interface type and a SelectableShape class. The SelectableShape is a service for classes that wish to implement the SceneShape interface type. If they find its implementation appropriate, and if they don't already extend another class, they are free to extend the class. But they aren't forced into anything—a class can implement the interface type in any way it chooses.

In general, it is a good idea to supply both an interface type and a class that implements some of its methods with convenient defaults.

 NOTE The Java library has a number of "interface type/abstract class" pairs, such as Collection/AbstractCollection and ListModel/AbstractListModel. The abstract class implements some of the methods of the interface type, making it easier for programmers to supply concrete classes that implement the interface type. It would be a good idea to follow that naming convention and rename the SelectableShape class into AbstractShape. We did not do so because students preferred the more descriptive name.

Here is the core code for the scene drawing program. The program is very similar to the car mover program of the preceding section. However, a SceneComponent holds an array list of SceneShape objects. Its paintComponent method draws the shapes. If a shape is selected, its selection decoration is drawn as well.

The mouse press handler of the SceneComponent searches all shapes in the scene, looks for the shape containing the mouse position, and toggles its selection state. Then the component is asked to repaint itself, so that the change in the selection state is properly painted.

The code for dragging shapes is exactly analogous to that of the car mover program. However, we now move all selected shapes.

Ch6/scene1/SceneComponent.java

```
 1  import java.awt.*;
 2  import java.awt.event.*;
 3  import java.awt.geom.*;
 4  import javax.swing.*;
 5  import java.util.*;
 6
 7  /**
 8     A component that shows a scene composed of shapes.
 9  */
10  public class SceneComponent extends JComponent
11  {
12     public SceneComponent()
13     {
14        shapes = new ArrayList<SceneShape>();
15
16        addMouseListener(new
17           MouseAdapter()
18           {
19              public void mousePressed(MouseEvent event)
20              {
21                 mousePoint = event.getPoint();
22                 for (SceneShape s : shapes)
23                 {
24                    if (s.contains(mousePoint))
25                       s.setSelected(!s.isSelected());
26                 }
27                 repaint();
28              }
29           });
30
31        addMouseMotionListener(new
32           MouseMotionAdapter()
33           {
34              public void mouseDragged(MouseEvent event)
35              {
36                 Point lastMousePoint = mousePoint;
37                 mousePoint = event.getPoint();
38                 for (SceneShape s : shapes)
39                 {
40                    if (s.isSelected())
41                    {
42                       double dx
43                          = mousePoint.getX() - lastMousePoint.getX();
44                       double dy
45                          = mousePoint.getY() - lastMousePoint.getY();
46                       s.translate((int) dx, (int) dy);
47                    }
48                 }
49                 repaint();
50              }
51           });
52     }
53
54     /**
```

```
55           Adds a shape to the scene.
56           @param s the shape to add
57        */
58        public void add(SceneShape s)
59        {
60           shapes.add(s);
61           repaint();
62        }
63
64        /**
65           Removes all selected shapes from the scene.
66        */
67        public void removeSelected()
68        {
69           for (int i = shapes.size() - 1; i >= 0; i--)
70           {
71              SceneShape s = shapes.get(i);
72              if (s.isSelected()) shapes.remove(i);
73           }
74           repaint();
75        }
76
77        public void paintComponent(Graphics g)
78        {
79           super.paintComponent(g);
80           Graphics2D g2 = (Graphics2D) g;
81           for (SceneShape s : shapes)
82           {
83              s.draw(g2);
84              if (s.isSelected())
85                 s.drawSelection(g2);
86           }
87        }
88
89        private ArrayList<SceneShape> shapes;
90        private Point mousePoint;
91   }
```

Ch6/scene1/SceneEditor.java

```
 1   import java.awt.*;
 2   import java.awt.geom.*;
 3   import java.awt.event.*;
 4   import javax.swing.*;
 5
 6   /**
 7      A program that allows users to edit a scene composed
 8      of items.
 9   */
10   public class SceneEditor
11   {
12      public static void main(String[] args)
13      {
14         JFrame frame = new JFrame();
15         frame.setDefaultCloseOperation(JFrame.EXIT_ON_CLOSE);
16
```

```
17          final SceneComponent scene = new SceneComponent();
18
19          JButton houseButton = new JButton("House");
20          houseButton.addActionListener(new
21             ActionListener()
22             {
23                public void actionPerformed(ActionEvent event)
24                {
25                   scene.add(new HouseShape(20, 20, 50));
26                }
27             });
28
29          JButton carButton = new JButton("Car");
30          carButton.addActionListener(new
31             ActionListener()
32             {
33                public void actionPerformed(ActionEvent event)
34                {
35                   scene.add(new CarShape(20, 20, 50));
36                }
37             });
38
39          JButton removeButton = new JButton("Remove");
40          removeButton.addActionListener(new
41             ActionListener()
42             {
43                public void actionPerformed(ActionEvent event)
44                {
45                   scene.removeSelected();
46                }
47             });
48
49          JPanel buttons = new JPanel();
50          buttons.add(houseButton);
51          buttons.add(carButton);
52          buttons.add(removeButton);
53
54          frame.add(scene, BorderLayout.CENTER);
55          frame.add(buttons, BorderLayout.NORTH);
56          frame.setSize(300, 300);
57          frame.setVisible(true);
58       }
59 }
```

 Special Topic 6.1

Refactoring

Martin Fowler has coined the term *refactoring* for restructuring code in a disciplined way. His book (*Refactoring*, Addison-Wesley, 2000) and Web site (http://www.refactoring.com) list a large number of refactoring rules. The rules have a simple format. Each rule starts with a brief explanation of the possible benefits of applying the restructuring and then contains "before" and "after" scenarios, separated by an arrow (⟹). Here is a typical example of a refactoring rule that we used in the preceding section:

Extract Superclass	
Symptom	You have two classes with similar features.
Remedy	Create a superclass and move the common features to the superclass.

In general, a refactoring rule teaches you how to make small transformations of your code. Some are quite mundane, for example:

Introduce Explaining Variable	
Symptom	You have an expression that is hard to understand.

Remedy	Put the value of the expression in a temporary variable whose name explains the purpose of the expression.
	
	 ``java
	car.translate(mousePoint.getX() - lastMousePoint.getX(),
	    mousePoint.getY() - lastMousePoint.getY());
	``
	 ⟱
	 ``java
	int xdistance = mousePoint.getX() - lastMousePoint.getX();
	int ydistance = mousePoint.getY() - lastMousePoint.getY();
	car.translate(xdistance, ydistance);
	``

It has been observed that programmers are often reluctant to make any changes in existing code, presumably because they are afraid of breaking it. The advocates of "relentless refactoring" suggest that programmers should be familiar with the refactoring rules and apply them whenever they see code that can be improved. In order to validate that the refactoring has not introduced any bugs, it is essential to run a test suite after the refactoring.

Refactoring rules are quite different from design patterns. Refactoring tells you how to improve code that has already been written. A design pattern tells you how to produce a better design so that you hopefully won't need to apply refactoring later.

6.4 The TEMPLATE METHOD Pattern

Consider the task of drawing the selection adornment of a shape. Selected shapes need to be drawn in a special way so that they can be visually distinguished. In the preceding section, each shape was responsible for drawing a special decoration when it was selected. However, that approach was not very satisfactory. Each shape class had to provide a separate mechanism for drawing the decoration. Figure 8 shows a better way that can be applied generically, independent of the particular shape: Move the shape by a small amount, draw it, move it again, and draw it again. That draws a thickened image of the shape.

This method can be supplied in the `SelectableShape` class:

```
public void drawSelection(Graphics2D g2)
{
   translate(1, 1);
   draw(g2);
   translate(1, 1);
   draw(g2);
   translate(-2, -2);
}
```

Of course, the abstract `SelectableShape` class doesn't know *how* the actual subclass will do the drawing and translating. It just knows *that* the subclass has these methods, and that calling them in this order will achieve the desired effect of drawing a thickened image of the shape.

> The Template Method pattern teaches how to supply an algorithm for multiple types, provided that the sequence of steps does not depend on the type.

The `drawSelection` method is an example of the TEMPLATE METHOD pattern. In this pattern, a superclass defines a method that calls *primitive operations* that a subclass needs to supply. Each subclass can supply the primitive operations as is most appropriate for it. The template method contains the knowledge of how to combine the primitive operations into a more complex operation.

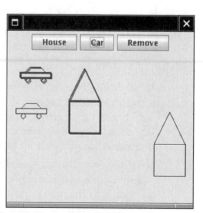

Figure 8

Highlighting a Shape

PATTERN

TEMPLATE METHOD

Context

1. An algorithm is applicable for multiple types.
2. The algorithm can be broken down into *primitive operations*. The primitive operations can be different for each type.
3. The order of the *primitive operations* in the algorithm doesn't depend on the type.

Solution

1. Define an abstract superclass that has a method for the algorithm and abstract methods for the primitive operations.
2. Implement the algorithm to call the primitive operations in the appropriate order.
3. Do not define the primitive operations in the superclass or define them to have appropriate default behavior.
4. Each subclass defines the primitive operations but not the algorithm.

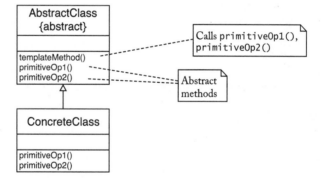

Here is the mapping of the pattern concepts to the shape drawing algorithm:

Name in Design Pattern	Actual Name
AbstractClass	SelectableShape
ConcreteClass	CarShape, HouseShape
templateMethod()	drawSelection()
primitiveOp1(), primitiveOp2()	translate(), draw()

> **TIP**   The TEMPLATE METHOD pattern teaches you how to deal with a set of subclass methods whose implementations are *almost* identical. To check whether you can apply the pattern, see whether you can express the *difference* between the various methods as another method. Then move the common code to the superclass and call a method for the variant part. You saw an example of that process in the drawSelection method of the SelectableShape class.

Ch6/scene2/SelectableShape.java

```java
1  import java.awt.*;
2  import java.awt.geom.*;
3
4  /**
5      A shape that manages its selection state.
6  */
7  public abstract class SelectableShape implements SceneShape
8  {
9      public void setSelected(boolean b)
10     {
11         selected = b;
12     }
13
14     public boolean isSelected()
15     {
16         return selected;
17     }
18
19     public void drawSelection(Graphics2D g2)
20     {
21         translate(1, 1);
22         draw(g2);
23         translate(1, 1);
24         draw(g2);
25         translate(-2, -2);
26     }
27
28     private boolean selected;
29 }
```

Ch6/scene2/HouseShape.java

```java
1  import java.awt.*;
2  import java.awt.geom.*;
3
4  /**
5      A house shape.
6  */
7  public class HouseShape extends SelectableShape
8  {
```

```
 9    /**
10       Constructs a house shape.
11       @param x  the left of the bounding rectangle
12       @param y  the top of the bounding rectangle
13       @param width  the width of the bounding rectangle
14    */
15    public HouseShape(int x, int y, int width)
16    {
17       this.x = x;
18       this.y = y;
19       this.width = width;
20    }
21
22    public void draw(Graphics2D g2)
23    {
24       Rectangle2D.Double base
25             = new Rectangle2D.Double(x, y + width, width, width);
26
27       // The left bottom of the roof
28       Point2D.Double r1
29             = new Point2D.Double(x, y + width);
30       // The top of the roof
31       Point2D.Double r2
32             = new Point2D.Double(x + width / 2, y);
33       // The right bottom of the roof
34       Point2D.Double r3
35             = new Point2D.Double(x + width, y + width);
36
37       Line2D.Double roofLeft
38             = new Line2D.Double(r1, r2);
39       Line2D.Double roofRight
40             = new Line2D.Double(r2, r3);
41
42       g2.draw(base);
43       g2.draw(roofLeft);
44       g2.draw(roofRight);
45    }
46
47    public boolean contains(Point2D p)
48    {
49       return x <= p.getX() && p.getX() <= x + width
50             && y <= p.getY() && p.getY() <= y + 2 * width;
51    }
52
53    public void translate(int dx, int dy)
54    {
55       x += dx;
56       y += dy;
57    }
58
59    private int x;
60    private int y;
61    private int width;
62 }
```

6.5   Protected Interfaces

In this section, we introduce the concept of a *protected interface*, consisting of operations that are intended only for subclasses. To motivate this concept, we introduce the CompoundShape class that stores shapes that are made up of several individual shapes. The CompoundShape class makes use of the GeneralPath class in the standard library.

To create a compound shape, you simply append individual shapes to a GeneralPath object:

```
GeneralPath path = new GeneralPath();
path.append(new Rectangle(. . .), false);
path.append(new Triangle(. . .), false);
g2.draw(path);
```

The value of false for the second parameter of the append method specifies that you do not want to add line segments that connect the individual shapes. The shapes can belong to any classes that implement the java.awt.Shape interface type.

There is a definite advantage of using GeneralPath: That class knows how to do containment testing and how to move its shapes. For example, the call

```
path.contains(aPoint)
```

tests whether the path contains the given point. Thus, there is no need to test the constituent shapes individually.

The CompoundShape class delegates the methods of the SceneShape interface to a GeneralPath object:

Ch6/scene3/CompoundShape.java

```
 1  import java.awt.*;
 2  import java.awt.geom.*;
 3
 4  /**
 5     A scene shape that is composed of multiple geometric shapes.
 6  */
 7  public abstract class CompoundShape extends SelectableShape
 8  {
 9     public CompoundShape()
10     {
11        path = new GeneralPath();
12     }
13
14     protected void add(Shape s)
15     {
16        path.append(s, false);
17     }
18
19     public boolean contains(Point2D aPoint)
20     {
21        return path.contains(aPoint);
22     }
23
```

```
24    public void translate(int dx, int dy)
25    {
26       path.transform(
27             AffineTransform.getTranslateInstance(dx, dy));
28    }
29
30    public void draw(Graphics2D g2)
31    {
32       g2.draw(path);
33    }
34
35    private GeneralPath path;
36 }
```

Now HouseShape can easily be defined as a subclass of this class (see Figure 9):

```
public class HouseShape extends CompoundShape
{
   public HouseShape(int x, int y, int width)
   {
      Rectangle2D.Double base = . . .;
      add(base);
      . . .
   }
}
```

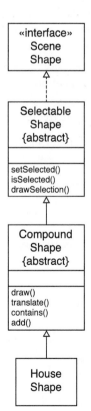

Figure 9

Inheritance Diagram of the
HouseShape Class

You may wonder why the `CompoundShape` class supplies an `add` method. Can't the `HouseShape` constructor simply call

```
path.append(base);
```

However, this code does not compile: `HouseShape` does not have the right to access the private `path` instance field of the superclass.

The obvious solution is to supply a public `add` method. But then any client can call that method and add potentially unsightly shapes to cars and houses.

> A protected feature can be accessed by the methods of all subclasses.

It is occasionally useful to consider subclass methods as more privileged than other code and to give them special access permissions. This is achieved with *protected* access control. A protected feature of a superclass is accessible by the methods of all subclasses. For example, the add method of the `CompoundShape` class is declared as `protected`:

```
public abstract class CompoundShape
{
    protected void add(Shape s);
    . . .
}
```

The `HouseShape` constructor can call the `add` method, but methods of other classes that are not subclasses of `CompoundShape` cannot.

Note that the `CompoundShape` class is declared as an abstract class, even though it has no undefined methods. It would make no sense to construct `CompoundShape` objects because nobody could call their add method. The add method can only be called by subclass methods such as the `HouseShape` constructor.

As an added security measure, methods can use protected features only on objects *of their own class*. This is to prevent the following attack:

```
public Attacker extends CompoundShape
    // Tries to call protected add method
{
    void uglify(HouseShape house)
    {
        . . .
        house.add(aShape);
        // Won't work—can only call add on other Attacker objects
    }
}
```

Could we declare the path instance field as protected?

```
public abstract class CompoundShape
{
    . . .
    protected GeneralPath path; // DON'T!
}
```

> Protected fields should be avoided. They have the same disadvantages as public fields.

Technically, this is legal. However, protected data is never a good idea. It is impossible to enumerate all classes that extend a given class. Thus, protected access is open-ended. After a protected field has been defined, its definition can never be modified because some subclass somewhere might rely on it.

In Java, protected visibility has another strike against it. Classes in the same *package* also have access to protected features, even if they don't belong to subclasses.

Some people use protected fields in the belief that subclasses have a better understanding of a superclass and thus can be trusted more than others. This is a dangerous belief that we do not encourage.

> A class can supply a public interface for all clients and a protected interface for subclasses.

However, *protected methods* can be helpful. They allow you to *distinguish between two interfaces:* the interface for class users and the interface for refining the class behavior through inheritance.

Because a class has no control over who will extend it, protected methods should be designed with the same care as public methods.

6.6   The Hierarchy of Swing Components

By repeated inheritance, you can organize a collection of related classes, factoring out common behavior. The result is a hierarchy of classes. In this section, we will investigate the hierarchy of user interface component classes that you find in the Java library. Figure 10 shows the inheritance diagram.

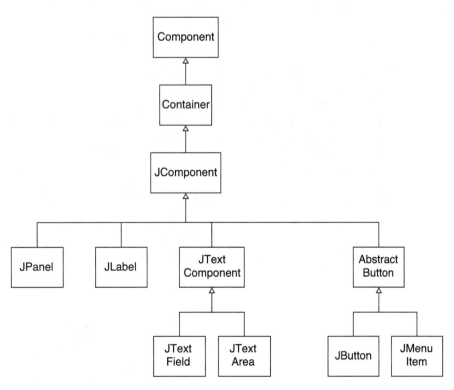

Figure 10

Inheritance Diagram of Swing Component Classes

This analyis is useful because it shows you a complex hierarchy from a real-world library. Furthermore, you use the Swing library whenever you program graphical user interfaces. You often need to know about the inheritance relationships between Swing classes. For example, if you know that the `JPanel` class extends the `Container` class, you can add components to a panel.

The base of the component hierarchy is the `Component` class. It has a large number of commonly used methods such as

```
int getWidth()
int getHeight()
Dimension getPreferredSize()
void setBackground(Color c)
```

Of course, all subclasses of the `Component` class inherit these methods.

The `Container` class is a subclass of `Component`. The most important property of a container is the ability to contain components, under the control of a layout manager. We discussed the container/component relationship as an example of the COMPOSITE pattern in Chapter 5.

To understand the component hierarchy in more detail, you need to know some Java history. The first release of Java used a GUI toolkit called *AWT (Abstract Windowing Toolkit)*. You still see traces of the AWT in package names such as `java.awt`. The AWT uses components that are *native* to the host windowing system. For example, when a Java program shows an AWT button in Windows, it looks exactly like all other Windows buttons. When the same program runs on the Macintosh, it creates a Macintosh button.

The advantage of this setup is clear: Java programs look just like all other applications on the same platform. However, as it turns out, there are subtle platform differences, particularly with the handling of mouse events, repainting, keyboard shortcuts, and so on. Those differences meant that programmers were never quite able to write Java programs that have the same behavior on multiple platforms. The promise of "write once, run anywhere" turned into the ugly reality of "write once, debug everywhere".

To solve that problem once and for all, the Swing toolkit was developed. Swing paints all components onto blank windows. The toolkit draws Swing buttons, scroll bars, and so on, pixel by pixel. When the user clicks the button or moves the scroll bar, then the toolkit redraws the component. In this way, Swing has complete control over the behavior of the components. You can configure Swing to draw the components in a style that imitates the host windowing system, or you can use the cross-platform style called "Metal" that you see in the screen captures in this book.

 INTERNET   You can also install alternative look and feel implementations and change the way your Java programs look. For example, the freely available "Napkin" look and feel at `http://napkinlaf.sourceforge.org` paints the user interface components as if they had been sketched out on a paper napkin—see Figure 11. This look and feel is used for building "mock ups" of user interfaces. Customers can try out mock user interfaces and check that they fulfill their requirements, without being led to believe that the product is almost done.

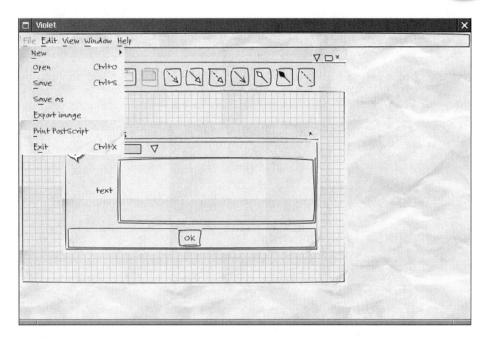

Figure 11

The Napkin Look and Feel

The `JComponent` class is the base of all Swing components. (There are other user interface components that preceded the Swing toolkit, such as the `Button` and `Panel` classes. These classes are less commonly used than the Swing classes, and we will not discuss them further. Note that all Swing components start with the letter `J`.)

The `JComponent` class is a subclass of `Container`, which doesn't actually make conceptual sense. After all, many of the Swing components are not meant to be containers for other components. However, the designers of the Swing classes were in a bind. They would have preferred a `JContainer` class that simultaneously extends `JComponent` and `Container`, but that is not possible in Java.

The `JComponent` class has several methods that are of interest to the GUI programmer, such as

```
void setBorder(Border b)
void setToolTipText(String tip)
```

A tooltip is a message that shows up when the user moves the mouse over a component. (In a look and feel for blind people—or temporarily "blind" people such as motorists— the tooltip may be spoken by a speech synthesizer.) Tooltips and borders are only available for Swing components, not for AWT components.

The `JComponent` class has a number of subclasses, such as the familiar `JLabel` and `JPanel`. Other familiar classes such as `JButton` and `JTextField` are not direct subclasses of

JComponent. There are intermediate classes—AbstractButton and JTextComponent—that capture commonalities with other classes. For example, JMenuItem is another subclass of AbstractButton. Superficially, buttons and menu items don't seem to have much in common, but they share quite a bit of behavior, such as the ability to notify an Action-Listener. Similarly, JTextField and JTextArea are subclasses of JTextComponent. The JTextComponent class defines methods such as getText and setText.

Special Topic 6.2

Multiple Inheritance

When the Swing designers added the JComponent class, they might have liked to add a JContainer class as well. Conceptually, a JContainer would extend both an AWT Container and a Swing JComponent (see Figure 12).

However, in Java, it is not possible for a class to have two direct superclasses. Therefore, the Swing designers chose to have JComponent extend Container.

Other object-oriented programming languages, such as C++ and Eiffel, allow classes to extend multiple superclasses. This feature is called *multiple inheritance*. As you just saw, multiple inheritance can be useful in practical programming situations.

Java does not have multiple inheritance because it can be complex to implement. Multiple inheritance has two major challenges:

- How to deal with name clashes—features with the same name that are inherited from multiple superclasses.
- How to share fields that are inherited through multiple paths.

The first problem can be addressed by renaming or scope resolution mechanisms. The second problem is more vexing. For example, the Component class defines width and height fields. Both Container and JComponent inherit these fields. If JContainer extends both of these classes, it inherits two copies of these fields. This is not desirable. Confusion would result if some methods manipulated the width and height fields from one superclass and others used the fields from the other superclass. In C++, implementors must use the *virtual base class* feature to achieve an object layout that avoids the duplication of inherited fields. In C++ notation, the inheritance is set up as follows:

```
class Container : virtual public Component { . . . };
class JComponent : virtual public Component { . . . };
class JContainer : public Container, public JComponent { . . . }
```

(In C++, the : symbol is the equivalent of the extends keyword in Java. C++ also distinguishes between public and private inheritance. Public inheritance behaves like inheritance in Java.)

Fields of a virtual base class are shared if a class inherits them through multiple inheritance paths. Thus, JContainer only inherits a single set of Component fields.

However, virtual base classes are problematic. The designers of intermediate classes (such as Container) must have the foresight to use virtual inheritance to provide for the possibility that someone might later want to combine the classes with multiple inheritance. But C++

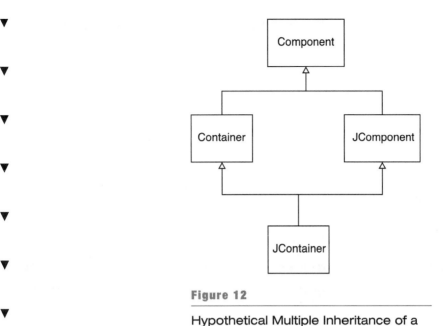

Figure 12

Hypothetical Multiple Inheritance of a
Swing Container Class

programmers are generally reluctant to use virtual base classes since the implementation is
somewhat inefficient.

The designers of the Java language decided that the complexity of multiple inheritance out-
weighs the benefits. However, it is permissible in Java to implement multiple interface types.
Since interface types cannot contribute instance fields, none of the implementation complexities of shared fields can arise.

6.7   The Hierarchy of Standard Geometric Shapes

In the preceding section, you learned about the hierarchy of Swing components. In this
section, we will look at another inheritance hierarchy of the Java library: the hierarchy of
geometric shapes. As you study this hierarchy, you will see much factoring out of common code, encounter another example of the TEMPLATE METHOD pattern, and learn
the secret behind the strange shape class names (such as `Rectangle2D.Double`).

To understand the twists and turns of the geometric shape classes, we need to delve into
the history of Java once again. The first version of Java contained a small number of
geometry classes that use integer coordinates. These classes are in the `java.awt` package.

- `Point`
- `Rectangle`
- `Polygon`

Java 2 introduced a much richer set of shapes in the `java.awt.geom` package.

- `Point2D`
- `Rectangle2D`
- `RoundRectangle2D`
- `Line2D`
- `Ellipse2D`
- `Arc2D`
- `QuadCurve2D`
- `CubicCurve2D`
- `GeneralPath`
- `Area`

All of these classes, except for the `Point2D` class, implement the `Shape` interface type.

The legacy `Point` and `Rectangle` classes are subclasses of `Point2D` and `Rectangle2D` respectively.

The four classes

- `Rectangle2D`
- `RoundRectangle2D`
- `Ellipse2D`
- `Arc2D`

are subclasses of the class `RectangularShape`. Of course, ellipses and elliptical arcs aren't strictly rectangular, but they have a rectangular bounding box. The class `Rectangular-Shape` has a number of useful methods that are common to these classes, such as

- `getCenterX`
- `getCenterY`
- `getMinX`
- `getMinY`
- `getMaxX`
- `getMaxY`
- `getWidth`
- `getHeight`
- `setFrameFromCenter`
- `setFrameFromDiagonal`

None of these are complex to implement, but they are all nice to have.

Figure 13 shows the inheritance hierarchy of the geometric shape classes. We omit the `QuadCurve2D`, `CubicCurve2D`, and `Area` classes that we won't use in this book.

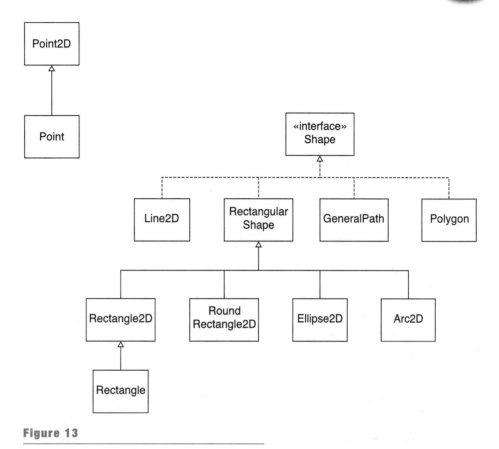

Figure 13

Inheritance Hierarchy of the Geometric Shape Classes

Now we are ready to explain the curious `Rectangle2D.Float` and `Rectangle2D.Double` classes.

First, why have two separate classes at all? Wouldn't it be simpler to store the coordinates in `double` values? Indeed, but the range of the `float` type is more than sufficient for the vast majority of graphical applications. After all, as long as the roundoff error of a calculation is less than a visible pixel, then it is not a concern for the user. In a program that manipulates a large number of graphical objects, the space savings of using `float` coordinates is substantial. A `float` value uses 4 bytes of storage and a `double` uses 8 bytes.

Why didn't the library designers then use `float` values for all graphical objects? First, there may well have been the nagging suspicion that some applications need double precision. Perhaps more importantly, it is somewhat painful to program with `float`: the constants have an F at the end, such as `0.0F`, and you often have to apply a `(float)` cast, such as `(float) Math.sqrt(. . .)`. Therefore, the library designers decided to give the programmer a choice.

`Float` and `Double` are inner classes, declared inside the `Rectangle2D` class. This explains the class names: `Rectangle2D.Float` is the `Float` class defined inside the `Rectangle2D`

Figure 14

Subclasses of the `Rectangle2D` Class

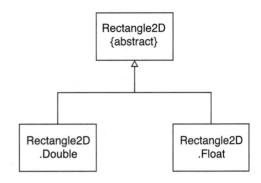

class. In this situation, the inner class was used only for naming reasons. The designers of the library felt that `Rectangle2D.Float` was a nicer name than, say, `FloatRectangle2D`.

Furthermore, `Float` and `Double` are subclasses of the `Rectangle2D` class (see Figure 14). They only define a small number of methods, in particular

- `double getX()`
- `double getY()`
- `double getWidth()`
- `double getHeight()`

Note that both the `Float` and `Double` classes return double values! Even for the `Float` class, most of the intermediate computations are done in double precision.

Here is an extract of the source code for the `Rectangle2D` class and its inner classes.

```
public abstract class Rectangle2D extends RectangularShape
{
    public static class Float extends Rectangle2D
    {
        public double getX() { return (double) x; }
        public double getY() { return (double) y; }
        public double getWidth() { return (double) width; }
        public double getHeight() { return (double) height; }

        public void setRect(float x, float y, float w, float h)
        {
            this.x = x;
            this.y = y;
            this.width = w;
            this.height = h;
        }

        public void setRect(double x, double y, double w, double h)
        {
            this.x = (float) x;
            this.y = (float) y;
            this.width = (float) w;
            this.height = (float) h;
```

```
      }
      . . .
      public float x;
      public float y;
      public float width;
      public float height;
   }

   public static class Double extends Rectangle2D
   {
      public double getX() { return x; }
      public double getY() { return y; }
      public double getWidth() { return width; }
      public double getHeight() { return height; }

      public void setRect(double x, double y, double w, double h)
      {
         this.x = x;
         this.y = y;
         this.width = w;
         this.height = h;
      }
      . . .
      public double x;
      public double y;
      public double width;
      public double height;
   }
   . . .
}
```

The `Rectangle2D` class has no instance fields.

 NOTE The keyword `static` for the inner classes denotes the fact that the inner class methods do not access the outer class instance fields and methods. An inner class that doesn't require access to the surrounding scope is called a *nested class*. Objects of nested classes do not contain a reference to an outer class object in the inner class.

Most of the work is done by methods of the `Rectangle2D` class, not the inner classes. Here is a typical method:

```
public boolean contains(double x, double y)
{
   double x0 = getX();
   double y0 = getY();
   return x >= x0
         && y >= y0
         && x < x0 + getWidth()
         && y < y0 + getHeight();
}
```

Depending on the actual type of the object, the `getX`, `getY`, `getWidth`, and `getHeight` methods of the `Float` or `Double` subclass are called to retrieve these values (in the `double` type). These methods are *only* implemented in the `Float` and `Double` subclasses; the `Rectangle2D` superclass does not provide a definition.

The contains method is another example of the TEMPLATE METHOD pattern:

Name in Design Pattern	Actual Name
`AbstractClass`	`Rectangle2D`
`ConcreteClass`	`Rectangle2D.Double`
`templateMethod()`	`contains()`
`primitiveOp1(), primitiveOp2(), . . .`	`getX(), getY(), getWidth(), getHeight()`

Fortunately, you only need to worry about all of these issues when you *construct* a rectangle. Then you need to be specific whether you want a `Float` or `Double` rectangle. Afterwards, just reference the object through a `Rectangle2D` variable:

```
Rectangle2D rect = new Rectangle2D.Double(5, 10, 20, 30);
```

Of course, all the other "2D" classes have the same setup, for example

```
Point2D pt = new Point2D.Float(5.0F, 10.0F);
```

6.8   The Hierarchy of Exception Classes

The Java library uses inheritance to categorize a large number of exception classes. To use exception handling effectively, it is essential that you understand the hierarchy of the standard exception classes, and that you know how to add custom exception classes to the hierarchy.

> Subclasses of `Error` describe fatal errors.

All exceptions must ultimately extend the class `Throwable`. The `Throwable` class has two subclasses, `Error` and `Exception`. Subclasses of the `Error` class denote fatal errors that cannot be remedied, such as memory exhaustion of the virtual machine or an assertion failure. Application programmers generally do not deal with these errors.

> Subclasses of `Runtime-Exception` are unchecked exceptions.

The `Exception` class is the superclass for exceptions that may occur on the application level. The most important subclass of the `Exception` class is the `RuntimeException` class. All subclasses of `Runtime-Exception` are *unchecked:* the compiler does not check whether your methods catch or declare them. Examples of unchecked exceptions are `NullPointerException` and `IndexOutOfBoundsException`.

On the other hand, subclasses of `Exception` that are not subclasses of `RuntimeException` are *checked exceptions.* You need to either catch them or list them in `throws` clauses. Examples are `IOException` and its subclasses.

Figure 15 shows an inheritance diagram of the most common exception classes.

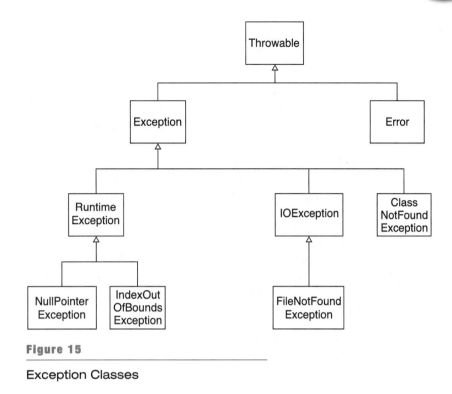

Figure 15

Exception Classes

You catch an exception in a `try` block of the form

```
try
{
    code that may throw exceptions
}
catch (ExceptionType₁ exception₁)
{
    handler for ExceptionType₁
}
catch (ExceptionType₂ exception₂)
{
    handler for ExceptionType₂
}
    . . .
```

> A `catch` clause catches exceptions of a given class or any of its subclasses.

A `catch` clause gains control if a statement inside the `try` block (or in a method that was called from the `try` block) throws an exception object that belongs to the class of the `catch` clause *or one of its subclasses*. For example, the clause

```
catch (IOException exception)
```

can catch an exception of type `FileNotFoundException`. The inheritance hierarchy of exception classes makes it possible for the code that throws an exception to be specific about the nature of the error (such as "file not found") without burdening the error handling code. The error handling code can catch exceptions at a more general level (such as "all I/O errors").

When you encounter an error condition in your code, and you want to throw an exception, then you need to make a decision whether to use an exception class in the standard library, or whether to design your own exception class. If you design your own class, you first need to decide whether the exception should be checked or unchecked. Recall that a checked exception should be used when an error condition is beyond the control of the programmer (such as a network failure), whereas an unchecked exception is appropriate when an error was caused by programmer inattention (such as a null pointer exception). Unchecked exceptions must be subclasses of `RuntimeException`.

When you design an exception class, you should provide two constructors: a default constructor and a constructor with a string parameter that signifies the reason for the exception. The latter constructor should simply pass the reason string to the superclass constructor. Here is a typical example. You want to throw an `IllegalFormatException` when a user enters information in the wrong format. Since user actions are beyond the control of the programmer, we design a checked exception. We inherit from the `Exception` class but not from `RuntimeException`.

```java
public class IllegalFormatException extends Exception
{
   public IllegalFormatException() {}
   public IllegalFormatException(String reason) { super(reason); }
}
```

Now we can throw an exception of this new class:

```java
if (. . .) throw new IllegalFormatException("number expected");
```

6.9   When Not to Use Inheritance

6.9.1 — Points and Circles

> Use inheritance for *is-a* relationships, aggregation for *has-a* relationships.

Recall that inheritance is used to model an *is-a* relationship. Use aggregation (instance fields) for *has-a* relationships.

For example, a car *has* a tire (in fact, it has four or five, counting the spare). A car *is* a vehicle.

It is easy to get this wrong. A tutorial that accompanied a popular C++ compiler showed how to form a subclass `Circle` that extends a `Point` class. Here is the Java equivalent:

```java
public class Point
{
   public Point(int x, int y) { . . . }
   public void translate(int dx, int dy) { . . . }

   private int x;
   private int y;
}
```

```
public class Circle extends Point // DON'T
{
    public Circle(Point center, int radius) { . . . }
    public void draw(Graphics g) { . . . }

    private int radius;
}
```

This does little good. By sheer accident, one of the methods of `Point` (namely `translate`) is applicable to `Circle` objects. But that is not a good enough reason to use inheritance. A circle *has* a center point—it isn't a point.

```
public class Circle // OK
{
    public Circle(Point center, int radius) { . . . }
    public void draw(Graphics g) { . . . }
    public void translate(int dx, int dy) { . . . }

    private Point center;
    private int radius;
}
```

The same tutorial goes on to derive `Rectangle` from `Point`. That doesn't work any better. In fact, treating the two corner points differently is downright weird.

```
public class Rectangle extends Point // DON'T
{
    public Rectangle(Point a, Point b) { . . . }
    public void draw(Graphics g) { . . . }
    public void translate(int dx, int dy) { . . . }

    private Point other;
}
```

One of the corner points is stored in the superclass; the other is an instance field. None of the methods can be inherited. The implementations of the methods look very strange because of the asymmetry between the point stored in the superclass and the point stored as an instance field:

```
void translate(int dx, int dy)
{
    super.translate(dx, dy);
    other.translate(dx, dy);
}
```

The authors of the tutorial had a reason for choosing this example. They wanted to demonstrate polymorphism of shapes:

```
ArrayList<Point> shapes = new ArrayList<Point>();
shapes.add(new Circle(. . .));
shapes.add(new Rectangle(. . .));
for (Point p : shapes)
{
    // Polymorphic calls
    p.translate(10, 10);
    p.draw(g);
}
```

Of course, that doesn't look right. Circles and rectangles aren't points, they are shapes. It would have made more sense to define an abstract class or an interface type Shape. Perhaps the authors of the tutorial felt that the concept of an abstract class or interface type was too advanced for students just starting with object-oriented programming.

In this situation, misusing inheritance resulted in code that was difficult to understand.

 TIP   As you just saw, the *is-a* test can tell you when you should use inheritance. However, you have to be careful when applying that test. You should only use the *is-a* relationship when comparing two *classes*. For example, "A Chevrolet is a car" is a relationship between classes (the class of Chevrolets and the class of cars). But now consider "My car is a Chevrolet". That is a relationship between an *object* (my car) and a class (the class of Chevrolets). An object can never inherit from a class. Thus, the *is-a* test does not apply here.

6.9.2 — Vectors and Stacks

The java.util package has a Stack class that extends a dynamic array class (the Vector class, a precursor of the ArrayList class):

```
public class Stack<T> extends Vector<T> // DON'T
{
    T pop() { . . . }
    T push(T item) { . . . }
    . . .
}
```

This is not a good idea. A stack isn't a special case of a dynamic array. Some things you can do to an array make no sense for a stack. When using inheritance, the stack class inherits *all* methods of the Vector class, whether appropriate or not. Consider this sequence of method calls:

```
Stack<String> s = new Stack<String>();
s.push("A");
s.push("B");
s.push("C");
s.remove(1); // Removes "B"
```

Don't use inheritance if it violates the Liskov substitution principle.

The code is legal but obviously makes no sense for a stack. You can't remove elements from the middle of a stack. Thus, the stack class violates the Liskov substitution principle.

In this situation, misusing inheritance leads to a possibly dangerous situation. Programmers can cause objects to have an invalid state by applying the wrong methods.

The appropriate solution is to use aggregation, not inheritance.

```
public class Stack<T>
{
```

```
        T pop() { . . . }
        T push(T item) { . . . }
        . . .
        private ArrayList<T> elements;
    }
```

In this chapter, you have learned how to use inheritance to design class hierarchies, and how to recognize situations in which inheritance is not appropriate.

Special Topic   6.3

Stacks

A *stack* lets you insert and remove elements at only one end, traditionally called the *top* of the stack. To visualize a stack, think of a stack of books (see Figure 16).

New items can be added to the top of the stack. Items are removed from the top of the stack as well. Therefore, they are removed in the order opposite from the order in which they were added, called *last in, first out* or *LIFO* order. For example, if you add items A, B, and C and then remove them, you obtain C, B, and A. Traditionally, the addition and removal operations are called push and pop, respectively.

The following sample code shows how to use a stack.

```
        Stack<String> s = new Stack<String>();
        s.push("A");
        s.push("B");
        s.push("C");

        // The following loop prints C, B, and A
        while (s.size() > 0)
            System.out.println(s.pop());
```

Figure 16

A Stack of Books

EXERCISES

Exercise 6.1. Start with the following class.

```
public class BankAccount
{
   public void deposit(double amount) { balance += amount; }
   public void withdraw(double amount) { balance -= amount; }
   public double getBalance() { return balance; }
   private double balance;
}
```

A checking account is just like a bank account, except that there is a service charge for deposits and withdrawals. Each month, the first five transactions are free. All further transactions cost $1. Define a subclass `CheckingAccount` with a constructor

```
CheckingAccount(double initialBalance)
```

and a method

```
void deductFees()
```

that deducts the fees and resets the transaction count. (The bank computer will call this method once a month. There is no transaction charge for deducting the fees.) You will also need to redefine the `deposit` and `withdraw` methods.

Exercise 6.2. Form subclasses `HourlyEmployee` and `SalariedEmployee` of the `Employee` class. Provide constructors

```
HourlyEmployee(String aName, double anHourlySalary)
SalariedEmployee(String aName, double anAnnualSalary)
```

Add a method `getWeeklySalary`. Assume that hourly employees work 40 hours per week, and that salaried employees are paid 1/52 of their annual salary every week.

Exercise 6.3. Explain the two different uses of the `super` keyword. How can you tell when `super` is used to invoke a constructor?

Exercise 6.4. Implement a class

```
public class LabeledPoint extends java.awt.Point
{
   public LabeledPoint(int x, int y, String text) { . . . }
   public void draw(Graphics g) { . . . }
   private String text;
}
```

The draw method should draw a small circle and the label. Which methods does this class inherit?

Exercise 6.5. Implement a class

```
public class LabeledRectangle extends Rectangle
{
   public LabeledRectangle(int x, int y, int width, int height,
         String text) { . . . }
   public void draw(Graphics g) { . . . }
   private String text;
}
```

The draw method should draw the rectangle and center the label string inside it.

Exercise 6.6. (hard) Make the class of Exercise 6.5 implement the java.awt.Shape interface type.

Exercise 6.7. Explain why a method in a subclass cannot throw more checked exceptions than the superclass method that it replaces. *Hint:* Show how the checking mechanism could be defeated.

Exercise 6.8. Find examples of final methods and final classes in the Java library.

Exercise 6.9. Consider the ArrayList<E> and LinkedList<E> classes of the standard library. What abstract class do they extend? What interface types does that abstract class implement? Draw a class diagram.

Exercise 6.10. Consider the HashSet<E> and TreeSet<E> classes of the standard library. What abstract class do they extend? What interface types does that abstract class implement? Draw a class diagram.

Exercise 6.11. Find examples of abstract classes and abstract methods in the Java graphics library.

Exercise 6.12. Consider the Number class in the standard Java library.

(a)   What are its subclasses?

(b)   Why are the methods byteValue and shortValue *not* abstract? (Note that all other methods are abstract.)

Exercise 6.13. Reorganize the code for the scene editor as follows: Define a class Scene-Frame that extends the JFrame class. Its constructor should set up the scene component and the buttons. The main method of the SceneEditor class should merely construct the SceneFrame and show it.

Exercise 6.14. Add more items to the scene editor (such as trucks, stop signs, and so on).

Exercise 6.15. Start with the classes in the Ch6/scene2 directory. Reorganize the Car-Shape, HouseShape, and SelectableShape classes so that the SelectableShape class stores the top left corner of the item. Move the translate method to the SelectableShape class.

Exercise 6.16. The scene editor user interface has an unnatural feel. When you click on a selected shape, intending to drag it to a different position, it is deselected instead. Implement an improved behavior that feels more natural.

Exercise 6.17. Most drawing programs indicate selected items by placing "grabbers" around the corners. Implement this feature in the scene editor by adding a method

```
Rectangle getBounds()
```

to the SceneShape interface type. In the drawSelection method of the SelectableShape class, call getBounds to determine the grabber locations. Is this an example of the TEM-PLATE METHOD pattern?

Exercise 6.18. A GeneralPath collects shapes and is itself a shape. What design pattern does it exemplify?

Exercise 6.19. Find examples of `protected` methods and `protected` fields in the Java library. Are the protected fields safe from modification by hostile code?

Exercise 6.20. The `JButton` class does not define an `addActionListener` method. In which superclass is that method defined?

Exercise 6.21. Suppose the class `Square` extends the `Rectangle` class. Does this inheritance pass the conceptual *is-a* test? Does it pass the "Liskov substitution" test?

Exercise 6.22. In this chapter, we criticized a design in which classes `Circle` and `Rectangle` extended a class `Point`. Implement a better design in which the `Circle` and `Rectangle` classes have a common supertype `Shape`. Should `Shape` be an interface type or an abstract class? (You need to place your classes in a separate package to avoid conflict with the `java.awt` classes.)

Exercise 6.23. Reimplement the `Stack<E>` class using aggregation instead of inheritance. (You need to place your class in a separate package to avoid conflict with `java.util.Stack`.)

The Java
Object Model

This chapter discusses five important concepts of object-oriented design. First, we study the Java *type system* and the important subtype relationship. We then have a close look at the Object class, the common superclass of all Java classes, and the services that it provides. We discuss the concept of *reflection*, which allows a program to analyze its own objects and classes, and examine *generic programming*, a recent feature of the Java language for implementing classes and methods with type parameters. The chapter concludes with an introduction to the concept of components, entities that encapsulate functionality at a conceptually higher level than objects. We look at the JavaBeans™ component model and investigate how components can be assembled into applications in a graphical user interface builder.

7.1   The Java Type System

7.1.1 — Types and Subtypes

> A *type* is a set of values together with a set of operations that can be applied to the values.

An important concept in a programming language is the notion of *type*. A type specifies a set of values and the operations that can be carried out with those values. For example, the `int` type specifies all 32-bit integers and the arithmetic operations on them. A class type specifies a set of objects, together with the methods that can be applied to them.

In a *strongly typed* language, the compiler and run-time system carry out checks to ensure that your programs never execute an operation on a value that would be forbidden under the type system rules. Java is strongly typed. Most attempts to apply an illegal operation are caught by the compiler. Others—such as invalid casts—are detected by the virtual machine and result in an exception. Other languages, in particular C and C++, do not have complete checks for type system rules. Those languages rely on the programmer to produce correct code.

Most type system rules of the Java language are validated during compilation. In order to support compile-time checking, variables have types. If you declare a variable of type `Employee`, it can only hold references to objects of type `Employee` or one of its subclasses. The compiler can check that all operations on the variable are legal. For example, a Java compiler finds the error in the code

```
Employee e = new Employee(); // This is Java
e.clear(); // Compile-time error; undefined method
```

Not all programming languages make an effort to check types at compile time. For example, a variable in JavaScript can hold values of any type. If you apply an operation that is not applicable for the value that is currently stored in the variable, then a run-time error occurs.

```
var e = new Employee(); // This is JavaScript
e.clear(); // Run-time error; undefined method
```

Of course, compile-time checking is safer than run-time checking. The compiler checks the entire program, whereas run-time checks may pass during testing and later fail during deployment when unforeseen values are stored in untyped variables.

In order to fully understand which values can be stored in which variables, we will describe the types of the Java programming language in a systematic way.

Every *type* in Java is one of the following:

1. A primitive type (int, short, long, byte, char, float, double, boolean)
2. A class type
3. An interface type
4. An array type
5. The null type

Examples for types are:

```
int
Rectangle
Shape
String[]
```

 NOTE If you have an array type, the type of the array elements is called the *component type* of the array. For example, the component type of the String[] array type is String.

NOTE The null type is defined in the Java language specification as the type with a single value, null. This solves a technical problem—every value, including null, should belong to one specific type.

Every *value* in Java is one of the following:

1. A value of a primitive type
2. A reference to an object of a class
3. A reference to an array
4. null

Examples for values are

```
13
new Rectangle(5, 10, 20, 30)
new int[] { 2, 3, 5, 7, 11, 13 }
null
```

Note that you cannot have a value of an interface type. Interface types are only used to declare variables, method parameters, or return types.

 NOTE According to the Java language specification, void is not a type. The void keyword is merely used to tag a method that returns no value.

> You can substitute a value of a subtype whenever a supertype value is expected.

An important relationship between types is the *subtype* relationship. A subtype contains a subset of the values of a given type. You can use a subtype whenever a supertype is specified. For example, JButton is a subtype of Component, so you can store JButton objects in Component variables. In general, if S is a subtype of T, the values of S can be assigned to variables of type T without a cast.

Here is the complete rule set for the subtype relationship between non-generic types. The rules for generic types are more complex—see Section 7.7. A type S is a *subtype* of the type T if

1. S and T are the same type.
2. S and T are both class types and S is a direct or indirect subclass of T.
3. S and T are both interface types and S is a direct or indirect subinterface of T.
4. S is a class type, T is an interface type, and S or one of its superclasses implements the interface type T or one of its subinterfaces.
5. S and T are both array types and the component type of S is a subtype of the component type of T.
6. S is not a primitive type and T is the type Object.
7. S is an array type and T is the type Cloneable or Serializable. (These types are explained later in this chapter.)
8. S is the null type and T is not a primitive type.

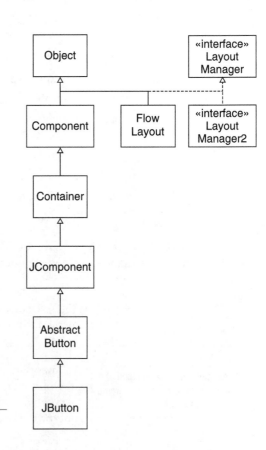

Figure 1

Examples of Subtype Relationships

For example (see Figure 1):

- `Container` is a subtype of `Component` because the class `Container` directly extends the class `Component`. (Rule 2)

- `JButton` is a subtype of `Component` because `JButton` extends `AbstractButton`, which extends `JComponent`, which extends `Container`, which extends `Component`. (Rule 2)

- `LayoutManager2` is a subtype of `LayoutManager` because the `LayoutManager2` interface type extends the `LayoutManager` interface type. (Rule 3)

- `FlowLayout` is a subtype of `LayoutManager` because `FlowLayout` implements the `LayoutManager` interface type. (Rule 4)

- `JButton[]` is a subtype of `Component[]` because `JButton` is a subtype of `Component`. (Rule 5)

- `int[]` is a subtype of `Object`. (Rule 6)

However, note that `int` is not a subtype of `long`, nor is `long` a subtype of `int`. Similarly, `int[]` is not a subtype of `Object[]`.

7.1.2 — Array Types

Array types are somewhat subtle in Java. Consider the rule that `S[]` is a subtype of `T[]` when `S` is a subtype of `T`. Let's look at a concrete example: an array of rectangles.

```
Rectangle[] r = new Rectangle[10];
```

Because `Shape[]` is a supertype, you can store the reference `r` in a variable of type `Shape[]`:

```
Shape[] s = r;
```

Note that `r` and `s` point to the same array of ten rectangle references (see Figure 2).

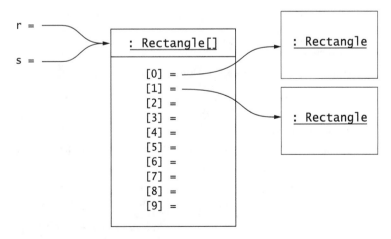

Figure 2

Two Array Variables of Different Types
Referring to the Same Array of Rectangles

At first, this seems to make sense. Of course, all s[i] are rectangles and hence shapes.

But now what stops you from storing a non-rectangle shape in the array?

```
s[0] = new Polygon(. . .);
```

The compiler accepts this statement because Polygon is a subtype of Shape, the type of s[0]. However, this code will throw an ArrayStoreException at runtime. Every array object remembers its component type. The virtual machine keeps track of all array stores and throws an exception if you try to store an object in an array whose class isn't a subtype of the array component type.

7.1.3 — Wrappers for Primitive Types

> Use wrapper classes whenever you need to supply primitive type values to services that require objects.

For efficiency's sake, primitive types aren't objects in Java. However, it is occasionally necessary to *wrap* primitive types into objects. There are eight wrapper classes:

```
Integer
Short
Long
Byte
Character
Float
Double
Boolean
```

NOTE   The wrapper classes are immutable. In particular, you cannot simulate "call by reference" by using wrappers.

For example, here is how you convert a value of type int into an Integer wrapper.

```
int n = 13;
Integer i = new Integer(n);
```

To unwrap a wrapped integer value, use the intValue method of the Integer wrapper class:

```
n = i.intValue();
```

There are corresponding methods such as doubleValue, booleanValue, and so on, in the other wrapper classes.

Starting with Java 5.0, the conversion between primitive types and the corresponding wrapper classes is automatic. For example,

```
int n = 13;
Integer i = n; // Automatically calls the Integer constructor
```

> Auto-boxing is the automatic conversion of a primitive type value into an object of a wrapper class.

This process is called *auto-boxing* (even though *auto-wrapping* might have been a better term). Conversion in the other direction is also automatic:

```
n = i; // Automatically calls the intValue method
```

Auto-boxing is particularly convenient if you need to store primitive type values in collections. For example, the type parameter of the `ArrayList<E>` class cannot be a primitive type. However, you can use an `ArrayList<Integer>`, and auto-boxing gives you the illusion that it contains `int` values:

```
ArrayList<Integer> luckyNumbers = new ArrayList<Integer>();
luckyNumbers.add(13); // Automatically calls the Integer constructor
```

NOTE   Be careful when comparing wrapper objects. The == operator only checks whether the wrapper objects are identical, not whether they have equal contents.

7.1.4 — Enumerated Types

An enumerated type is a type with a finite set of values. A typical example is a type `Size` with three values

```
SMALL
MEDIUM
LARGE
```

It is common to "fake" enumerated types by sequences of integers:

```
public static final int SMALL = 1;
public static final int MEDIUM = 2;
public static final int LARGE = 3;
```

However, this approach is not very satisfactory, because the compiler cannot check type errors. For example, consider the following code:

```
int size = LARGE;
size++;
```

> Use an enum instead of a sequence of integers to define enumerated types.

Now the value for `size` is no longer one of the three permitted values. Starting with Java 5.0, you can instead define an *enumerated type:*

```
public enum Size { SMALL, MEDIUM, LARGE };
```

The enum keyword defines a class with a private constructor and a finite number of instances. It is equivalent to the following:

```
public class Size
{
    private Size() {}

    public static final Size SMALL = new Size();
    public static final Size MEDIUM = new Size();
    public static final Size LARGE = new Size();
}
```

Note that the constructor for the `Size` class is *private*. Only the methods of the `Size` class can construct new instances. However, there are no such methods. Thus, the only three instances of the `Size` class that can ever exist are the three static members.

A user of the enumerated type can declare variables of type `Size` and initialize them with one of the three constant values:

```
Size imageSize = Size.MEDIUM;
```

You can use the `==` operator to compare enumeration values against each other. For example,

```
if (imageSize == Size.SMALL) . . .
```

 NOTE An enum variable can be `null`! For example, the `imageSize` variable in the preceding example has four possible values: `SMALL`, `MEDIUM`, `LARGE`, and `null`.

Because enumerated types are classes, you can add methods and instance fields. You can also supply constructors, but they can only be used to construct the enumeration values. For example,

```
public enum Size
{
    SMALL(0.5), MEDIUM(1), LARGE(2);
    private Size(double value) { this.value = value; }
    public double getValue() { return value; }
    private double value;
}
```

All enumeration classes automatically extend the `Enum` class, from which they inherit a number of useful methods. In particular, the `toString` method yields the name of an enumerated constant. For example, `Size.SMALL.toString()` returns the string `"SMALL"`. The `Enum` class implements the `Comparable` interface. The `compareTo` method compares enumeration instances in the order in which they are defined.

7.2   Type Inquiry

> The `instanceof` operator tests whether the type of an object is a subtype of a given type.

To test whether an expression *e* is a reference to an object of a given type or one of its subtypes, use the `instanceof` operator. The following condition tests whether *e* refers to an object of a subtype of the `Shape` interface type:

```
if (e instanceof Shape)
```

You might use this test before you apply a cast, to make sure that the cast does not fail. For example,

```
Object x = . . .;
if (x instanceof Shape)
{
    Shape s = (Shape) x; // Cast is guaranteed to succeed
    g2.draw(s);
}
```

The `instanceof` operator can test whether the type of a value is a subtype of a given type, but it won't give you the exact type. For example, if *e* `instanceof Shape` is `true`, then you don't know whether *e* is a `Rectangle` object or another shape. Testing *e* `instanceof`

Rectangle still doesn't give you a definite answer—*e* might belong to a subclass of Rectangle.

NOTE   If *e* is null, the test *e* instanceof T does not throw an exception but simply returns false.

> An object of the Class class is a descriptor for a type.

If you have any object reference, you can find the actual type of the object to which it refers with the getClass method. That method returns an object of type Class that describes the object's class.

```
Class c = e.getClass();
```

After you have a Class object, you can obtain a large amount of information about the class.

TIP   It can be hard to imagine Class objects. A Class object is a *type descriptor*. It contains information about a given type, such as the type name and the superclass. Figure 3 shows you the contrast between an Employee object and the Class object that describes the Employee class.

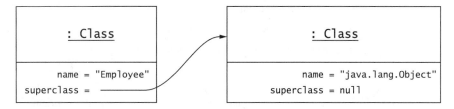
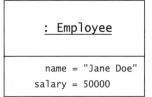

Figure 3

Contrasting an Employee Object with the Employee Class Object

To get the exact class name of a Java object, get its Class object and invoke the getName operation on it. The result is a string spelling out the class name. You can print it out for debugging purposes.

```
System.out.println(e.getClass().getName());
```

For example, if *e* is a Rectangle, then the class name is the string "java.awt.Rectangle".

The static `forName` method of the `Class` class is the converse of the `getName` method. Given a string that includes the package name, you get a `Class` object. For example,

```
Class c = Class.forName("java.awt.Rectangle");
```

> Adding the suffix `.class` to a type name yields the `Class` object that describes the type.

Instead of calling `Class.forName`, you can use *literal class objects*, by applying a suffix `.class` to a type name:

```
Class c = Rectangle.class;
```

NOTE You may wonder why you have to specify the full package name in `Class.forName("java.awt.Rectangle")`, but you can refer to `Rectangle.class` without the package name. Keep in mind that package lookup is a service of the compiler. If you import the `java.awt` package, then the compiler translates `Rectangle` into `java.awt.Rectangle`. In a running program, *all* classes (including those in the `java.lang` package) must be qualified with the package name.

NOTE The name `Class` is a misnomer—`Class` objects can describe *any type*, including primitive types, class types, and interface types. For example, `int.class` is the `Class` object that describes the `int` type.

NOTE The `Class` class has a type parameter. For example, `Rectangle.class` is an instance of `Class<Rectangle>`—in fact, it is the sole instance of that type. For simplicity, we omit the type parameter for now.

There is only one `Class` object for every type that has been loaded into the virtual machine. Therefore, you can use the `==` operator to test whether two class objects describe the same type. For example, here is how you can test whether the object *e* is an instance of the `Rectangle` class:

```
if (e.getClass() == Rectangle.class) . . .
```

This test is true if the class of *e* is exactly the `Rectangle` class.

TIP You should not use type inquiry as a substitute for polymorphism. When you find code of the form

```
if (e.getClass() == Employee.class) some action;
else if (e.getClass() == Manager.class) another action;
```

ask yourself how the variation of the action can be described by a method. Then supply two versions of the method, one in the `Employee` class and one in the `Manager` class, and call

```
e.action();
```

The mechanism of polymorphism automatically invokes the correct method, even if you later add other subclasses of `Employee`. Code with polymorphism is much easier to maintain and extend than code that uses type inquiry.

When getClass is applied to an array, the result is a Class object that describes the array type. The isArray method tests whether a type is an array type. The getComponentType method returns a Class object describing the component type.

```
double[] a = new double[10];
Class c = a.getClass();
if (c.isArray())
   System.out.println("Component type=" + c.getComponentType());
      // Prints Component type=double
```

NOTE   For historical reasons, the getName method produces strange-looking names for array types. For example, double[].class.getName() is

"[D"

and String[][].class.getName() is

"[[Ljava.lang.String;"

In general, an array type name is made up according to the following rules:

[type	array type
B	byte
C	char
D	double
F	float
I	int
J	long
Lname;	class or interface
S	short
Z	boolean

7.3   The Object Class

The Object class is the common superclass of all other Java classes.

All Java classes are subclasses of the Object class. A class that is defined without an extends clause is a direct subclass of Object. Therefore, the methods of the Object class apply to all Java objects (including arrays). The most important methods of the Object class are:

Method	Description
String toString()	Returns a string representation of the object
boolean equals(Object other)	Compares the object with another object
int hashCode()	Returns a hash code
Object clone()	Returns a copy of the object

7.3.1 — The toString Method

> The toString method yields a string that describes the state of an object.

The toString method is important because it is automatically applied

- When you concatenate an object with a string
- When you print an object with the print or println method of the PrintStream and PrintWriter classes
- When you pass an object reference *e* to an assert statement of the form assert *condition* : *e*;

For example,

```
Rectangle r = new Rectangle(5, 10, 20, 30);
String s = "r=" + r;
```

really executes code that is equivalent to

```
String s = "r=" + r.toString();
```

That sets s to the string

```
"r=java.awt.Rectangle[x=5,y=10,width=20,height=30]"
```

The Rectangle class has implemented the toString method to print out the class name, followed by the names and values of the instance fields.

Not all class implementors were that thoughtful. For example, if you print a GeneralPath object, you will get a printout somewhat like this:

```
java.awt.geom.GeneralPath@4abc9
```

The implementor of the GeneralPath class did not override toString, so the default implementation of the toString method in the Object class is used. That method returns the name of the class and the hash code of the object. (We will discuss hash codes later in this chapter.)

Because the toString method is a useful debugging aid, it is a good idea to implement it in your own classes. For example,

```
public class Employee
{
   public String toString()
   {
      return getClass().getName()
            + "[name=" + name
            + ",salary=" + salary
            + "]";
   }
   . . .
}
```

A typical string is

```
Employee[name=Harry Hacker,salary=35000]
```

However, if the class has a superclass, then you should first call its toString method and then add the fields of the subclass:

```
public class Manager extends Employee
{
   public String toString()
   {
      return super.toString()
             + "[bonus=" + bonus
             + "]";
   }
   . . .
}
```

A typical string is

```
Manager[name=Wendy Chen,salary=100000][bonus=20000]
```

 TIP The toString methods in your programs should always return the result of calling get-Class().getName(), not a hard-coded class name. Then the correct class name is produced for subclasses.

7.3.2 — Equality Testing

> The equals method tests whether two objects have equal contents.

The test

    x == y

tests whether x and y are two references to the same object.

In contrast, the test

    x.equals(y)

tests whether x and y are references to two objects that may be distinct but that have "equal" contents.

The default implementation of equals in the Object class simply tests for identity:

```
public class Object
{
   public boolean equals(Object obj)
   {
      return this == obj;
   }
   . . .
}
```

Each class needs to define what it means for its objects to be equal to another. For example, we may consider two Employee objects equal to each other if they have equal name and salary fields. Alternatively, one may take the position that two Employee objects are equal if they have the same ID number, without testing the name and salary values. The second definition might be more appropriate in an application where employee names and salaries are subject to change. Thus, it is up to each class how to define the notion of equality that is most appropriate for its objects.

The equals method is used by many methods in the collection classes. Here is a typical example, the indexOf method of the ArrayList class.

```
/**
    Searches for the first occurrence of the given argument, testing
    for equality using the equals method.
    @param elem an object
    @return the index of the first occurrence of the argument in this
    list; returns −1 if the object is not found.
*/
public int indexOf(Object elem)
{
    if (elem == null) . . .
    else
    {
        for (int i = 0; i < size; i++)
            if (elem.equals(elementData[i]))
                return i;
    }
    return -1;
}
```

Because so many methods in the Java library assume that objects have a well-defined notion of equality, it is important that you define the equals method for your own classes. In many cases, objects are equal if corresponding fields are equal:

```
public class Employee
{
    public boolean equals(Object otherObject) // Not complete — see below
    {
        Employee other = (Employee) otherObject;
        return name.equals(other.name)
                && salary == other.salary;
    }
    . . .
}
```

Note the use of equals to compare fields of a class type and == to compare fields of a primitive type.

However, it is not always this simple. For example, two sets should be considered equal if they contain the same elements in some order, not necessarily the same order. The equals method of the AbstractSet class, the common superclass of HashSet and TreeSet, tests that two sets have the same size and that one is contained in the other. Here is a slightly simplified version of the actual implementation.

```
public class AbstractSet . . .
{
    public boolean equals(Object otherObject)
    {
        if (!(otherObject instanceof Set)) return false;
        Collection other = (Collection) otherObject;
        if (size() != other.size()) return false;
        return containsAll(other);
    }
    . . .
}
```

There are some technical requirements that the Java Language Specification imposes on the `equals` method.

- It is *reflexive:* for any reference value x, x.equals(x) should return true.
- It is *symmetric:* for any reference values x and y, x.equals(y) should return true if and only if y.equals(x) returns true.
- It is *transitive:* for any reference values x, y, and z, if x.equals(y) returns true and y.equals(z) returns true, then x.equals(z) should return true.
- For any non-null reference value x, x.equals(null) should return false.

> The equals method must be reflexive, symmetric, and transitive.

The `equals` method of the `Employee` class in the preceding example violates two of these rules. First, it doesn't return `false` if `otherObject` is `null`. That's easy to fix:

```
public boolean equals(Object otherObject)
{
    if (otherObject == null) return false;
    . . .
}
```

What should happen if `otherObject` is not an `Employee` object? It seems reasonable that the `equals` method should then also return `false`.

```
public class Employee
{
    public boolean equals(Object otherObject)
    {
        if (getClass() != otherObject.getClass()) return false;
        . . .
    }
    . . .
}
```

This makes sense; if the classes aren't identical, the objects can't be truly equal.

Finally, it is a good idea to check whether `this == otherObject` at the beginning of the `equals` method. Many times, `equals` is called on identical objects, and then there is no point in checking for equal contents. Thus, the perfect `equals` method starts out like this:

```
public boolean equals(Object otherObject)
{
    if (this == otherObject) return true;
    if (otherObject == null) return false;
    if (getClass() != otherObject.getClass()) return false;
    . . .
}
```

Because a subclass has no access to the superclass state, its `equals` method must invoke the superclass version:

```
public class Manager extends Employee
{
    public boolean equals(Object otherObject)
    {
        if (!super.equals(otherObject)) return false;
        Manager other = (Manager) otherObject;
        return bonus == other.bonus;
```

```
            }
               . . .
         }
```

Special Topic   **7.1**

Consequences of the Symmetry Condition for Equality Testing

In many published examples, you will find that programmers use an `instanceof` test in the `equals` method. However, that test is often wrong, for a subtle reason. Consider this example:

```java
public class Employee
{
   public boolean equals(Object otherObject)
   {
      if (!(otherObject instanceof Employee)) return false; // DON'T
      . . .
   }
   . . .
}
public class Manager
{
   public boolean equals(Object otherObject)
   {
      if (!(otherObject instanceof Manager)) return false; // DON'T
      . . .
   }
}
```

Suppose you compare an `Employee` object e and a `Manager` object m that happen to have the same name and the same salary. Then `e.equals(m)` would be true, but `m.equals(e)` would be false. The symmetry condition is violated!

Using `getClass` instead of `instanceof` is much safer. You are automatically guaranteed that the symmetry condition holds.

However, not every use of `instanceof` in an `equals` method is an error. If a class is `final`, then it doesn't matter whether one uses `instanceof` or `getClass`, because a final class has no subclasses. Also, if you look again at the definition of equality of the `AbstractSet` class that you saw earlier in this section, you will note the test

```java
if (!(otherObject instanceof Set)) return false;
```

As you can see, an `AbstractSet` is willing to compare itself to any objects that implement the `Set` interface type. In order to preserve symmetry, all other classes that implement the `Set` interface must now support the same notion of equality. For sets, this is not a problem because the mathematical definition of a set specifies when two sets are equal.

However, in most programming situations, subclasses cannot simply inherit the notion of equality from their superclasses. As a rule of thumb, you should avoid the use of `instanceof` in `equals` methods.

7.3.3 — Hashing

> The hashCode method computes the hash code of an object. It must be compatible with the equals method.

The HashSet and HashMap classes of the Java library use hash tables to quickly locate elements. (See the special topic at the end of this section for more information on hash tables.) Because the Object class has a hashCode method, objects of any type can be stored in hash tables.

Of course, it is important that the hashCode be consistent with the equals method, that is,

- If x.equals(y), then x.hashCode() == y.hashCode().

The default implementation of hashCode in the Object class hashes the memory address of the object, which is consistent with the Object.equals method. But if you redefine the equals method in a subclass, you must also redefine hashCode, or the hash table will not function correctly.

A hash function computes an integer hash code from an object, so that different objects are likely to have different hash codes. Let's first look at how the standard library computes a hash code from a string. Clearly, the character values of the string must be combined to yield some integer. You could, for example, add up the character values:

```
int h = 0;
for (int i = 0; i < s.length(); i++)
    h = h + s.charAt(i);
```

However, that would not be a good idea. It doesn't scramble the character values enough. Strings that are permutations of another (such as "eat" and "tea") all have the same hash code.

Here is the method that the standard library uses to compute the hash code for a string.

```
int h = 0;
for (int i = 0; i < s.length(); i++)
    h = 31 * h + s.charAt(i);
```

For example, the hash code of "eat" is

$$31 * (31 * 'e' + 'a') + 't' = 100184$$

The hash code of "tea" is quite different, namely

$$31 * (31 * 't' + 'e') + 'a' = 114704$$

(Use a Unicode table to look up the character values: 'a' is 97, 'e' is 101, and 't' is 116.)

Now consider the Employee class. Two Employee objects are considered equal to one another if they have equal names and salaries. Therefore, we should compute the hash codes of the individual fields and combine them. It is best to multiply individual hash codes with relatively prime factors before adding them together, to minimize the risk of collisions.

Here is a definition of hashCode for the Employee class. Note that we wrap the double value before computing its hash code.

```
public class Employee
{
    public int hashCode()
    {
```

```
        return 11 * name.hashCode()
            + 13 * new Double(salary).hashCode();
    }
    . . .
}
```

Now equal `Employee` objects will yield the same hash code.

To emphasize that the `hashCode` computation is tied to the definition of the `equals` method, let's look at the `hashCode` implementation of the `AbstractSet` class. Two sets that are equal must yield the same hash code, even if the order of their elements differs. For that reason, the `AbstractSet` class simply adds up the hash codes of its elements.

```
public class AbstractSet . . .
{
    public int hashCode()
    {
        int h = 0;
        Iterator i = iterator();
        while (i.hasNext())
        {
            Object obj = i.next();
            if (obj != null) h += obj.hashCode();
        }
        return h;
    }
    . . .
}
```

The sum stays the same, even if the order of the elements changes.

Special Topic 7.2

Hash Tables

The technique of *hashing* can be used to find elements in a data structure quickly, without making a linear search through all elements. Hashing gives rise to the *hash table*, which can be used to implement sets and maps.

A *hash function* is a function that computes an integer value, the *hash code*, from an object in such a way that different objects are likely to yield different hash codes. The `Object` class has a `hashCode` method that other classes need to redefine. The call

```
    int h = x.hashCode();
```

computes the hash code of the object x.

It is possible that two or more distinct objects have the same hash code. That is called a *collision*. A good hash function minimizes collisions. For example, the `String` class defines a hash function for strings that does a good job of producing different integer values for different strings. Table 1 shows some examples of strings and their hash codes.

A hash code is used as an array index into a hash table. In the simplest implementation of a hash table, you could make an array and insert each object at the location of its hash code (see Figure 4).

String	Hash Code
"Adam"	2035631
"Eve"	70068
"Harry"	6949448
"Jim"	74478
"Joe"	74656
"Juliet"	−2065036585
"Katherine"	2079199209
"Sue"	83491

Table 1

Sample Strings and
Their Hash Codes

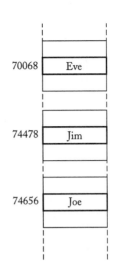

Figure 4

A Simplistic Implementation
of a Hash Table

Then it is a very simple matter to find out whether an object is already present in the hash table or not. Compute its hash code and check whether the array position with that hash code is already occupied. This doesn't require a search through the entire array.

However, there are two problems with this simplistic approach. First, it is not possible to allocate an array that is large enough to hold all possible integer index positions. Therefore, choose an array of some reasonable size and then reduce the hash code to fall inside the array:

```
int h = x.hashCode();
if (h < 0) h = -h;
h = h % size;
```

Second, it is possible that two different objects have the same hash code. After reducing the hash code for a smaller array size, it becomes even more likely that several objects collide and need to share a position in the array.

To store multiple objects in the same array position, use (short, we hope) link sequences for the elements with the same hash code (see Figure 5). These link sequences are called *buckets*.

Now the algorithm for finding an object x in a hash table is quite simple.

1. Compute the hash code and reduce it to fit the table. This gives an index h into the hash table.
2. Iterate through the elements of the bucket at position h. For each element of the bucket, check whether it is equal to x.
3. If a match is found among the elements of that bucket, then x is in the set. Otherwise, it is not.

In the best case, in which there are no collisions, all buckets either are empty or have a single element. Then checking for containment takes constant or $O(1)$ time.

More generally, for this algorithm to be effective, the bucket sizes must be small. If the table has only a few entries, then collisions are unavoidable, and each bucket will get quite full.

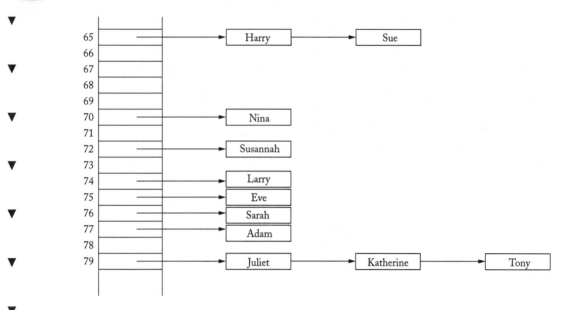

Figure 5

A Hash Table with Linked Lists to Store Elements with the Same Hash Code

Then the linear search through a bucket is time consuming. In the worst case, where all elements end up in the same bucket, a hash table degenerates into a linked list!

Therefore, it is recommended that the table be somewhat larger than the number of elements that you expect to insert. Then there is a good chance for avoiding collisions altogether. An excess capacity of about 30 percent is typical. According to some researchers, the hash table size should be chosen to be a prime number to minimize the number of collisions.

Adding an element is a simple extension of the algorithm for finding an object. First compute the hash code to locate the bucket in which the element should be inserted. Try finding the object in that bucket. If it is already present, do nothing. Otherwise, insert it.

Removing an element is equally simple. First compute the hash code to locate the bucket in which the element should be inserted. Try finding the object in that bucket. If it is present, remove it. Otherwise, do nothing.

As long as there are few collisions, an element can be added or removed in constant or $O(1)$ time.

7.4   Shallow and Deep Copy

> A deep copy or clone of an object is an object with distinct identity and equal contents.

As you know, a copy of an object reference is another reference to the same object. The clone method of the Object class is useful when you want to make a *deep copy* or *clone* of the object (see Figure 6).

```
Employee e = new Employee(. . .);
Employee cloned = e.clone();
```

Here we assume that the Employee class supplies an appropriate clone method.

Figure 6

Cloning an Object

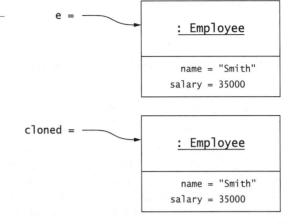

In general, a `clone` method is expected to fulfill these three conditions:

- `x.clone() != x`
- `x.clone().equals(x)`
- `x.clone().getClass() == x.getClass()`

That is, the clone should be a new object, but it should be equal to its original.

For reasons that will become apparent presently, cloning is a subtle process. Therefore, the `Object` class didn't dare to make `clone` a public method and made it `protected` instead. If a class wants to allow clients to clone its instances, it must redefine `clone` to a `public` method.

```
public class Employee
{
   public Employee clone()
   {
      return super.clone(); // Not complete
   }
   . . .
}
```

NOTE   When overriding the `Object.clone` method, we change the return type from `Object` to `Employee`. This is a feature of Java 5.0. In older versions of Java, it was not possible to constrain the return type when overriding a method.

> To define a `clone` method, a class must minimally implement the `Cloneable` interface type and override the `clone` method.

However, it isn't this simple. The designers of the `Object` class were so nervous about clonability that they added a second requirement. Any class willing to be cloned must implement the `Cloneable` interface type.

```
public class Employee implements Cloneable
{
   public Employee clone()
   {
```

```
        return (Employee) super.clone(); // Not complete
    }
    . . .
}
```

The `Cloneable` interface type is a curious interface type because it has *no methods:*

```
public interface Cloneable { }
```

It is a "tagging" interface type—you can only use it to test whether an object implements it:

```
if (x instanceof Cloneable) . . .
```

When the `Object` class finds that the object to be cloned isn't an instance of a class that implements `Cloneable`, it throws a `CloneNotSupportedException`. Unfortunately, this is a checked exception, so you must declare or catch it. Normally, we advocate declaring checked exceptions instead of catching them. But in this case, that would force the caller to handle an exception that will in fact never happen. Therefore, in this case, it is appropriate to "squelch" the exception:

```
public class Employee implements Cloneable
{
    public Employee clone()
    {
        try
        {
            return (Employee) super.clone();
        }
        catch (CloneNotSupportedException e)
        {
            return null; // Won't happen
        }
    }
    . . .
}
```

Why all the fuss? The `Object.clone` method makes a *shallow* copy. It makes a new object of the same type as the original and copies the values of all fields. If the fields are object references, the original and the clone can share common subobjects.

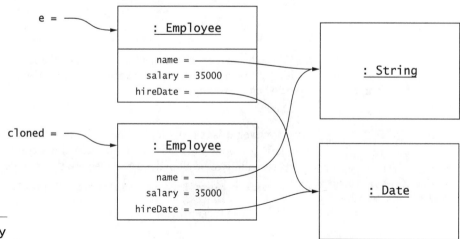

Figure 7

A Shallow Copy

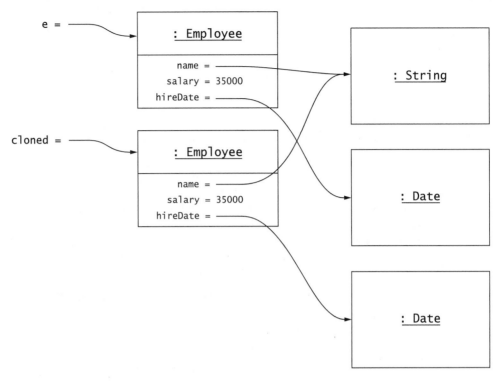

Figure 8

A "Sufficiently Deep" Copy

Consider an `Employee` class that stores the employee name, salary, and hire date. Figure 7 shows the shallow copy that `Object.clone` creates. As you can see, both the original and the clone share a `String` and a `Date` object.

The sharing of the `String` object is not a problem—strings are immutable. But sharing a `Date` is only reasonable if we know that none of the `Employee` methods mutates it. Otherwise, it too should be cloned.

Here is how you can define a "sufficiently deep" copy of the `Employee` class with a hire date (see Figure 8).

```java
public class Employee implements Cloneable
{
   public Employee clone()
   {
      try
      {
         Employee cloned = (Employee) super.clone();
         cloned.hireDate = (Date) hireDate.clone();
         return cloned;
      }
      catch (CloneNotSupportedException e)
      {
```

```
            return null;
        }
    }
    . . .
}
```

NOTE The `clone` method is defined for arrays. It makes a shallow copy of the array, that is, a new array of the same type and size whose elements are copies (but not clones) of the original elements.

Now you know why the `Object.clone` method is so paranoid. Its behavior—to make a shallow copy of all fields—is simply not appropriate for most subclasses. The designers of the `Object` class were in a position to express their paranoia in three ways: the `protected` attribute, the `Cloneable` interface type, and the checked `CloneNotSupportedException`.

The users of your classes aren't so lucky. The `Employee.clone` method is every bit as risky as `Object.clone`. A subclass must be very careful to override `clone` if it has mutable fields.

```
public class Manager extends Employee
{
    public Manager clone()
    {
        Manager cloned = (Manager) super.clone();
        clone mutable fields
        return cloned;
    }
    . . .
}
```

But unlike `Object.clone`, `Employee.clone` carries no warning. It is a public method that throws no exceptions. And, of course, since `Employee` implements `Cloneable`, all of its subclasses do too.

NOTE As you can see, tagging interface types such as `Cloneable` are not really useful for non-`final` classes. A tagging interface type is supposed to validate that a programmer understands a subtle issue. But interface types are inherited, so the validation automatically extends to subclasses, even though there is no guarantee that the subclass implementors have the same understanding.

NOTE You may wonder why the `clone` method doesn't make a deep copy by default. Arguably, a deep copy is a more reasonable default than a shallow copy. But it is not always appropriate. Sometimes, a cloned object should share some subobjects with the original object. Suppose, for example, that each `Employee` object has a field of type `Department` that signifies the department in which the employee works. A clone of an employee object should probably *not* make a deep copy of the department object. After all, there is a benefit of shared references to the same department object. If the department changes its name (say, from Personnel to Human Resources), then all employees automatically pick up the name change of the shared object. Thus, cloning truly is a subtle business, and each class needs to decide which fields to clone.

7.5 Serialization

> Serialization denotes the process of storing an object and its dependent objects in a stream.

In Java, it is simple to save objects to a stream *without converting them to an external representation*. For example, suppose you want to save an array of Employee objects to a file.

```
Employee[] staff = new Employee[2];
staff[0] = new Employee();
staff[1] = new Employee();
```

Construct an ObjectOutputStream that is associated with a FileOutputStream.

```
ObjectOutputStream out = new ObjectOutputStream(
      new FileOutputStream("staff.dat"));
```

Then write the array and close the stream.

```
out.writeObject(staff);
out.close();
```

Now the array *and all objects that it references* are saved to the file. To read the data back, reverse the process.

```
ObjectInputStream in = new ObjectInputStream(
      new FileInputStream("staff.dat"));
Employee[] staff = (Employee[]) in.readObject();
in.close();
```

Afterwards, the staff array is filled with Employee objects that are identical to the saved ones.

> Objects of classes that implement the Serializable interface type can be serialized in object streams.

Remarkably, the Employee class does not have to implement any methods to make this possible. This is in marked contrast to the toString and clone methods, which require programmers to supply an implementation. The only requirement is that the class (or one of its superclasses) implements the Serializable interface type.

```
public class Employee implements Serializable
{
   . . .
}
```

The Serializable interface type is a tagging interface type similar to Cloneable, with no methods.

To gain some respect for the serialization mechanism, let's understand how it works in a complex situation. Suppose that each Employee object has a field

```
private Employee buddy;
```

The buddy of an employee is another employee, perhaps one who is called to duty if an employee cannot show up for work. Figure 9 shows a scenario in which two employees are buddies of each other. Suppose the array of employees is serialized.

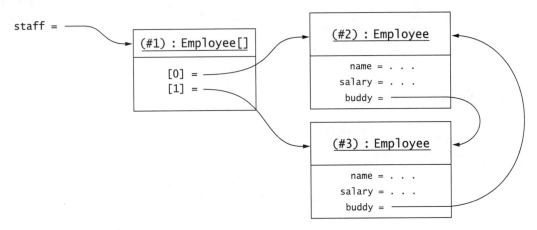

Figure 9

Objects with References Between Them to be Serialized

The serialized file contains the following information:

- Object #1, type = Employee[]
  - [0] component is Object #2, type = Employee
    - name field is . . .
    - salary field is . . .
    - buddy field is Object #3, type = Employee
      - name field is . . .
      - salary field is . . .
      - buddy field is Object #2 (already described)
  - [1] component is Object #3 (already described)

As you can see, every object gets a *serial number* (#1, #2, #3). When an object is saved for the first time, its fields are saved as well. However, when an object has been previously saved, then only the serial number is saved.

There are a few times when it is not desirable to have a field serialized explicitly. By marking the field as transient, it is simply not saved or restored. For example, when serializing an item in a scene, you may not want to save whether or not the item was currently selected. Then declare the selected flag like this:

```
private transient boolean selected;
```

Another reason for using the transient keyword is to avoid errors with instance fields of types that are not serializable. For example, the graphical shapes in the java.awt.geom package are not serializable. There is no good reason for this limitation. The programmers who implemented these classes simply neglected to implement the Serializable interface type. If your class has fields of that type, you must mark them as transient. (If you don't, then a NotSerializableException will be thrown when trying to write the object.) For example, in a serializable Car class, you would declare the tires as transient.

```
private transient Ellipse2D.Double frontTire;
```

NOTE   If you use transient fields, then the default serialization mechanism may not store sufficient information. To overcome that problem, you need to supply special methods

```
private void writeObject(ObjectOutputStream out)
private void readObject(ObjectInputStream in)
```

These methods must first call `defaultWriteObject`/`defaultReadObject` to write or read the superclass information and any non-transient fields, and then manually write or read the remaining information. You will find an example in the companion code to this book in `Ch7/serial2/Car.java`.

NOTE   Serialization is well suited for *short-term* storage of objects. However, if the definition of a class changes, then the serialization format also changes. As a consequence, you cannot read in files that contain objects of an older version of the class. A better alternative for long-term storage of classes whose definition may change over time is the long-term persistence storage for JavaBeans—see `http://java.sun.com/products/jfc/tsc/articles/persistence/index.html`.

7.6   Reflection

> Reflection denotes the ability of a program to analyze its objects and their capabilities.

Reflection is a mechanism by which a program can find out about the capabilities of its objects at runtime, and manipulate the objects whose capabilities it has discovered. Reflection is particularly useful for building programming tools. For example, the BlueJ environment uses reflection to enumerate the constructors and methods of arbitrary classes. Reflection is also an essential part of the JavaBeans component model that we describe at the end of this chapter.

In order to support reflection, a number of classes have been created to describe the various features of Java types. They are shown in the table below.

Reflection Class	Purpose
Class	Describes a type
Package	Describes a package
Field	Describes a field and allows inspection and modification of fields
Method	Describes a method and allows its invocation on objects
Constructor	Describes a constructor and allows its invocation
Array	Has static methods to analyze arrays

> **TIP** Just as the `Class` class can be demystified by thinking of it as a type descriptor, you should think of the other reflection classes as descriptors. For example, a `Method` object is not a method. It just describes a method. The object knows the method name and its parameter and return types. It knows how to call the method. But it doesn't know what the method does.

7.6.1 — Enumerating the Features of a Class

As you have seen, you can obtain the `Class` object that describes the type of any object. The `Class` object gives a wealth of information about the class:

- The superclass
- All interface types that the class implements
- The package of the class
- The names and types of all fields
- The names, parameter types, and return types of all methods
- The parameter types of all constructors

The `getSuperclass` method returns the `Class` object that describes the superclass of a given type. If the type does not have a superclass (because it is `Object` or not a class type), then the `getSuperclass` method returns `null`.

The `getInterfaces` method returns an array of `Class` objects describing the interface types that a class implements or an interface type extends. If the type doesn't implement or extend interface types, an array of length 0 is returned. Note that this method only returns the direct superinterface. That means you need to call this method on all superclasses and superinterfaces to obtain the complete collection of interface types that a class implements.

For example, the statement

```
Class[] interfaces = Rectangle.class.getInterfaces();
```

yields an array consisting of the two elements `Shape.class` and `Serializable.class`. Note that `Cloneable.class` is not in the array because it is not a direct superinterface.

The `getPackage` method returns a `Package` object that describes the package of a class. For example,

```
Package pkg = String.class.getPackage();
System.out.println(pkg.getName()); // Prints java.lang
```

> Using reflection, you can enumerate all fields, methods, and constructors of a class.

The `getDeclaredFields` method returns an array of `Field` objects for all fields that this class or interface declares. That includes public, private, protected, and package-visible fields. Both instance fields and static fields are included. However, fields from superclasses are not. If you want to have information on a specific field whose name you know, then you can call the `getDeclaredField` method to get a `Field` object describing the field with the given name. There is also a less useful `getFields` method that returns all public fields of the class and its superclasses.

The Field class has three methods to describe the field: getName gets the field name, getType gets the field type (as a Class object), and getModifiers gets an integer that has various bits set to indicate whether the field is public, private, protected, static, or final. Use the static isPublic, isPrivate, isProtected, isStatic, isFinal methods of the Modifier class to test the return value of getModifiers. For example, the following loop prints out the names of all static fields of the Math class.

```
Field[] fields = Math.class.getDeclaredFields();
for (Field f : fields)
   if (Modifier.isStatic(f.getModifiers()))
      System.out.println(f.getName());
```

The getDeclaredConstructors method of the Class class returns an array of Constructor objects that describes the constructors of the class. A class can have multiple constructors, each with different parameter types. The getParameterTypes method of the Constructor class returns an array of Class objects that describe the parameter types.

For example, calling

```
Constructor[] constructors = Rectangle.class.getDeclaredConstructors()
```

returns an array of seven Constructor objects, one for each of the constructors of the class. The double loop

```
for (Constructor c : constructors)
{
   Class[] params = c.getParameterTypes();
   System.out.print("Rectangle(");
   for (int i = 0; i < params.length; i++)
   {
      if (i > 0) System.out.print(", ");
      System.out.print(params[i].getName());
   }
   System.out.println(")");
}
```

prints the parameter types of all of them, yielding the output

```
Rectangle()
Rectangle(java.awt.Rectangle)
Rectangle(int, int, int, int)
Rectangle(int, int)
Rectangle(java.awt.Point, java.awt.Dimension)
Rectangle(java.awt.Point)
Rectangle(java.awt.Dimension)
```

Finally, the getDeclaredMethods method of the Class class returns an array of Method objects that describes each method. As with Constructor objects, the getParameter-Types method returns an array of parameter types. In addition, the getName method returns the method name, and the getReturnType method returns a Class object describing the return type.

You can also get the descriptor of a single method. Call the getDeclaredMethod method with the method name and the parameter types. The parameter types are needed because there may be multiple methods with the same name. For example, to obtain a `Method` object for the method

```
contains(int x, int y)
```

of the `Rectangle` class, you call

```
Method m = Rectangle.class.getDeclaredMethod("contains",
       int.class, int.class);
```

Similarly, to obtain a single `Constructor` object, you specify the parameter types, such as

```
Constructor c = Rectangle.class.getDeclaredConstructor();
        // Gets the default constructor because no parameters specified
```

You will see in the next section how to call a method that is described by a `Method` object.

NOTE   The `getDeclaredMethod` and `getDeclaredConstructor` methods are "varargs" methods that take a variable number of parameters of type `Class`. They are declared as

```
Method getDeclaredMethod(String name, Class... parameterTypes)
Constructor getDeclaredConstructor(Class... parameterTypes)
```

You supply zero or more parameters of type `Class`.

In the examples of this section, we showed you the effect of the reflection mechanism on known classes such as `String` and `Rectangle`. However, the real importance of the mechanism is to analyze classes that are not known when the program is compiled. For example, the BlueJ program lets you load arbitrary classes, and it enumerates their constructors and methods for you.

7.6.2 — Invoking Methods

A `Method` object describes a method of some class. Can you call the method? Sure you can. The `Method` class has an `invoke` method for that purpose. Give it the implicit and explicit parameter objects, and the method is invoked. Let's run through an example.

Suppose you want to call the `println` method of the `PrintStream` class the hard way, by getting the `Method` object and giving it `System.out` and `"Hello, World!"` as parameters.

First, get the `Method` object, as discussed in the preceding section: You want the `println` method of the `PrintStream` class that takes one parameter of type `String`.

```
Method m = PrintStream.class.getDeclaredMethod("println", String.class);
```

Then invoke m on the implicit parameter `System.out`, and supply the explicit parameters. In this case, there is just one explicit parameter, the string `"Hello, World!"`.

```
m.invoke(System.out, "Hello, World");
```

As a result, the string `"Hello, World!"` is printed to `System.out`.

The `invoke` method receives a variable number of parameters of type `Object`. The first parameter is the implicit parameter of the call. Supply `null` if you call a static method. The remaining parameters are the explicit parameters of the call.

Here is the complete program.

Ch7/reflect1/HardHello.java

```
1  import java.lang.reflect.*;
2  import java.io.*;
3
4  /**
5     This program prints "Hello, World!" the hard way,
6     using reflection.
7  */
8  public class HardHello
9  {
10    public static void main(String[] args)
11        throws NoSuchMethodException, IllegalAccessException,
12            InvocationTargetException
13    {
14      Method m = PrintStream.class.getDeclaredMethod(
15          "println", String.class);
16      m.invoke(System.out, "Hello, World!");
17    }
18 }
```

The `getDeclaredMethod` and `invoke` methods can throw a number of serious exceptions—if the method doesn't exist, if you call it with the wrong parameter types, if the method is not accessible (for example, because it is `private`), or if the method throws an exception during its execution.

If any of the method parameters are primitive types, they need to be wrapped into objects of the corresponding wrapper classes. As of Java 5.0, auto-boxing takes care of this issue.

If the method returns a value, the `invoke` method returns it as an `Object`. If the return type is a primitive type, then it is wrapped in a wrapper object. For example, if a method returns a `double`, then `invoke` returns a `Double` object. You can have it automatically unboxed, provided that you cast the returned value to the wrapper type.

For example, here is a call to `Math.sqrt(4.0)`:

```
Method m = Math.class.getDeclaredMethod("sqrt", double.class);
double r = (Double) m.invoke(null, 4.0); // r is 2.0
```

Why would anyone want to go through this trouble to call a method? There is of course no sense in calling a known method in this way. However, if a program needs to call a method that is not known when the program is compiled, then the dynamic invocation mechanism is required. For example, the JUnit program dynamically invokes all methods of a test class whose names start with `test`.

7.6.3 — Inspecting Objects

You can also use the reflection mechanism to dynamically look up the fields of objects as a program runs. Of course, fields are generally private, so you must override the normal access control mechanism. To allow access to a field, call its `setAccessible` method, like this:

```
Class c = obj.getClass();
Field f = c.getDeclaredField(name);
f.setAccessible(true);
```

It appears dangerous to allow a program to read and write private fields of any object. For that reason, the `setAccessible` call can be protected by installing a security manager. By default, basic Java applications do not install a security manager. However, applets, servlets, and other types of programs run with a security manager that disallows access to private fields. (For more information on security managers, see Horstmann and Cornell, *Core Java*, 7th ed., vol. 2, Sun Microsystems Press, 2005).

If you are granted access, you can read and write any field of the object:

```
Object value = f.get(obj);
f.set(obj, value);
```

Of course, f must be a `Field` object that describes a field of the class of `obj`; otherwise, the `get` and `set` methods throw an exception.

If the field type is a primitive type, then the `get` method returns a wrapper object. Conversely, the `set` method expects a wrapper object and unwraps it.

To read or write a static field, supply `null` for the object.

Let's run through an example. The following program spies on the internal state of a randomizer. When you run the program, you can observe how the `seed` field changes. Note the generic `spyFields` method that can show the fields of *any* object, not just a random number generator.

Ch7/reflect2/FieldTester.java

```
 1  import java.lang.reflect.*;
 2  import java.util.*;
 3
 4  /**
 5     This program shows how to use reflection to print
 6     the names and values of all nonstatic fields of an object.
 7  */
 8  public class FieldTester
 9  {
10     public static void main(String[] args)
11           throws IllegalAccessException
12     {
13        Random r = new Random();
14        System.out.print(spyFields(r));
15        r.nextInt();
16        System.out.println("\nAfter calling nextInt:\n");
17        System.out.print(spyFields(r));
18     }
19
20     /**
21        Spies on the field names and values of an object.
22        @param obj the object whose fields to format
23        @return a string containing the names and values of
24        all nonstatic fields of obj
25     */
26     public static String spyFields(Object obj)
27           throws IllegalAccessException
28     {
```

```
29          StringBuffer buffer = new StringBuffer();
30          Field[] fields = obj.getClass().getDeclaredFields();
31          for (Field f : fields)
32          {
33             if (!Modifier.isStatic(f.getModifiers()))
34             {
35                f.setAccessible(true);
36                Object value = f.get(obj);
37                buffer.append(f.getType().getName());
38                buffer.append(" ");
39                buffer.append(f.getName());
40                buffer.append("=");
41                buffer.append("" + value);
42                buffer.append("\n");
43             }
44          }
45          return buffer.toString();
46       }
47 }
```

Here is a typical output of the program.

```
java.util.concurrent.atomic.AtomicLong seed=214557382433043
double nextNextGaussian=0.0
boolean haveNextNextGaussian=false
```

After calling nextInt:

```
java.util.concurrent.atomic.AtomicLong seed=231457616363298
double nextNextGaussian=0.0
boolean haveNextNextGaussian=false
```

NOTE You may wonder why Java doesn't use a method such as spyFields to implement a generic toString method. However, it isn't always so simple. Suppose the Employee class has a field Employee buddy. If it happens that Harry's buddy is Joe, and Joe's buddy is Harry, then the mechanical implementation of toString would die in an infinite recursion.

7.6.4 — Inspecting Array Elements

The Field class allows you to read and write the value of an arbitrary field of an object. The Array class does a similar job for array objects. If a is any array, then you can read a value at index i as

```
Object value = Array.get(a, i);
```

You set a value as

```
Array.set(a, i, value);
```

You can find out the length of the array as

```
int n = Array.getLength(a);
```

To create a new array, call the static `newInstance` method with the desired component type and length. For example, here is how you can double the size of an array:

```
Object anew = Array.newInstance(
        a.getClass().getComponentType(),
        2 * Array.getLength(a) + 1);
System.arraycopy(a, 0, anew, 0, Array.getLength(a));
a = anew;
```

7.7   Generic Types

7.7.1 — Type Variables

> A generic type has one or more type variables.

A generic type is a type that is parameterized by one or more *type variables*. A generic type is *instantiated* when actual types are substituted for the type variable. For example, `ArrayList<E>` is a generic type, and `ArrayList<String>` is an instantiation.

In Java, type variables can only be instantiated with class or interface types, not with primitive types. For example, it is not possible to declare an `ArrayList<int>`.

When you define a generic class, you use type variables for the generic types of variables, fields, and methods. Here is a fragment of the definition of the `ArrayList<E>` class:

```
public class ArrayList<E>
{
    public E get(int i)
    {
        if (i < 0 || i >= size) throw new IndexOutOfBoundsException(. . .);
        return elementData[i];
    }

    public E set(int i, E newValue)
    {
        if (i < 0 || i >= size) throw new IndexOutOfBoundsException(. . .);
        E oldValue = elementData[i];
        elementData[i] = newValue;
        return oldValue;
    }
    . . .
    private E[] elementData;
    private int size;
}
```

When the generic class is instantiated, then the type variables are substituted with the actual types. For example, the instantiated class `ArrayList<String>` has methods

```
String get()
String set(int i, String newValue)
```

NOTE There is *no* subclass relationship between generic classes that are instantiated with subtypes. For example, `ArrayList<Rectangle>` is *not* a subclass of `ArrayList<Shape>`. The two classes are completely unrelated. In this regard, generic collections differ from the built-in array types.

Generic types are most commonly used for collections, with a type variable denoting the element type. However, there are many other uses as well. We have seen the generic `Comparable` interface

```
public interface Comparable<T>
{
    int compare(T other);
}
```

Here, the type variable specifies the parameter type of the `compare` method.

7.7.2 — Generic Methods

A generic method is a method with one or more type parameters. A generic method can be declared inside an ordinary class or a generic class. Here is an example of a generic method that is declared inside an ordinary class `Utils`.

```
public class Utils
{
    public static <E> void fill(ArrayList<E> a, E value, int count)
    {
        for (int i = 0; i < count; i++)
            a.add(value);
    }
}
```

The type parameter list `<E>` after the `public static` modifiers indicates that this method is generic. The type parameter is used to denote the type of the array elements and the fill value.

When you call a generic method, you need not specify type parameters. Instead, it is inferred from the call parameters. For example, consider the call

```
ArrayList<String> ids = new ArrayList<String>();
Utils.fill(ids, "default", 10);
```

The compiler matches the generic parameter types (`ArrayList<E>` and `E`) against the actual parameter types (`ArrayList<String>` and `String`). It then infers that `E` is `String` in this method call.

The type matching mechanism is rather sophisticated. Consider for example the call

```
ArrayList<Shape> shapes = new ArrayList<Shape>();
Utils.fill(shapes, new Rectangle(5, 10, 20, 30), 10);
```

Now the compiler needs to work harder when matching the generic parameter types (`ArrayList<E>` and `E`) against the actual parameter types (`ArrayList<Shape>` and `Rectangle`). Matching `E` with `Shape` succeeds since `Rectangle` is a subtype of `Shape`.

However, matching E with Rectangle does not succeed because ArrayList<Rectangle> is *not* a subtype of ArrayList<Shape>.

The compiler will figure out the appropriate method instantiation automatically. However, for greater clarity, you can specify the instantiation—place the actual type parameters before the method name, like this:

```
Utils.<Shape>fill(shapes, new Rectangle(5, 10, 20, 30), 10);
```

7.7.3 — Type Bounds and Wildcards

> Type variables can be constrained with bounds.

It is often necessary to specify constraints between the types that can be used in a generic class or method. Consider a generic method that appends elements from one array list to another:

```
public static <E> void append(ArrayList<E> a, ArrayList<E> b, int count)
{
   for (int i = 0; i < count && i < b.size(); i++)
      a.add(b.get(i));
}
```

This method is rather limited. It cannot be used to append an ArrayList<Rectangle> to an ArrayList<Shape>. Here, we will want to use two type bounds E and F to express the fact that the two array lists may have different types:

```
public static <E, F> void append(ArrayList<E> a, ArrayList<F> b, int count)
```

However, we can only append elements of a subtype. We use a *type bound* to express this fact:

```
public static <E, F extends E> void append(
      ArrayList<E> a, ArrayList<F> b, int count)
{
   for (int i = 0; i < count && i < b.size(); i++)
      a.add(b.get(i));
}
```

You use the the extends keyword to express that a type is a subtype of a given type as defined in Section 7.1.1. For example, you can append an ArrayList<Shape> and an ArrayList<Rectangle> because Rectangle is a subtype of the Shape type.

 NOTE Occasionally, you want to specify multiple type bounds; in that case, separate them with & symbols:

```
E extends Cloneable & Serializable
```

It is possible to simplify the declaration of the append method. Note that the type variable F is never used in the body of the function. We can eliminate it and replace it with a *wildcard*:

```
public static <E> void append(
      ArrayList<E> a, ArrayList<? extends E> b, int count)
{
   for (int i = 0; i < count && i < b.size(); i++)
      a.add(b.get(i));
}
```

The expression `? extends E` matches any subtype of `E`.

> Use a wildcard type for a generic type parameter that can be anonymous.

Wildcards can only be used as type parameters, inside `< >` brackets. You cannot not define a variable or an array of type `?`.

Wildcard type parameters restrict the methods that you can call. For example, the `set` method of `ArrayList<? extends E>` has the form

```
? extends E add(? extends E newElement)
```

You cannot call this method! If you call `b.add(x)`, the compiler only knows that `x` must belong to some subtype of `E`, but it does not know which type is required. Therefore, any such call is an error. However, the `get` method is still usable:

```
? extends E get(int i)
```

It returns an object of an unknown subtype of `E`, and you can safely use it as an object of type `E`.

Wildcards can also be bounded in the opposite direction. The expression `? super F` matches any supertype of `F`. We could have equally well defined the `append` method as

```
public static <F> void append(
    ArrayList<? super F> a, ArrayList<F> b, int count)
{
    for (int i = 0; i < count && i < b.size(); i++)
        a.add(b.get(i));
}
```

Note that the `add` method of `ArrayList<? super F>` has the form

```
boolean add(? super F newElement)
```

The method can safely receive any object of type `F`.

NOTE You will sometimes find unbounded wildcards such as `Class<?>` in the API documentation. This typically means that the API was defined before generics were introduced. You cannot call any methods that require type parameters (such as `newInstance`) on the resulting `Class` object, but you can call methods such as `getName`.

INTERNET Subtype relationships between generic types are more subtle than those for non-generic types in Section 7.1.1, particularly when wildcards are involved. For example, `ArrayList<Rectangle>` is *not* a subtype of `ArrayList<Shape>`, but it is a subtype of `ArrayList<? extends Shape>` or `ArrayList<?>`. For a full description of the rules, see Angelika Langer's Generics FAQ at `http://www.langer.camelot.de/GenericsFAQ/JavaGenericsFAQ.html`.

Let's look at a more complex example of using type bounds and wildcards. We want to write a generic `getMax` method that finds the largest element in an array list of objects. In general, we don't know how to compare array elements, but we can use a type bound to ensure that the element type is a subtype of the `Comparable` interface. Here is a first attempt:

```
public static <E extends Comparable<E>> E getMax(ArrayList<E> a)
{
```

```
        E max = a.get(0);
        for (int i = 1; i < a.size(); i++)
            if (a.get(i).compareTo(max) > 0) max = a.get(i);
        return max;
    }
```

Here, we use the type bound to express that the element type of the array should be a subtype of the type bound `Comparable<E>`. For example, you can call the `getMax` method with a `String[]` array but not with a `Rectangle[]` array—the `String` class implements `Comparable<String>`, but `Rectangle` does not implement `Comparable<Rectangle>`.

The definition of the `getMax` method is overly restrictive. Suppose you want to sort an `ArrayList<GregorianCalendar>`. The `GregorianCalendar` class is a subclass of the `Calendar` class which implements `Comparable<Calendar>`. Therefore, `GregorianCalendar` also implements `Comparable<Calendar>`, but *not* `Comparable<GregorianCalendar>`. This is not a problem—you can still find the largest entry, by using the superclass comparison.

Therefore, we should only require that the element type `E` implements `Comparable<S>` for some supertype `S` of `E`. Since we never need to know exactly what that supertype is, we can use a wildcard:

```
    public static <E extends Comparable<? super E>> E getMax(ArrayList<E> a)
```

7.7.4 — Type Erasure

> The raw type of a generic type is obtained by erasing the type variables.

The virtual machine that executes Java programs does not work with generic classes or methods. Instead, it uses *raw* types, in which the type variables are replaced with ordinary Java types. Each type variable is replaced with its bound, or with `Object` if it is not bounded.

The compiler *erases* the type variables when it compiles generic classes and methods. For example, the generic class `ArrayList<E>` turns into the following raw class:

```
    public class ArrayList
    {
        public Object get(int i)
        {
            if (i < 0 || i >= size) throw new IndexOutOfBoundsException(. . .);
            return elementData[i];
        }

        public Object set(int i, Object newValue)
        {
            if (i < 0 || i >= size) throw new IndexOutOfBoundsException(. . .);
            Object oldValue = elementData[i];
            elementData[i] = newValue;
            return oldValue;
        }
        . . .
        private Object[] elementData;
        private int size;
    }
```

As you can see, the type variable `E` has been replaced by `Object`. The result is an ordinary class.

The same process is applied to generic methods. After erasing the type parameter, the `getMax` method of the preceding section turns into an ordinary method:

```
public static Comparable getMax(ArrayList a)
{
   Comparable max = (Comparable) a.get(0);
   for (int i = 1; i < a.size(); i++)
      if (a.get(i).compareTo(max) > 0) max = a.get(i);
   return max;
}
```

Note that due to the type bound (`E extends Comparable<? super E>`) the type E has been erased to `Comparable`.

> In order to interface with legacy code, you can convert between generic and raw types.

Raw types are necessary when you interface with *legacy code* that was written before generics were added to the Java language. For example, if a legacy method has a parameter `ArrayList` (without a type variable), you can pass an `ArrayList<String>` or `ArrayList<Employee>`. This is not completely safe—after all, the legacy method might insert an object of the wrong type. The compiler will issue a warning, but your program will compile and run.

NOTE   When generic code compiles without warnings, the code is *typesafe:* no `ClassCastException` will be thrown at runtime. However, when you mix generic and raw collections, the compiler can no longer guarantee type safety. For example,

```
ArrayList<String> names = new ArrayList<String>();
ArrayList a = names;     // Compiles with warning
a.add(new Country( . . . ));    // Not an error
String n = names.get(0);    // ClassCastException thrown
```

7.7.5 — Limitations of Generics

Knowing about raw types helps you understand limitations of Java generics. For example, you cannot replace type variables with primitive types. Erasure turns type variables into the bounds type, such as `Object` or `Comparable`. The resulting types can never hold values of primitive types.

Another limitation is that you cannot construct new objects of a generic type. That is, the following method, which tries to fill an array list with copies of default objects, would be wrong:

```
public static <E> void fillWithDefaults(ArrayList<E> a, int count)
{
   for (int i = 0; i < count; i++)
      a.add(new E()); // ERROR
}
```

To see why this is a problem, carry out the type erasure process, as if you were the compiler:

```
public static void fillWithDefaults(ArrayList a, int count)
{
```

```
    for (int i = 0; i < count; i++)
        a.add(new Object()); // ERROR
}
```

Of course, if you start out with an ArrayList<Rectangle>, you don't want it to be filled with Object instances. But that's what the code would do after erasing types.

In situations such as this one, the compiler will report an error. You then need to come up with another mechanism for solving your problem.

You can pass a Class object to make new instances, using reflection. For example,

```
public static <E> void fillWithDefaults(ArrayList<E>,
        Class<? extends E> cl, int count)
        throws InstantiationException, IllegalAccessException
{
    for (int i = 0; i < count; i++)
        a.add(cl.newInstance());
}
```

Here, we use the fact that the Class class has a type parameter. That parameter determines the return type of methods such as newInstance:

```
class Class<T>
{
    public T newInstance()
            throws InstantiationException, IllegalAccessException { . . . }
    . . .
}
```

We require that the Class type parameter is a subtype of E. For example, the following call will compile:

```
ArrayList<Shape> shapes = new ArrayList<Shape>();
fillWithDefault(shapes, Rectangle.class)
```

The Rectangle.class object is an instance of Class<Rectangle>, and Rectangle is a subtype of Shape. But the call

```
fillWithDefault(shapes, String.class)
```

will not compile.

There are other technical limitations of generic classes that are consequences of the type erasure mechanism. Here are the most important ones:

- You cannot form arrays of parameterized types. For example, an array Comparable<E>[] is illegal. A remedy is to use an array list ArrayList<Comparable<E>>.

- You cannot reference type parameters of a generic type in a *static context*, that is, in static fields, methods, or inner classes. For example, the following is illegal:

```
public class MyClass<E>
{
    private static E defaultValue; // Error
    . . .
}
```

This code gives the impression as if there was a separate `defaultValue` for each instantiation type. However, after erasure, the class can only have one static field. Therefore, use of type variables in static contexts is outlawed.

- You can neither throw nor catch generic types. In fact, a generic type cannot extend `Throwable`.

- You cannot have type clashes after erasure. For example, `GregorianCalendar` cannot implement `Comparable<GregorianCalendar>` since it already inherits the `Comparable<Calendar>` interface, and the two interfaces are erased to the same raw type.

The following program contains the various sample methods that were discussed in the preceding sections.

Ch7/generic/Utils.java

```
1  import java.util.*;
2
3  public class Utils
4  {
5     public static <E> void fill(ArrayList<E> a, E value, int count)
6     {
7        for (int i = 0; i < count; i++)
8           a.add(value);
9     }
10
11    public static <E, F extends E> void append(ArrayList<E> a,
12          ArrayList<F> b, int count)
13    {
14       for (int i = 0; i < count && i < b.size(); i++)
15          a.add(b.get(i));
16    }
17
18    public static <E extends Comparable<? super E>>
19          E getMax(ArrayList<E> a)
20    {
21       E max = a.get(0);
22       for (int i = 1; i < a.size(); i++)
23          if (a.get(i).compareTo(max) > 0) max = a.get(i);
24       return max;
25    }
26
27    public static <E> void fillWithDefaults(ArrayList<E> a,
28          Class<? extends E> cl, int count)
29          throws InstantiationException, IllegalAccessException
30    {
31       for (int i = 0; i < count; i++)
32          a.add(cl.newInstance());
33    }
34 }
```

Ch7/generic/UtilsTester.java

```java
1  import java.util.*;
2  import java.awt.*;
3
4  public class UtilsTester
5  {
6      public static void main(String[] args)
7              throws InstantiationException, IllegalAccessException
8      {
9          ArrayList<String> ids = new ArrayList<String>();
10         Utils.fill(ids, "default", 10);
11         System.out.println(ids);
12
13         ArrayList<Shape> shapes = new ArrayList<Shape>();
14         Utils.fill(shapes, new Rectangle(5, 10, 20, 30), 2);
15         System.out.println(shapes);
16
17         ArrayList<Polygon> polys = new ArrayList<Polygon>();
18         Utils.fillWithDefaults(polys, Polygon.class, 10);
19         Utils.append(shapes, polys, 2);
20         System.out.println(shapes);
21
22         ArrayList<GregorianCalendar> dates
23             = new ArrayList<GregorianCalendar>();
24         Utils.fillWithDefaults(dates, GregorianCalendar.class, 5);
25         System.out.println(Utils.getMax(dates));
26     }
27 }
```

7.8   JavaBeans Components

7.8.1 — Components

> A software component is a building block that can be combined with other components into programs, usually by employing a program builder tool.

Objects form the building blocks of object-oriented programming. However, objects are too fine-grained to provide significant reusability of complex behavior. A software component is a construct that encapsulates more functionality than a single class, in such a way that you can compose an application from multiple components with only minimal additional programming.

In the early days of object-oriented programming, it was envisioned that classes would be sold as standardized "software ICs (integrated circuits)". Rather than programming another linked list from scratch, programmers would purchase a standard linked list class from a vendor. However, few customers wanted to buy a linked list since it isn't that hard to write your own or just use the library version. In order to be commercially viable, reusable software needed to supply more functionality.

The first successful example of reusable software was the market for Visual Basic controls (also called "ActiveX" controls). Typical Visual Basic controls are:

- A calendar control that lets users select a date from a pop-up calendar
- A graph control that draws multiple types of graphs

- A control that connects to a database and displays the results of a query as a scroll-able table
- A control that communicates with a Lego Mindstorms robot

These components have complex behavior, and it would not be economical to reimplement them in-house. There is an active market for developing and selling these kinds of components.

When you buy such a component, you need to *customize* it. For example, a graph component may have dozens of graph types, with many choices for fonts and colors. In your particular application, you will want to select just one or two choices.

Next, you need to *compose* the component with other components, such as a data source for the values that are being displayed in the graph.

This process of customization and composition typically takes place in a *builder environment*, a program that displays the components and that allows an operator (who need not be a programmer) to combine the components into a program (see Figure 10).

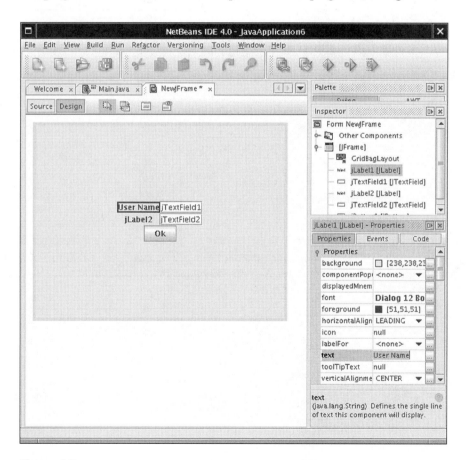

Figure 10

A Builder Environment

7.8.2 — JavaBeans

> A Java bean is composed of one or more classes that are packaged together, allowing a builder or execution enviroment to discover the methods, properties, and events that the bean exposes.

JavaBeans is the term for a component model used to create applications with a graphical user interface. A Java bean is an entity with three capabilities:

- The ability to execute methods (which are like object methods)
- The ability to expose *properties* (which are like object attributes)
- The ability to emit events (see Figure 11)

Just as with classes, the implementation details of a bean are private and not accessible to programmers using it. However, a Java bean is typically composed of multiple classes because its functionality is generally more complex than that of a single class.

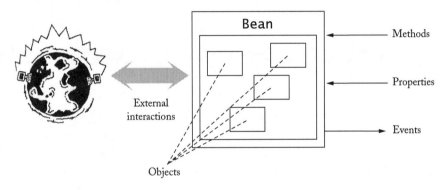

Figure 11

A Java Bean

INTERNET   Figure 12 shows a calendar bean that you can integrate into any application that requires users to input dates. You can download that bean from `http://www.toedter.com/en/jcalendar`.

	Sun	Mon	Tue	Wed	Thu	Fri	Sat
March ▼						2005	
10			1	2	3	4	5
11	6	7	8	9	10	11	12
12	13	14	15	16	17	18	19
13	20	21	22	23	24	25	26
14	27	28	29	30	31		

Figure 12

A Calendar Bean

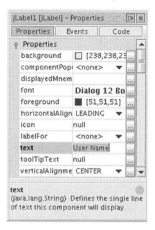

Figure 13

A Property Sheet

A Java bean is intended to be manipulated by a *builder environment* that allows for the modification and composition of components without programming. For example, a component's properties can be set with a *property sheet*, a dialog box that lists all properties of the component and allows them to be edited interactively (see Figure 13).

Because the Java language has no special support for components, each bean designates a single class to be the *facade* for the bean. That class contains methods that describe the bean methods, properties, and events. Clients of the bean call methods of the facade class, and those methods call on other classes in the bean.

PATTERN

FACADE

Context

1. A subsystem consists of multiple classes, making it complicated for clients to use.
2. The implementation of the subsystem is subject to change, but the functionality that it provides is stable.
3. In order to support reuse of components, you want to give a coherent entry point to the capabilities of the subsystem.

Solution

1. Define a facade class that exposes all capabilities of the subsystem as methods.
2. The facade methods delegate requests to the subsystem classes.
3. The subsystem classes do not know about the facade class.

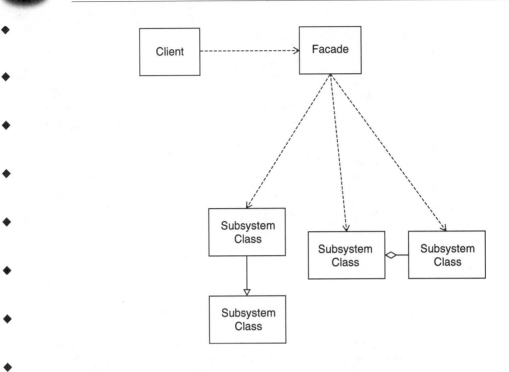

The following table shows the meaning of the names in the pattern when it is applied to a Java bean.

Name in Design Pattern	Actual Name
`Client`	Builder tool
`Facade`	Main bean class with which the builder tool interacts
`SubsystemClass`	Class used to implement bean functionality

7.8.3 — Bean Properties

A component property is a named value that denotes a characteristic of the component, and that can be accessed by component clients.

A *property* of a bean has a name and methods for getting and setting the property value. (Most properties are get-and-set, but there are also get-only and set-only properties.) What happens when you get or set the property is entirely up to the implementor. The implementor specifies methods that carry out the getting and setting. Note that a property is generally *not* the same as an instance field. For example, a property may be stored in a database. Even when a property is stored as an instance field, the getter and setter methods may do more work than just getting or setting the field value. For example, in a visual component, the setter for a `color` property may update a field and then call a repaint method, so that the changed property becomes visible.

> Component-oriented programming languages have special syntax for accessing properties. In Java, properties are implemented through methods that follow a strict naming convention.

Programming languages that support components have a convenient syntax for getting and setting properties. For example, in C# and Visual Basic, properties look like public instance fields of an object, even though they are actually manipulated through special methods. The statement

   b.*propertyName* = value

automatically calls the property setter, whereas

   value = b.*propertyName*

calls the property getter.

However, the Java programming language has no such syntax. When you implement properties of a Java bean, you need to provide a pair of methods that follows a *naming convention*. The get method starts with `get` and is followed by the name of the property, with the first letter capitalized. It must have no parameters, and its return type is the type of the property. The set method starts with `set`, followed by the name of the property, with the first letter capitalized, a single parameter whose type is the type of the property, and a return type of `void`.

```
public X getPropertyName()
public void setPropertyName(X x)
```

For example, the following two methods implement a `background` property:

```
public Color getBackground()
public void setBackground(Color c)
```

There is an exception for Boolean-valued properties. For them, the naming convention is

```
public boolean isPropertyName()
public void setPropertyName(boolean b)
```

That is, you use `is` as the prefix of the method for getting the Boolean property value, not `get`.

Finally, when a property is array-valued, you supply four methods, two for getting and setting the entire array, and two for getting and setting individual elements:

```
public X[] getPropertyName()
public void setPropertyName(X[] array)
public X getPropertyName(int i)
public void setPropertyName(int i, X x)
```

Remember to replace *PropertyName* with the capitalized name of the actual property.

If a property has a `get` method and no `set` method, it is considered get-only. Conversely, a property without a `get` method is set-only.

When a builder environment loads a bean, then the facade class is analyzed and searched for methods that start with `get` and `set`. (This search uses the reflection mechanism.) As long as the methods follow the naming convention exactly, then a property is deduced by taking the name of the method, removing the get or set prefix, and "decapitalizing" the remainder. That is, the first character is converted to lowercase *unless* both the first and second character are uppercase, in which case the first letter is not changed. Thus, get-Background yields a property background but getURL yields a property URL. (This kind of hokus-pokus is what you have to deal with when a programming language isn't able to express a useful concept and you have to fake it through coding conventions.)

Special Topic   7.3

Accessing Java Properties from JavaScript

Let's run a JavaScript experiment to appreciate the benefits of an easier syntax for properties. Rhino is a JavaScript interpreter that is tightly integrated with Java. That integration allows you to access JavaBeans properties with a simplified syntax.

Download the Rhino program from `http://www.mozilla.org/rhino`. Install it into a directory of your choice.

Open a shell window, change to the Rhino install directory, and launch the Rhino interpreter:

```
java -jar js.jar
```

You get a prompt

```
js>
```

Now you can type any JavaScript commands. Start by constructing a frame and a button.

```
importPackage(Packages.javax.swing);
var frame = new JFrame();
var button = new JButton();
```

(Note that JavaScript variables are untyped. Any variable can hold an object of any type.)

Now set the text property of the button:

```
button.text = "Hello, World!";
```

Behind the scenes, Rhino has discovered that the JButton class has getText and setText methods that correspond to a text property, and it calls the method button. setText("Hello, World!"). That's exactly the kind of functionality that the designers of JavaBeans had in mind. The programmer can use a convenient syntax, and the run-time environment automatically generates the equivalent method call.

Next, add the button to the content pane:

```
frame.add(button);
```

Finally, let's pack and show the frame:

```
frame.pack();
frame.visible = true;
```

The frame and the button are displayed immediately (see Figure 14).

```
File  Edit  View  Terminal  Tabs  Help
java -jar js.jar
Rhino 1.5 release 5 2004 03 25
js> importPackage(Packages.javax.swing);
js> var frame = new JFrame();
js> var button = new JButton();
js> button.text = "Hello, World!";
Hello, World!
js> frame.add(button);
javax.swing.JButton[,0,0,0x0,invalid,alignmentX=0.0,alignmentY=0.5,border=javax.
swing.plaf.BorderUIResource$CompoundBorderUIResource@23e5d1,flags=296,maximumSiz
e=,minimumSize=,preferredSize=,defaultIcon=,disabledIcon=,disabledSelectedIcon=,
margin=javax.swing.plaf.InsetsUIResource[top=2,left=14,bottom=2,right=14],paintB
order=true,paintFocus=true,pressedIcon=,rolloverEnabled=true,rolloverIcon=,rollo
verSelectedIcon=,selectedIcon=,text=Hello, World!,defaultCapable=true]
js> frame.pack();
js> frame.visible = true;
true
js>
```

Figure 14

Running the Rhino Interpreter

7.8.4 — Editing Bean Properties in a Builder Tool

In this section, we describe the process of editing bean properties in the NetBeans 4.0 development environment. Other development environments, such as Eclipse or JBuilder, have similar options.

INTERNET   The NetBeans development environment is available at no charge from http://www.netbeans.org.

Select File → New Project from the menu, then make a project of type Java Application in the General category. Then select File → New File from the menu and make a JFrame from in the Java GUI forms category (see Figure 15). You now see an empty JFrame. Locate the *component palette* and the JButton icon inside the palette. Click on the icon, and then click on the south end of the frame. The button is added to the frame, and you

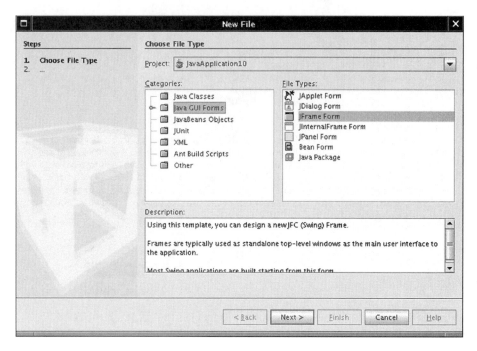

Figure 15

The New Template Wizard in NetBeans

see a property sheet that lists the properties of the button. You'll see properties such as `text`, `font`, and `background` (see Figure 16). By clicking on the properties, you can change them. Try it out: Change the button text to "Hello, World!" and the background color to pink. As you make the changes in the property sheet, the button is instantly updated.

What is going on? The builder tool has enumerated the properties of the `JButton` class and constructed a property sheet that shows the names of the properties. Then the builder tool invoked the getter methods for these properties to find the current button settings. It painted graphical representations of the property values next to the property names in the property sheet. Whenever you change the value of a property, the builder tool invokes the setter method with the new value, so that the button immediately shows the new setting.

As you can see, the builder tool allows developers to inspect and set properties visually. Many developers prefer this approach over writing code because they find it faster and more intuitive.

7.8.5 — Packaging a Bean

Since a bean is typically composed of multiple classes and other resources, such as icon files, it needs to be packaged for inclusion into a builder tool. You use the `jar` (Java

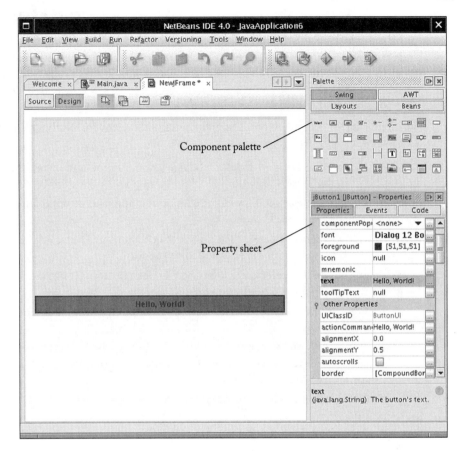

Figure 16

The Property Sheet of a Buttton

archive) packaging tool to bundle the files that make up the bean. Actually, a jar file can contain multiple beans. To specify which classes are the facade classes for the beans in the archive, you need to supply a *manifest file*. Here is a typical example:

Ch7/carbean/CarBean.mf

```
1 Manifest-Version: 1.0
2
3 Name: CarBean.class
4 Java-Bean: True
```

To make a jar file, first write the manifest file. Then run the jar program as

```
jar cvfm CarBean.jar CarBean.mf *.class
```

If your bean classes are in packages, then the subdirectory path in the archive must match the package name, such as edu/sjsu/cs/cs151/alice/CarBean.class.

Once the bean is packaged, you can load the archive into a builder tool. The builder tool will then analyze the contents and may display the discovered bean (or beans) in a toolbar.

If you have a builder tool such as NetBeans, you should run the following experiment. First, compile the CarBean class and package it into a file CarBean.jar. The CarBean is simply a JPanel that draws a car. It has two properties, x and y, that denote the *x*- and *y*-positions of the top-left corner of the car.

Then start your builder tool. We will describe the steps for NetBeans, but other builder tools have equivalent commands.

1. Choose the Tools → Palette Manager menu option and install the CarBean.jar file in the "Beans" palette.
2. Choose the File → New File menu option and use the wizard dialog box to make a new JFrame GUI form.
3. In the "Swing" palette, click on the JSlider button. Then click on the bottom of the JFrame. A slider is now added to the form.
4. In the "Beans" palette, click on the CarBean button. (It has a default icon because we didn't supply a prettier one.)
5. Click in the center of the JFrame. The CarBean is now added to the form. (See Figure 17.)
6. Right-click on the car and select the Properties menu option. In the property sheet for the car, set the values for the *x* and *y* properties to 50. The car moves toward the center of the panel.
7. If you like, build and execute the current application. Of course, the slider doesn't do anything yet.
8. In the builder tool, right-click on the slider and select the menu option Events → Change → stateChanged.
9. The builder tool pops up the source window and positions your cursor next to a comment

   ```
   // Add your handling code here:
   ```
10. Add the code

    ```
    carBean1.setX(jSlider1.getValue());
    ```
11. Compile and execute the program. Now the slider moves the car position.

What can you learn from this experiment? You produced a running program, using an approach that is very different from traditional programming.

- You composed the application by arranging pre-packaged components.
- You customized one of the components by setting its properties in the property sheet.
- You wrote only one line of code. If the Java language supported properties, that code would have been even simpler:

  ```
  carBean1.x = jSlider1.value;
  ```
- The builder tool supplied all the knowledge about frames and event handling.

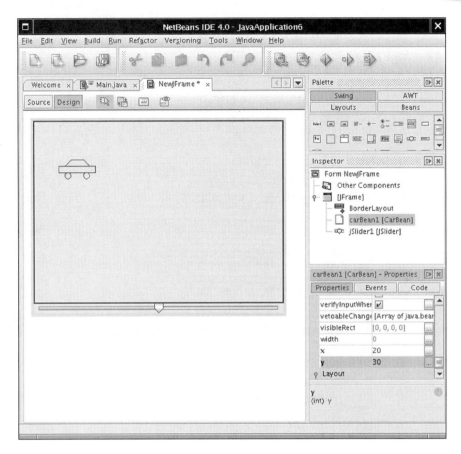

Figure 17

Composing Beans in a Builder Tool

This example concludes our discussion of Java components. As you have seen, components encapsulate complex functionality that may exceed the capabilities of a single class. Component properties may have arbitrary types and can be edited by component assembly tools. In Java, the component programmer provides getter and setter methods to identify properties and assembles component classes inside a JAR file.

Ch7/carbean/CarBean.java

```
1  import java.awt.*;
2  import java.awt.geom.*;
3  import javax.swing.*;
4
```

```
 5  /**
 6       A component that draws a car shape.
 7  */
 8  public class CarBean extends JComponent
 9  {
10     /**
11          Constructs a default car bean.
12     */
13     public CarBean()
14     {
15        x = 0;
16        y = 0;
17        width = DEFAULT_CAR_WIDTH;
18        height = DEFAULT_CAR_HEIGHT;
19     }
20
21     /**
22          Sets the x property.
23          @param newValue the new x position
24     */
25     public void setX(int newValue)
26     {
27        x = newValue;
28        repaint();
29     }
30
31     /**
32          Gets the x property.
33          @return the x position
34     */
35     public int getX()
36     {
37        return x;
38     }
39
40     /**
41          Sets the y property.
42          @param newValue the new y position
43     */
44     public void setY(int newValue)
45     {
46        y = newValue;
47        repaint();
48     }
49
50     /**
51          Gets the y property.
52          @return the y position
53     */
54     public int getY()
55     {
56        return y;
57     }
58
59     public void paintComponent(Graphics g)
60     {
```

```
61          Graphics2D g2 = (Graphics2D) g;
62          Rectangle2D.Double body
63              = new Rectangle2D.Double(x, y + height / 3,
64              width - 1, height / 3);
65          Ellipse2D.Double frontTire
66              = new Ellipse2D.Double(x + width / 6,
67              y + height * 2 / 3, height / 3, height / 3);
68          Ellipse2D.Double rearTire
69              = new Ellipse2D.Double(x + width * 2 / 3,
70              y + height * 2 / 3, height / 3, height / 3);
71
72          // The bottom of the front windshield
73          Point2D.Double r1
74              = new Point2D.Double(x + width / 6, y + height / 3);
75          // The front of the roof
76          Point2D.Double r2
77              = new Point2D.Double(x + width / 3, y);
78          // The rear of the roof
79          Point2D.Double r3
80              = new Point2D.Double(x + width * 2 / 3, y);
81          // The bottom of the rear windshield
82          Point2D.Double r4
83              = new Point2D.Double(x + width * 5 / 6, y + height / 3);
84
85          Line2D.Double frontWindshield
86              = new Line2D.Double(r1, r2);
87          Line2D.Double roofTop
88              = new Line2D.Double(r2, r3);
89          Line2D.Double rearWindshield
90              = new Line2D.Double(r3, r4);
91
92          g2.draw(body);
93          g2.draw(frontTire);
94          g2.draw(rearTire);
95          g2.draw(frontWindshield);
96          g2.draw(roofTop);
97          g2.draw(rearWindshield);
98       }
99
100      public Dimension getPreferredSize()
101      {
102         return new Dimension(DEFAULT_PANEL_WIDTH,
103             DEFAULT_PANEL_HEIGHT);
104      }
105
106      private int x;
107      private int y;
108      private int width;
109      private int height;
110
111      private static final int DEFAULT_CAR_WIDTH = 60;
112      private static final int DEFAULT_CAR_HEIGHT = 30;
113      private static final int DEFAULT_PANEL_WIDTH = 160;
114      private static final int DEFAULT_PANEL_HEIGHT = 130;
115   }
```

EXERCISES

Exercise 7.1. Which types can you use for variables but not for values in Java?

Exercise 7.2. What is the type of `null`?

Exercise 7.3. Which of the following types are subtypes of another type?

(a) `Object`
(b) `int`
(c) `long`
(d) `int[]`
(e) `Object[]`
(f) `int[][]`
(g) `Rectangle`
(h) `Rectangle[]`
(i) `Rectangle2D[]`
(j) `Comparable[]`

Exercise 7.4. Write a program that generates an `ArrayStoreException`. Why can't the validity of array stores be checked at compile time?

Exercise 7.5. When do you use wrapper classes for primitive types?

Exercise 7.6. What Java code do you use to test

(a)   Whether x belongs to the `Rectangle` class?
(b)   Whether x belongs to a subclass of the `JPanel` class (but not the `JPanel` class itself)?
(c)   Whether the class of x implements the `Cloneable` interface type?

Exercise 7.7. Give three distinct ways of obtaining the `Class` object that describes the `Rectangle` class.

Exercise 7.8. Why is there a `Class` object to represent `void` even though there is no `void` type? Why isn't there a `Class` object to represent the null type?

Exercise 7.9. Write a program that prompts the user for the name of a class and the values of construction parameters. Construct an instance of the class. Then prompt the user to enter the name of any method and its parameters, provided that they are primitive type values, strings, or `null`. Invoke the method on the constructed object and print the result if the method is not declared to be `void`. Continue applying methods until the user wishes to quit. If there are multiple methods that match the user inputs, then print an error message. Sample dialog:

```
Construct object: java.awt.Rectangle 5 10 20 30
Invoke method (blank line to quit): getWidth
20
Invoke method (blank line to quit): translate 10 10
```

```
Invoke method (blank line to quit): getX
15
```

Exercise 7.10. Write a method dumpClass that prints out the name of a class (including its package name), its superclass, and all of its constructors, methods, and fields, including parameter and field types and modifiers (such as static and final). Format the output to look as much as possible like a class definition. The input to the method should be either the Class object that describes the class or an object of the class.

Exercise 7.11. Use the method of Exercise 7.10 to peek inside an anonymous inner class that accesses a local variable from the enclosing scope. Explain the constructor and the instance fields.

Exercise 7.12. Write a method dumpArray that prints the elements of *any* array to System.out, using toString on the array elements if the array elements are objects.

Exercise 7.13. Explain why you can't simply use the spyFields of the FieldTest program as the basis for a generic toString method. That is, why can't you simply add

```
String toString() { return FieldTest.spyFields(this); }
```

to each of your classes?

Exercise 7.14. Remedy the problem of Exercise 7.13. Implement a FieldDumper class that can dump the fields of an object, then the fields of all referring objects, and so on, in such a way that there is no infinite recursion. *Hint:* Keep track of the objects that were already encountered in the dumping process, and only print an indication of the repetition if you encounter it again.

Exercise 7.15. Survey the source code for the standard Java library. How many classes implement the equals method? How many implement the equals method correctly, that is, so that it fulfills the axioms that are laid out in the Java API specification?

Exercise 7.16. Complete the definitions of the Manager and Employee classes and their toString, equals, and hashCode methods.

Exercise 7.17. Repeat Exercise 7.16 for an Employee class with a buddy field.

Exercise 7.18. Define toString, equals, and hashCode methods for the Day class of Chapter 3.

Exercise 7.19. Consider the following approach to cloning. Using serialization, save an object to a stream and read it back. You get a new object that appears to be a clone of the original, because all of its instance fields are distinct. Implement this approach to clone employees with a buddy field. Verify that the result is a proper clone.

Exercise 7.20. Give two limitations of the approach used in Exercise 7.19.

Exercise 7.21. Study the source code for the ArrayList class. It defines writeObject/readObject methods. What do these methods do, and why?

Exercise 7.22. Turn the MessageQueue class of Chapter 3 into a generic class Queue<E>.

Exercise 7.23. Write a generic class Pair<E> that stores two values of type E. Supply methods to get and set the first and second value of the pair.

Exercise 7.24. Make the `Pair` class of Exercise 7.23 cloneable and serializable. Introduce the required type bounds, and test with a `Pair<Rectangle>`.

Exercise 7.25. Supply a method

```
public static <E> Pair<E> getFirstLast(ArrayList<E> a)
```

in the `Utils` class that returns a pair consisting of the first and last element of a.

Exercise 7.26. Supply a method

```
public static <E, F . . .> void putFirstLast(ArrayList<E> a, Pair<F> p)
```

in the `Utils` class that places the first and last element of a into p. Supply appropriate type bounds.

Exercise 7.27. Supply a method `getMinMax` in the `Utils` class that returns a pair consisting of the smallest and largest element of a. Supply a constraint to express that T should be a subtype of an appropriate `Comparable` instantiation.

Exercise 7.28. Provide a generic class `EventListenerList<L>` that manages a list of event listeners of type L, similar to the `javax.swing.Event.EventListenerList` class. Your class should only manage listeners of a fixed type, and you need not be concerned with thread safety.

Exercise 7.29. What is the difference between the types `Class` and `Class<?>`? (*Hint:* Which methods can you call?)

Exercise 7.30. What are the Java bean properties of the `Rectangle` class?

Exercise 7.31. What are *all* Java bean properties of the `JSlider` class?

Exercise 7.32. Download the calendar bean from `http://www.toedter.com` and put it into a builder environment such as NetBeans. Make a screen shot that shows how you customize a `Calendar` object. What properties does the bean have? Which of them can your builder environment display?

Exercise 7.33. Modify the `CarBean` to have separate `width` and `height` properties.

Exercise 7.34. Modify the `CarBean` to have separate color properties for the base and the tires.

Exercise 7.35. Write JavaScript code that shows an instance of a `CarBean` inside a `JFrame`, after you set the color, dimension, and draw mode properties. Test your code with Rhino.

Exercise 7.36. Produce a `HouseBean` class with `width`, `height`, and `color` properties.

Exercise 7.37. Modify the application that was composed from the `CarBean` by adding two sliders: one to adjust the x property and another to adjust the y property. List the steps you carried out in the builder tool.

Exercise 7.38. Compose a more complex application from the `CarBean`: Animate the car by adding a timer bean to the frame. Wire the slider to the timer bean and the timer bean to the car. The slider should change the frequency of the timer, and every timer event should move the car by a small amount. List the steps you carried out in the builder tool.

Frameworks

In Chapter 6, you saw how the inheritance mechanism can be used to derive a new class that extends and customizes a given class. In this chapter we will go beyond simple inheritance and turn to larger clusters of classes, called *frameworks*, that collectively form the basis for customization. We will study how to use frameworks to derive new classes or even entire applications. Then we will turn to the design of a sample framework and show how that framework forms the basis of the Violet UML editor.

8.1   Frameworks

> A framework is a set of classes and interface types that structures the essential mechanisms of a particular domain.

A *framework* is a set of cooperating classes that implements the mechanisms that are essential for a particular problem domain. A programmer can create new functionality in the problem domain by extending framework classes. For example, Swing is a framework for the problem domain of graphical user interface programming. A programmer can implement new GUI programs by forming subclasses of JFrame, JComponent, and so on.

Unlike a design pattern, a framework is not a general design rule. It consists of classes that provide functionality in a particular domain. Typically, a framework uses multiple patterns.

> An application framework is a framework for creating applications of a particular type.

An *application framework* consists of a set of classes that implements services common to a certain type of application. To build an actual application, the programmer subclasses some of the framework classes and implements additional functionality that is specific to the application that the programmer is building. Thus, the first characteristic of an application framework is:

- An application framework supplies a set of classes that an application programmer augments to build an application, often by forming subclasses of framework classes.

> Inversion of control in a framework signifies that the framework classes, and not the application classes, are responsible for the control flow in the application.

The programmer has little or no influence on the order in which the methods of the programmer-supplied classes are called. The majority of activity occurs in the framework, and eventually some objects of the programmer-defined classes are constructed. Then the framework calls their methods in the order that it deems appropriate. This phenomenon is often called *inversion of control*.

- In an application framework, the framework classes, and not the application-specific classes, control the flow of execution.

It is the role of the framework to determine which methods to call at what time. Its designers have expert knowledge about control flow. It is the job of the application programmer to override those methods to fulfill the application-specific tasks.

 TIP   Designing a single class is an order of magnitude harder than designing a single method because you must anticipate what other programmers will do with it. Similarly, designing a framework is much harder than designing a class library or a single application because you must anticipate what other programmers want to achieve. A good rule of thumb for validating the design of a framework is to use it to build at least three different applications.

8.2   Applets as a Simple Framework

> An applet is a Java program that runs inside a browser.

> The applet package is a simple framework that demonstrates subclassing from framework classes and inversion of control.

Java applets are Java programs that run inside a Web browser (see Figure 1).

The java.applet package is a simple application framework: It contains superclasses to make applets, and the application programmer adds classes and overrides methods to make an actual applet. The main method is not supplied by the programmer of a specific applet. The sequencing of the operations that the programmer supplies is under the control of the framework.

To design an applet, you must write a class that extends the Applet class. You must override some or all of the following methods:

- init: Called exactly once, when the applet is first loaded. Purpose: Initialize data structures and add user interface elements.

- start: Called when the applet is first loaded and every time the user restores the browser window containing the applet. Purpose: Start or restart animations or other computationally intensive tasks.

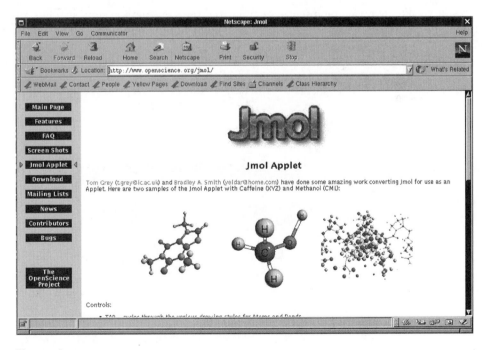

Figure 1

An Applet

- `stop`: Called when the user leaves the browser window containing the applet, and when the browser terminates. Purpose: Stop computationally intensive tasks when the applet is not being viewed.

- `destroy`: Called when the browser terminates. Purpose: Relinquish any resources that were acquired during `init` or other processing.

- `paint`: Called when the applet window needs repainting. Purpose: Redraw the window contents to reflect the current state of the applet data structures.

The sample applet at the end of this section is quite typical. The applet shows a scrolling banner (see Figure 2). A Web designer can customize the applet by specifying different messages, fonts, and delay timings. Here is a typical HTML file:

```
<applet code="BannerApplet.class" width="300" height="100">
<param name="message" value="Hello, World!"/>
<param name="fontname" value="Serif"/>
<param name="fontsize" value="64"/>
<param name="delay" value="10"/>
</applet>
```

The `init` method reads these parameters with the `getParameter` method. It then initializes a `Font` object and a timer. The timer moves the starting position of the string and calls `repaint` whenever the timer delay interval has lapsed.

The `start` method starts the timer and the `stop` method stops it. Thus, the message does not scroll when the applet is not visible. You can verify this by minimizing the browser window and restoring it again. The scrolling picks up where it left off when you minimized the window.

Finally, the `paint` method draws the string.

Figure 2

The Scrolling Banner Applet

You can see the typical characteristics of the framework in this example.

- The applet programmer uses inheritance to extend the Applet framework class to a specific program.

- The Applet class deals with the behavior that is common to all applets: interaction with the browser, parsing param tags, determining when the applet is visible, and so on. The applet programmer only fills in customized behavior for a particular program.

- Inversion of control means that the applet programmer is not concerned with the overall flow of control, but only fills in handlers for initialization, starting, stopping, and painting. When these methods are called is beyond the control of the applet programmer.

Ch8/applet/BannerApplet.java

```
 1 import java.applet.*;
 2 import java.awt.*;
 3 import java.awt.event.*;
 4 import java.awt.font.*;
 5 import java.awt.geom.*;
 6 import javax.swing.*;
 7
 8 public class BannerApplet extends Applet
 9 {
10    public void init()
11    {
12       message = getParameter("message");
13       String fontname = getParameter("fontname");
14       int fontsize = Integer.parseInt(getParameter("fontsize"));
15       delay = Integer.parseInt(getParameter("delay"));
16       font = new Font(fontname, Font.PLAIN, fontsize);
17       Graphics2D g2 = (Graphics2D) getGraphics();
18       FontRenderContext context = g2.getFontRenderContext();
19       bounds = font.getStringBounds(message, context);
20
21       timer = new Timer(delay, new
22          ActionListener()
23          {
24             public void actionPerformed(ActionEvent event)
25             {
26                start--;
27                if (start + bounds.getWidth() < 0)
28                   start = getWidth();
29                repaint();
30             }
31          });
32    }
33
34    public void start()
35    {
36       timer.start();
37    }
38
```

```
39    public void stop()
40    {
41       timer.stop();
42    }
43
44    public void paint(Graphics g)
45    {
46       g.setFont(font);
47       g.drawString(message, start, (int) -bounds.getY());
48    }
49
50    private Timer timer;
51    private int start;
52    private int delay;
53    private String message;
54    private Font font;
55    private Rectangle2D bounds;
56 }
```

8.3   The Collections Framework

The collections library is both a repository of common data structures and a framework for new collection classes.

As you know, the Java library contains useful data structures such as linked lists and hash tables. Most programmers are simply interested in the collection library as a provider of common data structures. However, the designers of these collection classes supplied more than just a set of useful classes. They provided a framework that makes it easy to add more collection classes in such a way that the new classes can interact with existing collections. We will demonstrate this capability by adding the queue class of Chapter 3 to the framework. We will then critically examine the collections framework.

8.3.1 — An Overview of the Collections Framework

A collection is a data structure that contains objects, which are called the *elements* of the collection. The *collections framework* specifies a number of interface types for collections. They include

- Collection: the most general collection interface type
- Set: an unordered collection that does not permit duplicate elements
- SortedSet: a set whose elements are visited in sorted order
- List: an ordered collection

The framework also supplies concrete classes that implement these interface types. Among the most important classes are

- HashSet: a set implementation that uses hashing to locate the set elements
- TreeSet: a sorted set implementation that stores the elements in a balanced binary tree
- LinkedList and ArrayList: two implementations of the List interface

These interface types and classes are shown in Figure 3.

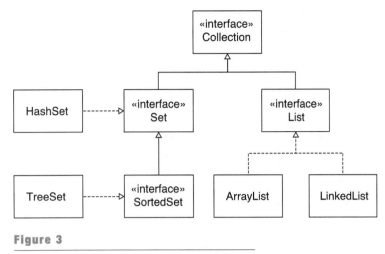

Figure 3

Collection Interface Types and Implementing Classes

All collection classes and interfaces are generic types; the type parameter denotes the type of the collected elements.

 NOTE The collections framework also defines a Map interface type and implementations HashMap and TreeMap. A map associates one set of objects, called the *keys*, with another set of objects, called the *values*. An example of such an association is the map of applet parameters that associates parameter names with parameter values. However, the Map type is not a subtype of the Collection type. Programmers generally prefer to use methods that locate map values from their keys. If a map was implemented as a collection, programmers would need to work with a sequence of key/value pairs.

For simplicity, we will not consider maps in our discussion of the collections framework.

8.3.2 — The Collection and Iterator Interface Types

The two fundamental interface types of the collections framework are Collection and Iterator. A collection is any class that can hold elements in some way. Individual collection classes may have different disciplines for storing and locating elements. For example, a linked list keeps elements in the order in which they were inserted, whereas a sorted set keeps them in ascending sort order. An iterator is a mechanism for visiting the elements of the collection. We discussed iterators already in Chapters 1 and 3. Recall that the Iterator<E> interface type has three methods:

```
boolean hasNext()
E next()
void remove()
```

The Collection<E> interface extends the Iterable<E> interface type. That interface type has a single method

```
Iterator<E> iterator()
```

NOTE *Any* class that implements the `Iterable<E>` interface type can be used in the "for each" loop. Therefore, you use the "for each" loop with all collections.

The `Collection<E>` interface type has the following methods:

```
boolean add(E obj)
boolean addAll(Collection<? extends E> c)
void clear()
boolean contains(Object obj)
boolean containsAll(Collection<?> c)
boolean equals(Object obj)
int hashCode()
boolean isEmpty()
Iterator<E> iterator()
boolean remove(Object obj)
boolean removeAll(Collection<?> c)
boolean retainAll(Collection<?> c)
int size()
Object[] toArray()
E[] toArray(E[] a)
```

That is a hefty interface type. It would be quite burdensome to supply all of these methods for every collection class. For that reason, the framework supplies a class `Abstract-Collection` that implements almost all of these methods. For example, here is the implementation of the `toArray` method in the `AbstractCollection<E>` class.

```
public Object[] toArray()
{
    Object[] result = new Object[size()];
    Iterator e = iterator();
    for (int i = 0; e.hasNext(); i++)
        result[i] = e.next();
    return result;
}
```

This is again the TEMPLATE METHOD pattern at work: The `toArray` method is synthesized from the primitive operations `size` and `iterator`.

NOTE Because it is impossible to construct an array from a generic type parameter, this method returns an `Object[]` array, not an array of type `E[]`.

The `AbstractCollection` class leaves only two methods undefined. They are

```
int size()
Iterator<E> iterator()
```

Any concrete collection class must minimally supply implementations of these two methods. However, most concrete collection classes also override the `add` and `remove` methods.

NOTE The `AbstractCollection` class defines the `add` method as a dummy operation that throws an `UnsupportedOperationException`. That default is reasonable for immutable collections.

8.3.3 — Adding a New Collection to the Framework

In this section, you will see how to fit the queue class of Chapter 3 into the collections framework.

We will enhance the queue class of Chapter 3 and define a generic class `BoundedQueue` that extends the `AbstractCollection` class (see Figure 4).

We have to make a slight change to the `add` method. The collections framework requires that the `add` method return `true` if adding the element modifies the collection. The queue class always returns `true`, but a set class would return `false` if the element to be added was already present in the set.

Finally, we need to supply an iterator that visits the queue elements. You will find the code at the end of this section.

> A class that is added to the collections hierarchy can benefit from the mechanisms that the framework provides.

What is the benefit of adding the queue class to the collections framework? The Java library contains a number of mechanisms that work for arbitrary collections. For example, all collections have an `addAll` method that does a bulk addition of all elements of one collection to another. You can pass a `BoundedQueue` object to this method. Moreover, the `Collections` class that you encountered in Chapter 4 has static methods for a number of common algorithms, such as finding the minimum and maximum element in any collection. Thus, a large number of methods can be applied to `BoundedQueue` objects when the class becomes a part of the framework.

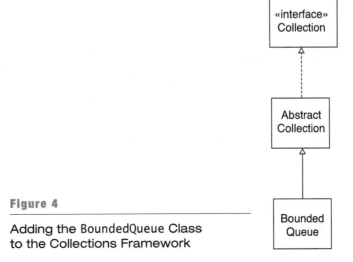

Figure 4

Adding the `BoundedQueue` Class
to the Collections Framework

NOTE   As of Java 5.0, the standard library has a `Queue` interface type. That interface type has been designed primarily for threadsafe queues. For simplicity, our `BoundedQueue` class doesn't implement it.

NOTE   Because it is not possible to construct arrays with a generic type, the `BoundedQueue` stores its value in an `Object[]` array. Casts are used when accessing elements of type E. The compiler flags these casts as unsafe because it cannot verify their correctness. You can do better—see Exercise 8.7.

Ch8/queue/BoundedQueue.java

```
 1  import java.util.*;
 2
 3  /**
 4      A first-in, first-out bounded collection of objects.
 5  */
 6  public class BoundedQueue<E> extends AbstractCollection<E>
 7  {
 8     /**
 9         Constructs an empty queue.
10         @param capacity the maximum capacity of the queue
11         @precondition capacity > 0
12     */
13     public BoundedQueue(int capacity)
14     {
15        elements = new Object[capacity];
16        count = 0;
17        head = 0;
18        tail = 0;
19     }
20
21     public Iterator<E> iterator()
22     {
23        return new
24           Iterator<E>()
25           {
26              public boolean hasNext()
27              {
28                 return visited < count;
29              }
30
31              public E next()
32              {
33                 int index = (head + visited) % elements.length;
34                 E r = (E) elements[index];
35                 visited++;
36                 return r;
37              }
38
39              public void remove()
40              {
```

```
41                    throw new UnsupportedOperationException();
42                }
43
44            private int visited = 0;
45          };
46    }
47
48    /**
49        Removes object at head.
50        @return the object that has been removed from the queue
51        @precondition size() > 0
52    */
53    public E remove()
54    {
55        E r = (E) elements[head];
56        head = (head + 1) % elements.length;
57        count--;
58        return r;
59    }
60
61    /**
62        Appends an object at tail.
63        @param anObject the object to be appended
64        @return true since this operation modifies the queue.
65        (This is a requirement of the collections framework.)
66        @precondition !isFull()
67    */
68    public boolean add(E anObject)
69    {
70        elements[tail] = anObject;
71        tail = (tail + 1) % elements.length;
72        count++;
73        return true;
74    }
75
76    public int size()
77    {
78        return count;
79    }
80
81    /**
82        Checks whether this queue is full.
83        @return true if the queue is full
84    */
85    public boolean isFull()
86    {
87        return count == elements.length;
88    }
89
90    /**
91        Gets object at head.
92        @return the object that is at the head of the queue
93        @precondition size() > 0
94    */
95    public E peek()
96    {
```

```
97          return (E) elements[head];
98      }
99
100     private Object[] elements;
101     private int head;
102     private int tail;
103     private int count;
104 }
```

Ch8/queue/QueueTester.java

```
1  import java.util.*;
2
3  public class QueueTester
4  {
5     public static void main(String[] args)
6     {
7        BoundedQueue<String> q = new BoundedQueue<String>(10);
8
9        q.add("Belgium");
10       q.add("Italy");
11       q.add("France");
12       q.remove();
13       q.add("Thailand");
14
15       ArrayList<String> a = new ArrayList<String>();
16       a.addAll(q);
17       System.out.println("Result of bulk add: " + a);
18       System.out.println("Minimum: " + Collections.min(q));
19    }
20 }
```

8.3.4 — The Set Interface Type

As you have seen, the Collection interface type defines methods that are common to all collections of objects. That interface type has two important subtypes, Set and List. Let's discuss the Set interface first. Its definition is

```
public interface Set<E> extends Collection<E> { }
```

Perhaps surprisingly, the Set interface type adds *no methods* to the Collection interface type. Why have another interface type when there are no new methods?

Conceptually, a set is a collection that eliminates duplicates. That is, inserting an element that is already present has no effect on the set. Furthermore, sets are *unordered* collections. Two sets should be considered equal if they contain the same elements, but not necessarily in the same order.

That is, the add and equals methods of a set have conceptual restrictions when compared to the same methods of the Collection interface type. Some algorithms may require sets, not arbitrary collections. By supplying a separate interface type, a method can require a Set parameter and thus refuse collections that aren't sets.

8.3.5 The List Interface Type

The Java collections framework defines a "list" as an ordered collection in which each element can be accessed by an integer index. The List<E> interface type adds the following methods to the Collection<E> interface type:

```
void add(int index, E obj)
boolean addAll(int index, Collection<? extends E> c)
E get(int index)
int indexOf(E obj)
int lastIndexOf(Object obj)
ListIterator<E> listIterator()
ListIterator<E> listIterator(int index)
E remove(int index)
E set(int index, E element)
List<E> subList(int fromIndex, int toIndex)
```

As you can see, most of these methods are concerned with the index positions.

The ListIterator<E> interface type is a subtype of Iterator<E>. Here are the added methods:

```
int nextIndex()
int previousIndex()
boolean hasPrevious()
E previous()
void add(E obj)
void set(E obj)
```

Recall from Chapter 1 that an iterator is conceptually located between two elements. The nextIndex and previousIndex methods yield the index positions of the neighbor elements. These methods are conceptually tied to the fact that the list iterator visits an indexed collection.

The other methods are unrelated to indexing. They simply allow backwards movement and element replacement.

Of course, the best-known class that implements the List interface type is the ArrayList class. More surprisingly, the LinkedList class also implements the List interface type. That flies in the face of everything that is taught in a data structures class. Accessing elements in a linked list by their index is slow: To visit the element with a given index, you must first visit all of its predecessors.

This is indeed a weakness in the design of the collections framework. It would have been an easy matter to supply two interface types: OrderedCollection for linked lists and IndexedCollection for arrays.

The library programmers belatedly noticed this problem when they implemented the binarySearch method in the Collections class. The binary search algorithm locates an element in a *sorted* collection. You start with the middle element. If that element is larger than the element you are looking for, you search the first half. Otherwise, you search the second half. Either way, every step cuts the number of elements to consider in half. The algorithm takes $O(\log_2(n))$ steps if the collection has n elements, *provided* you can access an individual element in constant time. Otherwise, the algorithm is completely pointless and it would be faster to use a sequential search that simply looks at all elements.

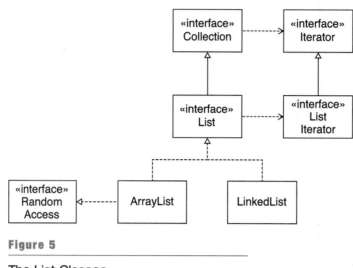

Figure 5

The List Classes

To fix this problem, version 1.4 of the library added an interface type `RandomAccess` that has no methods. It is simply a tagging interface type, to be used with an `instanceof` test. For example, a search method can test whether a `List` supports fast element access or not:

```
if (list instanceof RandomAccess)
    // Use binary search
else
    // Use linear search
```

The `ArrayList` class implements this interface type, but the `LinkedList` class does not.

As so often in software design, it is better to be familiar with the foundations of computer science and apply them correctly than to try to patch up one's design errors later.

Figure 5 shows the `List` interface type and the classes that implement it.

8.3.6 — Optional Operations

If you look at the API documentation of the collections framework, you will find many methods that are tagged as "optional operations". Among them is the `add` method of the `Collection` interface type. The `AbstractCollection` class defines the `add` method so that an `UnsupportedOperationException` is thrown when it is called. The optional operations are controversial, but there is a good reason why the library designers make use of them. The need for optional operations arises from certain *views*. A view is an object of a class that implements one of the interface types in the collections framework, and that permits restricted access to a data structure.

The collections framework defines a number of methods that yield views. Here is a typical example. An array is a built-in Java type with no methods. The `asList` method of the `Arrays` class turns an array into a collection that implements the `List` interface type:

```
String[] strings = { "Kenya", "Thailand", "Portugal" };
List<String> view = Arrays.asList(strings);
```

You can apply the `List` methods to the `view` object and access the array elements. The `view` object *does not copy* the elements in the array. The `get` and `set` methods of the view object are defined to access the original array. You can think of the view as a shallow copy of the array.

What is the use? A `List` has a richer interface than an array. You can now take advantage of operations supplied by the collections framework, such as bulk add:

```
anotherCollection.addAll(view);
```

The `addAll` method asks the view for an iterator, and that iterator enumerates all elements of the original array.

However, there are some operations that you cannot carry out. You cannot call the `add` or `remove` methods on the view. After all, it is not possible to change the size of the underlying array. For that reason, these methods are "optional". The `asList` view simply defines them to throw an `UnsupportedOperationException`.

Would it have been possible to define a separate interface type that omits the `add` and `remove` methods? The problem is that you soon have an inflation of interface types. Some views are read-only, other views (such as the one returned by the `asList` method) allow modifications, as long as the size of the collection stays the same. These are called "modifiable" in the API documentation. Having three versions of every interface type (read only, modifiable, and resizable) adds quite a bit of complexity. The drawback of the "optional" operations is that the compiler cannot check for errors.

NOTE   The `Collections` utility class has convenient static methods that give unmodifiable views of collections, lists, sets, and so on. These views are useful if you want to give a client of a class the ability to view a collection but not to modify it. For example, the `Mailbox` class of Chapter 2 can give out an unmodifiable list of messages like this:

```
public class Mailbox
{
   public List<Message> getMessages()
   {
      return Collections.unmodifiableList(messages);
   }
   . . .
   private ArrayList<Message> messages;
}
```

The `Collections.unmodifiableList` method returns an object of a class that implements the `List` interface type. Its accessor methods are defined to retrieve the elements of the underlying list, and its mutator methods fail by throwing an `UnsupportedOperationException`.

8.4 A Graph Editor Framework

8.4.1 The Problem Domain

> The problem domain for our graph editor framework is the interactive editing of graphs that consist of nodes and edges.

> An application that is based on the graph editor framework defines specific behavior for the nodes and edges.

In this section we will introduce a simple application framework in which the programmer has to add a number of classes to complete an application. The problem domain that we address is the *interactive editing of graphs*. A *graph* is made up of *nodes* and *edges* that have certain shapes.

Consider a class diagram. The nodes are rectangles, and the edges are either arrows or lines with diamonds. A different example is an electronic circuit diagram, where nodes are transistors, diodes, resistors, and capacitors. Edges are simply wires. There are numerous other examples, such as chemical formulas, flowcharts, organization charts, and logic circuits.

Traditionally, a programmer who wants to implement, say, a class diagram editor, starts from scratch and creates an application that can edit only class diagrams. If the programmer is lucky, code for a similar program, say a flowchart editor, is available for inspection. However, it may well be difficult to separate the code that is common to all diagrams from the flowchart-specific tasks, and much of the code may need to be recreated for the class diagram editor.

> The graph editor framework encapsulates those aspects that are common to all graph editing applications.

In contrast, the graph editor framework encapsulates those aspects that are common to all graph editors, in particular the user interface and the handling of commands and mouse events. The framework provides a way for specific diagram types to express their special demands that go beyond the common services.

8.4.2 The User Interface

Many of the tasks, such as selecting, moving, and connecting elements, are similar for all editors. Let's be specific and describe the user interface that our very primitive editor will have. The screen is divided into two parts, shown in Figure 6.

On the top is a *toolbar*, a collection of buttons. There is one button for each node type and one for each edge type. We will see later how a specific application supplies the icons for the buttons. The leftmost button is the *grabber* tool that is used for selecting nodes or edges. Exactly one of the tool buttons is active at any time.

There are also menu options for loading and saving a diagram, and for deleting selected nodes and edges.

In the middle is the diagram drawing area. The mouse is used for drawing. The program user can click the mouse on a node, an edge, or in empty space. The user can also use the mouse to connect nodes or to drag a node to a new position. The mouse actions depend on where the user clicks or drags, and what the currently selected tool is.

Figure 6

An Instance of the Graph
Editor Framework

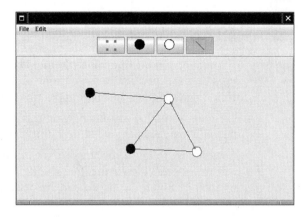

- When the current tool is a node, clicking on an empty space inserts a new node. Its type is that of the currently selected node in the toolbar.

- When the current tool is the grabber, clicking inside a node or on an edge selects that node or edge.

- When the current tool is the grabber, starting a drag operation inside an existing node moves the node as well as the edges that are connected to it.

- When the current tool is an edge, starting a drag operation inside an existing node and dragging the cursor inside another existing node inserts a new edge. Its type is that of the currently selected edge in the toolbar.

Of course, programs written with this framework are rather limited in their functionality. There is no provision to supply text labels for edges and nodes. There is no support for common commands such as cut/copy/paste or undo/redo. These features can be handled by an extended version of this framework. This example is kept as simple as possible to show the main concept: the separation of framework code and application-specific code.

8.4.3 — Division of Responsibility

The framework programmer is responsible for generic mechanisms, whereas the application programmer needs to supply code that is specific to a particular application.

When designing a framework, one must divide responsibilities between the framework and specific instances of the framework. For example, it is clear that the code to draw a transistor-shaped node is not part of the general framework—only of the electronic circuit instance.

Drawing the shapes of nodes and edges is the responsibility of the application programmer. The same holds for *hit testing:* finding out whether a node or edge is hit by a mouse click. This can be tricky for odd shapes and cannot be the responsibility of the framework.

On the other hand, drawing the toolbar and managing the mouse clicks is the job of the framework. An application programmer need not be concerned with these aspects of a graph editor at all.

> A concrete graph class must enumerate all node and edge types for the given graph.

This brings up a very interesting problem. The framework must have some idea of the node and edge types in the application so that each type of node or edge can be painted as an icon in a button. Just as importantly, it must be possible to add new nodes and edges of the types that are specified in the buttons. The application programmer must tell the framework about the node and edge types that can occur in a particular kind of graph.

There are several ways of achieving this task. For example, a concrete graph could produce a list of class names or Class objects to describe the node and edge classes.

However, we follow a slightly different approach. In our graph editor framework, a concrete graph must give the framework *prototype objects*. For example, the application instance in Figure 6 was created by defining a node class, CircleNode, an edge class, LineEdge, and a SimpleGraph class that specifies two node prototypes and an edge prototype.

```
public class SimpleGraph extends Graph
{
    public Node[] getNodePrototypes()
    {
        Node[] nodeTypes =
            {
                new CircleNode(Color.BLACK),
                new CircleNode(Color.WHITE)
            };
        return nodeTypes;
    }

    public Edge[] getEdgePrototypes()
    {
        Edge[] edgeTypes =
            {
                new LineEdge()
            };
        return edgeTypes;
    }
}
```

When the toolbar is constructed, it queries the graph for the node and edge prototypes and adds a button for each of them. The nodes and edges draw themselves in the paintIcon method of the button icon object.

When a user inserts a new node or edge, the object corresponding to the selected tool button is *cloned* and then added to the graph:

```
Node prototype = node of currently selected toolbar button;
Node newNode = (Node) prototype.clone();
Point2D mousePoint = current mouse position;
graph.add(newNode, mousePoint);
```

Why use prototype objects and not classes? Note that the two circle nodes are instances of the same class, one with a black fill color and the other with a white fill color. Thus, cloning prototype objects is a bit more economical than instantiating classes.

> The Prototype pattern teaches how a system can instantiate classes that are not known when the system is built.

This mechanism is an example of the PROTOTYPE pattern. The prototype pattern gives a solution to the problem of dealing with an open-ended collection of node and edge types whose exact nature was not known when the framework code was designed.

PATTERN

PROTOTYPE

Context

1. A system needs to create several kinds of objects whose classes are not known when the system is built.
2. You do not want to require a separate class for each kind of object.
3. You want to avoid a separate hierarchy of classes whose responsibility it is to create the objects.

Solution

1. Define a prototype interface that is common to all created objects.
2. Supply a prototype object for each kind of object that the system creates.
3. Clone the prototype object whenever a new object of the given kind is required.

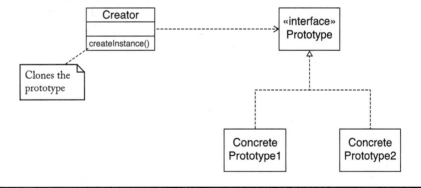

For example, in the case of the node and edge types, we have

Name in Design Pattern	Actual Name
Prototype	Node
ConcretePrototype1	CircleNode
Creator	The GraphPanel class that handles the mouse operation for adding new nodes to the graph

8.4.4 — Framework Classes

> The Node and Edge interface types describe the behavior that is common to all nodes and edges.

The framework defines the interface types Node and Edge. The methods of these interface types define the shapes of the nodes and edges.

Both Node and Edge have a draw method that is used when painting the graph and a contains method that is used to test whether the mouse point falls on a node or an edge.

Both interface types have a getBounds method that returns the rectangle enclosing the node or edge shape. That method is needed to compute the total size of the graph as the union of the bounding rectangles of its parts. The scroll pane that holds the graph panel needs to know the graph size in order to draw the scroll bars.

The Edge interface type has methods that yield the nodes at the start and end of the edge.

The getConnectionPoint method in the Node interface type computes an optimal attachment point on the boundary of a node (see Figure 7). Since the node boundary may have an arbitrary shape, this computation must be carried out by each concrete node class.

The getConnectionPoints method of the Edge interface type yields the two end points of the edge. This method is needed to draw the "grabbers" that mark the currently selected edge.

The clone method is declared in both interface types because we require all implementing classes to supply a public implementation of the clone method. That method is required to clone prototypes when inserting new nodes or edges into the graph. (Recall that the clone method of the Object class has protected visibility.)

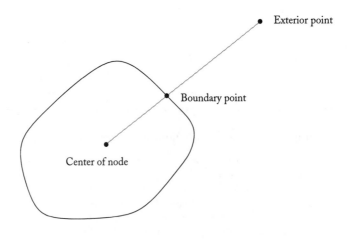

Figure 7

Node Connection Points

Ch8/graphed/Node.java

```java
1  import java.awt.*;
2  import java.awt.geom.*;
3  import java.io.*;
4
5  /**
6      A node in a graph.
7  */
8  public interface Node extends Serializable, Cloneable
9  {
10     /**
11         Draws the node.
12         @param g2 the graphics context
13     */
14     void draw(Graphics2D g2);
15
16     /**
17         Translates the node by a given amount.
18         @param dx the amount to translate in the x-direction
19         @param dy the amount to translate in the y-direction
20     */
21     void translate(double dx, double dy);
22
23     /**
24         Tests whether the node contains a point.
25         @param aPoint the point to test
26         @return true if this node contains aPoint
27     */
28     boolean contains(Point2D aPoint);
29
30     /**
31         Gets the best connection point to connect this node
32         with another node. This should be a point on the boundary
33         of the shape of this node.
34         @param aPoint an exterior point that is to be joined
35         with this node
36         @return the recommended connection point
37     */
38     Point2D getConnectionPoint(Point2D aPoint);
39
40     /**
41         Gets the bounding rectangle of the shape of this node.
42         @return the bounding rectangle
43     */
44     Rectangle2D getBounds();
45
46     Object clone();
47  }
```

Ch8/graphed/Edge.java

```java
1  import java.awt.*;
2  import java.awt.geom.*;
3  import java.io.*;
4
```

```
 5 /**
 6    An edge in a graph.
 7 */
 8 public interface Edge extends Serializable, Cloneable
 9 {
10    /**
11       Draws the edge.
12       @param g2 the graphics context
13    */
14    void draw(Graphics2D g2);
15
16    /**
17       Tests whether the edge contains a point.
18       @param aPoint the point to test
19       @return true if this edge contains aPoint
20    */
21    boolean contains(Point2D aPoint);
22
23    /**
24       Connects this edge to two nodes.
25       @param aStart the starting node
26       @param anEnd the ending node
27    */
28    void connect(Node aStart, Node anEnd);
29
30    /**
31       Gets the starting node.
32       @return the starting node
33    */
34    Node getStart();
35
36    /**
37       Gets the ending node.
38       @return the ending node
39    */
40    Node getEnd();
41
42    /**
43       Gets the points at which this edge is connected to
44       its nodes.
45       @return a line joining the two connection points
46    */
47    Line2D getConnectionPoints();
48
49    /**
50       Gets the smallest rectangle that bounds this edge.
51       The bounding rectangle contains all labels.
52       @return the bounding rectangle
53    */
54    Rectangle2D getBounds(Graphics2D g2);
55
56    Object clone();
57 }
```

The programmer using this framework must define specific node and edge classes that realize these interface types:

```
class Transistor implements Node { . . . }
class Wire implements Edge { . . . }
```

For the convenience of the programmer, the framework also supplies an abstract class AbstractEdge that provides reasonable implementations of some, but not all, of the methods in the Edge interface type. Whenever these default implementations are appropriate, a programmer can extend that class rather than having to implement all methods of the interface type. There is no corresponding AbstractNode class since all of the methods of the Node interface type require knowledge of the node shape.

Ch8/graphed/AbstractEdge.java

```java
1  import java.awt.*;
2  import java.awt.geom.*;
3
4  /**
5     A class that supplies convenience implementations for
6     a number of methods in the Edge interface type.
7  */
8  public abstract class AbstractEdge implements Edge
9  {
10     public Object clone()
11     {
12        try
13        {
14           return super.clone();
15        }
16        catch (CloneNotSupportedException exception)
17        {
18           return null;
19        }
20     }
21
22     public void connect(Node s, Node e)
23     {
24        start = s;
25        end = e;
26     }
27
28     public Node getStart()
29     {
30        return start;
31     }
32
33     public Node getEnd()
34     {
35        return end;
36     }
37
```

```
38     public Rectangle2D getBounds(Graphics2D g2)
39     {
40        Line2D conn = getConnectionPoints();
41        Rectangle2D r = new Rectangle2D.Double();
42        r.setFrameFromDiagonal(conn.getX1(), conn.getY1(),
43              conn.getX2(), conn.getY2());
44        return r;
45     }
46
47     public Line2D getConnectionPoints()
48     {
49        Rectangle2D startBounds = start.getBounds();
50        Rectangle2D endBounds = end.getBounds();
51        Point2D startCenter = new Point2D.Double(
52              startBounds.getCenterX(), startBounds.getCenterY());
53        Point2D endCenter = new Point2D.Double(
54              endBounds.getCenterX(), endBounds.getCenterY());
55        return new Line2D.Double(
56              start.getConnectionPoint(endCenter),
57              end.getConnectionPoint(startCenter));
58     }
59
60     private Node start;
61     private Node end;
62  }
```

> The Graph class supplies methods for adding, finding, and removing nodes and edges.

The Graph class collects the nodes and edges. It has methods for adding, removing, finding, and drawing nodes and edges. Note that this class supplies quite a bit of useful functionality. This is, of course, characteristic of frameworks. In order to supply a significant value to application programmers, the framework classes must be able to supply a substantial amount of work.

Nevertheless, the Graph class is abstract. Subclasses of Graph must override the abstract methods

```
public abstract Node[] getNodePrototypes()
public abstract Edge[] getEdgePrototypes()
```

These methods are called when a graph is added to a frame. They populate the toolbar with the tools that are necessary to edit the graph. For example, the getNodePrototypes method of the SimpleGraph class specifies two circle node prototypes.

Ch8/graphed/Graph.java

```
1  import java.awt.*;
2  import java.awt.geom.*;
3  import java.io.*;
4  import java.util.*;
5  import java.util.List;
6
7  /**
8      A graph consisting of selectable nodes and edges.
```

```
 9  */
10  public abstract class Graph implements Serializable
11  {
12     /**
13        Constructs a graph with no nodes or edges.
14     */
15     public Graph()
16     {
17        nodes = new ArrayList<Node>();
18        edges = new ArrayList<Edge>();
19     }
20
21     /**
22        Adds an edge to the graph that joins the nodes containing
23        the given points. If the points aren't both inside nodes,
24        then no edge is added.
25        @param e the edge to add
26        @param p1 a point in the starting node
27        @param p2 a point in the ending node
28     */
29     public boolean connect(Edge e, Point2D p1, Point2D p2)
30     {
31        Node n1 = findNode(p1);
32        Node n2 = findNode(p2);
33        if (n1 != null && n2 != null)
34        {
35           e.connect(n1, n2);
36           edges.add(e);
37           return true;
38        }
39        return false;
40     }
41
42     /**
43        Adds a node to the graph so that the top left corner of
44        the bounding rectangle is at the given point.
45        @param n the node to add
46        @param p the desired location
47     */
48     public boolean add(Node n, Point2D p)
49     {
50        Rectangle2D bounds = n.getBounds();
51        n.translate(p.getX() - bounds.getX(),
52              p.getY() - bounds.getY());
53        nodes.add(n);
54        return true;
55     }
56
57     /**
58        Finds a node containing the given point.
59        @param p a point
60        @return a node containing p or null if no nodes contain p
61     */
62     public Node findNode(Point2D p)
63     {
```

```
64        for (int i = nodes.size() - 1; i >= 0; i--)
65        {
66            Node n = nodes.get(i);
67            if (n.contains(p)) return n;
68        }
69        return null;
70     }
71
72     /**
73         Finds an edge containing the given point.
74         @param p a point
75         @return an edge containing p or null if no edges contain p
76     */
77     public Edge findEdge(Point2D p)
78     {
79        for (int i = edges.size() - 1; i >= 0; i--)
80        {
81            Edge e = edges.get(i);
82            if (e.contains(p)) return e;
83        }
84        return null;
85     }
86
87     /**
88         Draws the graph.
89         @param g2 the graphics context
90     */
91     public void draw(Graphics2D g2)
92     {
93        for (Node n : nodes)
94            n.draw(g2);
95
96        for (Edge e : edges)
97            e.draw(g2);
98     }
99
100    /**
101        Removes a node and all edges that start or end with that node.
102        @param n the node to remove
103    */
104    public void removeNode(Node n)
105    {
106       for (int i = edges.size() - 1; i >= 0; i--)
107       {
108           Edge e = edges.get(i);
109           if (e.getStart() == n || e.getEnd() == n)
110               edges.remove(e);
111       }
112       nodes.remove(n);
113    }
114
115    /**
116        Removes an edge from the graph.
117        @param e the edge to remove
118    */
119    public void removeEdge(Edge e)
```

```
120    {
121        edges.remove(e);
122    }
123
124    /**
125        Gets the smallest rectangle enclosing the graph.
126        @param g2  the graphics context
127        @return  the bounding rectangle
128    */
129    public Rectangle2D getBounds(Graphics2D g2)
130    {
131        Rectangle2D r = null;
132        for (Node n : nodes)
133        {
134            Rectangle2D b = n.getBounds();
135            if (r == null) r = b;
136            else r.add(b);
137        }
138        for (Edge e : edges)
139            r.add(e.getBounds(g2));
140        return r == null ? new Rectangle2D.Double() : r;
141    }
142
143    /**
144        Gets the node types of a particular graph type.
145        @return  an array of node prototypes
146    */
147    public abstract Node[] getNodePrototypes();
148
149    /**
150        Gets the edge types of a particular graph type.
151        @return  an array of edge prototypes
152    */
153    public abstract Edge[] getEdgePrototypes();
154
155    /**
156        Gets the nodes of this graph.
157        @return  an unmodifiable list of the nodes
158    */
159    public List<Node> getNodes()
160    {
161        return Collections.unmodifiableList(nodes);
162    }
163
164    /**
165        Gets the edges of this graph.
166        @return  an unmodifiable list of the edges
167    */
168    public List<Edge> getEdges()
169    {
170        return Collections.unmodifiableList(edges);
171    }
172
173    private ArrayList<Node> nodes;
174    private ArrayList<Edge> edges;
175 }
```

The graph editor uses the following classes for editing the graph:

- GraphFrame: a frame that manages the toolbar, the menu bar, and the graph panel.

- ToolBar: a panel that holds toggle buttons for the node and edge icons.

- GraphPanel: a panel that shows the graph and handles the mouse clicks and drags for the editing commands.

We do not list these classes here. The implementations are straightforward but a bit long. The graph frame attaches the toolbar and graph panel, sets up the menu, and loads and saves graphs using object serialization, as discussed in Chapter 7. The toolbar sets up a row of buttons with icon objects that paint the nodes and edges, and which are scaled down to fit inside the buttons. The mouse handling of the graph panel is similar to that of the scene editor in Chapter 6.

Interestingly enough, the Node and Edge interface types are rich enough that the framework classes do not need to know anything about particular node and edge shapes. The mechanics of mouse movement, rubber banding, and screen update are completely solved at this level and are of no concern to the programmer using the framework. Because all drawing and mouse operations are taken care of in the framework classes, the programmer building a graphical editor on top of the framework can simply focus on implementing the node and edge types.

8.4.5 — Turning the Framework into an Application

The classes for the simple graph editor are summarized in Figure 8. The bottom four classes are application-specific. All other classes belong to the framework.

Let's summarize the responsibilities of the programmer creating a specific diagram editor:

- For each node and edge type, define a class that implements the Node or Edge interface type and supply all required methods, such as drawing and containment testing. For convenience, you may want to subclass the AbstractEdge class.

- Define a subclass of the Graph class whose getNodePrototypes and getEdge-Prototypes methods supply prototype objects for nodes and edges.

- Supply a class with a main method such as the SimpleGraphEditor class below.

Note that the programmer who turns the framework into an application supplies only application-specific classes and does not implement the user interface or control flow. This is characteristic of using a framework.

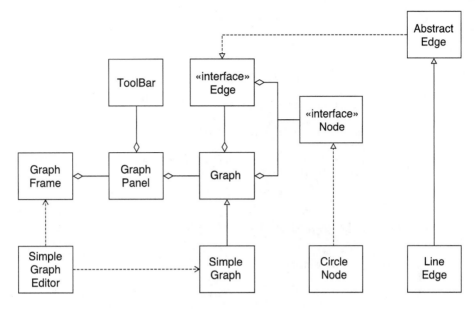

Figure 8

Application and Framework Classes

Ch8/graphed/SimpleGraph.java

```java
 1  import java.awt.*;
 2  import java.util.*;
 3
 4  /**
 5     A simple graph with round nodes and straight edges.
 6  */
 7  public class SimpleGraph extends Graph
 8  {
 9     public Node[] getNodePrototypes()
10     {
11        Node[] nodeTypes =
12           {
13              new CircleNode(Color.BLACK),
14              new CircleNode(Color.WHITE)
15           };
16        return nodeTypes;
17     }
18
19     public Edge[] getEdgePrototypes()
20     {
21        Edge[] edgeTypes =
22           {
23              new LineEdge()
24           };
25        return edgeTypes;
26     }
27  }
```

Ch8/graphed/SimpleGraphEditor.java

```
1  import javax.swing.*;
2
3  /**
4      A program for editing UML diagrams.
5  */
6  public class SimpleGraphEditor
7  {
8      public static void main(String[] args)
9      {
10         JFrame frame = new GraphFrame(new SimpleGraph());
11         frame.setVisible(true);
12     }
13 }
```

Ch8/graphed/CircleNode.java

```
1  import java.awt.*;
2  import java.awt.geom.*;
3
4  /**
5      A circular node that is filled with a color.
6  */
7  public class CircleNode implements Node
8  {
9      /**
10         Construct a circle node with a given size and color.
11         @param aColor the fill color
12     */
13     public CircleNode(Color aColor)
14     {
15         size = DEFAULT_SIZE;
16         x = 0;
17         y = 0;
18         color = aColor;
19     }
20
21     public Object clone()
22     {
23         try
24         {
25             return super.clone();
26         }
27         catch (CloneNotSupportedException exception)
28         {
29             return null;
30         }
31     }
32
33     public void draw(Graphics2D g2)
34     {
35         Ellipse2D circle = new Ellipse2D.Double(
36             x, y, size, size);
37         Color oldColor = g2.getColor();
38         g2.setColor(color);
```

```
39          g2.fill(circle);
40          g2.setColor(oldColor);
41          g2.draw(circle);
42      }
43
44      public void translate(double dx, double dy)
45      {
46          x += dx;
47          y += dy;
48      }
49
50      public boolean contains(Point2D p)
51      {
52          Ellipse2D circle = new Ellipse2D.Double(
53                  x, y, size, size);
54          return circle.contains(p);
55      }
56
57      public Rectangle2D getBounds()
58      {
59          return new Rectangle2D.Double(
60                  x, y, size, size);
61      }
62
63      public Point2D getConnectionPoint(Point2D other)
64      {
65          double centerX = x + size / 2;
66          double centerY = y + size / 2;
67          double dx = other.getX() - centerX;
68          double dy = other.getY() - centerY;
69          double distance = Math.sqrt(dx * dx + dy * dy);
70          if (distance == 0) return other;
71          else return new Point2D.Double(
72                  centerX + dx * (size / 2) / distance,
73                  centerY + dy * (size / 2) / distance);
74      }
75
76      private double x;
77      private double y;
78      private double size;
79      private Color color;
80      private static final int DEFAULT_SIZE = 20;
81  }
```

Ch8/graphed/LineEdge.java

```
1  import java.awt.*;
2  import java.awt.geom.*;
3
4  /**
5     An edge that is shaped like a straight line.
6  */
7  public class LineEdge extends AbstractEdge
8  {
```

```
9    public void draw(Graphics2D g2)
10   {
11       g2.draw(getConnectionPoints());
12   }
13
14   public boolean contains(Point2D aPoint)
15   {
16       final double MAX_DIST = 2;
17       return getConnectionPoints().ptSegDist(aPoint)
18           < MAX_DIST;
19   }
20 }
```

8.4.6 — Generic Framework Code

> The generic framework code does not need to know about specific node and edge types.

In the last section you saw how to customize the framework to a specific editor application. In this section we will investigate how the framework code is able to function without knowing anything about the types of nodes and edges.

The framework code is too long to analyze here in its entirety, and some technical details, particularly of the mouse tracking, are not terribly interesting. Let's consider two operations: adding a new node and adding a new edge.

First let's look at adding a new node. When the mouse is clicked outside an existing node, then a new node of the current type is added. This is where the clone operation comes in. The getSelectedTool method of the ToolBar class returns an object of the desired node type. Of course, you cannot simply insert that object into the diagram. If you did, all nodes of the same type would end up in identical positions. Instead you invoke clone and add the cloned node to the graph. The mousePressed method of the mouse listener in the GraphPanel class carries out these actions.

```
public void mousePressed(MouseEvent event)
{
    Point2D mousePoint = event.getPoint();
    Object tool = toolBar.getSelectedTool();
    . . .
    if (tool instanceof Node)
    {
        Node prototype = (Node) tool;
        Node newNode = (Node) prototype.clone();
        graph.add(newNode, mousePoint);
    }
    . . .
    repaint();
}
```

Figure 9 shows the sequence diagram. Note how the code is completely independent of the actual node type in a particular application.

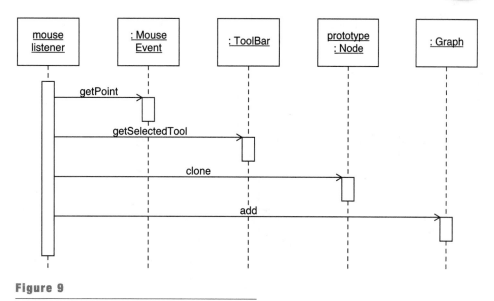

Figure 9

Inserting a New Node

Next, consider a more involved action, adding a new edge. When the mouse is clicked, we must first determine whether the click is inside an existing node. This operation is carried out in the findNode method of the Graph class, by calling the contains method of the Node interface:

```
public Node findNode(Point2D p)
{
    for (Node n : nodes)
        if (n.contains(p)) return n;
    return null;
}
```

If the mouse is clicked inside an existing node and the current tool is an edge, we remember the mouse position in the rubberBandStart field of the GraphPanel class.

```
public void mousePressed(MouseEvent event)
{
    . . .
    Node n = graph.findNode(mousePoint);
    if (tool instanceof Edge)
    {
        if (n != null) rubberBandStart = mousePoint;
    }
    . . .
}
```

In the mouseDragged method, there are two possibilities. If the current tool is not an edge, then the purpose of the dragging is to move the selected node elsewhere. We don't

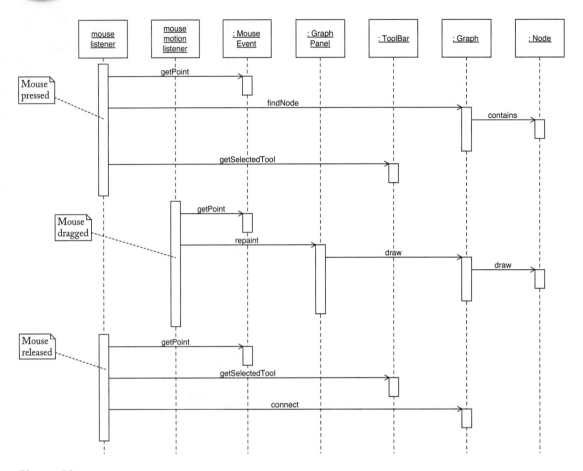

Figure 10

Inserting a New Edge

care about that case right now. However, if we are currently inserting an edge, then we want to draw a "rubber band", a line that follows the mouse pointer.

```java
public void mouseDragged(MouseEvent event)
{
    Point2D mousePoint = event.getPoint();
    . . .
    lastMousePoint = mousePoint;
    repaint();
}
```

The repaint method invokes the paintComponent method of the GraphPanel. It draws the graph and, if rubberBandStart is not null, the rubber banded line.

```java
public void paintComponent(Graphics g)
{
```

```
Graphics2D g2 = (Graphics2D) g;
graph.draw(g2);
if (rubberBandStart != null)
   g2.draw(new Line2D.Double(rubberBandStart, lastMousePoint));
   . . .
}
```

When the mouse button goes up, we are ready to add the edge.

```
public void mouseReleased(MouseEvent event)
{
   Object tool = toolBar.getSelectedTool();
   if (rubberBandStart != null)
   {
      Point2D mousePoint = event.getPoint();
      Edge prototype = (Edge) tool;
      Edge newEdge = (Edge) prototype.clone();
      graph.connect(newEdge, rubberBandStart, mousePoint);
      rubberBandStart = null;
      repaint();
   }
}
```

Figure 10 shows the sequence diagram.

These scenarios are representative of the ability of the framework code to operate without an exact knowledge of the node and edge types.

8.5   Enhancing the Graph Editor Framework

8.5.1   Editing Node and Edge Properties

In this section, we will discuss an important enhancement of the graph editor framework: the ability to edit properties of nodes and edges. We add a menu option Edit → Properties that pops up a dialog box to edit the properties of the selected node or edge (see Figure 11).

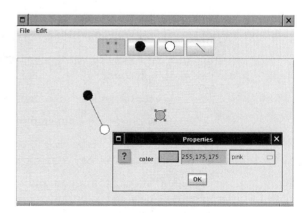

Figure 11

Editing a Node Property

Clearly, such a facility is necessary to enable users to select colors, line styles, text labels, and so on. The challenge for the framework designer is to find a mechanism that allows arbitrary node and edge classes to expose their properties, and then to provide a generic user interface for editing them.

> To enable a graph editor application to edit the properties of nodes or edges, an application programmer simply implements them as JavaBeans properties. The graph editor framework contains the code for editing the properties.

Fortunately, this problem has been solved elsewhere. Recall from Chapter 7 that GUI builders are able to edit arbitrary properties of JavaBeans components. We will therefore require the implementors of nodes and edges to expose editable properties using the JavaBeans convention: with get and set methods. To edit the properties, we supply a property sheet dialog box that is similar to the property editor in a GUI builder.

For example, the CircleNode class can expose a Color property simply by providing two methods

```
public void setColor(Color newValue)
public Color getColor()
```

No further work is necessary. The graph editor can now edit node colors.

Let's consider a more complex change: to support both solid and dotted lines. We will define an enumerated type LineStyle with two instances:

```
LineStyle.SOLID
LineStyle.DOTTED
```

(See Chapter 7 for a discussion of the implementation of enumerated types in Java.)

The LineStyle enumeration has a convenience method

```
Stroke getStroke()
```

That method yields a solid or dotted stroke object. The LineEdge method uses that object in its draw method:

```
public void draw(Graphics2D g2)
{
   Stroke oldStroke = g2.getStroke();
   g2.setStroke(lineStyle.getStroke());
   g2.draw(getConnectionPoints());
   g2.setStroke(oldStroke);
}
```

The effect is either a solid or dotted line that joins the connection points.

Of course, we need to add getters and setters for the line style to the LineEdge class.

Altogether, the following changes are required to add colored nodes and dotted lines to the simple graph editor:

- Add setColor and getColor methods to CircleNode.

- Supply a LineStyle enumeration.

- Enhance the LineEdge class to draw both solid and dotted lines, and add getLineStyle and setLineStyle methods.

It is a simple matter to support additional graph properties, such as line shapes, arrow shapes, text labels, and so on.

8.5.2 — Another Graph Editor Instance: A Simple UML Class Editor

Figure 12 shows a simple UML class diagram editor that has been built on top of the graph editor framework.

The editor is essentially the same as the Violet UML editor. However, it supports only class diagrams, and it lacks some convenience features such as keyboard shortcuts, image export, and snap-to-grid.

> To build a simple UML editor, add class node and class relationship edge classes to the graph editor framework.

Of course, the node and edge classes of this editor are more complex. They format and draw text, compute edges with multiple segments, and add arrow tips and diamonds. It is instructive to enumerate the classes that carry out this new functionality. None of these classes are difficult to implement, although there is an undeniable tedium to some of the layout computations.

- The RectangularNode class describes a node that is shaped like a rectangle. It is the superclass of ClassNode.

- The SegmentedLineEdge class implements an edge that consists of multiple line segments. It is the superclass of ClassRelationshipEdge.

- ArrowHead and BentStyle classes are enumerations for arrow heads and edge shapes, similar to the LineStyle class of the preceding section.

- MultiLineString formats a string that may extend over multiple lines. A Class-Node uses multiline strings for the class name, the attributes, and the methods.

- Finally, the ClassDiagramGraph class adds the ClassNode and various edge proto-types to the toolbar.

The basic framework is not affected at all by these changes. The implementor of the UML editor need not be concerned about frames, toolbars, or event handling. Even the editing of properties is automatically provided because the framework supplies a dialog

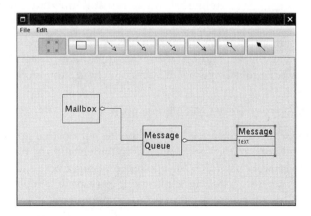

Figure 12

A Simple UML Class Diagram Editor

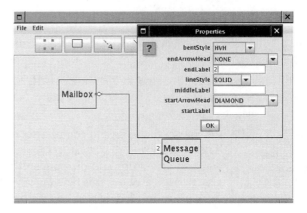

Figure 13

The Edge Property Editor

box that manipulates the JavaBeans properties (see Figure 13). Thus, the framework allows the implementor of any particular graph type to focus on the intricacies of the nodes and edges of just that graph.

8.5.3 — Evolving the Framework

> The Violet UML editor uses an enhanced version of the graph editor framework. The simple graph editor can take advantage of the enhancements with no changes in application code.

The Violet UML editor uses an enhanced version of the graph editor framework that adds a number of useful features such as graphics export, a grid for easier alignment, and simultaneous display of multiple graphs. The companion code for this book does not include the Violet code because some of it is rather lengthy. You can find the source code at http://horstmann.com/violet.

Remarkably, you can still integrate the simple graph editor with its circle nodes and line edges into the enhanced framework (see Figure 14).

This demonstrates another advantage of using a framework. By decoupling the framework and the application code, the application designers can take advantage of the framework evolution, without having to change the application-specific code.

8.5.4 — A Note on Framework Design

In this chapter, you have learned how to put existing application frameworks to use. In order to use a framework, you have to understand the requirements that the designer of the framework set forth for application programmers. For example, to turn the graph editor framework into an application, you have to supply subclasses of Graph, Node, and Edge. Other frameworks have similar requirements.

Designing your own framework is a far bigger challenge than using a framework. You need to have a thorough understanding of the problem domain that the framework addresses. You need to design an architecture that enables application programmers to

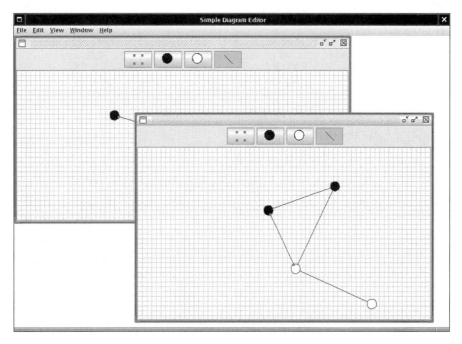

Figure 14

The Simple Graph Editor Takes Advantage of the
Enhanced Framework

add application-specific code, without changing the framework code. The design of the framework should shield application programmers from internal mechanisms and allow them to focus on application-specific tasks. On the other hand, you need to provide "hooks" that allow application programmers to modify the generic framework behavior when applications require nonstandard mechanisms. It is notoriously difficult to anticipate the needs of application programmers. In fact, it is commonly said that a framework can only claim to have withstood the test of time if it is the basis of at least three different applications. Rules for the effective design of application frameworks are an area of active research at this time.

EXERCISES

Exercise 8.1. The java.io package contains pluggable streams, such as PushbackInputStream and ZipInputStream. Explain why the stream classes form a framework. Describe how a programmer can add new stream classes to the framework, and what benefits those classes automatically have.

Exercise 8.2. Search the Web for application frameworks until you have found frameworks for three distinct problem domains. Summarize your findings.

Exercise 8.3. Turn the scene editor of Chapter 6 into an applet.

Exercise 8.4. Write an applet that can display a bar chart. The applet should obtain the chart values from a set of param tags.

Exercise 8.5. Explain the phenomenon of "inversion of control", using the graph editor framework as an example.

Exercise 8.6. Re-implement the BoundedQueue class as a subtype of the Queue interface type in the standard library.

Exercise 8.7. Prove the following class invariant for the BoundedQueue<E> class:

- All values in the elements array belong to a subtype of E.

Why does this invariant show that the class implementation is safe, despite the compiler warnings? Why can't the compiler determine that the implementation is safe?

Exercise 8.8. Suppose the designers of the collections framework had decided to offer separate interface types for ordered collections (such as linked lists) and indexed collections (such as array lists). Explain the changes that must be made to the framework.

Exercise 8.9. Suppose the designers of the collections framework had, instead of allowing "unsupported operations", supported three kinds of data structures: read-only, modifiable, and resizable. Explain the changes that must be made to the framework. How do the basic interface types change? Which classes need to be added? Which methods need to be added to the Arrays and Collections classes?

Exercise 8.10. The RandomAccess interface type has no methods. The Set interface type adds no methods to its superinterface. What are the similarities and differences between the functionality that they are designed to provide?

Exercise 8.11. The standard C++ library defines a collections framework (known as STL) that is quite different from the Java framework. Explain the major differences.

Exercise 8.12. Contrast the algorithms available in the Java collections framework with those of the standard C++ library.

Exercise 8.13. Enhance the SimpleGraphEditor to support both circular and rectangular nodes.

Exercise 8.14. Enhance the SimpleGraphEditor to support lines with arrow tips.

Exercise 8.15. Enhance the SimpleGraphEditor to support text annotations of lines. *Hint:* Make a label property.

Exercise 8.16. Enhance the SimpleGraphEditor to support multiple arrow shapes: v-shaped arrow tips, triangles, and diamonds.

Exercise 8.17. Add cut/copy/paste operations to the graph editor framework.

Exercise 8.18. Design a sorting algorithm animation framework. An algorithm animation shows an algorithm in slow motion. For example, if you animate the merge sort algorithm, you can see how the algorithm sorts and merges intervals of increasing size. Your framework should allow a programmer to plug in various sorting algorithms.

Exercise 8.19. Design a framework for simulating the processing of customers at a bank or supermarket. Such a simulation is based on the notion of *events*. Each event has a time stamp. Events are placed in an event queue. Whenever one event has finished processing, the event with the earliest time stamp is removed from the event queue. That time stamp becomes the current system time. The event is processed, and the cycle repeats. There are different kinds of events. Arrival events cause customers to arrive at the bank. A stream of them needs to be generated to ensure the continued arrival of customers, with somewhat random times between arrivals. This is typically done by seeding the event queue with one arrival event, and having the processing method schedule the next arrival event. Whenever a teller is done processing a customer, the teller obtains the next waiting customer and schedules a "done processing" event, some random time away from the current time. In the framework, supply an abstract event class and the event processing mechanism. Then supply two applications that use the framework: a bank with a number of tellers and a single queue of waiting customers, and a supermarket with a number of cashiers and one queue per cashier.

Multithreading

In this chapter, you will learn how to manage programs that contain multiple *threads*—program units that can be executed in parallel. You will learn how to start new threads and how to coordinate the threads of a program. Thread programming poses a number of complexities. The order in which threads are executed is not deterministic. You need to ensure that the behavior of a program is not affected by variations in execution order. Furthermore, you need some way of synchronizing the threads. One thread may need a result that is being computed by another thread. Another common problem occurs when multiple threads simultaneously try to modify a shared object; you will learn how to deal with these issues in this chapter.

9.1 Thread Basics

9.1.1 — Threads and the Runnable InterfaceType

When you use a computer, you often run multiple programs at the same time. For example, you may download your e-mail while you write a report in your word processor. The operating system of your computer is able to run multiple programs at the same time, switching back and forth between them. Technically speaking, a modern operating system can concurrently execute multiple *processes*. The operating system frequently switches back and forth between the processes, giving the illusion that they run in parallel. Actually, if a computer has multiple central processing units (CPUs), then some of the processes really can run in parallel, one on each processor.

It is often useful for a single program to carry out two or more tasks at the same time. For example, a Web browser can load multiple images into a Web page at the same time. A program can do a lengthy computation in the background, while responding to user commands in the foreground. Or an animation program can show moving figures, with separate tasks computing the layout of each separate figure. Of course, you can obtain effects such as these by implementing a loop that first does a little bit of the first task, then a little bit of the second, and so on. But such programs get complex quickly, because you have to mix the code for doing the work with the code to control the timing.

> A thread of execution is a program unit that is executed independently of other parts of the program.

In Java, you can implement each of several tasks as a *thread of execution*. A thread is a program unit that is executed independently of other parts of the program. The Java virtual machine executes each thread for a short amount of time and then switches to another thread. You can visualize the threads as programs executing in parallel to each other.

There is an important difference between processes and threads. Modern operating systems isolate processes from each other. For example, processes can't overwrite each other's memory. Obviously, this isolation is an important safety feature. But it also makes the switching between processes rather slow. Threads, on the other hand, run within a single process so switching between threads is very fast. But multiple threads share memory and are able to corrupt each other's data if programmers are not careful.

Threads let you concentrate on the task that you want to carry out, without having to worry how that task is alternated with other tasks. If you need to carry out two tasks in parallel, you simply start a thread for each of them.

Running a thread is simple—just follow these steps:

1. Define a class that implements the Runnable interface type. That interface type has a single method called run.

   ```java
   public interface Runnable
   {
       void run();
   }
   ```

2. Place the code for the task into the run method of the class.

3. Create an object of the class.

4. Construct a `Thread` object and supply the `Runnable` object in the constructor.

5. Call the `start` method of the `Thread` object to start the thread.

> The `start` method of a `Thread` object starts a new thread that executes the `run` method of its `Runnable`.

Let's look at a concrete example. You want to run two threads in parallel, each of which prints ten greetings.

Each thread executes this loop.

```
for (int i = 1; i <= REPETITIONS; i++)
{
    System.out.println(i + ": " + greeting);
    Thread.sleep(DELAY);
}
```

After printing the greeting, let each thread sleep for a short amount of time. That gives the other thread a chance to run. Every thread should occasionally yield control to other threads. Otherwise the thread is *selfish*. On some platforms, a selfish thread can prevent other threads from making progress.

> The `sleep` method puts the current thread to sleep for a given number of milliseconds.

The static `sleep` method of the `Thread` class puts the current thread to sleep for a given number of milliseconds. In our case, the thread sleeps for 100 milliseconds or 1/10th of a second.

> When a thread is interrupted, the most common response is to terminate the `run` method.

There is, however, one technical problem. Putting a thread to sleep is potentially risky—a thread might sleep for so long that it is no longer useful and should be terminated. As you will see later in this chapter, a thread is terminated by *interrupting* it. When a sleeping thread is interrupted, an `InterruptedException` is generated. This is a checked exception, declared by the `sleep` method. You need to catch that exception in your run method. The simplest way to handle thread interruptions is to give your run method the following form:

```
public class MyRunnable implements Runnable
{
    public void run()
    {
        try
        {
            do work
        }
        catch (InterruptedException exception)
        {
        }
        clean up, if necessary
    }
    . . .
}
```

Here is the complete class of the `Runnable` that produces a sequence of greetings.

Ch9/greeting/GreetingProducer.java

```
1  /**
2     An action that repeatedly prints a greeting.
3  */
4  public class GreetingProducer implements Runnable
5  {
```

```
6    /**
7         Constructs the producer object.
8         @param aGreeting the greeting to display
9    */
10   public GreetingProducer(String aGreeting)
11   {
12        greeting = aGreeting;
13   }
14
15   public void run()
16   {
17      try
18      {
19         for (int i = 1; i <= REPETITIONS; i++)
20         {
21            System.out.println(i + ": " + greeting);
22            Thread.sleep(DELAY);
23         }
24      }
25      catch (InterruptedException exception)
26      {
27      }
28   }
29
30   private String greeting;
31
32   private static final int REPETITIONS = 10;
33   private static final int DELAY = 100;
34 }
```

This class is not a thread. It is merely a class that defines an action in its run method. To execute that action in a thread, you create a thread and start it.

```
Runnable r = new GreetingProducer("Hello, World!");
Thread t = new Thread(r);
t.start();
```

Figure 1 shows the relationships between these classes.

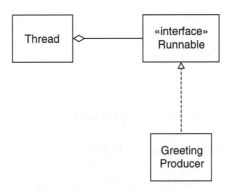

Figure 1

A Thread and Its Runnable

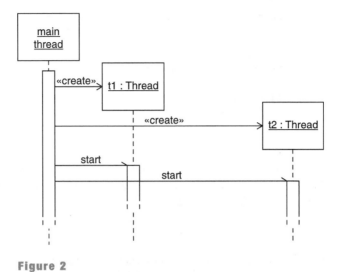

Figure 2

Starting Two Threads

> A thread terminates when the run method of its Runnable terminates.

The `start` method creates a new thread in the Java virtual machine. That thread calls the `run` method of the `Runnable` object. The thread terminates when the `run` method returns or throws an uncaught exception.

NOTE You can also define threads by forming subclasses of the `Thread` class and overriding the run method in the subclass. However, there are other mechanisms for executing `Runnable` objects without having to create new threads. In particular, you can execute a `Runnable` in a *thread pool*. A thread pool contains a number of threads that are already constructed, ready to execute the run method of any `Runnable`. By using a thread pool, you amortize the high cost of constructing a new thread. This is particularly important for programs that launch a very large number of short-lived threads, such as Web servers. See the API documentation of the `Executors` class in the `java.util.concurrent` package for details.

To run two threads in parallel, simply construct and start two `Thread` objects. The following test program does just that. Figure 2 shows the sequence diagram.

Ch9/greeting/ThreadTester.java

```
1  /**
2     This program runs two threads in parallel.
3  */
4  public class ThreadTester
5  {
6     public static void main(String[] args)
7     {
```

```
8       Runnable r1 = new GreetingProducer("Hello, World!");
9       Runnable r2 = new GreetingProducer("Goodbye, World!");
10
11      Thread t1 = new Thread(r1);
12      Thread t2 = new Thread(r2);
13
14      t1.start();
15      t2.start();
16   }
17 }
```

Note that the main method runs in its own thread, the *main thread* of the program. The main thread terminates after starting t2, but both t1 and t2 still execute. The program only ends when all of its threads terminate.

NOTE This observation also explains why graphical user interfaces keep running long after the main method exited. When the first frame of an application is shown, a *user interface* thread is started. That thread processes user interface events such as mouse clicks and key presses. The user interface thread only terminates if the program is forced to exit, for example by calling the System.exit method or by closing a frame with the EXIT_ON_CLOSE setting.

9.1.2 — Scheduling Threads

Here is a sample output of the thread tester program. Each thread runs for a short amount of time, called a *time slice*. Then the scheduler activates another thread. Therefore, both producer threads take turns, and the two sets of greetings are interleaved.

```
1: Hello, World!
1: Goodbye, World!
2: Hello, World!
2: Goodbye, World!
3: Hello, World!
3: Goodbye, World!
4: Hello, World!
4: Goodbye, World!
5: Hello, World!
5: Goodbye, World!
6: Hello, World!
6: Goodbye, World!
7: Hello, World!
7: Goodbye, World!
8: Goodbye, World!
8: Hello, World!
9: Goodbye, World!
9: Hello, World!
10: Goodbye, World!
10: Hello, World!
```

> The thread scheduler allows each thread to execute for a short amount of time, called a time slice.

If you look closely at the output, you will find that the two threads aren't *exactly* alternating. Sometimes, the second thread seems to jump ahead of the first thread. This shows an important characteristic of threads. The thread scheduler gives no guarantee about the order in which threads are executed. Moreover, there will always be slight variations in running times, especially when calling operating system services (such as input and output). Thus, you should expect that the order in which each thread gains control appears to be somewhat random.

Let's have a closer look at the algorithm that the scheduler uses to pick the next thread to run. Each thread has

- A thread state
- A priority

The thread state is one of the following (see Figure 3):

- new (before start is called)
- runnable
- blocked
- dead (after the run method exits)

 NOTE   There is no separate state to indicate whether a runnable thread is actually running.

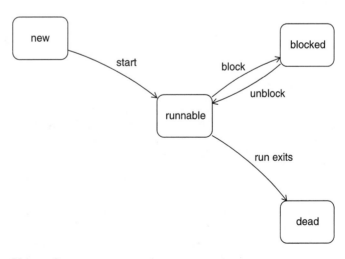

Figure 3

Thread States

A thread can enter the blocked state for several reasons that we will discuss in the remainder of this chapter. They include:

- Sleeping
- Waiting for input/output
- Waiting to acquire a lock (see Section 9.2.3)
- Waiting for a condition (see Section 9.2.4)

Once a thread is blocked in a particular way, it stays blocked until the event for which it is waiting has occurred. For example, a sleeping thread can only become runnable again after the sleep time has elapsed.

The scheduler will activate a new thread when one of three events occurs:

- A thread has completed its time slice
- A thread has blocked itself
- A thread with a higher priority has become runnable

> The thread scheduler selects among the runnable threads with the highest priority value.

When the scheduler is about to activate the next thread, it looks at all threads that are currently runnable, computes the highest priority value, and then picks one among the threads whose priority equals that highest value. The Java standard does not specify which thread among the eligible ones should be scheduled. A scheduler could pick one at random, or use a round-robin scheme that gives each thread a chance.

NOTE Priority values are system-dependent and not portable. Application programmers should generally not adjust thread priorities. Just stick to the normal priority that each thread has by default. Then the scheduler will simply pick among the runnable threads.

9.1.3 — Terminating Threads

A thread terminates when the run method of its Runnable returns. This is the normal way of terminating a thread—implement the run method so that it returns when it determines that no more work needs to be done.

However, sometimes you need to terminate a running thread. For example, you may have several threads attempting to find a solution to a problem. As soon as the first one has succeeded, you can terminate the other ones. In the initial release of the Java library, the Thread class had a stop method to terminate a thread. However, that method is now deprecated—computer scientists have found that stopping a thread can lead to dangerous situations if the thread holds a lock on shared resources. Instead of simply stopping a thread, you should notify the thread that it should terminate itself. The thread needs to cooperate, by releasing any resources that it currently holds and doing any other required cleanup.

To notify a thread that it should clean up and terminate, use the `interrupt` method.

```
t.interrupt();
```

This call doesn't terminate the thread; it merely sets a flag in the thread data structure.

> A thread should check whether it has been interrupted.

The run method should check whether its thread has been interrupted. In that case, it should do any necessary cleanup and exit. The most practical strategy for dealing with thread interruptions is to surround the entire work portion of the run method with a `try` block that catches the `InterruptedException`. Then the run method has the form

```
public void run()
{
    try
    {
        while (more work to do)
        {
            do work
            Thread.sleep(DELAY);
        }
    }
    catch (InterruptedException exception)
    {
    }
    clean up
}
```

This code works because the `sleep` mehod checks the "interrupted" flag. If the flag is set, the `sleep` method clears it and throws an `InterruptedException`.

Occasionally, it is inconvenient to call `sleep`—then you should check the "interrupted" flag manually:

```
if (Thread.currentThread().isInterrupted()) . . .
```

TIP You may find code that *squelches* the `InterruptedException`, like this:

```
try  // Bad!
{
    Thread.sleep(DELAY);
}
catch (InterruptedException exception)
{
}
```

Apparently, the `try/catch` clause was added to "shut up" the compiler's complaint about the checked exception that the `sleep` method may throw. Don't do that. If such a thread is interrupted, then the interruption is ignored and the thread simply keeps on running.

Sometimes, you need to call a method such as `sleep` inside a method that cannot throw a checked exception (for example, an event handler). In that case, catch the `Interrupted-Exception` and reactivate the "interrupted" flag of the thread.

```
try
{
    Thread.sleep(DELAY);
```

```
    }
    catch (InterruptedException exception)
    {
        Thread.currentThread().interrupt();
    }
```

Of course, then you need to check for interruptions elsewhere.

NOTE Strictly speaking, nothing in the Java language specification says that a thread must terminate when it is interrupted. It is entirely up to the thread what it does when it is interrupted. Interrupting is a general mechanism for getting the thread's attention, even when it is sleeping. However, in this chapter, we will always terminate a thread that is being interrupted.

9.2   Thread Synchronization

9.2.1   Corrupting a Shared Data Structure

When threads share access to a common object, they can conflict with each other. To demonstrate the problems that can arise, we will investigate a sample program in which two threads insert greetings into a queue, and another thread removes them. Each producer thread inserts 100 greetings, and the consumer thread removes all of them.

We use the bounded queue of Chapter 8.

The run method of the Producer class contains this loop:

```
int i = 1;
while (i <= greetingCount)
{
    if (!queue.isFull())
    {
        queue.add(i + ": " + greeting);
        i++;
    }
    Thread.sleep((int) (Math.random() * DELAY));
}
```

The run method of the Consumer class simply removes the greetings from the queue. In a more realistic program, the consumer would do something with these objects, but here we just print them.

```
int i = 1;
while (i <= greetingCount)
{
    if (!queue.isEmpty())
    {
        String greeting = queue.remove();
        System.out.println(greeting);
        i++;
```

```
        }
        Thread.sleep((int) (Math.random() * DELAY));
    }
```

When the program runs, it displays output similar to the following.

```
1: Hello, World!
1: Goodbye, World!
2: Hello, World!
3: Hello, World!
. . .
99: Goodbye, World!
100: Goodbye, World!
```

At least that is what *should* happen. However, there is a small chance that the program will corrupt the queue and not work correctly.

Have a look at the source code to see if you can spot the problem. We will analyze the flaw in the next section.

Ch9/queue1/ThreadTester.java

```
1  /**
2      This program runs two threads in parallel.
3  */
4  public class ThreadTester
5  {
6      public static void main(String[] args)
7      {
8          BoundedQueue<String> queue = new BoundedQueue<String>(10);
9          queue.setDebug(true);
10         final int GREETING_COUNT = 100;
11         Runnable run1 = new Producer("Hello, World!",
12                 queue, GREETING_COUNT);
13         Runnable run2 = new Producer("Goodbye, World!",
14                 queue, GREETING_COUNT);
15         Runnable run3 = new Consumer(queue, 2 * GREETING_COUNT);
16
17         Thread thread1 = new Thread(run1);
18         Thread thread2 = new Thread(run2);
19         Thread thread3 = new Thread(run3);
20
21         thread1.start();
22         thread2.start();
23         thread3.start();
24     }
25 }
```

Ch9/queue1/Producer.java

```
1  /**
2      An action that repeatedly inserts a greeting into a queue.
3  */
4  public class Producer implements Runnable
5  {
```

```
6      /**
7          Constructs the producer object.
8          @param aGreeting the greeting to insert into a queue
9          @param aQueue the queue into which to insert greetings
10         @param count the number of greetings to produce
11     */
12     public Producer(String aGreeting, BoundedQueue<String> aQueue,
13             int count)
14     {
15         greeting = aGreeting;
16         queue = aQueue;
17         greetingCount = count;
18     }
19
20     public void run()
21     {
22         try
23         {
24             int i = 1;
25             while (i <= greetingCount)
26             {
27                 if (!queue.isFull())
28                 {
29                     queue.add(i + ": " + greeting);
30                     i++;
31                 }
32                 Thread.sleep((int) (Math.random() * DELAY));
33             }
34         }
35         catch (InterruptedException exception)
36         {
37         }
38     }
39
40     private String greeting;
41     private BoundedQueue<String> queue;
42     private int greetingCount;
43
44     private static final int DELAY = 10;
45 }
```

Ch9/queue1/Consumer.java

```
1  /**
2      An action that repeatedly removes a greeting from a queue.
3  */
4  public class Consumer implements Runnable
5  {
6      /**
7          Constructs the consumer object.
8          @param aQueue the queue from which to retrieve greetings
9          @param count the number of greetings to consume
10     */
11     public Consumer(BoundedQueue<String> aQueue, int count)
12     {
```

```
13            queue = aQueue;
14            greetingCount = count;
15        }
16
17        public void run()
18        {
19            try
20            {
21                int i = 1;
22                while (i <= greetingCount)
23                {
24                    if (!queue.isEmpty())
25                    {
26                        String greeting = queue.remove();
27                        System.out.println(greeting);
28                        i++;
29                    }
30                    Thread.sleep((int) (Math.random() * DELAY));
31                }
32            }
33            catch (InterruptedException exception)
34            {
35            }
36        }
37
38        private BoundedQueue<String> queue;
39        private int greetingCount;
40
41        private static final int DELAY = 10;
42    }
```

Ch9/queue1/BoundedQueue.java

```
 1    /**
 2          A first-in, first-out bounded collection of objects.
 3    */
 4    public class BoundedQueue<E>
 5    {
 6        /**
 7             Constructs an empty queue.
 8             @param capacity the maximum capacity of the queue
 9        */
10        public BoundedQueue(int capacity)
11        {
12            elements = new Object[capacity];
13            head = 0;
14            tail = 0;
15            size = 0;
16        }
17
18        /**
19             Removes the object at the head.
20             @return the object that has been removed from the queue
21             @precondition !isEmpty()
22        */
```

```
23      public E remove()
24      {
25         if (debug) System.out.print("removeFirst");
26         E r = (E) elements[head];
27         if (debug) System.out.print(".");
28         head++;
29         if (debug) System.out.print(".");
30         size--;
31         if (head == elements.length)
32         {
33            if (debug) System.out.print(".");
34            head = 0;
35         }
36         if (debug)
37            System.out.println("head=" + head + ",tail=" + tail
38                  + ",size=" + size);
39         return r;
40      }
41
42      /**
43         Appends an object at the tail.
44         @param newValue the object to be appended
45         @precondition !isFull();
46      */
47      public void add(E newValue)
48      {
49         if (debug) System.out.print("add");
50         elements[tail] = newValue;
51         if (debug) System.out.print(".");
52         tail++;
53         if (debug) System.out.print(".");
54         size++;
55         if (tail == elements.length)
56         {
57            if (debug) System.out.print(".");
58            tail = 0;
59         }
60         if (debug)
61            System.out.println("head=" + head + ",tail=" + tail
62                  + ",size=" + size);
63      }
64
65      public boolean isFull()
66      {
67         return size == elements.length;
68      }
69
70      public boolean isEmpty()
71      {
72         return size == 0;
73      }
74
75      public void setDebug(boolean newValue)
76      {
77         debug = newValue;
78      }
```

```
79
80     private Object[] elements;
81     private int head;
82     private int tail;
83     private int size;
84     private boolean debug;
85 }
```

9.2.2 — Race Conditions

If you run the program of the preceding section several times, you may find that the consumer thread gets stuck and won't complete. Even though 200 greetings were inserted into the queue, it can't retrieve them all. At other times, it may complete, but print the same greetings repeatedly.

To see better what is happening, turn debugging on by calling

```
queue.setDebug(true);
```

The debug messages show the queue status.

You may need to run the program quite a few times to get it to misbehave. Activating the queue debugging messages increases the chance of observing the failure.

Here is one of many scenarios that demonstrates how a problem can occur.

1. The first thread calls the `add` method of the `BoundedQueue` class and executes the following statement:

    ```
    elements[tail] = newValue;
    ```

2. The second thread calls the `add` method on the same `BoundedQueue` object and executes the statements

    ```
    elements[tail] = newValue;
    tail++;
    ```

3. The first thread executes the statement

    ```
    tail++;
    ```

The consequences of this scenario are unfortunate. Step 2 overwrites the object that the first thread stored in the queue. Step 3 increments the tail counter past a storage location without filling it. When its value is removed later, some random value will be returned (see Figure 4).

This situation is an example of a *race condition*. Both threads, in their race to complete their respective tasks, rush to store objects in the queue and to increment the tail index. The end result depends on which of them happens to win the race.

> A race condition occurs if the effect of multiple threads on shared data depends on the order in which the threads are scheduled.

What is the likelihood of corruption? If you turn off the debugging mode and run the program on a fast computer, then you may not see the problem for a long time. Testing the program only under auspicious circumstances can give you the *dangerous illusion* of correctness. Of course, the problem hasn't gone

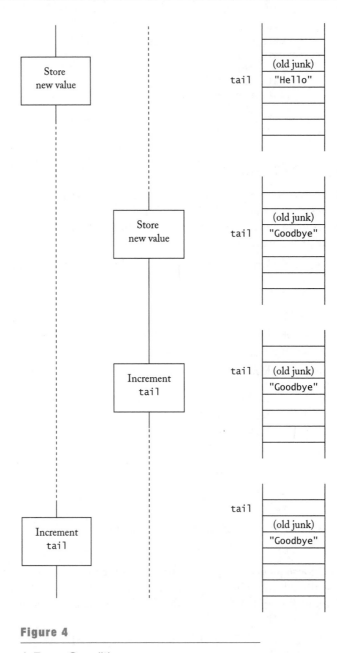

Figure 4

A Race Condition

away; it just has become much less frequent, and therefore more difficult to observe. To really fix the race conditions, you need to ensure that only one thread manipulates the queue at any given moment. That is the topic of the next section.

9.2.3 — Locks

> A thread can acquire a lock. When another thread tries to acquire the same lock, it is blocked. When the first thread releases the lock, the other threads are unblocked.

To solve problems such as the one that you observed in the preceding section, a thread can temporarily acquire ownership of a *lock*. While the thread owns the lock, no other thread can acquire the same lock. If another thread tries to do so, it is temporarily blocked. When the first thread unlocks the lock, it releases ownership and the other thread becomes unblocked.

As of Java 5.0, there are two kinds of locks:

- Objects of the `ReentrantLock` class or another class that implements the `Lock` interface type in the `java.util.concurrent.locks` package.

- Locks that are built into *every* Java object.

We discuss the `Lock` interface first because it is easier to understand, and it is also a bit more flexible than the built-in locking mechanism.

You use the following idiom to ensure that a block of code is exclusively executed by a single thread:

```
aLock = new ReentrantLock();
. . .
aLock.lock();
try
{
    protected code
}
finally
{
    aLock.unlock();
}
```

The `finally` clause ensures that the lock is unlocked even when an exception is thrown in the protected code.

Let's see how locks avoid the unfortunate scenario of the preceding section. Assuming the body of the add method is protected by a lock, the troublesome scenario that we considered in the preceding section plays out differently.

1. The first thread calls the add method and acquires the lock. The thread executes the following statement:

    ```
    elements[tail] = newValue;
    ```

2. The second thread also calls the add method on the same queue object and wants to acquire the same lock. But it can't—the first thread still owns the lock. Therefore, the second thread is blocked and cannot proceed.

3. The first thread executes the statement

    ```
    tail++;
    ```

4. The first thread completes the add method and returns. It releases the lock.

5. The lock release unblocks the second thread. It is again runnable.

6. The second thread proceeds, now successfully acquiring the lock.

Of course, the remove method must be protected by the same lock. After all, if one thread calls add, we don't want another thread to execute the remove method on the same object.

Note that each queue needs to have a separate lock object. It is perfectly acceptable if two threads operate on different BoundedQueue objects.

9.2.4 — Avoiding Deadlocks

Unfortunately, protecting the bodies of the add and remove methods with locks is not enough to ensure that your program will always run correctly. Consider these actions of the producer:

```
if (!queue.isFull())
{
    queue.add(i + ": " + greeting);
    i++;
}
```

Now suppose the producer thread has ascertained that the queue is not yet full, and then its time slice has elapsed. Another thread gains control and fills up the queue. The first thread is reactivated and proceeds where it left off, adding a message to the full queue. The queue is again corrupted.

Clearly, the test should be moved inside the add method. That ensures that the test for sufficient space is not separated from the code for adding the element. Thus, the add method should look like this:

```
public void add(E newValue)
{
    queueLock.lock();
    try
    {
        while (queue is full)
            wait for more space
        . . .
    }
    finally
    {
        queueLock.unlock();
    }
}
```

A deadlock occurs if no thread can proceed because each thread is waiting for another to do some work first.

But how can you wait for more space? You can't simply call sleep inside the try block. If a thread sleeps after locking queueLock, no other thread can remove elements because that block of code is protected by the same lock. The consumer thread will call remove, but it will simply be blocked until the add method exits.

But the add method doesn't exit until it has space available. This is called a *deadlock* or, more poetically, a *deadly embrace*.

NOTE   Technically speaking, threads are not completely deadlocked if they sleep and periodically wake up and carry out a futile check. Some computer scientists call this situation a "live lock". A true deadlock can be achieved if two threads try to acquire two separate locks, with one thread locking the first and attempting to lock the second, and the other thread acquiring the second lock and then attempting to lock the first. How to resolve such deadlocks is beyond the scope of this book.

> Calling await on a Condition object makes the current thread wait and allows another thread to acquire the lock.

The methods of the Condition interface are designed to resolve this issue. Each lock can have one or more associated Condition objects— you create them by calling the newCondition method, like this:

```
private Lock queueLock = new ReentrantLock();
private Condition spaceAvailableCondition
    = queueLock.newCondition();
private Condition valueAvailableCondition
    = queueLock.newCondition();
```

It is useful to create a condition object for each condition that needs to be monitored. In our example, we will monitor two conditions, whether space is available for insertion and whether values are available for removal.

Calling await on a condition object temporarily releases a lock and blocks the current thread. The current thread is added to a set of threads that are waiting for the condition. For example, the add method starts with the loop

```
public void add(E newValue)
{
    . . .
    while (size == elements.length)
        spaceAvailableCondition.await();
    . . .
}
```

> A waiting thread is blocked until another thread calls signalAll or signal on the condition object for which the thread is waiting.

When a thread calls await, it enters a blocked state. To unblock the thread, another thread must execute the signalAll method on the same condition object. The signalAll method unblocks all threads waiting for the condition, making them all runnable again.

You call the signalAll method whenever the state of an object has changed in a way that might benefit waiting threads. In our queue example, this is the case after an object has been removed. At that time, the threads that are waiting for available space should be unblocked so that they can finish adding elements. Here is how you should modify the remove method:

```
public E remove()
{
    . . .
    E r = elements[head];
    . . .
    spaceAvailableCondition.signalAll(); // Unblock waiting threads
    return r;
}
```

The `valueAvailableCondition` is maintained in the same way. The `remove` method starts with the loop

```
while (size == 0)
    valueAvailableCondition.await();
```

After the add method has added an element to the queue, it calls

```
valueAvailableCondition.signalAll();
```

Note that the test for a condition *must* be contained in a `while` loop, not an `if` statement:

```
while (not ok to proceed)
    aCondition.await();
```

The condition must be retested after the thread returns from the call to `await`.

NOTE   There is also a `signal` method, which randomly picks just *one* thread that is waiting on the object and unblocks it. The `signal` method can be more efficient than the `signalAll` method, but it is useful only if you know that every waiting thread can actually proceed. In general, you don't know that, and `signal` can lead to deadlocks. For that reason, we recommend that you always call `signalAll`.

With the calls to `await` and `signalAll` in the add and `remove` methods, we can launch any number of producer and consumer threads without a deadlock. If you run the sample program, you will note that all greetings are retrieved without ever corrupting the queue. Here is the source code for the modified queue.

Ch9/queue2/BoundedQueue.java

```java
1  import java.util.concurrent.locks.*;
2
3  /**
4      A first-in, first-out bounded collection of objects.
5  */
6  public class BoundedQueue<E>
7  {
8      /**
9          Constructs an empty queue.
10         @param capacity the maximum capacity of the queue
11     */
12     public BoundedQueue(int capacity)
13     {
14         elements = new Object[capacity];
15         head = 0;
16         tail = 0;
17         size = 0;
18     }
19
20     /**
21         Removes the object at the head.
22         @return the object that has been removed from the queue
23     */
24     public E remove() throws InterruptedException
```

```
25    {
26       queueLock.lock();
27       try
28       {
29          while (size == 0)
30             valueAvailableCondition.await();
31          E r = (E) elements[head];
32          head++;
33          size--;
34          if (head == elements.length)
35             head = 0;
36          spaceAvailableCondition.signalAll();
37          return r;
38       }
39       finally
40       {
41          queueLock.unlock();
42       }
43    }
44
45    /**
46       Appends an object at the tail.
47       @param newValue the object to be appended
48    */
49    public void add(E newValue) throws InterruptedException
50    {
51       queueLock.lock();
52       try
53       {
54          while (size == elements.length)
55             spaceAvailableCondition.await();
56          elements[tail] = newValue;
57          tail++;
58          size++;
59          if (tail == elements.length)
60             tail = 0;
61          valueAvailableCondition.signalAll();
62       }
63       finally
64       {
65          queueLock.unlock();
66       }
67    }
68
69    private Object[] elements;
70    private int head;
71    private int tail;
72    private int size;
73
74    private Lock queueLock = new ReentrantLock();
75    private Condition spaceAvailableCondition
76          = queueLock.newCondition();
77    private Condition valueAvailableCondition
78          = queueLock.newCondition();
79 }
```

TIP Note that the await method can throw an InterruptedException. It would be a bad idea to catch the InterruptedException inside the add and remove methods. These methods have no way of knowing what the current thread wants to do if it is interrupted. In most cases, it is best to let methods throw an InterruptedException if they call the await or sleep methods.

9.2.5 — Object Locks

The Lock and Condition interface types were added in Java 5.0 to address limitations of the original synchronization primitives of the Java language. In this section, we will examine those primitives.

Every Java object has an associated *object lock*. It is very easy to acquire and release the lock belonging to the implicit parameter of a method: simply tag the method with the synchronized keyword.

Consider for example the BoundedQueue class. We can protect a queue object simply by declaring its methods to be synchronized.

```java
public class BoundedQueue<E>
{
    public synchronized void add(E newValue) { . . . }
    public synchronized E remove() { . . . }
    . . .
}
```

When a thread calls q.add(e), it tries to acquire the lock of q. It succeeds unless another thread owns that lock. Upon exiting the add method, the lock is automatically released.

Each object lock comes with one condition object. To wait on that condition, call wait. To signal that the condition has changed, call notifyAll or notify. For example, here is the add method:

```java
public synchronized void add(E newValue)
        throws InterruptedException
{
    while (size == elements.length) wait();
    elements[tail] = anObject;
    . . .
    notifyAll();
}
```

Note that the wait, notifyAll, and notify methods belong to the Object class and not the Thread class. If you call x.wait(), the current thread is added to the wait set of the condition belonging to the lock of the object x. Most commonly, you will call wait(), which adds the current thread to the wait set of this. Similarly, the call notifyAll() unblocks all threads that are waiting for this.

The BoundedQueue class of the preceding section used two conditions, to monitor whether the queue was full or empty. Here, we use the implicit object lock, and we only have a single condition. Whenever the queue contents changes in any way, all waiting threads will be woken up.

Figure 5

Visualizing Object Locks

As you can see, using synchronized methods is simpler than using `Lock` and `Condition` objects, but it is also a bit more confusing because three different concepts are combined: the object whose state must be protected, the lock, and the condition.

One way to visualize the locking behavior is to imagine that the object is an old-fashioned telephone booth with a door, and the threads are people wanting to make telephone calls. (See Figure 5.) The telephone booth can accommodate only one person at a time. If the booth is empty, then the first person wanting to make a call just goes inside and closes the door. If another person wants to make a call and finds the booth occupied, then the second person needs to wait until the first person leaves the booth. If multiple people want to gain access to the telephone booth, they all wait outside.

To visualize the condition behavior, suppose that the coin reservoir of the telephone is completely filled. No further calls can be made until a service technician removes the coins. You don't want the person in the booth to go to sleep with the door closed. The `wait` method makes the person leave the booth temporarily, waiting for the situation to improve. That gives other people (one of whom is hopefully a service technician) a chance to enter the booth. At some point, a service technician enters the booth, empties the coin reservoir, and shouts a notification. Now all the waiting people compete again for the telephone booth.

NOTE In the 1970s, Per Brinch Hansen and Tony Hoare invented the *monitor* construct for managing thread interactions. A monitor is analogous to a Java class in which every method is synchronized and every instance field is private. Those restrictions are eminently sensible:

they guarantee that the object state cannot be corrupted by interfering threads. The Java synchronization primitives are unfortunately rather half-baked. They are neither as safe as monitors nor as efficient as explicit locks. In a fiery critique (http://brinch-hansen.net/papers/1999b.pdf), Per Brinch Hansen wrote: "It is astounding to me that Java's insecure parallelism is taken seriously by the programming community, a quarter of a century after the invention of monitors and Concurrent Pascal. It has no merit."

Should you use `Lock` and `Condition` objects or implicit locks and `synchronized` methods in your code? It depends. The implicit object locks have a few limitations:

- There is only a single condition. If the only available condition is "something has changed", some threads may be woken up even though they have no realistic chance of proceeding.

- It is not possible to interrupt a thread that is trying to acquire an implicit lock.

- You cannot specify a timeout for trying to acquire an implicit lock.

Synchronized methods were invented for a specific purpose: to ensure the integrity of a data structure. We suggest that you use them for that purpose. If you have a data structure that is accessed by multiple threads, declare all of its methods as `synchronized` and all of its instance fields as private. You will never have surprising race conditions.

However, synchronized methods can be tricky to use to implement other thread coordination problems. The `java.util.concurrent` package offers several pre-built classes for managing threads. We will see one of them, the `LinkedBlockingQueue`, in the next section.

Here is the complete code for the `BoundedQueue` class with synchronized methods.

Ch9/queue3/BoundedQueue.java

```
 1  /**
 2       A first-in, first-out bounded collection of objects.
 3  */
 4  public class BoundedQueue<E>
 5  {
 6      /**
 7          Constructs an empty queue.
 8          @param capacity the maximum capacity of the queue
 9      */
10      public BoundedQueue(int capacity)
11      {
12          elements = new Object[capacity];
13          head = 0;
14          tail = 0;
15          size = 0;
16      }
17
18      /**
19          Removes the object at the head.
20          @return the object that has been removed from the queue
21      */
22      public synchronized E remove()
23              throws InterruptedException
24      {
```

```
25        while (size == 0) wait();
26        E r = (E) elements[head];
27        head++;
28        size--;
29        if (head == elements.length)
30            head = 0;
31        notifyAll();
32        return r;
33    }
34
35    /**
36        Appends an object at the tail.
37        @param newValue the object to be appended
38    */
39    public synchronized void add(E newValue)
40            throws InterruptedException
41    {
42        while (size == elements.length) wait();
43        elements[tail] = newValue;
44        tail++;
45        size++;
46        if (tail == elements.length)
47            tail = 0;
48        notifyAll();
49    }
50
51    private Object[] elements;
52    private int head;
53    private int tail;
54    private int size;
55 }
```

▼ ▦ **Special Topic** ▶ **9.1**

Synchronized Blocks

▼

Synchronized methods automatically manipulate the lock that is associated with the implicit
parameter of a method. You can manually manipulate the lock of any object by programming
a *synchronized block*. The syntax is

▼

```
synchronized (anObject)
{
    code
}
```

▼

This statement acquires the lock of the given object, executes the code, and then releases the
lock. Of course, if the lock is already owned by another thread, then the thread executing the

▼ statement blocks.

Consider this example from the standard Java library. The `toString` method of the `Date` class
uses a static formatter to format `Date` objects. Here is a slight simplification of the code.

▼

```
public String toString()
{
```

```
            if (formatter == null)
                formatter = new SimpleDateFormat(
                    "EEE MMM dd HH:mm:ss zzz yyyy", Locale.US);
            synchronized (formatter)
            {
                formatter.setTimeZone(TimeZone.getDefault());
                return formatter.format(this);
            }
        }
```

If the `format` method was interrupted in the middle of formatting one date and started to format another, the internal state of the formatter object would become corrupted. The synchronized block ensures that two threads cannot simultaneously execute the call to `formatter.format`.

Most people find code with synchronized blocks hard to read. Explicit locks or synchronized methods are better alternatives.

 Special Topic   **9.2**

Volatile Fields

Acquiring a lock is a time-consuming operation. Some programmers try to avoid locks and synchronized methods for simple methods, in the mistaken belief that nothing is going to go wrong. However, as computers with multiple processors are becoming more common, even seemingly harmless-looking code can be problematic. Suppose, for example, we added a method to the `BoundedQueue` class that reports the current size of the queue:

```
    public int getSize() { return size; } // Not threadsafe
```

Unfortunately, this method is not threadsafe. If one thread updates the `size` field, the change may not be *visible* in another thread. This can happen if the two threads are executed by different processors. For performance reasons, each processor duplicates frequently accessed memory locations in a high-speed memory cache. (Ordinary memory is quite a bit slower than modern CPUs!) If each processor caches a copy of the `size` field, then they only see changes made by the other processor when the cache and memory are synchronized. The Java virtual machine issues the (relatively slow) synchronization instructions when you use locks. But otherwise, all bets are off. Perhaps, one thread keeps adding elements to the queue, but the other always sees the size as 0.

Tagging the `getSize` method as `synchronized` solves this problem. There is also another way—you can tag the `size` field as `volatile`:

```
    private volatile int size;
```

The virtual machine ensures that changes to volatile fields are properly synchronized. However, this is an advanced technique that is only needed to enhance performance. It is best to first program for safety, using locks for all methods of a shared data structure. Use optimizations such as volatile fields only after you have collected measurements that demonstrate a significant speedup.

9.3 Animations

One popular use for thread programming is animation. A program that displays an animation shows different objects moving or changing in some way as time progresses. This is often achieved by launching one or more threads that compute how parts of the animation change.

As you saw in Chapter 4, you can use the Swing `Timer` class for simple animations without having to do any thread programming. However, more advanced animations are better implemented with threads.

In this section, you will see a particular kind of animation, namely the visualization of the steps of an algorithm. Algorithm animation is an excellent technique for gaining a better understanding of how an algorithm works.

 INTERNET Many algorithms can be animated—type "Java algorithm animation" into your favorite Web search engine, and you'll find lots of links to Web pages with animations of various algorithms.

Most algorithm animations have a similar structure. The algorithm runs in a separate thread that periodically updates a drawing of the current state of the algorithm and then sleeps. After a short amount of time, the algorithm thread wakes up and runs to the next point of interest in the algorithm. It then updates the drawing and sleeps again. This sequence is repeated until the algorithm has finished.

In our sample program, we will animate a merge sort algorithm that works just like the `Arrays.sort` method of the standard Java library. The `MergeSorter.sort` method sorts an array of objects.

```
Double[] values = . . .;
Comparator<Double> comp = . . .;
MergeSorter.sort(values, comp);
```

The array is initialized with a sequence of random `Double` values.

We supply a comparator that pauses the sorter thread before yielding the result of the comparison. When the sorter thread is paused, the user interface thread draws the contents of the array (see Figure 6).

```
Comparator<Double> comp = new
   Comparator<Double>()
   {
      public int compare(Double d1, Double d2)
      {
         update drawing data
         pause the thread
         return d1.compareTo(d2);
      }
   };
```

Figure 6

Animating a Sort Algorithm

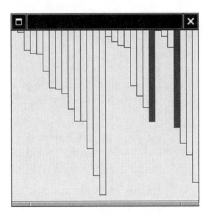

The Sorter class implements the Runnable interface type. Its run method calls Merge-Sorter.sort. The sort algorithm repeatedly calls the comparator during the sorting process. Each time, the animation is paused. When the pause has elapsed, the comparator returns the result of the comparison, and the algorithm continues.

The main program shows the array drawing panel and then starts the sorting thread. When you run the program, you will see the merge sort algorithm in action. You can observe how the algorithm repeatedly sorts subarrays and merges them together.

Ch9/animation1/Sorter.java

```
1  import java.util.*;
2
3  /**
4     This runnable executes a sort algorithm.
5     When two elements are compared, the algorithm
6     pauses and updates a panel.
7  */
8  public class Sorter implements Runnable
9  {
10    /**
11       Constructs the sorter.
12       @param values  the array to sort
13       @param panel  the panel for displaying the array
14    */
15    public Sorter(Double[] values, ArrayComponent panel)
16    {
17       this.values = values;
18       this.panel = panel;
19    }
20
21    public void run()
22    {
23       Comparator<Double> comp = new
24          Comparator<Double>()
25          {
```

```
26              public int compare(Double d1, Double d2)
27              {
28                 panel.setValues(values, d1, d2);
29                 try
30                 {
31                    Thread.sleep(DELAY);
32                 }
33                 catch (InterruptedException exception)
34                 {
35                    Thread.currentThread().interrupt();
36                 }
37                 return (d1).compareTo(d2);
38              }
39           };
40        MergeSorter.sort(values, comp);
41        panel.setValues(values, null, null);
42     }
43
44     private Double[] values;
45     private ArrayComponent panel;
46     private static final int DELAY = 100;
47  }
```

Ch9/animation1/ArrayComponent.java

```
1  import java.awt.*;
2  import java.awt.geom.*;
3  import javax.swing.*;
4
5  /**
6     This panel draws an array and marks two elements in the
7     array.
8  */
9  public class ArrayComponent extends JComponent
10 {
11    public synchronized void paintComponent(Graphics g)
12    {
13       if (values == null) return;
14       Graphics2D g2 = (Graphics2D) g;
15       int width = getWidth() / values.length;
16       for (int i = 0; i < values.length; i++)
17       {
18          Double v = values[i];
19          Rectangle2D bar = new Rectangle2D.Double(
20             width * i, 0, width, v);
21          if (v == marked1 || v == marked2)
22             g2.fill(bar);
23          else
24             g2.draw(bar);
25       }
26    }
27
28    /**
29       Sets the values to be painted.
30       @param values the array of values to display
31       @param marked1 the first marked element
```

```
32        @param marked2 the second marked element
33     */
34     public synchronized void setValues(Double[] values,
35           Double marked1, Double marked2)
36     {
37        this.values = (Double[]) values.clone();
38        this.marked1 = marked1;
39        this.marked2 = marked2;
40        repaint();
41     }
42
43     private Double[] values;
44     private Double marked1;
45     private Double marked2;
46  }
```

Ch9/animation1/AnimationTester.java

```
1  import java.awt.*;
2  import javax.swing.*;
3
4  /**
5     This program animates a sort algorithm.
6  */
7  public class AnimationTester
8  {
9     public static void main(String[] args)
10    {
11       JFrame frame = new JFrame();
12       frame.setDefaultCloseOperation(JFrame.EXIT_ON_CLOSE);
13
14       ArrayComponent panel = new ArrayComponent();
15       frame.add(panel, BorderLayout.CENTER);
16
17       frame.setSize(FRAME_WIDTH, FRAME_HEIGHT);
18       frame.setVisible(true);
19
20       Double[] values = new Double[VALUES_LENGTH];
21       for (int i = 0; i < values.length; i++)
22          values[i] = Math.random() * panel.getHeight();
23
24       Runnable r = new Sorter(values, panel);
25       Thread t = new Thread(r);
26       t.start();
27    }
28
29    private static final int VALUES_LENGTH = 30;
30    private static final int FRAME_WIDTH = 300;
31    private static final int FRAME_HEIGHT = 300;
32 }
```

One drawback of our animation program is that it runs at a fairly brisk pace. To improve the program, let's add two buttons labeled "Run" and "Step". The "Step" button runs the algorithm until the next step and then pauses the algorithm. By repeatedly clicking on the "Step" button, you can observe the algorithm one step at a time.

In a situation such as this one, it can be difficult to coordinate the button clicks in the user interface thread and the pauses in the sorter thread. In single-step mode, we want the sorter thread to wait until the user clicks the "Step" button.

We want a shared object that allows the two threads to communicate. When the sorter thread has finished a step, it should ask the shared object for permission to proceed. The thread blocks until the permission is issued. When the user clicks the "Step" button, the shared object should be instructed to issue a permission, unblocking the waiting sorter thread.

We could design a class with this behavior, but it is easier and safer to use an existing class instead. The java.util.concurrent library has a number of professionally implemented classes for thread synchronization—see *Core Java*, 7th Ed., Vol. 2, Chapter 2, by Cay Horstmann and Gary Cornell for more details. The LinkedBlockingQueue class has the behavior that we need. Whenever a button is clicked, we add a command string "Step" or "Run" to the queue. The take method of the LinkedBlockingQueue removes a value, blocking if none is available.

The compare method waits until a command string is available in the queue. If the command is "Run", the thread simply pauses for a short delay, just as in the first version of the program, then adds the "Run" command back into the queue. In either case, the thread proceeds until it calls the take method again, blocking until the next command is available.

```java
public int compare(Double d1, Double d2)
{
    . . .
    String command = queue.take();
    if (command.equals("Run"))
    {
        Thread.sleep(DELAY);
        queue.add("Run");
    }
    . . .
}
```

Here is the code for the Sorter class and the main program. This example concludes our introduction to Java threads. As you have seen, the Java synchronization primitives are at a fairly low level. It is a good idea to use them as building blocks for higher-level synchronization mechanisms (such as the LinkedBlockingQueue) that are conceptually easier to understand.

Ch9/animation2/Sorter.java

```java
 1 import java.util.*;
 2 import java.util.concurrent.*;
 3
 4 /**
 5    This runnable executes a sort algorithm.
 6    When two elements are compared, the algorithm
 7    pauses and updates a panel.
 8 */
 9 public class Sorter implements Runnable
10 {
```

```
11      public Sorter(Double[] values, ArrayComponent panel,
12          BlockingQueue<String> queue)
13      {
14         this.values = values;
15         this.panel = panel;
16         this.queue = queue;
17      }
18
19      public void run()
20      {
21         Comparator<Double> comp = new
22             Comparator<Double>()
23             {
24                public int compare(Double d1, Double d2)
25                {
26                   try
27                   {
28                      String command = queue.take();
29                      if (command.equals("Run"))
30                      {
31                         Thread.sleep(DELAY);
32                         if (!"Step".equals(queue.peek()))
33                            queue.add("Run");
34                      }
35                   }
36                   catch (InterruptedException exception)
37                   {
38                      Thread.currentThread().interrupt();
39                   }
40                   panel.setValues(values, d1, d2);
41                   return d1.compareTo(d2);
42                }
43             };
44         MergeSorter.sort(values, comp);
45         panel.setValues(values, null, null);
46      }
47
48      private Double[] values;
49      private ArrayComponent panel;
50      private BlockingQueue<String> queue;
51      private static final int DELAY = 100;
52   }
```

Ch9/animation2/AnimationTester.java

```
1  import java.awt.*;
2  import java.awt.event.*;
3  import javax.swing.*;
4  import java.util.concurrent.*;
5
6  /**
7     This program animates a sort algorithm.
8  */
9  public class AnimationTester
10 {
```

```
11    public static void main(String[] args)
12    {
13       JFrame frame = new JFrame();
14       frame.setDefaultCloseOperation(JFrame.EXIT_ON_CLOSE);
15
16       ArrayComponent panel = new ArrayComponent();
17       frame.add(panel, BorderLayout.CENTER);
18
19       JButton stepButton = new JButton("Step");
20       final JButton runButton = new JButton("Run");
21
22       JPanel buttons = new JPanel();
23       buttons.add(stepButton);
24       buttons.add(runButton);
25       frame.add(buttons, BorderLayout.NORTH);
26       frame.setSize(FRAME_WIDTH, FRAME_HEIGHT);
27       frame.setVisible(true);
28
29       Double[] values = new Double[VALUES_LENGTH];
30       for (int i = 0; i < values.length; i++)
31          values[i] = Math.random() * panel.getHeight();
32
33       final BlockingQueue<String> queue
34             = new LinkedBlockingQueue<String>();
35       queue.add("Step");
36
37       final Sorter sorter = new Sorter(values, panel, queue);
38
39       stepButton.addActionListener(new
40          ActionListener()
41          {
42             public void actionPerformed(ActionEvent event)
43             {
44                queue.add("Step");
45                runButton.setEnabled(true);
46             }
47          });
48
49       runButton.addActionListener(new
50          ActionListener()
51          {
52             public void actionPerformed(ActionEvent event)
53             {
54                runButton.setEnabled(false);
55                queue.add("Run");
56             }
57          });
58
59       Thread sorterThread = new Thread(sorter);
60       sorterThread.start();
61    }
62
63    private static final int FRAME_WIDTH = 300;
64    private static final int FRAME_HEIGHT = 300;
65    private static final int VALUES_LENGTH = 30;
66 }
```

Exercises

Exercise 9.1. Modify the `ThreadTester` program to execute the following instructions:

```
Runnable r1 = new GreetingProducer("Hello, World!");
Runnable r2 = new GreetingProducer("Goodbye, World!");
r1.run();
r2.run();
```

Note that the outputs are not interleaved. Explain.

Exercise 9.2. In the program in Section 9.1, is it possible that both threads are sleeping at the same time? That neither of the two threads is sleeping at a particular time? Explain.

Exercise 9.3. In Java, a graphical user interface program has more than one thread. Explain how you can prove that.

Exercise 9.4. Give an example why you would want to terminate a thread in a Web browser program.

Exercise 9.5. Suppose the following threads are alive.

Thread	State
Thread-0	Runnable
Thread-1	Sleeping
Thread-2	Runnable
Thread-3	Waiting

The scheduler is about to give a time slice to a new thread. Among which of these threads does it choose?

Exercise 9.6. Suppose threads in the following table are alive.

Thread	State	Priority
Thread-0	Runnable	Normal
Thread-1	Sleeping	High
Thread-2	Runnable	Normal
Thread-3	Waiting	High
Thread-4	Runnable	Low

The scheduler is about to give a time slice to a new thread. Among which of these threads does it choose?

Exercise 9.7. What is the difference between a thread that sleeps by calling `sleep` and a thread that waits by calling `await`?

Exercise 9.8. What happens when a thread calls `await` and no other thread calls `signal-All` or `signal`?

Exercise 9.9. Write a program that has multiple threads that make deposits and withdrawals in a shared bank account program without using locks. Demonstrate how the bank account can become corrupted.

Exercise 9.10. Use synchronized methods to overcome the corruption problem of Exercise 9.9.

Exercise 9.11. Use a `ReentrantLock` to implement a threadsafe `BankAccount` class.

Exercise 9.12. Suppose you call `wait` instead of `await` on a condition object in the `BoundedQueue` class that uses a `ReentrantLock`. Will the call compile? What will it do?

Exercise 9.13. List three other scenarios in which the queue in Section 9.2.1 can get corrupted.

Exercise 9.14. The special topic on synchronized blocks explains how the `Date` class guarantees that no two threads call the static formatter in the `toString` method at the same time. Discuss what would happen if two threads executed the `toString` method before the static formatter was constructed. What can you do to avoid constructing two instances of the formatter?

Exercise 9.15. It is always a good idea to look for classes in the standard library instead of building your own, particularly when thread safety is an issue. Which Java library classes can you use if you need a threadsafe queue?

Exercise 9.16. The `MailSystem` class in Chapter 2 is not threadsafe. Fix it (and any non-threadsafe classes on which it depends) so that multiple connections can have simultaneous access.

Exercise 9.17. In Chapter 2, the mail system was acccessed through a console interface. In Chapter 4, it was accessed through a GUI interface, allowing for multiple simultaneous connections. Explain why it is safe to use the original `MailSystem` class in both implementations.

Exercise 9.18. Modify the animation program in Chapter 4 so that various cars are moving at different speeds. Use a separate thread for each car.

Exercise 9.19. Modify the algorithm animation program so that it becomes a framework for animating different sorting algorithms. Demonstrate the framework by animating the selection sort algorithm.

Exercise 9.20. Modify the algorithm animation program so that it becomes a framework for animating algorithms of any kind. The algorithm needs to supply a mechanism for drawing the current state of the data structure on which it operates. Demonstrate the framework by animating the "Towers of Hanoi" algorithm.

Exercise 9.21. Write a program WordCount that counts the words in one or more files. Start a new thread for each file. For example, if you call

```
java WordCount report.txt address.txt Homework.java
```

then the program might print

```
address.txt: 1052
Homework.java: 445
report.txt: 2099
```

Exercise 9.22. Modify the program of Exercise 9.21 so that it prints the total of the words in all files after the last counting thread has completed.

More Design Patterns

In this chapter, we discuss a number of important design patterns. As in Chapter 5, we relate the patterns to examples in the Java class library whenever possible, so that you can remember them easily. You can read the sections of this chapter in any order, or just use them as a reference.

10.1   The ADAPTER Pattern

If you have ever had to hook up a laptop computer in a foreign country, you are probably familiar with the concept of an *adapter*. The power plug of your computer may not fit into the wall outlet, and the foreign telephone plug may not fit into your computer modem. To solve these problems, travelers often carry a set of adapter plugs that convert one kind of plug into another.

In object-oriented programming, you often have similar problems. For example, in Chapter 4, we designed a class CarIcon that implements the Icon interface type. Suppose we want to add a car icon into a user interface container. But you add components, not icons, into containers. What we need is an intermediary that adapts the Icon interface type to the Component interface type.

> The ADAPTER pattern teaches how to use a class in a context that requires a different interface.

It is an easy matter to provide such an adapter. The Icon interface type has methods for painting and for sizing the icon. A component has methods for the same purpose, but with minor differences. The adapter simply translates one set of methods into the other. Using the following adapter class, you can reuse the existing icon and add icon components into a container.

Ch10/adapter/IconAdapter.java

```java
 1  import java.awt.*;
 2  import javax.swing.*;
 3
 4  /**
 5      An adapter that turns an icon into a JComponent.
 6  */
 7  public class IconAdapter extends JComponent
 8  {
 9      /**
10          Constructs a JComponent that displays a given icon.
11          @param icon the icon to display
12      */
13      public IconAdapter(Icon icon)
14      {
15          this.icon = icon;
16      }
17
18      public void paintComponent(Graphics g)
19      {
20          icon.paintIcon(this, g, 0, 0);
21      }
22
23      public Dimension getPreferredSize()
24      {
25          return new Dimension(icon.getIconWidth(),
26              icon.getIconHeight());
27      }
28
29      private Icon icon;
30  }
```

Ch10/adapter/IconAdapterTester.java

```java
1  import java.awt.*;
2  import javax.swing.*;
3
4  /**
5     This program demonstrates how an icon is adapted to
6     a component. The component is added to a frame.
7  */
8  public class IconAdapterTester
9  {
10    public static void main(String[] args)
11    {
12       Icon icon = new CarIcon(300);
13       JComponent component = new IconAdapter(icon);
14
15       JFrame frame = new JFrame();
16       frame.add(component, BorderLayout.CENTER);
17       frame.setDefaultCloseOperation(JFrame.EXIT_ON_CLOSE);
18       frame.pack();
19       frame.setVisible(true);
20    }
21 }
```

Note that the IconAdapter holds a reference to the icon object that is being adapted.

The IconAdapter only redefines two methods of the JComponent class. For the other methods, the JComponent superclass supplies reasonable implementations.

This example can easily be generalized to a design pattern. You use the ADAPTER pattern when you would like to use an existing class but its interface doesn't match the one you need.

PATTERN

◆   **ADAPTER**

Context

1. You want to use an existing class without modifying it. We'll call this class the *adaptee*.

2. The context in which you want to use the class requires conformance to a *target* interface that is different from that of the adaptee.

3. The target interface and the adaptee interface are conceptually related.

Solution

1. Define an adapter class that implements the target interface.

2. The adapter class holds a reference to the adaptee. It translates target methods to adaptee methods.

3. The client wraps the adaptee into an adapter class object.

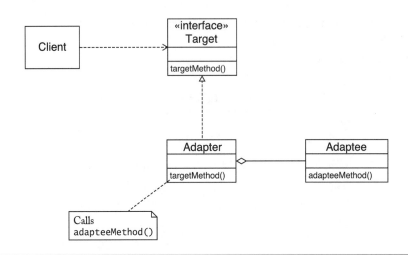

For example, in the case of the icon adapter, we have:

Name in Design Pattern	Actual Name
Adaptee	Icon
Target	JComponent
Adapter	IconAdapter
Client	The class that wants to add icons into a container
targetMethod()	paintComponent(), getPreferredSize()
adapteeMethod()	paintIcon(), getIconWidth(), getIconHeight()

There is another use of the ADAPTER pattern in the Java stream library. Recall that an input stream reads bytes, whereas a reader reads characters. The difference between bytes and characters is significant in many languages. In some encoding schemes (such as ASCII), a character is encoded as a single byte. But in many encoding schemes (for example, the Unicode UTF-8 encoding or the JIS encoding for Japanese characters), a variable number of bytes is required to encode characters. Therefore, you should use a reader object whenever you read text input.

What do you do if you have an input stream and need a reader? Use the InputStream-Reader adapter. That adapter turns an input stream into a reader whose read method reads bytes and translates them into characters, using a particular encoding scheme.

For example, System.in is an InputStream. To turn it into a reader, you use the following instructions:

```
Reader reader = new InputStreamReader(System.in);
    // Uses the default character encoding
```

or

```
Reader reader = new InputStreamReader(System.in, "UTF-8");
    // Uses the specified character encoding
```

In the case of the input stream reader adapter, we have:

Name in Design Pattern	Actual Name
`Adaptee`	`InputStream`
`Target`	`Reader`
`Adapter`	`InputStreamReader`
`Client`	The class that wants to read text from an input stream
`targetMethod()`	read (reading a character)
`adapteeMethod()`	read (reading a byte)

10.2 Actions and the COMMAND Pattern

The user interfaces of many programs give you multiple ways of issuing a particular command. For example, to cut a block of text in a word processor, you may select Edit → Cut from the menu, click on a toolbar button with a scissors icon, or simply type the CTRL+X key combination.

That is pretty easy to implement, of course. Simply route the event handlers for the menu, the toolbar button, and the keypress to the code that carries out the "cut" command. But there is more to a command than just the code that carries out the operation. For example, if there is nothing to cut, then the menu item and toolbar button should be *disabled*. A disabled menu item or button usually has a different visual appearance. It is therefore helpful if the "cut" command can remember whether it is currently enabled or disabled. Thus, a command has both behavior and state.

The `Action` interface type of the Swing library lets you implement commands that can be enabled or disabled. Moreover, actions can store various informational items, such as icons and descriptions.

The `Action` interface type extends the `ActionListener` interface type. That is, you specify the command action in an `actionPerformed` method. You use the `setEnabled` method to enable or disable an action.

An action stores properties, including

- The action name, displayed on menu items and buttons

- An icon, also displayed on menu items and buttons

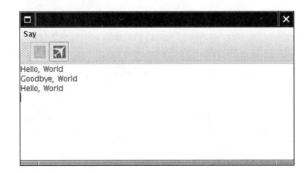

Figure 1

Using Actions for Menus and Toolbars

You set these properties with the putValue method, by using predefined constants in the Action type. For example,

```
helloAction.putValue(Action.NAME, "Hello");
helloAction.putValue(Action.SMALL_ICON, new ImageIcon("hello.png"));
```

Once you have action objects, it is very simple to add them to menus and toolbars.

```
menu.add(helloAction);
toolbar.add(helloAction);
```

The menu and toolbar retrieve the action name and icon and display them (see Figure 1). When the menu item or toolbar button is selected, the actionPerformed method of the action object is called.

The AbstractAction class implements the Action interface type. You will want to extend the AbstractAction class rather than implement the Action interface type (see Figure 2).

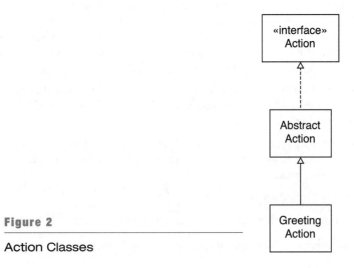

Figure 2

Action Classes

In our example program, we define a class `GreetingAction` and construct two instances, one to say "Hello, World", and one to say "Goodbye, World". Each action is added to both the menu and the toolbar. After being selected, each command disables itself and enables the other. As a result, the user must select the "Hello" and "Goodbye" commands in sequence.

> The COMMAND pattern teaches how to implement commands as objects whenever a command has both behavior and state.

Swing actions are an example of the COMMAND pattern. The command pattern tells you to implement commands as objects rather than methods. If a command is an object, it can have state. For example, a Swing action object remembers whether it is currently enabled. There is a second advantage. You can *collect* command objects. Collecting command objects has several useful applications. For example, you can define macros, that is, commands that are composed of other commands, or you can keep a sequence of recently issued commands so that you can "undo" them.

PATTERN

COMMAND

Context

1. You want to implement commands that behave like objects, either because you need to store additional information with commands, or because you want to collect commands.

Solution

1. Define a *command* interface type with a method to execute the command.
2. Supply methods in the command interface type to manipulate the state of command objects.
3. Each *concrete command* class implements the command interface type.
4. To invoke the command, call the `execute` method.

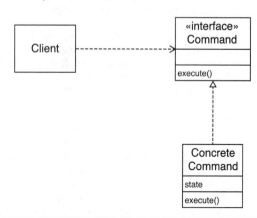

For example, in the case of Swing actions, we have:

Name in Design Pattern	Actual Name
Command	Action
ConcreteCommand	A subclass of AbstractAction
execute()	actionPerformed()
state	Name and icon

Ch10/command/CommandTester.java

```
1  import java.awt.*;
2  import javax.swing.*;
3
4  /**
5     This program demonstrates action objects. Two actions
6     insert greetings into a text area. Each action can be
7     triggered by a menu item or toolbar button. When an
8     action is carried out, the opposite action becomes enabled.
9  */
10 public class CommandTester
11 {
12    public static void main(String[] args)
13    {
14       JFrame frame = new JFrame();
15       JMenuBar bar = new JMenuBar();
16       frame.setJMenuBar(bar);
17       JMenu menu = new JMenu("Say");
18       bar.add(menu);
19       JToolBar toolBar = new JToolBar();
20       frame.add(toolBar, BorderLayout.NORTH);
21       JTextArea textArea = new JTextArea(10, 40);
22       frame.add(textArea, BorderLayout.CENTER);
23
24       GreetingAction helloAction = new GreetingAction(
25          "Hello, World", textArea);
26       helloAction.putValue(Action.NAME, "Hello");
27       helloAction.putValue(Action.SMALL_ICON,
28          new ImageIcon("hello.png"));
29
30       GreetingAction goodbyeAction = new GreetingAction(
31          "Goodbye, World", textArea);
32       goodbyeAction.putValue(Action.NAME, "Goodbye");
33       goodbyeAction.putValue(Action.SMALL_ICON,
34          new ImageIcon("goodbye.png"));
35
36       helloAction.setOpposite(goodbyeAction);
37       goodbyeAction.setOpposite(helloAction);
```

```
38            goodbyeAction.setEnabled(false);
39
40            menu.add(helloAction);
41            menu.add(goodbyeAction);
42
43            toolBar.add(helloAction);
44            toolBar.add(goodbyeAction);
45
46            frame.setDefaultCloseOperation(JFrame.EXIT_ON_CLOSE);
47            frame.pack();
48            frame.setVisible(true);
49        }
50  }
```

Ch10/command/GreetingAction.java

```
1   import java.awt.event.*;
2   import javax.swing.*;
3
4   /**
5       This action places a greeting into a text field
6       and afterwards disables itself and enables its
7       opposite action.
8   */
9   public class GreetingAction extends AbstractAction
10  {
11      /**
12          Constructs a greeting action.
13          @param greeting the string to add to the text area
14          @param textArea the text area to which to add the greeting
15      */
16      public GreetingAction(String greeting, JTextArea textArea)
17      {
18          this.greeting = greeting;
19          this.textArea = textArea;
20      }
21
22      /**
23          Sets the opposite action.
24          @param action the action to be enabled after this action was
25          carried out
26      */
27      public void setOpposite(Action action)
28      {
29          oppositeAction = action;
30      }
31
32      public void actionPerformed(ActionEvent event)
33      {
34          textArea.append(greeting);
35          textArea.append("\n");
36          if (oppositeAction != null)
37          {
38              setEnabled(false);
```

```
39              oppositeAction.setEnabled(true);
40          }
41      }
42
43      private String greeting;
44      private JTextArea textArea;
45      private Action oppositeAction;
46  }
```

10.3 The FACTORY METHOD Pattern

Recall how a Java collection produces an iterator for traversing its elements. The
Collection interface type defines a method

```
Iterator iterator()
```

Each subclass of Collection (such as LinkedList or our own Queue class in Chapter 8)
implements that method in a different way. Each iterator method returns an object of a
class that implements the Iterator interface type, but the implementations of these subtypes are completely different. An iterator through a linked list keeps a reference to the
last visited node. Our queue iterator keeps an index of the last visited array element.

You may wonder why the designers of the collections framework decided to have a
method that produces iterator objects. It would have been just as simple if every collection had a companion iterator. Then you would simply construct the iterator, like this:

```
LinkedList list = . . . ;
Iterator iter = new LinkedListIterator(list);
```

However, this approach has a drawback. If you don't know the exact type of the collection, you don't know which iterator type to construct.

```
Collection coll = . . . ;
Iterator iter = new ???(coll);
```

The iterator method does not have this problem. Because of polymorphism, the call

```
Iterator iter = coll.iterator();
```

calls the iterator method of the class to which the collection object belongs. That
method constructs an object of some class that implements the Iterator interface type.
(Actually, the iterator classes are often anonymous classes.)

> The FACTORY METHOD pattern
> teaches how to supply a
> method that can be overridden
> to create objects of varying
> types.

A method such as iterator is called a *factory method*. A factory
method is more flexible than a constructor. It can construct objects of
subclasses, not just a fixed class.

FACTORY METHOD

Context

1. A type (which we will call the *creator*) creates objects of another type (which we call the *product*).
2. Subclasses of the creator type need to create different kinds of product objects.
3. Clients do not need to know the exact type of product objects.

Solution

1. Define a creator type that expresses the commonality of all creators.
2. Define a product type that expresses the commonality of all products.
3. Define a method, called the *factory method*, in the creator type. The factory method yields a product object.
4. Each concrete creator class implements the factory method so that it returns an object of a concrete product class.

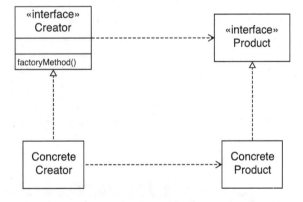

For example, in the case of iterators in the collections framework, we have:

Name in Design Pattern	Actual Name
Creator	Collection
ConcreteCreator	A subclass of Collection
factoryMethod()	iterator()
Product	Iterator
ConcreteProduct	A subclass of Iterator (which is often anonymous)

Not all methods that create new objects are factory methods in the sense of this design pattern. For example, consider the DateFormat class. If you want to format a Date object, you can obtain a formatter like this:

```
DateFormat formatter = DateFormat.getDateInstance();
Date now = new Date();
String formattedDate = formatter.format(now);
```

The getDateInstance method actually returns an object of type SimpleDateFormat, a subclass of DateFormat. But it is a static method. It is not possible to have creator subclasses that redefine the getDateInstance method. This example only uses half of the FACTORY METHOD pattern. We can form subclasses of the product but not the creator.

10.4   The PROXY Pattern

A *proxy* is a person who is authorized to act on another person's behalf. For example, you may send a proxy to a meeting who telephones you whenever a vote needs to be cast and then votes according to your instructions. Similarly, in software design, a proxy is an object that is a stand-in for another object.

There are many reasons to use proxies. Here we will look at a common application: to delay the instantiation of an object. For example, it is somewhat expensive to load an image. If a user never looks at the image, then it is not necessary to load it. To minimize the cost of image loading, it makes sense to defer the construction of image objects until there is a demand for them.

Consider the application shown in Figure 3. All but the top image are hidden when the frame window is first displayed. Image loading can be deferred until the user clicks on a tab.

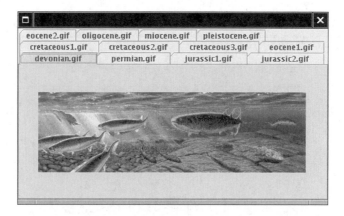

Figure 3

A Tabbed Image Viewer

Of course, it is desirable to implement the deferred loading so that the application programmer doesn't have to think about it. That is where the proxy comes into play.

The application generates a series of JLabel objects, each of which has an image icon. Normally, an application programmer would construct a label like this:

```
JLabel label = new JLabel(new ImageIcon(imageName));
```

However, for delayed loading, we will instead supply a proxy object to the label.

```
JLabel label = new JLabel(new ImageProxy(imageName));
```

The ImageProxy class implements the Icon interface type. It remembers the image name and loads the image as soon as it is needed. For example, the paintIcon method of the proxy class ensures that the image is loaded, and then passes the request on to the actual image object. The application generates a series of JLabel objects, each of which has an image icon.

```
public void paintIcon(Component c, Graphics g, int x, int y)
{
    if (image == null) image = new ImageIcon(name);
    image.paintIcon(c, g, x, y);
}
```

You will find the complete source code at the end of this section.

The PROXY pattern teaches how an object can be a placeholder for another object.

Note that the client of the image does not realize that the image loading is delayed. The client has the impression that the proxy is "the real thing".

PATTERN

◆   ## PROXY

Context

◆
1. A class, called the *real subject,* provides a service that is specified by an interface type, called the *subject* type.

◆
2. There is a need to modify the service in order to make it more versatile.

3. Neither the client nor the real subject should be affected by the modification.

◆   ### Solution

1. Define a *proxy* class that implements the subject interface type. The proxy holds a reference to the real subject, or otherwise knows how to locate it.

◆
2. The client uses a proxy object.

3. Each proxy method invokes the same method on the real subject and provides the necessary modifications.

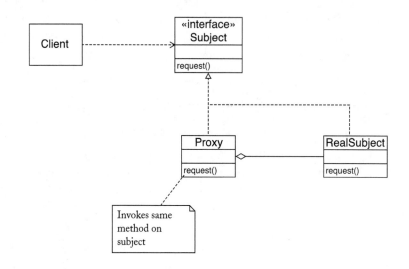

For example, in the case of the image proxy, we have:

Name in Design Pattern	Actual Name
Subject	Icon
RealSubject	ImageIcon
Proxy	ImageProxy
request()	The methods of the Icon interface type
Client	JLabel

Computer scientists jokingly say that "every problem in computer science can be solved by an additional level of indirection". In our example, the image proxy provides a level of indirection: The client calls the proxy which then calls the actual image. The additional indirection solved the problem of on-demand instantiation. Another use for proxies arises when a program needs to invoke a method on an object that is located on a remote computer. To enable remote method calls, the method parameters must be encoded and sent across a network connection. The programmer making remote calls should not be burdened with the mechanics of the network communication. Instead, the Java Remote Method Invocation (RMI) mechanism supplies proxy objects. An RMI proxy object appears to the programmer as if it was a local object carrying out the desired method, when in fact it merely transmits the method parameters to the remote object and relays the response back to the caller.

Ch10/proxy/ImageProxy.java

```java
 1  import java.awt.*;
 2  import javax.swing.*;
 3
 4  /**
 5     A proxy for delayed loading of image icons.
 6  */
 7  public class ImageProxy implements Icon
 8  {
 9     /**
10         Constructs a proxy for delayed loading of an image file.
11         @param name the file name
12     */
13     public ImageProxy(String name)
14     {
15        this.name = name;
16        image = null;
17     }
18
19     public void paintIcon(Component c, Graphics g, int x, int y)
20     {
21        ensureImageLoaded();
22        image.paintIcon(c, g, x, y);
23     }
24
25     public int getIconWidth()
26     {
27        ensureImageLoaded();
28        return image.getIconWidth();
29     }
30
31     public int getIconHeight()
32     {
33        ensureImageLoaded();
34        return image.getIconHeight();
35     }
36
37     /**
38         Loads the image if it hasn't been loaded yet. Prints
39         a message when the image is loaded.
40     */
41     private void ensureImageLoaded()
42     {
43        if (image == null)
44        {
45           System.out.println("Loading " + name);
46           image = new ImageIcon(name);
47        }
48     }
```

```
49
50    private String name;
51    private ImageIcon image;
52 }
```

Ch10/proxy/ProxyTester.java

```
1  import java.awt.*;
2  import javax.swing.*;
3
4  /**
5     This program demonstrates the use of the image proxy.
6     Images are only loaded when you press on a tab.
7  */
8  public class ProxyTester
9  {
10    public static void main(String[] args)
11    {
12       JTabbedPane tabbedPane = new JTabbedPane();
13       for (String name : imageNames)
14       {
15          JLabel label = new JLabel(new ImageProxy(name));
16          tabbedPane.add(name, label);
17       }
18
19       JFrame frame = new JFrame();
20       frame.add(tabbedPane);
21
22       frame.setSize(FRAME_WIDTH, FRAME_HEIGHT);
23       frame.setDefaultCloseOperation(JFrame.EXIT_ON_CLOSE);
24       frame.setVisible(true);
25    }
26
27    private static final String[] imageNames =
28    {
29       "devonian.gif",
30       "permian.gif",
31       "jurassic1.gif",
32       "jurassic2.gif",
33       "cretaceous1.gif",
34       "cretaceous2.gif",
35       "cretaceous3.gif",
36       "eocene1.gif",
37       "eocene2.gif",
38       "oligocene.gif",
39       "miocene.gif",
40       "pleistocene.gif"
41    };
42
43    private static final int FRAME_WIDTH = 500;
44    private static final int FRAME_HEIGHT = 300;
45 }
```

10.5 The SINGLETON Pattern

A singleton class has exactly one instance.

A *singleton* class is a class that has a single object. That unique object constitutes a global facility for all clients. For example, consider a program with various classes that need to generate random numbers. It is not a good idea to construct many independent random number generators. As you may know, the sequence of numbers that a random number generator emits is not truly random but the result of a deterministic calculation. For that reason, computer-generated random numbers should really be called *pseudo-random numbers*. In most algorithms for generating a sequence of pseudo-random numbers, you start with a *seed* value and transform it to obtain the first value of the sequence. Then you apply the transformation again for the next value, and so on.

NOTE The Java library uses a *linear congruential generator*. The seed is transformed according to the equation

```
seed = (seed * 25214903917 + 11) % 2⁴⁸
```

Typically, the seed of a random number generator is set to the time at its construction, to some value obtained by measuring the time between user keystrokes, or even to the input from a hardware device that generates random noise. However, for debugging purposes, it is often helpful to set the seed to a known quantity. Then the same program can be run multiple times with the same seed and thus with the same sequence of pseudo-random numbers. For this debugging strategy to be effective, it is important that there is one global random number generator.

Let us design a class `SingleRandom` that provides a single random number generator. The key to ensuring that the class has a single instance is to make the constructor private. The class constructs the instance and returns it in the static `getInstance` method.

```java
public class SingleRandom
{
   private SingleRandom() { generator = new Random(); }

   public void setSeed(int seed) { generator.setSeed(seed); }
   public int nextInt() { return generator.nextInt(); }

   public static SingleRandom getInstance() { return instance; }

   private Random generator;
   private static SingleRandom instance = new SingleRandom();
}
```

Note that the static field `instance` stores a reference to the unique `SingleRandom` object. Don't worry about the fact that this class has a static field of its own type. Recall that a static field is merely a "global" variable. In Java, every field must be declared in some class. We find it convenient to place the `instance` field inside the `SingleRandom` class itself.

Clients have only one way of obtaining a `SingleRandom` object, by calling the static `getInstance` method.

```
int randomNumber = SingleRandom.getInstance().nextInt();
```

> The SINGLETON pattern teaches how to implement a class that has exactly one instance.

Static fields of a class are initialized when the virtual machine loads the class. Since a class must be loaded before any of its methods can be called, the static `instance` field is initialized with the singleton object before the first call to the `getInstance` method occurs.

Alternatively, you can delay the construction of the instance until the `getInstance` method is called for the first time.

```
public static synchronized SingleRandom getInstance()
{
    if (instance == null) instance = new SingleRandom();
    return instance;
}
```

Note that this method needs to be synchronized to avoid a race condition if two threads call it at the same time.

PATTERN

◆ SINGLETON

Context

1. All clients need to access a single shared instance of a class.

2. You want to ensure that no additional instances can be created accidentally.

Solution

1. Define a class with a private constructor.

2. The class constructs a single instance of itself.

3. Supply a static method that returns a reference to the single instance.

The SINGLETON pattern is not as common as you may think. It only applies to classes that are guaranteed to have a unique instance. Consider for example the `Toolkit` class that you can use to determine the screen size and other aspects of the windowing system. The static `getDefaultToolkit` method returns a toolkit object.

```
Toolkit kit = Toolkit.getDefaultToolkit();
```

However, this is not an example of the SINGLETON pattern. It is possible to construct other toolkit objects besides the default toolkit object.

Utility classes such as the `Math` class are not singleton classes either. A utility is a class with only static methods. You don't construct *any* objects of such a class.

10.6   The VISITOR Pattern

Compound objects often have a complex structure, composed of individual elements. Some elements may again have child elements. The elements belong to various element classes. An operation on an element visits its child elements, applies the operation to them, and combines the results (see Figure 4). An example is a user interface container that is made up of components, some of which contain additional components. The `Component` and `Container` classes in the `java.awt` package contain numerous operations, such as `getPreferredSize` and `repaint`, that are recursively applied to child elements.

However, it is not easy to add new operations to such a design. Suppose we want to support a new operation for user interface containers and components. That operation would need to be added to the `Component` class and the various subclasses. But an application programmer cannot add methods to library classes.

The VISITOR pattern teaches how a library designer can supply an extensible mechanism that solves this problem. Each element class supports a single method

```
void accept(Visitor v)
```

Here, `Visitor` is an interface type. You supply a separate visitor class for each operation. An element and its children accept the visitor. In its most basic form, the `accept` method looks like this:

```
public void accept(Visitor v)
{
   v.visit(this);
}
```

By defining an appropriate `visit` method, a programmer can carry out arbitrary operations on the elements.

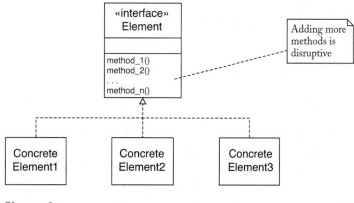

Figure 4

It Is Difficult to Add Operations to a
Hierarchy of Element Classes

However, there is a problem. A particular operation may need to carry out different actions for each element type. We cannot rely on polymorphism as a solution. In Java, polymorphism can only be put to work with a fixed set of operations, since a polymorphic operation must be a method, and a class can only have a fixed number of predefined methods. Instead, we can use a trick, *provided that there is only a fixed number of element classes.* Supply separate methods for each element type in the Visitor interface type:

```
public interface Visitor
{
    void visitElementType₁(ElementType₁ element);
    void visitElementType₂(ElementType₂ element);

    . . .

    void visitElementTypeₙ(ElementTypeₙ element);
}
```

For example, consider a directory tree that is made up of directory nodes and file nodes. The visitor interface for such a structure has two methods:

```
void visitDirectoryNode(DirectoryNode node)
void visitFileNode(FileNode node)
```

A particular visitor simply supplies the actions for the various element types in these methods.

To ensure that the appropriate method is called for each element, the accept methods must be implemented carefully. The accept method for a given element type must call the correct visitation method:

```
public class ElementTypeᵢ
{
    public void accept(Visitor v)
    {
        v.visitElementTypeᵢ(this);
    }
    . . .
}
```

For example,

```
public class DirectoryNode
{
    public void accept(Visitor v)
    {
        v.visitDirectoryNode(this);
    }
    . . .
}
```

Of course, these methods are completely mechanical.

To see the visitation mechanism in action, let us flesh out the example with the file and directory nodes. The File class in the java.io package describes either a file or a directory. You call the isDirectory method to find out whether a File object is actually a directory. If a File object really is a directory, then you can call the listFiles method to get an array of its files and subdirectories. That is a confusing design. We'll clarify it by supplying separate types for file and directory nodes, and supporting the VISITOR pattern.

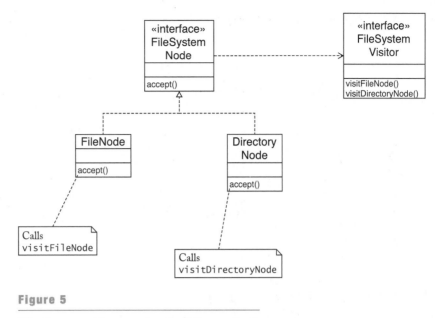

Figure 5

File System Classes for the VISITOR Pattern

The `FileSystemNode` interface type defines the accept method. The `FileNode` and `DirectoryNode` classes are simple wrappers around the `File` class (see Figure 5).

We also supply an actual visitor. The `PrintVisitor` prints the name of the visited node. If the node is a directory, it also visits its children, incrementing the indentation level. A typical printout looks like this:

```
..
command
 CommandTester.java
 GreetingAction.java
 hello.png
 goodbye.png
visitor
 FileNode.java
 DirectoryNode.java
 PrintVisitor.java
 VisitorTester.java
 FileSystemNode.java
 FileSystemVisitor.java
```

Ch10/visitor/FileSystemNode.java

```
1 /**
2     The common interface for file and directory nodes.
3 */
4 public interface FileSystemNode
5 {
6     void accept(FileSystemVisitor v);
7 }
```

Ch10/visitor/FileNode.java

```java
1  import java.io.*;
2
3  public class FileNode implements FileSystemNode
4  {
5     public FileNode(File file)
6     {
7        this.file = file;
8     }
9
10    public File getFile() { return file; }
11
12    public void accept(FileSystemVisitor v)
13    {
14       v.visitFileNode(this);
15    }
16
17    private File file;
18 }
```

Ch10/visitor/DirectoryNode.java

```java
1  import java.io.*;
2
3  public class DirectoryNode implements FileSystemNode
4  {
5     public DirectoryNode(File directory)
6     {
7        this.directory = directory;
8     }
9
10    public void accept(FileSystemVisitor v)
11    {
12       v.visitDirectoryNode(this);
13    }
14
15    public File getDirectory() { return directory; }
16
17    public FileSystemNode[] getChildren()
18    {
19       File[] files = directory.listFiles();
20       FileSystemNode[] children = new FileSystemNode[files.length];
21       for (int i = 0; i < files.length; i++)
22       {
23          File f = files[i];
24          if (f.isDirectory())
25             children[i] = new DirectoryNode(f);
26          else
27             children[i] = new FileNode(f);
28       }
29       return children;
30    }
31
32    private File directory;
33 }
```

Ch10/visitor/FileSystemVisitor.java

```
1  /**
2      The visitor interface type for visiting file system nodes.
3  */
4  public interface FileSystemVisitor
5  {
6      /**
7          Visits a file node.
8          @param node the file node
9      */
10     void visitFileNode(FileNode node);
11
12     /**
13         Visits a directory node.
14         @param node the directory node
15     */
16     void visitDirectoryNode(DirectoryNode node);
17 }
```

Ch10/visitor/PrintVisitor.java

```
1  import java.io.*;
2
3  public class PrintVisitor implements FileSystemVisitor
4  {
5      public void visitFileNode(FileNode node)
6      {
7          for (int i = 0; i < level; i++) System.out.print(" ");
8          System.out.println(node.getFile().getName());
9      }
10
11     public void visitDirectoryNode(DirectoryNode node)
12     {
13         for (int i = 0; i < level; i++) System.out.print(" ");
14         System.out.println(node.getDirectory().getName());
15         level++;
16         for (FileSystemNode c : node.getChildren())
17             c.accept(this);
18         level--;
19     }
20
21     private int level = 0;
22 }
```

Ch10/visitor/VisitorTester.java

```
1  import java.io.*;
2
3  public class VisitorTester
4  {
```

```
 5    public static void main(String[] args)
 6    {
 7       DirectoryNode node = new DirectoryNode(new File(".."));
 8       node.accept(new PrintVisitor());
 9    }
10 }
```

It is instructive to consider what happens when the `accept` method is called on the parent node (see Figure 6). That node is a `DirectoryNode`. Therefore, the `accept` method calls `v.visitDirectoryNode`. Because `v` is a `PrintVisitor`, the `visitDirectoryNode` method of the `PrintVisitor` class is called. This call pattern is called *double dispatch* because it uses polymorphism twice, first to select the node type and then to select the visitor type.

In some programming languages (such as Nice—see http://nice.sourceforge.net), you can define methods that have multiple polymorphic parameters. However, in Java, dynamic method dispatch only takes the implicit parameter into account. You can think of the visitor pattern as a technique for overcoming this limitation.

Recall that the purpose of this mechanism is to enable an open-ended collection of operations on the directory tree. For example, to find all files that contain a given keyword, you can supply a different visitor.

> The VISITOR pattern teaches how to support an open-ended set of operations on an object structure with a fixed set of element types.

Note that the visitor pattern only applies if there is a fixed number of element classes. Adding a new element class would force a change in the `Visitor` interface type and all visitor classes.

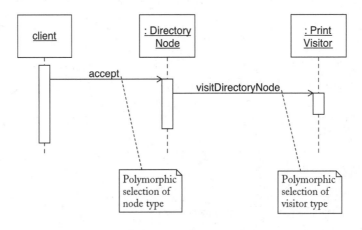

Figure 6

Double Dispatch

PATTERN

VISITOR

Context

1. An object structure contains element classes of multiple types, and you want to carry out operations that depend on the object types.

2. The set of operations should be extensible over time.

3. The set of element classes is fixed.

Solution

1. Define a *visitor* interface type that has methods for visiting elements of each of the given types.

2. Each element class defines an `accept` method that invokes the matching element visitation method on the visitor parameter.

3. To implement an operation, define a class that implements the visitor interface type and supplies the operation's action for each element type.

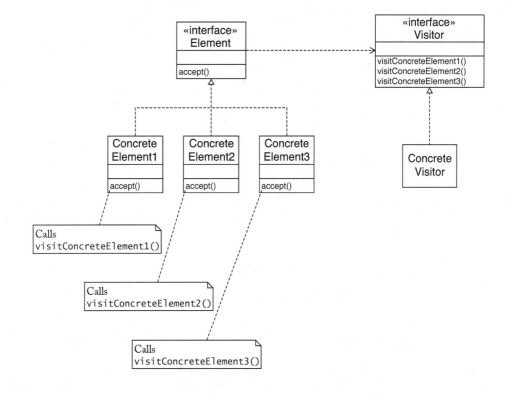

For example, in the case of the file and directory node structure, we have:

Name in Design Pattern	Actual Name
Element	FileSystemNode
ConcreteElement	FileNode, DirectoryNode
Visitor	FileSystemVisitor
ConcreteVisitor	PrintVisitor

10.7 Other Design Patterns

We conclude this chapter with a table that shows the design patterns that we have not yet discussed from the "Gang of Four" book. The table contains a short description of each pattern so that you can tell at a glance when you need to learn more about it.

You have now come to the end of this book on object-oriented design with Java. In the course of this book, you have studied material from three areas:

1. Object-oriented design

   - The design methodology
   - CRC cards and UML diagrams
   - Design patterns

2. Advanced Java

   - Interface types, polymorphism, and inheritance
   - Inner classes
   - Reflection
   - Generic types
   - Multithreading
   - Collections

3. User interface programming

   - Building Swing applications
   - Event handling
   - Graphics programming

You have seen how object-oriented design principles and design patterns are used in the Java library. These knowledge areas will form a solid foundation for your study of advanced computer science topics as well as for practical programming.

Pattern Name	Description	Example
ABSTRACT FACTORY	An abstract class defines methods that construct related products. Concrete factories create these product sets.	An abstract class specifies methods for constructing buttons, menus, and so on. Each user interface "look and feel" supplies a concrete subclass.
BRIDGE	An abstraction and its implementation have separate inheritance hierarchies.	A hierarchy of window types has separate implementations in various operating systems.
BUILDER	A builder class has methods to build parts of a complex product, and to retrieve the completed product.	A document builder has methods to build paragraphs, tables, and so on.
CHAIN OF RESPONSIBILITY	A request is passed to the first handler in a chain. Each handler acts on the request (or chooses not to act) and passes the request on to the next handler.	An event handling mechanism passes a mouse or keyboard event to a component, which then passes it to the parent component.
FLYWEIGHT	Use shared objects instead of large numbers of separate objects with identical state.	A word processor uses shared objects for styled characters rather than a separate object for each character.
INTERPRETER	A class hierarchy represents grammar rules. The interpreter recursively evaluates a parse tree of rule objects.	A program interactively evaluates mathematical expressions by building and evaluating a parse tree.
MEDIATOR	An object encapsulates the interaction of other objects.	All components in a dialog box notify a mediator of state changes. The mediator updates affected components.
MEMENTO	An object yields an opaque snapshot of a part of its state, and can later return to its state from that snapshot.	An "undo" mechanism requests a memento from an object before mutating it. If the operation is undone, the memento is used to roll the object back to its old state.
STATE	A separate object is used for each state. State-dependent code is distributed over the various state classes.	An image editor has different drawing states. Each state is handled by a separate "tool" object.

Table 1

Other Design Patterns

EXERCISES

Exercise 10.1. Consider the `enumeration` and `list` methods of the `Collections` class. To what extent do they follow the ADAPTER pattern?

Exercise 10.2. Explain why `MouseAdapter` and `WindowAdapter` are not adapters in the sense of the ADAPTER pattern.

Exercise 10.3. The `Iterable` interface type is attractive because it allows objects to be used in a "for each" loop. Design an adapter that adapts `InputStream` to the `Iterable<Integer>` interface type.

Exercise 10.4. Repeat Exercise 10.3, but now follow the DECORATOR pattern.

Exercise 10.5. Write an adapter that adapts a `Map` to an `AbstractTableModel`. The API documentation for the `AbstractTableModel` class tells you that you need to supply three methods:

```
public int getRowCount()
public int getColumnCount()
public Object getValueAt(int row, int column)
```

Then populate a `SortedMap` with key/value pairs and show the map inside a `JTable`.

Exercise 10.6. The STRATEGY and COMMAND patterns both suggest using objects in place of methods. What is the difference in intent between these two patterns?

Exercise 10.7. Is an `ActionListener` a command object in the sense of the COMMAND pattern?

Exercise 10.8. Use `Action` objects to implement the "Add House", "Add Car", and "Remove" commands in the scene editor of Chapter 6.

Exercise 10.9. Is the `BorderFactory` class of the Java library an example of the FACTORY METHOD pattern?

Exercise 10.10. Supply an interface type `LogFormatter` that can be used to write objects to a log file. The interface type has methods `logObject`, `logCollection`, and `logMap` to log single objects, collections, and maps. Supply an interface type `LogFile` with a factory method `getFormatter` that returns a `LogFormatter` object. Supply concrete subclasses `TextLogFile` and `HTMLLogFile` that log information in plain text and HTML format.

Exercise 10.11. The technique of "copy on write" minimizes copies by allowing multiple clients to share an object. However, if a client calls a mutator method, then the object is copied just before the mutator is applied. Implement a `CopyOnWriteList` proxy that implements copy on write for `List` objects.

Exercise 10.12. The image proxy has the disadvantage that the entire image is loaded when you only need the width and height. Improve the implementation of the `ImageProxy` class by calling the `getImage` method of the `Toolkit` class and attaching an

`ImageObserver` to track the loading process. Consult the API documentation for details about these classes.

Exercise 10.13. Look at the documentation and the source code of the `BorderFactory` method. It holds out the possibility that shared borders are used whenever possible. Are any of the shared borders actually singletons?

Exercise 10.14. Implement a singleton logger that a graphical application can use to log messages to a frame containing a `JTextArea`. Supply a static method `getInstance` that yields the logger and a method `log` that adds a string to the text area.

Exercise 10.15. Why doesn't the `Component` hierarchy in the Java library support the VISITOR pattern?

Exercise 10.16. Supply a visitor for the directory and file nodes that counts all files and directories that it encounters.

Exercise 10.17. Supply a visitor for the directory and file nodes that collects the names of all files that contain a given keyword.

Glossary

Abstract class   A class that cannot be instantiated.

Accessor method   A method that accesses an object but does not change it.

Activation bars   The bars in a sequence diagram that indicate when a method is called.

ADAPTER pattern   A design pattern that teaches how to use a class in a context that requires a different interface.

Aggregation   The *has a* relationship between classes.

Analysis phase   The phase of a software project that concerns itself solely with an understanding of the problem domain and the problem to be solved, not with any design or implementation strategy.

Anonymous array   An array reference that is not stored in a named variable.

Anonymous class   A class that does not have a name.

Anonymous object   An object reference that is not stored in a named variable.

Application framework   A framework for building application programs.

Array   A collection of values of the same type stored in contiguous memory locations, each of which can be accessed by an integer index.

Array list   A Java class that implements a dynamically growing array of objects.

Ascent   The vertical extent above the baseline of a font's characters.

Assertion   A claim that a certain condition holds in a particular program location.

Association   A relationship between classes in which one can navigate from objects of one class to objects of the other class, usually by following object references.

Attribute   A named property that an object is responsible for maintaining.

AWT (Abstract Windowing Toolkit)   The Java toolkit for interacting with platform-specific user-interface components and events.

Builder environment   A program that allows for the interactive construction of application programs or components. NetBeans is a builder environment.

Call by reference   Passing the location of a value as a method parameter so that the method can modify it.

Call by value   Passing a copy of a value as a method parameter.

Cast Explicitly converting a value from one type to a different type. For example, the cast from a floating-point number x to an integer is expressed in Java by the cast notation (int) x.

Checked exception An exception that the compiler checks. All checked exceptions must be declared or caught.

Class A programmer-defined data type.

Class diagram A diagram that depicts classes and their relationships.

Class file A file containing the Java virtual machine instructions for loading a class and executing its methods.

Class invariant A logical condition that is fulfilled by all objects of a class after the completion of any constructor or method.

Class method See static method.

Class variable See static field.

Clone A copy of an object that has the same state as the original.

Cloning Making a copy of an object whose state can be modified independently of the original object.

Cohesion A class is cohesive if its features support a single abstraction.

Collaborator A class on which another class depends.

Collections framework The set of Java classes for implementing collections.

COMMAND pattern A design pattern that teaches how to implement commands as objects whenever a command has both behavior and state.

Command line The line the user types to start a program in DOS or UNIX or a command window in Windows. It consists of the program name followed by any necessary arguments.

Compiler A program that translates code in a high-level language (such as Java) to machine instructions (such as bytecode for the Java virtual machine).

Component See user interface component, software component.

COMPOSITE pattern A design pattern that teaches how to combine several objects into an object that has the same behavior as its parts.

Composition A stronger form of aggregation in which the contained objects do not have an existence independent of their container.

Condition object An object that manages threads that currently cannot proceed.

Constructor A method that initializes a newly instantiated object.

Content pane The part of a Swing frame that holds the user interface components of the frame.

Controller (in the model-view-controller architecture) The object that processes user interaction.

Coupling The degree to which classes are related to each other by dependency.

CRC card An index card representing a class, listing its responsibilities and its collaborating classes.

Deadlock A state in which no thread can proceed because each thread is waiting for another to do some work first.

Deadly embrace A set of blocked threads, each of which can only be unblocked by the action of other threads in the set.

DECORATOR pattern A design pattern that teaches how to form a class that adds functionality to another class while keeping its interface.

Deep copy Copying an object and all objects to which it refers.

Dependency The *uses* relationship between classes, in which one class needs services provided by another class.

Deprecation Tagging a feature as obsolete and putting its users on notice that it may be removed.

Descent The vertical extent below the baseline of a font's characters.

Design pattern A description of a design problem and a proven solution.

Design phase The phase of a software project that concerns itself with the discovery of the structural components of the software system to be built, not with implementation details.

Double dispatch The invocation of a polymorphic operation that depends on the types of two parameters by calling two separate methods.

Edge A connection between two nodes in a graph.

Epoch A fixed point in time, such as January 1, 1970, 0:00 GMT.

Event adapter A class that implements an event listener interface by defining all methods to do nothing.

Event class A class that contains information about an event, such as its source.

Event listener An object that is notified by an event source when an event occurs.

Event source An object that can notify other classes of events.

Exception A class that signals a condition that prevents the program from continuing normally. When such a condition occurs, an object of the exception class is thrown.

Explicit parameter A parameter of a method other than the object on which the method is invoked.

FACADE pattern A design pattern that teaches how to simplify a subsystem consisting of multiple classes by introducing a facade class that exposes all capabilities of the subsystem as methods.

Factory method A method that constructs a new object.

FACTORY METHOD pattern A design pattern that teaches how to supply a method that can be overridden to create objects of varying types.

Field See instance field, static field.

Framework A collection of classes that provides mechanisms for a particular problem domain.

Functional specification A detailed specification of the externally observable behavior of a software system.

Generic class A class with one or more type parameters.

Generic method A method with one or more type parameters.

Generic programming Providing program components that can be reused in a wide variety of situations.

Generic type A type variable that can be replaced by an actual type.

Graph A set of nodes and edges, where each edge connects a pair of nodes.

Graphics context A class through which a programmer can cause shapes to appear on a window or off-screen bitmap.

Guillemets The « and » punctuation symbols.

Hash collision Two different objects for which a hash function computes identical values.

Hash function A function that computes an integer value from an object in such a way that different objects are likely to yield different values.

Hash table A data structure in which elements are mapped to array positions according to their hash function values.

Identity That characteristic that distinguishes an object from all others.

Immutable class A class without a mutator method.

Implementation invariant A class invariant that refers to the private implementation of the class.

Implementation phase The phase of software development that concerns itself with realizing the design in a programming environment.

Implementing an interface type Implementing a class that declares itself as an implementor of the interface type and that supplies methods of the interface type.

Implicit parameter The object on which a method is invoked. For example, in the call x.f(y), the object x is the implicit parameter of the method f.

Inheritance The *is a* relationship between a more general superclass and a more specialized subclass.

Inner class A class that is defined inside another class.

Instance field A variable defined in a class for which every object of the class has its own value.

Instance method A method with an implicit parameter; that is, a method that is invoked on an instance of a class.

Instance of a class An object whose type is that class.

Instantiation The process of creating an instance.

Interface invariant A class invariant that refers to the interface of the class but not to the private implementation.

Interface of a class The methods and fields of a class that are not private.

Interface type A type with no instance variables and only abstract methods and constants.

Interrupting a thread Signaling an interruption to a thread, usually to terminate it.

Invariant A condition that is not changed by a transformation such as a method call or a loop iteration.

Inversion of control Placing the responsibility for control flow outside the classes that specify the behavior of a program.

Invoking a method Calling a method.

Iterator An object that can inspect all elements in a container such as a linked list.

ITERATOR pattern A design pattern that teaches how to access the elements of an aggregate object.

Julian day number The number of days from January 1, 4713 BCE.

Law of Demeter A design guideline that states that a method should not operate on global objects or objects that are a part of another object.

Layout manager A class that arranges user interface components inside a container.

Lazy evaluation Delaying a computation until its result is requested.

Lifeline The vertical line below an object in a sequence diagram that indicates the time during which the object is alive.

Linear congruential generator A sequence of random numbers that is generated by repeated transformation of a seed value according to the rule `seed = (seed * a + b) %` n for fixed *a*, *b*, and *n*.

Linked list A data structure that can hold an arbitrary number of objects, each of which is stored in a link object, which contains a pointer to the next link.

Liskov substitution principle The rule that states that you can use a subclass object whenever a superclass object is expected.

Listener class See event listener.

Literal class object A `Class` object of the form C.`class`, where C is the name of a class.

Lock A data structure that ensures that only one thread can execute a set of statements.

Magic number A number that appears in a program without explanation.

Manifest file A file that describes the contents of an archive file.

Map A container that stores associations between key and value objects.

Method A sequence of statements that has a name, may have formal parameters, and may return a value. A method can be invoked any number of times, with different values for its parameters.

Model (in the model-view-controller architecture)   The object that contains the state of a data structure, independent of any visual presentation.

Model/view/controller architecture   An architecture that decouples the state, visual representations, and manipulation mechanisms of a data structure.

Multiple inheritance   Inheriting from two or more superclasses.

Mutator method   A method that changes the state of an object.

Node   A component of a graph.

Numeric type   A type representing numbers, with special support provided by the programming language. In Java, the numeric types are `char`, `short int`, `long`, `float`, and `double`.

OBSERVER pattern   A design pattern that teaches how an object can notify other objects about events.

Operator overloading   Assigning a new function to an operator that is selected if the operator has arguments of a specific type.

Overloading   Using the same name or symbol for a set of functions. The actual function is selected according to the types of the arguments.

Overriding   Redefining a method in a subclass.

Package   A collection of related classes. The `import` statement is used to access one or more classes in a package.

Package visibility   Accessibility from the methods of the classes in the same package.

Panel   A user interface component with no visual appearance. It can be used to group other components, or as the superclass of a component that defines a method for painting.

Parameterized type   A family of types with features that depend on generic type variables. By binding the type variables to actual types, a specific type is instantiated.

Pattern   See design pattern.

Pointer   A data structure that describes the memory address of a value.

Polymorphism   Selecting a method among several methods that have the same name on the basis of the actual types of the implicit parameters.

Postcondition   A condition that is true after a method has been called.

Precondition   A condition that must be true when a method is called if the method is to work correctly.

Primitive type   In Java, a number type or the `boolean` type.

Private feature   A feature that is accessible only by methods of the same class or an inner class.

Process   A sequence of instructions that executes under the control of the operating system.

Property   A named value that is managed by a component.

Property sheet   A table that lists property names and values.

Proportionally spaced font   A font whose characters have varying widths.

Protected visibility   Accessibility from the methods of all subclasses and the classes in the same package.

PROTOTYPE pattern   A design pattern that teaches how a system can instantiate objects of classes that are not known when the system is built.

PROXY pattern   A design pattern that teaches how an object can be a placeholder for another object.

Pseudo-random numbers   Numbers that appear to be random but are generated by a mathematical formula.

Queue   A collection of items with "first in, first out" retrieval.

Race condition   A condition in which the effect of multiple threads on shared data depends on the order in which the threads are scheduled.

Refactoring   Restructuring code to increase its quality.

Reference   A value that denotes the memory location of an object.

Reflection   The ability of a program to analyze its objects and their capabilities.

Responsibility   A high-level task that a class is expected to carry out.

Runnable thread   A thread that can proceed provided it is given a time slice to do work.

Seed   An initial value for a sequence of numbers.

Selfish thread   A thread that does not yield control to other threads.

Sequence diagram   A diagram that depicts a sequence of method calls.

Serialization   The process of saving an object, and all objects that it references, to a stream.

Shallow copy   Copying only the reference to an object.

Side effect   An effect of a method other than returning a value.

Singleton class   A class that has exactly one instance.

SINGLETON pattern   A design pattern that teaches how to implement a class that has exactly one instance.

Slider   A user interface component for specifying a continuous range of values.

Software component   A building block that can be combined with other components into programs, usually by employing a program builder tool.

Stack   A data structure with "last in, first out" retrieval. Elements can be added and removed only at one position, called the top of the stack.

Stack trace   A printout of the call stack, listing all currently pending method calls.

State   The current value of an object, which is determined by the cumulative action of all methods that were invoked on it.

State diagram   A diagram that depicts state transitions and their causes.

Static field   A variable defined in a class that has only one value for the whole class; a static field can be accessed and changed by any method of that class.

Static method   A method with no implicit parameter.

Stereotype descriptor   An adornment in a UML diagram that specifies a stereotypical role such as "interface".

STRATEGY pattern   A design pattern that teaches how to supply variants of an algorithm.

Strongly typed language   A programming language whose compiler ensures that operations will only be executed if they conform to the type system rules.

Subclass   A class that inherits variables and methods from a superclass but adds instance variables, adds methods, or redefines methods.

Subtype   A type that can be used when its supertype is expected.

Superclass   A general class from which a more specialized class (a subclass) inherits.

Synchronized block   A block of code that is controlled by a lock. To start execution, a thread must acquire the lock. Upon completion, it relinquishes the lock.

Synchronized method   A method that is controlled by a lock. In order to execute the method, the calling thread must acquire the lock.

TEMPLATE METHOD pattern   A design pattern that teaches how to supply an algorithm for multiple types, provided that the sequence of steps does not depend on the type.

Text field   A user interface component for text entry.

Thread   A program unit that is executed independently of other parts of the program.

Thread pool   A collection of threads that have been constructed in anticipation of their use.

Time slicing   Scheduling threads by giving each thread a small amount of time in which to do its work, then giving control to another thread.

Toolbar   A user interface component that holds a set of buttons.

Total ordering   An ordering relationship in which all elements can be compared to each other.

Type   A named set of values and the operations that can be carried out with them.

Type descriptor   A data structure that describes properties of a type.

Type parameter   A parameter in a generic class or method that can be replaced with an actual type.

Type system   A system of types and their relationships.

Typesafe enumeration   An idiom for implementing an enumerated type as a class with a set of named objects.

UML, the unified modeling language   A notation for specifying, visualizing, constructing, and documenting the artifacts of software systems.

Unchecked exception   An exception that the compiler doesn't check.

Unicode   A standard code that assigns code values consisting of two bytes to characters used in scripts around the world. Java stores all characters as their Unicode values.

Unit test A test of a method by itself, isolated from the remainder of the program.

Use case A sequence of actions that yields a result that is of value to an actor.

User interface component A building block for a graphical user interface, such as a button or a text field. User interface components are used to present information to the user and allow the user to enter information to the program.

Variable A symbol in a program that identifies a storage location that can hold different values.

View (in the model-view-controller architecture) The object that provides a visual representation of the underlying data.

Virtual base class In C++, a class whose fields are not replicated if they are repeatedly inherited.

VISITOR pattern A design pattern that teaches how to support an open-ended set of operations on an object structure with a fixed set of element types.

Wildcard An anonymous type parameter in a generic class or method.

Index

Photo Credits

Chapter 2

Page 44: Photodisc/Punchstock.

Chapter 5

Page 177: Rob Meinychuk/Digital Vision.
Page 185: EyeWire, Inc./Getty Images.

Chapter 9

Page 383: Creatas/Punchstock.